Meet Me on the Battlefield

YOU WANDERED IN ON A CHAPTER OF A BOOK FROM THE LIBRARY OF MY JOURNEY AND THINK YOU KNOW ME?

MEET ME ON THE BATTLEFIELD

ENJOY THE WATER...OR NOT.

A. S. E.

Paperback ISBN-13: 978-1-6312-9603-1
Ebook ISBN-13: 978-1-6312-9604-8

DEDICATED TO ...

BH, MY BEST friend. You're the only one who knows EXACTLY who I once was, who I am, and who I can be. You're more than my best friend, You're my EVERYTHING. I can't imagine ever living without You again. I want to thank You for reminding me of who I am when I forget. Thank You for loving me when I no longer want to love myself. Thank You for making the dark parts of me a majestic art that is constantly being molded and redefined by Your Almighty hands. Thank You for Your grace in sending me a borrowed angel. Thank You for Your mercy in allowing me to yet live through waters that were meant to drown me. I love You. I can't tell You how much, so I vow to spend the remainder of my life showing You.

Nayalee Kaya, my daughter and borrowed angel. You will always be nothing short of my hero. In you, the Father gifted me an anchor to help me not stray too far from His path. In you, the Father gifted me purpose to never give up the fight, come what may. In you, the Father gifted me strength to boldly and readily stand on the front lines to face the ultimate adversary. In you, the Father gifted me comfort in knowing He deems me capable of caring for something as precious and special as your soul. Thank you for singing me to sleep when you see me lying awake staring at the ceiling. Thank you for bringing me water and reminding me to stay hydrated. Thank you for reminding me to eat when I'm caught up in my work. Thank you for rubbing my head and cupping my face when you see my mind running faster than I can keep up with. Thank you for trying to cater to my every need as best as your little 5-year-old self can. Thank you for being my praise and worship buddy and my prayer partner. Thank you for randomly telling me how much God loves me and that He sees me. Thank you for knowing. You hear things I never say, and you see things I never show. You are truly my borrowed guardian angel.

Sabrena Sharie, my younger sister. You are such an inspiration to me, and I love you beyond anything I could describe. You're my tender bear. I'm so grateful to have grown up with you. We've shared laughs, cries, and hurts together. You're more than a conqueror and your resilience makes me want to be the best big sister I can to you in every way possible. Thank you for giving me hugs against my will and being the sunshine of my life. Thank you for never letting me sink to deep into my thoughts and binge-watching inspirational movies with me when I need it. Thank you for making me laugh and encouraging me when things get tough. Thank you for being my spiritual sister and gently pulling me back when you see me drifting away from myself. Thank you for being my 'Cindy ReeRee'. You are an extraordinary mother and amazing auntie to Nay, but you're an even lovelier daughter of The Most High. God bless you.

Lakriesha Williams, my older sister. Your brain is one I admire, but not as much as your homemade chocolate chip cookies! I'm kidding. You are an incredible soul and I love you. I know we didn't really have a lot of time to bond as kids, but I'm beyond amazed and inspired at the woman, wife and mother you've become. Thank you for the wonderful brother and nephew you've blessed me with. May God continue to bless and keep you and yours until we meet again!

Antuaine Dunn, my oldest brother. The memories I have of you are all times you were exactly what I always imagined a big brother being. You pushed me to challenge anything standing in my way. You taught me to swim in the deep, wrestle, and pop my knuckles. You also taught me determination and gave me standards to try and live up to. One of the proudest moments of my life was when you asked me for the jersey I wore on tour with Charlie Wilson and Anthony Hamilton. You told me you wanted to frame it right next to your other framed jerseys from your favorite sports teams. Your approval meant the world to me growing up and still does. Thank you for giving me one of the best sisters and most beautiful nieces and nephew I could have. May God bless and keep you and yours until we meet again!

Xavier Summerville, my older brother. The very first time I met you, I couldn't stop looking at you and feeling so grateful to have another big brother in my life. I want you to know that I've always felt proud of being able to call you a brother of mine. Your chill attitude and beautiful smile is something I've always admired. We haven't really gotten many chances to bond in our adult lives, but my love for you is just as strong as it was back then. May God bless and keep you and yours until we meet again!

Bryan Chatman, my older brother. When we met, I was married and struggling. I thank you for always being that person I can have an intellectually spiritual conversation with. I have cherished the long hours we spent talking about the vast depth of Christ. Like my other siblings, I haven't had the opportunity to spend much time with you, but I cherish you as my brother. May God bless and keep you and yours until we meet again!

Mother, there's something extremely important I pray you know. I am so grateful for the love and support you've shown me in telling my 'not so pretty' story to the world. I am so proud God gifted you to me as my mother! Grandma Stella would be overjoyed if she could see you today. You are my queen and you've planted a seed I could never repay you for! You planted the yearning for God in my life. Despite all our flawed experiences, I came from YOU. The wise woman you see in me today started with YOU! Thank you for all the silent, comforting squeezes on my shoulders. Thank you for believing in me more than anyone else I've ever known! Thank you for tolerating me even when you didn't quite understand me. You have been and will continue to be my Superwoman, from the hair on your beautiful head to your curvy arched feet. I love you, Ma. Always and forever.

Last, but not least, Dad. Where do I begin? You and I have undoubtedly had our differences, but I couldn't be more proud of the relationship we're growing today! We've come so far and still have far to go, but I want you to know that you're never a failure unless you give up. Something tells me the lion in the both of us won't allow either of us to do that. Dad, I love you and need you, still. I can remember how we cried together during my marital separation until we somehow found humor and laughed amid the sadness. Thank you for always being the one I can call and vent to. Thank you for all the times you listened to me without saying a word, letting me counsel myself with you there as merely a witness to my own words. Thank you for the droplets of simple, yet profound advice you share with me in wake of my anxiety. One special quote I will always live by is when you told me, "Baby, one step at a time. Sometimes that means one day, one hour, one minute and even one second. Focus on that one, and soon you'll reach your goal." I've lived by those words, and because of them I've finished my first book! Lastly, thank you for the unwavering support you've shown for me writing my story. I know much of the past is ugly, but your strong support has encouraged me and made me believe that we can face the ugly together for the sake of the beauty of Christ's redeeming power. I've always known you as a man of great pride, and that's caused you many great falls. But it's also taught me many great lessons. It means the world to me that you've laid your pride aside to exalt the name of The Most High. Thank you for believing in me. I love you so much! May God continue the great work in you He's already started.

Acknowledgements

I MUST BE HONEST in saying I've never written a book before. The closest I've come to composing anything like this are the hundreds of journals I've collected over the years. Huge thanks to Mom, Dad, and Ree for being my cheer squad.

There is one special lady I must thank. She walked up to me at a domestic violence conference and told me I was pregnant with a book. She's since, been more like a fairy godmother to me, constantly calling and pushing me through my rough patches of not wanting to write anymore. She was the first amazing author to tell me I had something special to share. Deidra Bynum, my big sis and motivator, I thank you from the pit of my heart for allowing God to use you in such a way to help me deliver this baby to the world. I am forever grateful to you.

This book could not have come together without the anointed efforts of my super smart, valedictorian big sister, Keisha, who edited this book with me. When things got tough, you dropped the meal you were cooking and drove in the middle of the night to meet me and talk me through my anxiety. I am so grateful to have you in my life and thanks for making me a better writer in the process.

Thanks to all of Xulon Press, my cheer squad, Paulette and everyone else for your feedback and encouragement during the process of writing and preparing this book.

All thanks and praise to The Most High, my BH, my Father for watering my spirit with this amazing inspiration to share with the world. May it be acceptable in Your sight and may Your will be seen, heard, and done. May You travel this journey with every single reader that picks up this voyage, and may You speak to their hearts, open their minds, and touch their spirits.

Preface

I, ASE, FORMERLY known La'Porsha Renae, have scribed a 7-book memoir series that journeys far beneath my surface.

Book #1 is set in the deep waters of my childhood. From the choppy waves of my southern experiences as a young child through the dark, complex caves and trenches of my teenage years, I invite you on a deep-dive into my unique beginnings. My story is no fairytale, but you will never be the same after embarking upon this voyage.

Narrated by my older and wiser being for the very first and last time, I invite you to explore the caves of my waters and gardens past the pearly gates of the deepest parts of my heart, through the mind and eyes of my younger self. You will laugh, cry, hurt, and experience a unique mixture of joy, pain, sorrow, rage, and wonder on this astonishing quest to self-love and self-discovery. As most caves are, parts of this exhibition may become a bit dark, so please, do not hesitate to take a rest or breather before continuing this journey. Meet me on the battlefield.

Have We Met?

"You wandered in on a chapter of a book from the library of my journey and think you know me?" ~A. S. E.

La'Porsha Renae Mays, the child; that's what my parents named me. La'Porsha Jennings, the wife; that's what my ex-husband called me. La'Porsha Renae, the famous singer; that's what the world called me. ASE., the redeemed daughter; that's what I Am named me.

Names are profoundly crucial to one's identity. Attached to each of mine are many caves that we'll be exploring throughout this memoir series. I want to tell you the caves are full of exciting, magical wonders, and some are. But most of them are dreaded with unfathomable dark gardens that I only dare speak of in a desperate attempt to shed light on others who may be trapped in caves that echo their screams back at them in lonely silence.

Often, we, or someone we know, wander through intricate gardens in lonely waters. We grow tired and decide to take a rest under a tree that appears able to shield and shade us from our torture, but we are then often met by vigorous, thick vines ready to coil mercilessly around our throats and summon our last breath. Some souls can fight and break free, while others give way to death's grip.

Reading this, you may think me melodramatic, but you will soon enough find that my description of what has taken place in my life countless times, as well as in the lives of many others suffering, only begin to scrape the surface. Let's begin, shall we?

Family Tree

"To understand the tree,
you must study the root and discover the seed." ~A. S. E.

I WAS BORN TO a loving, God-fearing mother, Carolyn, and hard-working, jack of all trades dad, Edward.

My mother's father was never really an active part of her life, and her mother, Grandma Stella, though big-hearted and sweet, wasn't regarded by my mother as the best example for her growing up. My mother saw many behaviors in Grandma Stella that she vowed to herself and God at the tender age of twelve that she would never carry into her own future family. My mother has four sisters, all of whom are fathered by different men except her twin sister, my favorite aunt.

My dad's father, Granddaddy Joe, is a legend among all his children and grandchildren for his enthusiastic tales of being extraordinarily strong in the days of his youth, as well as being gifted in making music.

There are many heroic stories about my Granddaddy Joe. Many have witnessed him holding up cars with his strength to allow someone to work underneath them. There are also many stories about him pulling tractors by his teeth. I must say that's one story I believe with all my heart because the proof is in the fact that there's not a single tooth left in his mouth.

He's known to be a man who'd give the shirt off of his back to a stranger in need or give his last five dollars to someone hungry on the street. He was said to have been one of the strongest men you'd ever meet. My Granddaddy Joe was said to have made the guitar and harmonica talk, and I've been blessed to witness the gut-wrenching sound of his singing. I'd be a fool not to credit him with passing down those soul-shaking vocals to me.

My father's mother, Grandma Ruthie, takes the cake for being legendary in my eyes. She was a feisty, little woman that always took care of her grown children, their children, and their children's children every holiday, birthday, and most of all, every Sunday dinner. Her cooking was always very Southern, but too moist for my taste. I've always been big on the texture of food and am extremely quick to get squeamish if things are too wet or soggy.

I remember Grandma Ruthie caught me throwing away a chicken leg that had gristles and fat on it. Since she was old school, she tried to make me get out the plate that I'd sort of laid on the top of the trash and eat that chicken leg! I didn't eat it, but from that point on, I was careful not to fix a plate of food that I knew I wouldn't want to eat.

Grandma Ruthie believed in many superstitions that I was always interested in hearing about. The main one I remember was that she thought it to be terrible luck to whistle in the house, something I did very often. She wasn't shy about telling me to stop.

The thing I'd look forward to most when visiting her home, though, is the sharp way she'd cut Granddaddy Joe down just before he'd reach the end of whatever story he'd be telling. It was epic! It never failed to draw the most aching laugh from my gut.

The way it would happen is Granddaddy Joe would be getting an exhilarating climax in his story, and I'd see Grandma Ruthie staring at him almost as if she was waiting for him to reach his height. Just as he would engage his entire face and body in expressing his story, she'd yell, "Shut up, Joe! Just shut up wit' all that lyin'!"

My aunts and uncles, all my cousins, my parents, siblings, and I would all burst into uncontrollable laughter. We all knew the more Granddaddy Joe spoke, the more it brewed the festering, boiling pot in Grandma Ruthie's gut until finally, she'd let it rip!

I was raised with my beautiful, yet meddlesome, younger sister, Sabrena Sharie. We all called her 'Ree' for short. For a brief time, my oldest brother, Antuaine Dunn, and older sister, Lakreisha Staples, whose name is now Lakreisha Williams, would come to live with us, also.

I loved my family and my siblings, but not because I wanted to. I loved them because I had to. The truth was I despised God placing me with my family throughout most of my childhood. I know that sounds horrible, but it's true. I never quite fit in with them, and even in my adult years, I would discover that I'd only be able to maintain healthy relationships with them from long distances.

Before we plunge into the deep of my caves, let's take a moment to swim among the current of my family's personalities. Doing this will later serve extremely helpful in understanding the perplexing dynamic between my family and myself.

The General

"A mother is the first angel or demon a child will every meet." ~A. S. E.

My mother was the Empress of my life, the green thumb of my gardens, and the warmth of my waters. Through the eyes of my early child self, she could do no wrong. All I ever wanted to do was make her proud of me. My mother was the runt of her sisters and described her childhood as one with some happy moments, but often, harsh circumstances. There were many good times, but there seemed to be even more sorrowful ones to reflect on.

My mother would often tell me stories about her childhood experiences. From what I understand, she grew up being noticeably different from her sisters and most of her peers. She, much like myself, felt God placed her into the wrong family and lived as an outcast in her own home. My mother was closest to her twin sister but still felt a sense of loneliness.

She told me that Grandma Stella, her mother, had a very kind-hearted and jolly spirit. Despite being extremely sensitive, she was very playful and would amuse herself by chasing my mother around with potatoes that had started growing stems out of themselves and pretty much loved to laugh at anyone, as long as the joke wasn't on her.

My mother would have my sister and me on the floor laughing when she'd tell us stories like the time her crying mother was chased by a horse and had to eventually surrender the red chitterling bucket full of pecans she'd worked so hard to pick. Another instance was the time her mother started crying and screaming because my Granddaddy Pup called the junkyard for old cars a 'graveyard.' Then, there's the time she and my Granddaddy Pup argued about the measly dollar and fifty cents she gave him for lunch due to him being an irresponsible drunk, which would only be enough to purchase a pack of crackers and a can of mini weaners. The funniest story was the time she tried to buy my mother and her sisters some encyclopedias for school but couldn't keep up the bill. The book owner gave her 3 options: sell her dog, stand on the street with a cup, begging for money to pay for the books, or go to jail.

But then, my mother would also share sad moments of her childhood like the time Grandma Stella and Granddaddy Pup were being chased and shot at with a shotgun by her former lover down a railroad track. One of the saddest stories was about the time my seven-year-old mother and her oldest sister went looking for their mother only to find her drunk and staggering the highway.

Grandma Stella ended up falling, despite her daughters' efforts to walk her home. They were near a steep creek bank, and since her daughters were too little to hold her up in her current state, she rolled down the bank almost plunging into the water while my mother and her sister stood as helpless witnesses; screaming, crying, and pleading for their mother to get up. A stranger saw them in their distress and pulled over to carry their mother back up the bank and drove them home.

My mother thought of herself to be the sister who was sometimes mistreated by Grandma Stella. She told me that she was forbidden to do most of the things her other sisters could do. The more she reflects on those times now, the more she thinks there was a possibility that Grandma Stella saw how different she was compared to her peers and wanted to protect her.

My mother was often teased by her peers, including her sisters, at times. She was called names like 'Nun' because she despised sex and 'No Teeth' because when she spoke, she didn't show her top row of teeth and would often talk with her lips barely parted. While most children laughed and giggled at foul, sexually inappropriate things, my mother would be ready to fight any boy who dared to try and tease or touch her in a sexually inappropriate manner.

My mother said she was a quiet but feisty child and would often fight bullies without hesitation, whether she was being bullied or she saw someone else being bullied. She was also one who struggled to learn in school. She felt the teachers didn't take enough time with her and didn't teach her in a way she could understand things. So, by the time she reached the 10th grade, she decided to drop out of school and attend a job corps program to obtain her GED, as well as a certificate in Culinary Arts.

My mother was extremely crazy about the Rambo character played by Sylvester Stallone. In some ways, I think my mother thought of herself to be somewhat of a lady Rambo. Think I'm joking? Okay, let's see.

There's the time my mother told me about her fight with a fifth-grade boy over a coloring paper. She said her teacher allowed them to choose a page out of a coloring book to color every Friday, and this day, she chose a Tom Sawyer page. She loved Tom Sawyer's character.

A boy approached her and asked if she would trade papers with him, but my mother refused. So, the boy got angry. He reached over with a pair of scissors and cut my mother's coloring page. The teacher stepped out for a minute, but upon her return, she found the boy with cat-like scratches all over his face. He was bleeding.

My mother says the teacher didn't want to paddle her because she was one of the teacher's favorite students. But the teacher knew she couldn't let my mother get away with what she'd done. "You should have waited and reported it to me when I came back in the classroom," the teacher explained. My mother understood and accepted her paddling.

Then there's the time my mother told me about a mean girl who wanted the desk my mother chose and took it from her in a nasty, humiliating way. She said that she had gone to class and picked out a desk that was right in front of the classroom and laid her books on top of it to claim it. She still had a little time before the tardy bell, so she decided to do a quick bathroom break before class.

When she returned, a bully had scattered all my mother's books across the floor and was sitting inside the desk my mother chose. The class laughed and pointed at the girl that was behind it all. "Why did you knock my books all over the floor? You could have easily moved them to another desk if you wanted to sit here!" she told the girl.

The girl didn't respond and just stared at my mother with a devilish grin. "Please pick my books up off the floor," my mother requested. She asked the girl three times to get her books, but the girl just ignored her. My mother bent over and got her books. Then, she looked at the girl and said, "three o'clock."

My mother said a crowd of students followed the girl, and another group followed her after school. She spotted the girl by her congregation, approached her, and jumped on her. They fought all the way to the girl's house. They rolled into a ditch, and my mother noticed a two by four wooden piece. She picked it up, but just as she did, one of her sisters stood in the way of her using it on the girl. My mother says though she was unsatisfied with the girl's beatdown, she left her alone.

She didn't just fight for herself, she fought for others.

"One day, while walking home, a boy decides to pick on a girl by calling her names and making her cry. When she didn't respond to him and kept walking, he amped up the bulling to jumping up in the air and coming down with a closed fist on her back. He kept doing it, and I encouraged the girl to fight back, but she was afraid. I went nose to nose with him and told him he had one more time to hit her, and I would *have* him. *"You ain't nothin' but a lil' punk. How you gon' hit somebody that ain't fightin' back?"* I asked. He wouldn't hit her or me and just stood there, huffin' and puffin'," she said.

My mother says she was never 'inspired' to fight unless someone touched her. She could ignore words and rarely ever responded to teasing. She recalled the time a group of mean girls taunted her while the class waited for a substitute teacher to arrive. "A mean girl and her clique came in class, teasing and taunting me. *"Girl, what's wrong with you? You don't never talk. Can you even talk? You don't never play with us or nothin'. You just sit there lookin' and quiet and everything. You got teeth in yo' mouth?*" they taunted. "*Put yo' finger in there and find out,*" she said. The teacher walked back in, and the girl backed off.

As my mother got older, she didn't fight as much. That is until she went to job corps. My mother got into two fights during her 2-year culinary program, and they were pretty huge. One was with a girl who had heard an untrue rumor about my mother gossiping about her. "Somebody told me you been talkin' about me," the girl said. "I don't know who you are, but you are not my concern. I'm here for one reason and one reason only," my mother replied. The girl dismissed what my mother said and attacked. They tussled all the way to the lobby, where my mother got a broomstick and whipped...her...down.

The other fight was called the Jumanji fight, in which case, my mother was a mad monkey. "I had no idea a flamboyant male classmate was competing with me. I was a hard worker and paid no mind to anyone around me. When he heard that I'd completed all of my objectives and was getting ready to graduate, he became furious. My instructor informed me that he was disturbed with me, and the moment she did, he came in screaming at her and me accusing me of cheating and her of showing favoritism and marking completion marks without me earning it. I said my work spoke for itself and left him to the instructor and went to sit down in the kitchen area. He followed me in there, took a knife, and stabbed the counter my hand was rested on with the knife, landing centimeters away from my fingers. Then he noticed the look of death I had on my face and asked what I was gonna do. While waving his hand in my face, his long fingernails scratched me. All kitchen devices became missiles. I hopped on top of the counter like a mad monkey and threw utensils, glasses, plates, bowls, and knives at him like they were frisbees. He scurried to hide under a nearby table, and the instructor came in, asking him what he did to cause this uproar in me. She couldn't calm me, so she told the other students to get security. They came and snatched me down. It took three of them to hold me. Because the scratch under my eye was visible and witnesses vouched for me, he was expelled while they only revoked my weekend off-campus pass for that week," she said.

My mother was a petite woman, so she didn't fight her goliaths fairly. She was resourceful in taking down a bully.

A huge girl and her cousin transferred from a notoriously troubled job corps to save themselves from getting kicked out of the program for good. One got stuck being one of my mother's roommates and had a habit of peeing in the bed. My mother and another roommate tried to tell the girl that she needed to take better care of herself, but the girl didn't take heed to their advice.

One day, the girl wet her bed while her cycle was on, but she just covered it with her blanket. They avoided reporting her to the hall monitor or telling anyone to save her from embarrassment but approached her about it because it had their room unbearably foul.

They approached her, and she got mad and told her cousin, and they decided to plan to jump my mother. "I prepared for her by putting all of my padlocks in a sock. She approached me and stood nose to nose. I told her, "It was said you wanted me, so here I am. I never throw the first blow, so go if you ready, but make it count, cause when I get you, Ima *have* you."

The girl backed down from fighting my mother because of what she saw in my mother's hand.

So, now do you believe that my mother thought she was Rambo? I thought you might, after those stories.

Despite her difficult circumstances, my mother chose to not perceive her mother's teachings to be a waste. She decided to become the exact opposite that she'd seen her mother portray. My mother was determined not to drink, smoke, party, speak profanely, dress provocatively or fornicate and was dead set on making sure that her children were fathered by one man, who would be none other than her husband. She told me she accepted God at the age of twelve and found anything that wasn't of Him to be detestable.

My mother said that Grandma Stella was never really a God-fearing woman until the last few years of her life. She began feeling a conviction about her behaviors and habits and made a diligent effort to put an end to the ways of her flesh and seek out God's path to redemption and eternal salvation. Not just by my mother's account, but by the reports of everyone that knew Grandma Stella, she started banning smoking and drinking from her house, she married my Granddaddy Pup to become righteous in the eyes of God and put an end to her fornication. She even became a more delightful person to those she once harshly judged for whatever her reasons may have been.

My mother said Grandma Stella had diabetes and died of an aneurism at the age of forty-nine, just two and a half months shy of her 50th birthday, where she was scheduled to be honored by her children with a special program. But before this unfortunate tragedy, Grandma Stella came to my mother, begging her to cook and show her a healthier way to eat.

She admitted to being afraid of dying and wanted to try and reverse the effect that diabetes had taken on her body. My mother says that she'd been too caught up with being a young mother of two and newlywed to an unfaithful husband to focus on her mother's request. This is something my mother often reflects on with a heart-load of regret since she was specifically skilled in cooking for people with medical issues from her time spent at job corps and often wonders if she could have made a difference in her mother's fate.

God warned me about Grandma Stella's approaching death through a reoccurring dream that I would have every single day. Grandma Stella cared for my younger sister and me while my mom would go to work, and she would lay us down for a nap while she went and sat in her rocking chair in the living room. Every single time I laid down, I woke up screaming and crying, "Grandma! Grandma! I don't want you to die, Grandma!" I'd run and hop straight in her arms in the rocking chair, and she'd always soothe me with the same words, "Aw, baby, Grandma ain't going nowhere. I'm right here. See?" she'd say with a huge smile that pushed her already high cheekbones right into her squinty little beady eyes.

It took her a while to ask me what my dream was about, but one day she asked. "Baby, tell me what you dreamed." "It was a T-rex dinosaur, and it was trying to get you. You was running, and I was running right in front of you. The family was waiting on us to make it to this giant garage that would protect us from the dinosaur, and I always make it. But then, everybody would start yelling to close the gate, saying that if we let you in, we let the dinosaur in. You cry and run to us yelling to keep the gate open, but the family closed the gate, and the dinosaur catch' you and swallow' you. And then I wake up," I said, sobbing. "Well, baby, ain't no dinosaur about to eat Grandma. I'm still here," she said. She would always rock me to comfort in that rocking chair. I was four years old when I started having that dream, and a couple months later, the dinosaur of an aneurism took her.

My mother never quite understood me, but she was always extremely interested in my thoughts and would often encourage me at my deepest lows. She always knew exactly what to say to comfort and strengthen my spirit.

She was also always going to bat for me against my dad, trying to get him to understand or empathize with me. He says she would always say to him about me, "Duke, it's something special about that child. She's just not normal." On the flip side of that, she would also try to get me to empathize with my dad's shortcomings as well. She'd tell me to pity him, but not hate him.

She'd tell me often that she was incredibly proud of me and loved me very much. But even more so, she'd warn me that I was being pursued by a greater enemy than my eyes could see. She also went as far as to make me an artsy bracelet with a white bow as a token of awareness for me. She took a piece of paper and colored three columns of red, green, and yellow on it. She wrapped the paper with clear tape and connected the ends with a bow of praying hands and a heart. The red stood for stopping my anger. The yellow stood for breathing through my emotions and being observant. The green only meant 'go' when I'd prayed and received the 'okay' from God about the situation at hand.

The white bow was connected to the ends of the paper and formed into a bracelet that I wore every single day for a few years straight.

She'd go on and on about how extraordinary I was and how my artistic ways were a dead giveaway that there was something incredibly special that I was meant to do. She took notice of the multiple talents I'd begun cultivating like drawing, sketching, singing, and writing poetry. She also noticed that I had been endowed with wisdom beyond my earthly years. She said the enemy wanted to stop me from achieving my purpose, and that's why he was always attacking my heart.

My mother was extremely fond of both her children equally for very different reasons. She never really made either of us feel as if she loved one more than the other and made sure that my sister and I always knew we were the most important aspects of her life.

She was also a lovely and physically attractive woman who, in my opinion, was out of my dad's league. Don't get me wrong, my dad was alright, but my mother was all that and some. She had this pear-shaped body that was dramatically accented by her protruding hip bones. She was a woman I knew God took his time with because her hip bones were uniformed identically to her high-sitting cheekbones that sat like two mountains on each side of her face even without her smiling. Her eyes were deep and compassionate until she grew angry. Then, they became deep and full of fierce fire. Her lashes were long, and her lips were thin and centered her heart-shaped face. She was fit and had shaped arms that carried lots of strength.

My mother always resembled Angela Bassett to me, which led me to become one of Angela's most dedicated fans. If you've ever seen Angela's acting during a scene of anger or sorrow, that was my mother whenever she was hurt. She rarely ever cried, but when she did, it ripped out my soul and made me willing to do whatever to whoever had done the damage. Most of the time, my dad would be on the receiving end of that.

My mother's nurturing spirit had a feisty twin spirit of overwhelming authority. She was the 'dad' of our household, and my dad knew it. She had the first hunch about something being off, and the last say on any matter that would affect the family. She feared nothing and was passionate about warning my sister and me of the dangers of the world. Often times, when we'd be in our own little worlds playing, my mother would summon us to the living-room couch and speak to us about something profound and random like being kidnapped by strangers and trusting no one to never turn against us.

My mother's soft spot was for children. She would do some severe damage to anyone who would dare mistreat a child because she always declared them innocent and too helpless to defend themselves. She was spontaneous and fun, and would much of the time, become more popular amongst my peers than I was. She was like the girl version of Peter Pan.

Despite her serious, almost paranoid side, my mother was extremely playful, much like her own mother, and would chase me around with bugs and anything else she knew I was afraid of. She even tricked me into thinking an alligator was behind me while we were pulled over under a bridge in floodwaters, looking at a turtle that would become our pet. I fell for these tricks because we lived in Louisiana, and alligators were always around, even if you didn't see them.

Her playing would most times cause friction between us. She liked to wrestle and physically 'tap' us and chase us. I didn't like playing with her because she was never aware of how hard her hands actually were. Eventually, I would get to the point of screaming at her to stop. She would stop, but I would be haunted by the somber and disappointed look on her face about not being able to horseplay with me. It was her way of bonding with me, and though it was something my younger sister couldn't get enough of, it wasn't my cup of tea.

My dad had compassion for me when it came to my mother's meddling. He would often scold her about how she needed to stop teasing so much before it caused me to seriously hurt myself one day. I would literally almost break the bones in my body, trying to run from whatever she was chasing me with.

This ended up backfiring on my mother in my teen and adult years. One day, she decided to stand on the opposite side of my bedroom door and wait for me to eventually open the door to come out. Well, I opened the door and was met by her bucked eyes and widely opened mouth. Before I could process it was my mother, I slammed the door right on her nose and bruised it.

For a while, my mother gave up on trying to scare me until I became pregnant with my daughter. I was asleep on the couch, and my mother decides she's going to crawl around the couch on the floor and put her face in mine and startle me. Without thinking, I slapped her backward, and she laughed until she cried. That was her last time trying to scare me while I was pregnant.

My mother would be her truest self whenever she linked up with her twin sister. When those two would get together, there would be countless stares in public and uncontrollable laughter from their children. It's really something you'd need to be an eyewitness to even begin to imagine.

My mother was only extraverted around people she knew and trusted, which wasn't really many people besides her two children. My sister and I were her best friends, and she didn't believe in hosting company at her home. She was notoriously private and paranoid about people coming to her house. She used to say, "If nowhere else, your home should be a place of undisturbed peace."

I can honestly say that my mother did all she could with the tools she had to try and ensure that to be a true statement for her family. Unfortunately, the reality became that despite her aggressive efforts, her home would be destroyed in some of the most tragically sinister ways.

You see, when she made her vow to God at the age of twelve to commit to one man, the enemy heard her as well. He sent a lost soul to a broken one and convinced them to marry and build a home in quicksand.

The Captain

"A great captain knows that he isn't really the One steering the ship, and a foolish one sinks the ship with his great pride."
~ A. S. E.

MY DAD WAS an extremely hard worker who made sure we always had everything we needed, pertaining to food and shelter, and most of what our young hearts could desire. When we were toddlers, he would be the parent advocating for us to be able to eat our trick-or-treat candy after bedtime and convincing my mother to let us skip nap times on our birthdays.

According to the home videos I've seen, he and I were very close when I was a toddler, and he'd been quite the hands-on dad. But he struggled with demons that were allowed to parade themselves through our home and rip our family apart several times. My sister and I were left vulnerable to them and suffered the consequences. My dad was exceedingly unfaithful to my mother and would often desire more practices and possessions of the world than treasures of the Kingdom of God. The friction between my dad and I began when I became aware of the presence of those demons.

My dad was raised in a home that attended church service every Sunday morning. His mother and dad were both working people who got married at the tender ages of fourteen and seventeen years old.

My dad said his dad made sure the family had what they needed as far as food and money, but hadn't really been a guided example to my dad and his brothers of what it took to become a man of God and lead a family in Christ.

My dad was extremely scholarly in school but was often targeted by teachers and administration because he was also quite the troublemaker. He described himself as more of a chameleon, being able to fit in with any and everyone. My dad never really stood for anything and fell for everything.

In his teen years, my dad was quite the rolling stone and sewed many oats that wouldn't be discovered until years after he married my mother. My dad met my mom at church service. My mother was an usher, and my dad noticed her while she was teaching children's Sunday school. He said that at that moment, he saw she had a way with children and thought of her to be an excellent prospect for his wife and the mother of *his* future children.

My dad pursued my mother by asking one of her sisters to tell her that he liked her. My mother said she thought he was ugly and annoying at first, but later became attracted to him because of his strong work ethic. She said he was a go-getter and was always mowing someone's lawn or finding odd jobs to make money. My mother also admired how my dad would try to use a prestigious vocabulary when conversing with his peers.

My Grandma Stella wasn't a fan of my dad, and she didn't approve of his and my mother's relationship. My mother said that while her other sisters were allowed to go out on dates with their boyfriends, she was forbidden to go out and date my dad. Somehow, my mother managed to still see him and get to know him as best she could.

My dad recalls how my Grandma Stella always thought he was wearing eye make-up because of how long his lashes were, and since my dad's eyelids are naturally a shade darker than his face, he always appeared to be wearing eyeshadow.

My dad was what some would consider a hunk. He was buff and wore his jet-black hair short and well-groomed. He had a connecting mustache-beard situation going on and a small goatee tucked under the curve of his bottom lip.

My mother often said my dad reminded her of Rambo, but I don't know why. I mean, from what I know, every time there was an altercation with someone, he'd show up with a gun. He wasn't really as resourceful as my mother and didn't 'fight' that often. I believe this was because he was a 'pretty boy' and didn't want to get his face messed up.

My dad's protective nature concerning my mother didn't help things between Grandma Stella and him, either.

One day, my mother lost track of time and stayed out later than her mother permitted. She ran into my dad and his cousin near the school and decided she would hang out with them for a minute. My dad had sent his cousin away so that he could walk with my mother for a little while. It was at this time that my dad tried to break things entirely off with my mother because he was tired of not being able to see her due to Grandma Stella's strict way with my mother.

When it started to get late, my dad said that he was about to leave and head home. As he was getting in the car, he noticed my mother walking in the opposite direction of her house. "Where are you going?" he asked. "Well, I ain't got you no more, and it's late, so I'm in trouble. Ma gon' try to whip me, and I'm tired of whippings, so I ain't goin' back," my mother answered.

My dad shooed his cousin away once more and tried to make my mother go back home, but she adamantly refused. My dad then lied to my mother and told her that he had some money saved up and promised her that they could run away together but said that he needed time to get it all figured out. It was this story that convinced my sixteen-year-old mother to go with him to his sister's house.

They stayed together all night and slept in an old school bus. They weren't at all intimate, and when morning came, his sister noticed my mother and warned my dad to get her home, or he would be arrested because he was eighteen, and she was a minor. They had been informed that the authorities were looking for my mother.

My dad drove my mother back home, and when they arrived, Grandma Stella was standing in the doorway, holding a belt. My dad and mother got out of the car and stood, staring at Grandma Stella for a long while. "You get in here," Grandma Stella said, pointing to my mother. "and you leave!" she instructed my dad.

My dad showed hesitation to leave because he didn't want my mother to get a whipping. "What? You lookin' at this?" Grandma Stella asked, referencing the belt in her hand. "I'm not gon' hit 'er. Go on," she said.

My mother's twin sister met her where she stood and reassured my mother that she told Grandma Stella not to whip her and that it was safe to go in the house.

My dad was a smoker and was very sexually active by the time he and my mother started seeing each other. My mother told me that once, my dad touched her glutes, and she slapped him into a shock. She also said that their first kiss had been terrible because it was all wet and sloppy and tasted like 'straight cigarettes.'

My mother hated cigarettes so much, she told me that any time her mother would ask her to light a cigarette from the stove, she would purposely burn it and bring it back to her mother almost completely gone.

My dad was nowhere near ready to commit to my mother and tried on numerous different occasions to break things off with her but had already won her heart and her commitment.

My dad never proposed to my mother, she told him they were getting married. They each gave each other alternatives; my dad explained to my mother that he was already sexually active and made it seem like it was something he couldn't 'turn off' long enough to wait on marriage. My mother told my dad that unless he waited for her, stopped smoking, and quit drinking, he would lose her forever.

My dad eventually wore my mother down at the age of sixteen after she left home to attend a jobs corps program, and they came together. But by this time, my mother had lowered her Godly standards. She wasn't aware at the time, but at this moment, she chose to dance with my dad instead of walking with God.

As a result of the blood covenant made between my dad and mother, she signed a deal with the devil. The enemy knew the promise my mother had made to herself in her youth and knew that she was now locked in for the long haul. He knew how hurt my mother had been when her own father instructed her not to call him 'dad' so that he could pick up young women. He knew that she would do anything to not be what she'd seen her mother be and give herself to multiple men. No, she'd be faithful, no matter the cost, because she'd think her loyalty to my dad equated to her devotion to God. He also knew that my dad was not ready for marriage or a family and would produce seed that the enemy could have his way with from lack of leadership.

The enemy's plans were coming along quite well.

My mother required more of my dad than anyone else had. He relied on her to push him in whatever direction would allow him to accomplish great things. She was his conscience, and though he fought her nail and tooth on various subjects, he found comfort in knowing he had someone in his life that cared more about him that he did.

This still wasn't enough to keep my dad faithful to my mother. He had been cheating on my mother with my older sister's mother, who'd been conceived even before my mother went away to job corps. By the time my mother was about to complete her job corps program and return to the delta, he was also sleeping with another woman who he tried to break things off with right before my mother came home. The break-off didn't go well, and the woman refused to accept my dad not wanting relations with her anymore. He says she began harassing his family and his parents, cursing his parents out and calling my mother everything but a child of God.

He dodged her and went to the police department to try and get a restraining order, but nothing was done about the harassment. Finally, after the woman had been looking for him everywhere, she showed up in his sister's yard while he was babysitting his nephews and nieces. She began cursing and telling my dad to send my mother out of the house. She thought my mother was there with him.

My dad had told his cousin about 'settling' things with the woman, but his cousin says he didn't expect things to be that bad, so he didn't try and talk him out of it. My dad's mother lived right around the corner from his sister's house, and when the woman showed up to his mother's house, he assaulted the woman by beating her up right where she stood in his mother's yard. He got arrested the day before he was supposed to pick my mother up from completing her program. My dad sent his cousin to pick her up, and he broke the news about my dad to my mother upon arrival.

My mother decided she couldn't face Grandma Stella or her sisters because she was told my dad's incident was all over the news. She spent her first night back home in a hotel room, crying and hating life.

The next day, my mother mustered up the nerve to return to Grandma Stella's house and was met with nothing short of what she expected. Her family stared in her face, bursting to tell all to her. They appeared sympathetic, but then Grandma Stella asked my mother what was next for her. When my mother replied that she was prepared to wait on my dad's release from prison, Grandma Stella blew a top and tried her best to convince my mother that she deserved much better than what she was subjecting herself to. But my mother, headstrong about being in love with my dad, was unwaveringly committed to him, no matter what.

My mother had no contact with my dad during his stay in jail, but after he was sentenced and transferred to a prison, she started receiving messages through my dad's mother that he wanted to contact her. My mother asked her mother if it would be alright for my dad to call, but Grandma Stella denied her request and said that my dad couldn't write there, either. My dad started writing to his cousin around the corner, and the cousin transferred the letters to my mother.

My mother and her oldest sister had a big fight one day. The sister ended up finding the letter that my mother had written to my dad, expressing how unhappy she was living there and how depressed she was about her step-dad being a drunk and how she wasn't getting along with the family. Her sister gave the letter to Grandma Stella, and she became furious about my mother conversing with my dad about what went on in her house.

My mother jumped on her sister for being messy, and her sister convinced Grandma Stella to put her out. My mother then moved in with Grandma Ruthie and got a job as a waitress at a restaurant. My mother made sure to attend every visitation my dad was permitted, and she was faithful in waiting for him.

My dad was sentenced to ten years, with five years suspended and only served half of that time due to good behavior and taking up the trade of welding. That hadn't been the only good thing that came out of my dad's incarceration. He had also learned sketching and drawing techniques that he would later pass on to me in a rare moment of he and I bonding over art. My dad had also learned to make a mean mackerel salad that was one of our favorite meals to share.

Every time he would have a moment of spare time from working and wasn't tired, he would randomly announce to the family that he was thinking about making his famous mackerel salad. My sister and I would be ecstatic! He would even make a separate bowl for me because he usually made it spicy and knew I couldn't really handle spicy foods well.

When he was released, he and my mother bought a trailer home together. My dad was able to use his welding trade to get a well-paying job, and they lived together for three years before conceiving me.

My dad finally married my mother three months after my birth but was unfaithful during her pregnancy with me and afterward. My mother left him just shy of my 1st birthday to go to California and live with her twin sister, but he followed and convinced her to come back. That was the birth of a never-ending cycle.

My dad had already fathered a 3-year-old baby boy, my oldest brother, Antuaine, by the time he and my mother began their courtship, if you could call it that. My brother was a sweet kid with a big heart. We actually have a video of him teaching me to do the butterfly. His heart was bright and honest, and I loved my big brother. During the short time he came to live with us, we got along great, and I found myself always trying to be just like him.

I remember going to the waterpark once with the entire family, and my dad and brother swam in the twelve-foot deep water. I didn't want to miss out on the fun, and I didn't want my strong, daring brother to think of me as weak or less than he was, so I joined them.

I stood on the edge for a long while, leaning forward and looking in. My big brother came behind me and coached me like an army drill sergeant. "Come on, na! What you gon' do? You can just stand here lookin' at it. Jump!" he barked. "I am! Just give me a minute," I said. My dad laughed at our exchange. "You got ten seconds to jump or be thrown in," he said. I didn't jump, so he picked me up and threw me in.

The experience was a bit divine. I looked down and couldn't make out the bottom. Then I looked up and saw the sun shining through the water. I stretched my arms out and allowed myself to sink for a moment because the feeling of the water swallowing me felt magical. Then I dog paddled my way back to the top.

"Girl! I was scared you weren't comin' back up! I was about to come down there lookin' for you," my dad said. "Yeah, you sho' took a long time? What were you doin'?" my brother asked. I smiled and said, "I was enjoying the water. I'm good." They both raised their hands to give me high fives for being a part of the group that swam in the deep, while the rest of the family stayed in the three-foot water.

My mother didn't meet his second child, my older sister, LaKriesha until my sister was 8 years old. My mother encouraged my dad to get involved with her, and she eventually came to live with us when she reached the 4th grade and left us when she reached the 9th grade.

My older sister and I didn't get along at all. She was always trying to counsel me and tell me to talk about my' feelings'. I was mean and shut off, but that didn't stop her from prying. "Why are you so angry all the time?" she would ask. "I'm not angry," I would say. She always came off as trying to be a second mother and would often boss Ree and me around. Ree didn't mind, but I did.

There was one instance I remember during the time my dad had been diagnosed with cancer. It was hard seeing him laid up that way, and this was his second time having it, so we were on pins and needles about it. The doctors had told him he had about a 50/50 chance of surviving. The family had even somewhat starting to prepare to lose him.

While my mother was at the hospital spending time with my dad, my older sister and Grandma Ruthie was left to look after my younger sister and me. She wanted to pick out our clothes for school and lay them on the bed. I decided to go to my dresser and pick out my own clothes. "Um, where is the outfit I picked out for you to wear?" she asked when I came into the kitchen. "I can pick out my own clothes," I said. "What's wrong with the ones on the bed?" she asked. "Nothing wrong, but I wanted to wear something I picked out," I said. "You're acting really childish right now," she said. "And you're acting like my mother right now when you're not," I said. "Okay, well, since I'm not your mother, you can make your own breakfast too. Ree, you want some waffles and eggs?" she asked my sister. "Yeah!" Ree said. "That's fine by me. I'll just get some cereal," I said. "Okay," she said.

My older sister and I had sweet moments together also, though they were quite rare. I remember her letting me make her face up with my play cosmetics. I felt awful about it because my sister had sensitive skin and broke out terribly after I'd packed her face with all that cheap make-up. She kept trying to reassure me that it was alright.

When I got older, my sister gave me my first dildo to try and serve as a form of therapy since, by this time, my comfortability with sexual intimacy had been tainted by traumatic experiences. It wasn't the best thing to do, but her heart was in the right place. I would talk with her and say how I was never getting married or letting another man touch me, so she thought it'd be beneficial to have that particular time to 'recondition' myself so that I'd be able to accept my future beau.

When I had entered my preteen years, my dad received a letter in the mail revealing to us that he'd fathered another son, my older brother Xavier and that the boy wanted a blood test because he wanted to know his real dad. My parents said Xavier's mom had even given him the same nickname my dad had; Duke. So, my parents suspected that she already knew that my dad was Xavier's dad. It came as a shock to all of us, but we were excited about welcoming a new brother into our sibling circle.

In my early adult years, I discovered that we had another older brother, Bryan, that had never met his dad...my dad. Finally, my little sister, Ree, and I said we'd make a social media ad stating that if anyone didn't have a dad and thought they looked like my dad, to contact us. Honestly, with all the infidelity committed by my dad throughout the marriage, I wouldn't be surprised if there are more siblings yet to be discovered.

As I mentioned earlier, old home videos show my dad to be very loving and involved with my sister and me. He was adventurous, spontaneous, and loved having fun. He even dressed up as his mother one Halloween to take me trick-or-treating. At Christmas time, he was always making sure we had more than we could ever use within a year.

My dad was always the one pushing us in our academic learning and would often participate in whatever parent-child activity our school would be hosting.

As we got older, my dad would take my younger sister, Ree, and me fishing and was a man who loved the outdoors. He'd wake up at 5 a.m., asking my sister and me who wanted to join him on the fishing trip. I hated fishing trips because of my severe allergies, but I loved being able to eat junk food and draw or sketch while my dad and younger sister fished.

My dad cherished Ree because she was like the son he and my mother never had together. She was very hands-on with him in the great outdoors. She'd offer to cut the grass on the riding lawn mower, rake the leaves, accompany him in his workshop, and boy did they have the same appetite for the same types of food.

Ree and my dad especially bonded over our 4-H program in school. My dad even helped us raise a bunch of chickens from the time they were baby chicks. This was an experience my dad and sister loved. But I remember going to the cage with my dad and him pointing out a hurting chick. I think the chick's leg started off being broken, and because of this, the other chicks pecked at it, causing the chick to bleed and terribly suffer.

When we saw the chick, it was mangled and suffering, so my dad broke the neck to put it out of its misery. I remember feeling enraged and wanting to kill every other chick in the cage. I related deeply to that mangled chick. I had been that chick, mangled throughout my grade school years, and because other children didn't understand what I was going through, they picked and pecked. Somehow, being nipped at by my peers, and sometimes picked apart by my parents' lack of a Godly foundation, I got my neck broken, except this didn't end my misery at all.

Ree was oblivious to my dad's indiscretions, and this would later cause more damage in the future. She was often mad at me for always bumping heads with my dad.

My dad often underestimated my illnesses. He didn't understand them, so he dismissed them as me being dramatic or just trying to get out of work. My nose would be swollen from sneezing, and I often snorted in an attempt to reach the itch in my throat. Many times, when I sneezed, I did not allow my mouth to spew out spit and would cut my sneeze short; at least that's what my dad called it.

He always threatened to give me a whipping if I didn't "stop snorting up mucus and sneeze right." My mother would try to explain to him that he should have more compassion for me because of my suffering. We lived in Louisiana, where it was often hot and humid. If a fan or air conditioner wasn't running, I fell victim to active sinus infections, vigorous sneeze attacks, sore throats, and migraine headaches.

I grew up allergic to mosquitos, grass, rainwater, mold, dust, dander, and most cleaning products. Because of this, I spent most of my time indoors. And when my mother would clean the house, I would go outside in the front yard for a while until she was done mopping or cleaning the kitchen and bathroom.

My dad also had in his mind that I was 'being weak' about my allergies and that if I would only spend more time around all the things I was allergic to, I would grow immune to them and not have allergies anymore. So, he would often try and not turn on the fans and air-conditioning and would insist that I needed to 'go outside for some fresh air.'

These were just a couple of the things that caused me to resent and hate my dad. The strife between my mother and dad, and between my dad and me, made my skin grow thick and my heart grow ice cold. My younger sister understood none of this.

The Private

"Forever young isn't a privilege, it's a tragedy."
~A. S. E.

MY YOUNGER SISTER, Ree, was such a happy kid. She made friends wherever we went and seemed to be a favorite in the household. She was kind and loved sharing with me, but she was extremely meddlesome, too. My sister would do disgusting things behind my parents' backs like, stick her tongue out at me with a load of mucus on it to make me gag.

She had a strong stomach, but a cowardly spirit. She was afraid of the spirit realm. She never really saw things like I did, but she felt them and would always beg to sleep with me in my room. I wanted to be left alone, so I ignored her knocking on my door until she'd give up and go back to her own room.

One day, a while after I'd turned ten years old, my parents suggested I prove to her that her room was safe and told me to spend the night in her room while she spent the night in mine. I reluctantly agreed. That night, I saw a dark figure swaying back and forth in her closet, but I'd been so used to seeing spirits that I simply ignored the figure and fell asleep.

When I woke up the next morning, I felt a heavy pressure on top of me and couldn't rise from the bed, but I didn't see anything. I remembered my mother telling me to call on the name of "Jesus" and try to touch something cold if that ever happened to me, so I called on my Savior, and I reached for the white dresser that was beside the bed and was able to bounce up. I ran into the living room where I heard my parents talking and told them what happened.

While I was sharing my experience with them, they both just kept looking from each other back to me with almost "knowing" glares. I told them that I wanted my sister to move into my room and that they could make my sister's old bedroom a place for guests. I was very adamant, almost demanding about them making the change as soon as possible. Ree never slept in that room again after that night, and soon after, my parents invested in a bunk bed to replace my queen-sized bed. I missed my privacy, but I felt better knowing my sister wasn't sharing a room with that dark figure I saw. She was extremely grateful.

Ree's fear of spirits caused her to go to the bathroom and not wipe good enough, trying not to be alone too long. This slowed up when my mother grew tired of seeing chunks of 'waste' in her underwear when it came time to wash clothes. My mother fixed this problem in one of the most hilarious and unbelievable ways.

"Girls! Get in here," she called out. My sister and I found her in the living room standing with both of our underwear in her hands. "I'm tired of this! You are too big to be messing up your underwear like this. There is no excuse for me finding chunks of booboo in your panties! Since you don't care about me having to smell and clean your underwear, here! Wear 'em and smell 'em for yourself!" she said.

She placed my sister's 'streaked' underwear right on top of her head with the inside liner right on her nose. "Don't think you off the hook. Your underwear stay wet and smelling like pee! You ain't wipin' good either, so here!" she said, placing my underwear over my head as well. We weren't allowed to take them off and my sister and I cried and laughed at the same time. We cried because we didn't want our underwear on our heads, but when we turned to face each other and saw how ridiculous the other looked, our insides were tickled beyond control. I think we were just glad to have to endure it together.

My sister and I had many nights of fun, especially when it was storming outside. We would enclose our bunk bed with sheets and blankets and would role-play with baby dolls, which wasn't really a good idea. Sometimes, the toys were in drama-filled relationships that we had no business pretending about.

Ree was always the bright, gentle flower of the family. She was just a sweet person, for the most part, and she adored my dad and had much respect for him. Ree and I really did want to be friends growing up, but our different childhood experiences made that a little more complicated. She saw me as cold and locked away, and she never understood why. She saw me as mean and disrespectful to our dad and would later start to feel a little angry about that.

Ree was a very cliquey type of girl in school. She probably had one good friend out of about four bad ones. Most of her friends were snobby little mean-girl monsters that I despised. My sister and her friends thought I had no heart and would often express their distaste for me. My sister would beg my parents not to let me hang around her and her friends because I embarrassed her with the showdowns I would have with her clique of pests. She also swore that I always said things to purposely embarrass her in front of her friends.

The way I saw it, the only reason she was embarrassed was that she hadn't grown the thick skin I had yet, and she still cared way too much about what people thought about her. I was disgusted at how she sometimes tried to be a pleaser to undeserving crowds. I admired her greatly and thought she was better than her company, by far.

Later, my sister grew to love and need my ruthlessness. The older she got, the more beautiful she became, and the more the other girls of her grade began sneering and picking on her. During summer camp, students would literally come to my class and ask the teacher for me to be excused, saying that it was an emergency with my sister. Every time, I'd run to my sister's defense and simply return to my own age group when I was finished.

As we both got older, she became more and more popular and well-liked by her teachers. She was such a scholar and made excellent grades.

The same was true for me until I reached 9th grade when good grades went to war with terrible happenings.

I remember trying to warn my mother and younger sister about how things would change once she grew older and reached high school, but my mother got fighting mad at me and claimed I was just jealous of my sister. She said I was a pathetic, negative person and needed to bridle my tongue. I remember this hurt me because I was only trying to warn them about what I'd already been living.

My mother knew I was an unhappy person, but I hoped she would know that my hatred for my life and certain people in it had nothing to do with jealousy.

This pretty much sums up my family's personalities, our family dynamic, as well as my relationships with each member. Now, let's dive deeper into *my* personal childhood experiences with myself, my God, and my enemy.

Born...on the Battlefield

"I was born a blank canvas.
Life is my paint, and The Creator is my brush."
~A. S. E.

How are you doing thus far? Have you enjoyed the current? Aw, that wasn't so bad, was it? Well, I pray your oxygen is at a healthy level. We are now beginning the deep dive that will take us to the cave gardens. Don't panic. It's quite a way down but we'll take our time, I promise.

I know many parents consider their children unique and genius. I believe my own daughter to be somewhere along those lines. But I was unique in a most peculiar way. Sure, I was pretty smart as a toddler. Heck, I even memorized an entire 'wordy' Three Little Pigs book and recited it word for word at the age of two. I couldn't yet read! My mother tried multiple times to have me recite the book on camera to try and make me famous, but when the recording light came on, I would always get silly and not cooperate. I'd say that was God protecting me from fame too soon.

However, my smarts aren't what I believe made me a peculiar child. My mother says that when I was just an infant, my eyes were following something near the ceiling that she couldn't see. I watched something go back and forth and smiled and cooed at its presence. The look of joy and peace on my face put my mother's nerves at ease. Still, as any parent would be, she remained curious as to what I saw.

I don't have any memory of that night; I was an infant. But my memory does start at a fairly young age. I remember bits and pieces of when I was two and three, but my memory is vivid, beginning at the age of four.

My mother says I was extremely picky about who I let hold me, and often gave mean stares to people when they cooed at me. I was severely allergic to cigarette smoke and, for that reason, I wasn't able to visit Grandma Ruthie in her home, because she allowed people to smoke there.

My mother and dad planned to have my younger sister, Ree, when I turned two years old. They thought I needed a playmate. They were wrong, but oh well, she came and now honestly, I wouldn't have it any other way.

Before she was born, my mother's twin sister warned her not to allow me and the newborn baby to sleep in the same room. She said something about toddlers not taking well to new babies. When Ree arrived, my mother placed both of us in the same bedroom anyway and walked in late one night to find me punching my younger sister in the face, repeatedly. Ree didn't even cry! My mother says she just blinked and stared at me after every blow. My mother lit my behind up that night, as she should have.

Basically, I was a mean, proper kid who couldn't quite figure out how to adjust my ancient spirit to this new family and the modern world I'd entered, just yet. My accent was strong and southern, nothing like my family's tongue. My parents had absolutely no idea where that came from. I was addicted to Disney movies that made me look deeper and discover not such obvious messages. I loved the forest scene of *Snow White* when she frantically runs away, and the scene in *The Lion King*, when adult Simba walks up and takes his kingdom back while the majestic music plays in the background. There was one more movie about a girl with a star and pink skirt that I loved. I haven't been able to discover that movie or its title, but it was my favorite.

That is, until my true love, *The Little Mermaid*, entered my life. I wanted to be so much like Princess Ariel that once when I was older, I took a green blanket and tied the ends with rubber bands to resemble a fishtail, and tied the other end of the blanket around my waist. I jumped in our pool and...sank right to the bottom. I literally almost drowned and had to vigorously fight my way out of my make-shift tail and swim to the water's surface.

I related so much to her because I loved music! I didn't know it at the time, but I would also grow to enjoy singing and swimming. I've always been incredibly drawn to the water. It almost seemed to call me.

I remember my parents having a dead starfish and conch shell in the bathroom. Before I understood what they were, I would place both to my ear to hear the ocean. It was one of my favorite wonders, and the sea would seem to be trying to tell me a secret every time I lifted the crystalized sea creatures.

I lost myself in fairy tales and cartoons. They served as a great escape, because I felt like I was escaping to a place that I fit into more than earth. I absolutely hated being on earth. I often looked to the sky for long periods, wishing that even if just for a glance, I'd be able to see beyond my limited human sight. I wanted to see things with my spirit.

I honestly believe that God searched and knew my heart. He heard my unspoken words because things rapidly became crystal clear, starting around about the age of four. I began seeing many creatures that others couldn't. I would just stare at them, and they would stare back. They never spoke to me, but strange enough, they didn't scare me either.

Honestly, the more I saw these creatures, the more afraid of humans I became because I felt they were hiding their true identities. My mother started reading the story of the Three Little Pigs to me, and I would always get spooked by the wolf's eyes because of the way they were illustrated in that particular book. The eyes were the same color as mine, hazel. After a while, I began to be afraid of my own eyes!

I would literally go to the bathroom and stare into the mirror, trying to see if I could get a glance of what I really looked like. The longer I stared into my eyes, the more my look seemed to change. I started doing this often and eventually accepted the fact that the only way I would meet the spirit under my coat of flesh was when I died and entered the third phase of my life.

I began seeing people in a deeper light...or more profound darkness than before, and my spirit would react to whatever kind of spirit they were. I also started having dreams a lot at this age. I can only remember a select few, which were the ones that came true not long after I had them.

In the beginning, I wouldn't really talk about my dreams to anyone, not even my parents. It wasn't because I didn't think they were a big deal, but most of them scared me and made me never want to even allow mention of them to leave my lips.

Growing up, babies were terrified of looking me in the eyes. This made me feel horrible, like some sort of monster. I just told myself that maybe they were only not used to seeing hazel-colored eyes. Perhaps that was the case, maybe not. All I know is that I became intrigued and almost desperate to meet myself. There was this spirit living inside of me that would be led by one master or the other.

Neither force wasted any time introducing themselves to me. I believe this happened because I was a target even from inside my mother's womb. The enemy used none other than my dad. My mother says she stayed angry at him her entire pregnancy and swears that's the reason I came out looking just like him.

I grew up despising my dad, which honestly makes me sad to think about. My dad did many things wrong, but I recognize it was because he was lost, and unfortunately, I wasn't old enough to know how to lead him back to the light just yet. So, I rejected him, even when he *was* trying to turn his life around.

You see, I didn't realize it then, but from my dad's point of view, he was married to a woman with love for God he didn't understand. To make matters worse, he procreated a 'knowing' child who always called him out on his ignorance and shortcomings.

The union of my parents basically went like this. My mother was strong-willed and utterly dependent on God. She chased after Him and spent her entire marriage, trying to get back to the place she was spiritually before she chose my dad over God. She wasn't a scholar on academics, but she could make a case for the Lord anywhere, anytime.

My dad was always bucking against my mother, not because he thought she was wrong, but because his selfish pride wouldn't acknowledge that she was right. He did this because my mother was right most of the time and always made my dad look ignorant on many different levels.

Because they entered an unevenly yoked union, one was always judgmental towards the other, and one was always giving up since they felt they could never obtain or catch up to the spiritual level of the other person. I honestly believe that if they had not been together and stayed together, both of them would have flourished in God a long time ago. They held each other back.

As I began acknowledging and understanding the dynamic of my parents' relationship, I voiced my opinions about things and entered conversations I probably should have stayed out of. Though I was wise beyond my years, I was still extremely young and had much studying and living and learning to do before becoming equipped enough to be the voice of reason for my parents.

Basic Training

"They say beauty is in the eye of the beholder...I had to learn that every beholder isn't necessarily worthy or ready for my beauty."
~A. S. E.

I HADN'T ALWAYS BEEN so strong-minded and ready to face adversity. I was quite the push-over when I was a young girl, I'd say from the time I was about five until about nine. My sister and I were sheltered from many things, one being vulgar tv shows, and we didn't know much slang.

Because of this, I stuck out like a sore thumb amongst my peers. There was one incident on the school bus that attested to this fate. Two boys were whooping and hollering and fighting and cursing. Suddenly, a loud chant came from all the other kids on the bus. "Jerry, Jerry, Jerry!" they chanted. I leaned over to as quietly as I could, and asked someone, "Which one is Jerry?"

The person I asked was overwhelmed with laughter and yelled out to the rest of the bus, "Hey man, this girl just asked me 'which one Jerry'!" he shouted. The entire busload of kids, including the two boys who were fighting, screamed and laughed, and I was overcome with embarrassment. I slid back in my seat and looked out of the window. I suppose maybe I could've view myself as a hero, because I literally stopped a fight.

I often lost myself in drawings or writings. If I wasn't locked away in my room conversing with my spirit guide, I was enjoying the company of my many pets. I had a dog named Star who was a black and white Siberian husky, a cat named Snowflake who was a black cat with a white drop on her paw, and two hamsters whose names I've forgotten. I was an introvert who kept to myself, but if I was approached incorrectly, I'd make it my goal to make whoever did it regret it. I didn't become this way, though, until my mother demanded that I stand up for myself.

I was brutally bullied in school and would often come home with extensive, dark bruises from being kicked and other marks from being pushed down or beat up on the school bus. I had a large plug of hair pulled from my scalp in the second grade by a girl who wanted the swing I was using. Boys would trip me and pull my clothes, and when they'd get in trouble, they would say they did it because they liked me. I was even pushed down a flight of stairs by one boy and punched in the face by another.

I was bullied in many ways, sometimes even sexually. In the second grade, I took this French class because it was a required class at the school I attended. I loved it! We'll call my teacher Mr. Angelfish. He was Canadian with long blond hair, and I found him to be the most handsome man I knew. But what made him attractive to me was how I would see him treat his even more beautiful wife. Her hair was long and dark brown, and every time we would have a school festival or fun day, those two would be shining together brighter than the sun. I could tell that they really loved each other, and their kindness was something I aspired to obtain.

Mr. Angelfish noticed that a boy kept talking to me and trying to get my attention. So, he moved me. Though, on a Friday afternoon, we were watching a movie about colors and shapes in French. That same boy who was quite mischievous with a reputation for flirting with all the girls and picking on any boy who wasn't as cool as he thought he was, scooted up right behind me on the alphabet floor mat. I was wearing a uniform khaki skort, a skirt with shorts attached underneath. I had a dark blue uniform collar shirt tucked in and had wrapped my sweater jacket around my waist.

There were many of us on the floor mat huddled together to watch the movie, so no one really paid any attention to the boy inching up behind me. I started to feel a hand easing in my skort from behind. I reached my hand to grab his hand and moved it away from me. He leaned in and whispered, "I just wanna play with your panty line, pretty eyes." "No, stop, or I'll tell," I responded. "And let the whole class know you're a tattle-tell and get me in trouble just for liking you? No, you won't. Don't move my hand again," he said.

He was right. I was already disliked by almost every girl in school and picked on by every boy. Me tattling on him would make things worse. I remember staring at Mr. Angelfish, watching him sit at his desk and work on 'teacher stuff.' I wanted him to see me and catch the boy messing with me, but he never looked up. I remember feeling small and invisible. This would be part of my dilemma with many boys throughout my school years. Any time an adult *would* find out, mostly adult women teachers, they would always say ignorant things like, "Well, child, boys will be boys."

I never did tell my mother about things like that, because I knew she'd probably go after the boys *and* their parents with a vengeance.

My mother grew up being an introvert, but she was a fighter and would often make bullies regret their decision to become one. She was dead set on me abiding by the rules, though, so she sat me down and had me thoroughly read my handbook. She told me to know my rights and taught me the way to stop getting bullied. She told me to first, report the incident to the teacher. If the bullying continued, she told me to go to the counselor or assistant principal, and then finally to the principal if the issue was still unresolved. She made it clear that if the bullying persisted after these steps were taken, I should defend myself and not worry about getting in trouble because I'd have a paper trail of reports that went unresolved.

I listened carefully to my mother's advice and did exactly as I was told. Each time my reports went ignored, I grew sick to my stomach with fear because I didn't know how to fight and quite frankly wasn't interested in learning. My mother tried to teach me some pressure points to hit so that I'd be able to stop the bullies long enough to get away, but it didn't prove useful because whenever those times came, I would just blank out and come to when it was all over.

However, when I'd finally snap out of the trance, my unfortunate opponent was always the one bleeding and in pain. Once I saw what I was capable of, I hated myself. I hated knowing that I was the one to cause another human being to bleed. I would have rather dealt with being bullied. I put in extreme effort to avoid fighting at all costs, but I would still be pushed to that point by a few people. I only partook in three actual fights, even though there were more instances where I quickly defended myself well enough to get the person to stop bothering me.

Eventually, my parents decided to drive me to school instead of having me ride the school bus. All it took was the school administration to see my mother once, and they became more attentive to making sure the bullies were punished.

I remember coming home to my mother, sobbing hard, asking her why they hated me. That day, a girl had been verbally picking on me, calling me dike and tramp because I didn't have a boyfriend. At that time, I loved learning and hated boys or anything that had to do with dating. I wanted to become a teacher and I was head-strong in my books. I was in the 6th grade when this happened. She'd also said that I was too bright and boujee to hang with the blacks and too dark and dirty to hang with the whites.

She was always leading a large group of ghetto, hackling hyenas. One of her followers decided to throw an electric pencil sharpener at my head and caused my ear to bleed. I stared at the teacher with a look of asking on my face, trying to see if she would do anything about what had just happened. The entire class "oohed," but the teacher simply shook her head and went back to whatever she was doing at her desk.

I stood up and asked who threw the pencil sharpener at my head, even though I already knew who did it. Everyone pointed to the girl I suspected, and she stood up, walked to me, stood chest to face with me, bragging about what she did and asked me what I was going to do about it. I blacked out.

When I snapped out of it, I heard the class yelling at me to stop, saying that I was going to kill her. I looked down and realized that I'd been stomping on the girl's face and had made her nose bleed. I started to shake and cry. I kept asking was she okay and what I could do to help. I was escorted to the nurse's office, and they were puzzled by my tears.

Next thing I knew, my dad had arrived at the nurse's office. He tried to get me to explain what happened, but I couldn't. I was stoned with tears rolling down my face. They told him that, according to the other students, a girl had started a fight with me by throwing a pencil sharpener. But they also said that I'd overreacted and had been excessive in what I'd done. They said I grabbed the girl by her hair and had been banging her head inside of a tin desk and then started kicking her in the face.

I didn't understand what I was hearing completely, but with each word that I was able to process, I felt more and more like a monster. I became hysterical and cried even harder. All I kept asking in a barely audible voice was if the girl was okay. The nurses told me she was being taken to the hospital, but they believed she would be fine. When my dad and I got in the car, he drove me home in silence. When we arrived at our home driveway, he asked me one question. "So, did you win?" I nodded my head 'yes' with tears in my eyes. He told me that he was sorry it came to this, but that he was proud of me for standing up for myself.

Although being bullied was extremely traumatic and terrifying, that didn't raise a candle to the war that had been waged on my soul. I was left vulnerable to the evil in heavenly places that diligently sought to destroy me.

At this moment, I recommend we stop and take a breather before continuing. If you're an adult with children, maybe take a moment to think about ways you can open communication between you and your children to discuss their social lives. If you're a child or young adult, maybe take a moment to figure out a way to start a conversation with your parents or guardian about your social struggles among your peers. Whatever you do, don't remain silent. Silence kills.

Tear Gas

"The enemy knows to attack the two 'pressure points' that always cause humans to stumble or bend; your eyes and below the belt."
~A. S. E.

We've made it. We've finally reached the first cave.

The cave we're about to explore probably has the most wicked garden of all my caves. The spirit of this garden attacked my identity, my value, my virtue, my dignity, my self-esteem. Then, it left me alone with the whispers in my head to deal with it all. This is the spirit that would bring me to many cheated deaths throughout my lifetime.

The first time my innocence had ever been tainted was when I was four years of age. My parents had decided to leave me with a family member to go and celebrate the honeymoon they never had. It was then that I'd be molested by two of my cousins. They were only a few years older than I was, and were still young children themselves, but I remember feeling like I was a "nothing." I felt low and dirty, and I felt like I'd done something wrong just by being a girl and not being a boy. They've, since, apologized to me, and we've all managed to remain close and push the incident to the back of our minds.

The second time my innocence was tried was with a much older cousin who had mental issues. He never touched my private parts, but he always wanted to kiss on my neck. My parents caught him in the act and whipped both of us, him for doing it and me for not saying anything. This went on until I was about six years old.

Once he stopped, the baton was then passed to another cousin of mine, who had also been molested by him. I had my first experience of oral sex with her. She was only two years older than I was. She'd been watching a show that had shown two women doing sexual things to each other, and she wanted to act out what she saw. *I was six years old, and she was eight years old.*

"Let's try something," she said. "Okay, like what?" "Come here," she said, leading me to the closet of my sister's room. This was before I discovered the evil that lived there. We closed the door, and she pulled down my pants, knelt down, and performed oral sex on me. I kept jumping back from the tickling, but she told me to stay still. *I was six years old, and she was eight years old.*

I couldn't control my gasps. My cousin kept shushing me, and after a few minutes, she told me it was my turn. I did what I saw her do. *I was six years old, and she was eight years old.*

When we were finished, she wanted to lay down like they did on tv, so we laid down and just talked about our dreams and what we wanted to be when we grew up. We both knew that we couldn't keep doing what we had just done, but we were at least comfortable and grateful that it was with each other, best friends, and not a boy...or man.

That was our first and last experience with each other, but we were close friends before and after the incident. She was beautiful, and I always thought I wanted to grow up to be just like her, even in our teen years. She was fearless and didn't let her vulnerability show to anyone. Though we were cousins, in our hearts, we were sisters.

While we were talking, I ended up telling her about the boy cousin that had been kissing on me. That's when she revealed he'd been doing the same to her. He was her older brother. She said that she didn't want to tell him no because she didn't want him to move on to her little sister.

One day, when we were about a year or two older, we decided to ask both of our little sisters about whether or not he touched them or anything, and they both laughed and said no in disbelief that we even asked. We then met back up in the closet and discussed it among ourselves. "So, he never touched them? Why did he do us like that?" she asked. "I don't know. Maybe he thinks we're weak or maybe he knows we're not tattle tells like they are," I said.

Whatever the case had been, we regretted ever being touched by him as well as the one incident we'd done with each other. I didn't discover the truth until my teen years when we'd had a revealing heart-to-heart conversation while we were both very drunk. She wasn't just molested by the boy at the time...there was something even more despicable happening that led her to come to me for a sort of 'comfort.'

Just know, this situation was part of a sinister masterpiece executed against us by the evil one.

Life was a great struggle for her, but she harkened the diligent call of God and, against all the odds, has started her journey of true healing from her traumas. She and I remain lifetime sisters, and my admiration for the fighter inside of her has never grown dim.

I tried to deal with the confusing feelings I started to have by focusing on my best Kindergarten friend. He was a white boy with crystal blue eyes. We did everything together. It may sound crazy, but I'm convinced he loved me, and I loved him, but not in a romantic way. I wouldn't say that we were in love, but we cared an awful lot about each other. When one of us was hurting, so was the other person. We were the best in everything that we did. We were inseparable. He'd gained my trust after taking up for me when a boy wouldn't stop trying to smack my glutes. He ran and tattled on the boy so that I wouldn't have to. He knew what scrutiny came from the other kids for being a tattle-tell, but he didn't care about what others thought about him.

One day after he pushed me on the swing for recess, the bell rang, and he told me that he really liked me more than anyone else at school. I smiled, and he kissed me on the cheek and ran to class before me.

Our friendship lasted until we were in the 3rd grade. My bestie was having a huge birthday party, but he wasn't allowed to invite me. He had tears in his eyes while trying to explain to me it was because I was black. I was devastated. I never even thought of our skin color until that very moment. We were no longer friends after that. It was a big deal because everyone had known us to be besties.

Later in life, I saw him in a restaurant with his mother. The moment he noticed me, he ran over to speak with me. His very next words after "Oh my gosh. Hi!" were "I'm sorry." I smiled and held up my hand as to say the past is the past. I haven't seen him since then.

I remember going through a stage of feeling ugly, nasty, and useless. My mother would always tell me about how high her standards were as a child, and how she started loving God at the age of twelve. I wanted to be just like her, but the more she spoke, the more I thought I couldn't.

She would tell me things like my private parts were special and should never be touched by anyone until I grew up and got married. She would say to me to always keep my legs closed, but she didn't know that *many* people had already touched me there.

The irony was that each time she spoke, she thought she was inspiring me, but every warning about 'being clean and pure to God' was a dagger in my heart. I would think to myself, *What about girls like me?*

For a while, this question led me to become the rope of a tug-of-war between condemnation and redemption. I understood neither in depth enough to realize I had a choice of whether to live in one or the other.

My mother taught from a place of prevention, not realizing that I'd already crossed over and needed to be taught from a place of redemption. I needed to know there was some sort of fix to my brokenness, some kind of way to regenerate what I'd lost, and some type of way to wash the mud off of my innocence, and reclaim it. I needed to know about the power of the cleansing and redeeming blood of Christ.

Without realizing it, I grew angry at God and started to distance myself, thinking that I could never be like the favored Mary that birthed Jesus.

I want to take a moment to say to you what I wish I knew then. To women, men, boys, and girls who have entered into sexual relations outside of the will of God, to those who have been molested, forced to have sex, or persuaded and conned by someone you trust to come into unhealthy sexual practices, you may not be the virgin Mary who birthed Jesus. But I want you to remember that she wasn't the only Mary the Son of God loved.

Like me, you may be Mary Magdalene; a woman or man with demons and spirits, a woman or man with uncleanness, a loose woman or man of many sexual partners and predators. Your hymen or virginity may have been broken by a family member, or by a wolf coming in the name of God, or maybe by a boyfriend, girlfriend or even a group of boys or men. Perhaps it was an older woman who claimed to taint you out of love or told you this would bring you honor and favor among them.

I want you to know that Christ is waiting for permission to break the hymen of your heart and He wants to come inside of you and restore all that has been lost or stolen or tainted. He wants you...bad. Give Him the chance to show you what true love, honor, and intimacy looks and feels like. He wants to be your everything.

I struggled to accept this and, therefore, struggled to believe myself to be one of God's beloved. I rebelled against Him out of hatred for myself stemming from all who'd entered my sacred gates without the right.

Another female cousin was into role-playing with me, and this went on until I was about nine. She always played the man's role. There was a lot of kissing and finger stimulation. I knew it was wrong, and while I felt convicted about my actions, but I also felt that there was no use in trying to be anything other than a sex object for people to release their pressures on.

One evening, I saw a sadness in her eye that translated to me as the perfect opportunity to speak to her heart. I knew she didn't want to do what we were doing, but she felt trapped in the same question of self-value that I was.

"Hey, you know I love you, right?" I asked. "Yeah," she answered, with tears welling up in her eyes. "Tell me what you're thinking," I said. "Well, I know what we do is wrong, but I feel like either way, God doesn't really love me. Like, I'm not into girls, I don't even know why I do this with you, but I think I'm looking for something. I want to feel loved, and honestly, Porsha, I don't feel like anyone really loves me the way I need to be," she sobbed.

She was a girl of low self-esteem, and I understood exactly where she was coming from. Somehow, I knew those were her thoughts all along because she'd always play the male part. She felt unpretty, useless, unattractive, and unworthy. She often struggled with her weight and was always ridiculed by family members and by some of her peers. She would tell me stories of how kids would treat her at school that would bring tears to my eyes.

"I've felt exactly how you do now. How about we help each other and give God another chance to love us the right way, together?" I asked. "Porsha, do you think He'll forgive us? I mean, we've done some pretty bad things for a pretty long time." "Girl, if we don't do it again, it's wiped away. We can start over, I promise. I can't tell you how many times I've started over with God. One minute I love Him, and the next, I'm angry with Him about something I don't understand," I said.

We talked about God for the rest of the night, well into the dawn of morning. I spoke to her about visions and dreams I had about God, and it scared her. She asked me to pray with her, and we prayed and repented together. Once again, my heart for God was softened, and I began taking my faith very seriously and started trying to learn more about *why* God made me and *who* God made me.

After severing the unhealthy practices with my cousin, I started feeling free again. I felt hopeful and looked forward to growing with God. It felt as if I'd survived the tear gas that was sprayed directly into my eyes. My vision became more clear about God's love and His way. I became a little stronger in being able to recognize the enemy's lying whispers to me about myself.

Nine was the age I started journaling. I wrote about everything that I felt I couldn't talk to my parents about. I recently ran across some intense entries. But the one that sticks out to me was the one I wrote at this age, begging to be taken back up to be with God. I wrote about how I hated not being with him and being on this planet full of selfish people. I sealed that passionate letter with my own blood and smeared the blood across the page as a sign of urgent yearning.

When I came across that letter recently, I burned the page with my old dried blood on it. I remembered the day I wrote it and tried to keep my mind from revisiting that moment. Not long after the blood sealed letter was written, though, my blood began to flow differently.

When I turned 10 years old, everything changed in my world. It started on my 10th birthday. I woke up that morning, went to the bathroom, peed, and wiped. Red. I was startled. My mother had told me this day would come, but neither one of us expected it would start so soon and on the morning of my 10th birthday. I called my mother in the bathroom and couldn't even speak. I just showed her the stained tissue. "Porsh, your period is on?" she asked in disbelief. "I guess so, Ma. You tell me." My mother began to smile, almost excited. "Oh my gosh, and on the morning of your birthday! Wow!" she exclaimed. "So, what do I do now?" I asked, feeling nervous and a little disgusted. "Well, you have two choices. We can put you a pad in your underwear, or we could try a tampon." "I don't want nothing inside me, Ma." "Well, I know, baby, but what about your party and the birthday dress we picked out? You don't want to keep worrying about showing all day, right? Just try the tampon. If you don't like it, we'll do the pads."

My mother tried to tell me to prop my leg up and push the tampon, but the moment I tried, I felt weak and said I couldn't do it. So, she decided to try and teach me by doing it for me this one time. I complained about the pain, but eventually, she got the tampon halfway in. I walked funny to the huge vanity mirror on the other side of the bathroom and looked at my reflection. I thought, "Something's inside of me," I saw my face flush white and fainted. Literally. I just passed out.

My mother carried me to my sister's room that was right across the hallway and laid me on the bed, dabbing a cold towel on my forehead. When I came to, we both laughed hysterically and agreed that I'd stick to pads for now. "Child, I don't know what you gon' do when you get married," my mom hackled. "What you mean?" I asked. "This is what your husband gotta do to you on the wedding night. This is the same process as *sex*," she laughed. "Then I'm not getting married," I told her. She laughed even harder. She didn't know it at the time, but that was an added resentment to my initial 4-year-old-dislike for being a girl.

I remember feeling so angry that morning. "Ma, why women have to go through all this. Why we have to bleed, and men don't? Why do they have to poke us to have kids? Why can't we poke them? It just seems like God made us to suffer. I'm really starting to feel like God hates women!" "Porsha, baby, no. God loves his creation. Having a period is a beautiful thing. This helps you to be able to have children. Now as far as us being the ones to get poked, you have to take that up with God. He's the only one that knows why he made us the way he did," she said, trying to contain her laughter after seeing me get upset.

"Well, ain't nobody poking me because I don't want a man. All they do is hurt you anyway. And I don't want kids, because I don't want to be with a man to get them," I barked. "Aw, baby, you say that now, but someday God will give you a man that loves Him and will be able to treat you the way you deserve. And when you love that man, you're gonna want to have children with him because you're going to want to see what you and he can make together. I know it doesn't seem like it now, but marriage is beautiful when it's done God's way with God's love," she said. I was tired of talking about it, so I gestured to my mom that the conversation was over. She offered to rid me of the tampon and put a pad in my underwear, and I eagerly agreed.

Rising War

"An easy indicator that you're on the right 'narrow' path is when you see the enemy amp up his efforts in destroying you."
~A. S. E.

LOOKING BACK, IT seems the new flow of my blood or my turning 10 years old was what particular beings had been waiting for to introduce themselves and pursue my heart and mind. This was the age I met my spirit guide and began speaking with it.

It was around this time that I started showing a dramatically increased interest in music. I fell head over heels for 'Controversy' by Prince and 'Purple Rain' after sneaking to watch the movie on BET after dark. But I also grew intrigued by classical music and found my body reacting to orchestral masterpieces in a very sensual way. My listening experience wasn't average. I remember being so emotionally drawn and bound by the music, I would sit paralyzed...inhaling every...single... stroke of every...single...instrument.

I looked forward to this erotic experience every night. One day, I came home from school and began my 'session' early. I spent the afternoon breathing music well into the night. It was time to go to bed, so I turned off my lights. But to my surprise, my room still looked extremely light. It looked like I turned my lights off during the daytime.

I was confused and started looking around because I could have sworn I felt something different...something strange, but I saw nothing. After scanning my room many times, I laid back in my bed and starred at the ceiling. Something told me to look again, and there my spirit guide was...sitting on my bed.

I should have been afraid, but I wasn't. It seemed to be a familiar energy to me like I'd seen something like it before. It had no face, but it was shaped like an 'almost' human. It appeared to have long hair, and I got a regal sense from it.

Ah! That was it! I'd seen this same figure at a previous home my family had lived in. I used to spend lots of time on the porch of our old home. We had a picnic table in the front yard, and it was there I saw a figure sitting at the table. I was a bit spooked then and went to tell my mother what I had seen. When I came back outside, the figure was gone.

Now, it had returned to me. I remember repeatedly saying 'Hello' to the figure but getting no response. Odd enough, I felt comfort and peace and fell asleep much quicker than I usually would. When I woke up, the figure was gone. I didn't see it for a couple of days, but then it returned. It appeared to face me and didn't speak much.

It seemed to only answer certain questions like ones about God or faith, and even then, it would take me asking many questions to even receive one answer. The answers were always short, but warm and would sound like the voice was right beside my ear.

Because of this dynamic, my spirit guide became something I vented my frustrations about life to. I grew to trust and love my spirit guide, but I kept it a secret from my family and school associates. The only person that knew was Shelly, but we'll get to that a little later.

I never heard my spirit guide laugh, but I would always feel it's smile when I'd speak on something I was ignorant about concerning God or when I'd ask innocent questions with 10-year-old frustration.

I didn't know it at the time, but when my mother had been about 6 years old, she was visited by a similar spirit. Her mother had left her and her siblings home alone to go clubbing when my mother saw a figure of light shaped like a kneeling woman on her mother's bed.

She says she was hysterical and screamed to the top of her lungs. None of her siblings could calm her and they became afraid to even go to the bathroom alone, so they traveled in groups of three. She said she never saw the figure again. This makes me wonder if her spirit guide was passed to me. What if my mother hadn't been afraid? Would it have stuck around?

This was also the age I began being ruthlessly hunted by the enemy. The voices started at this age, and the figures grew strong in appearance. I could see them as clear as my own reflection in a mirror just cleaned by Windex.

I was able to ask or tell my guide anything. Sometimes, our meetings would be choppy because I began sleeping a lot. I would literally hibernate for two days. I loved sleeping but this was also the age my prophetic dreams increased. They were the gift of foresight whenever God saw it fit to reveal certain things to me. I didn't consider them gifts at the time. I thought of my dreams as curses, because I would never be shown anything good or exciting. I was always shown things I would have to warn my family or others about. For a while, I didn't even share my dreams. I would wake up moody or bothered, but when asked about what was wrong, I wouldn't be honest or open up about anything. That is until I was visited by Grandma Stella one night.

That night, I dreamt that I woke up, walked out of my room to the back door of the house, and stepped outside into a brutal warzone with fire everywhere and huge figures fighting with one another. They seemed significantly bigger than normal humans. I was in awe and forgot that I'd walked out into the middle of a raging war. I caught the attention of an enemy, and the figure charged towards me, but another character blocked it from reaching me. The kind figure turned to look at me but wouldn't speak. It merely pointed me to a broad tent sitting right in the middle of the yard, unscathed by the battle going on above and around it.

I walked towards the tent with the kind figure protecting me from evil characters charging at me until finally, I peeled the entrance apart and entered the tent. There in the middle of the tent, I saw my Grandma Stella! She was beautiful and just as warm as I remembered her.

She beckoned me to sit down in front of her with my legs crossing each other like she was sitting. Before I took my seat, I couldn't compose myself, and ran to her, jumped in her arms, and gave her a big bear hug the way I used to do when I'd have my nightmare before she passed on. "Grandma Stella! Hey! I miss you so much, Grandma! I miss you so much!" I exclaimed. She chuckled and hugged me back.

When I took my seat, she asked, "How are you, child?" "I'm good, Grandma. What's going on? Why are things fighting each other outside?" I asked. "That's what Grandma needs to talk to you about. Porsha, I need you to do something very important for me, okay? Will you do Grandma a favor?" she asked, smiling with those same high cheekbones and squinted beady eyes. "Yeah, Grandma. I'll do it. I promise."

She looked down and then back at me. "Porsha, do you have any idea what's happening outside this tent right now?" she asked. "No. I don't know anything," I said, with a fear-stricken face. "Porsha, baby, those creatures fighting outside are angels and spirits. They're fighting over you and your family. Listen to me carefully, Porsha. I need you to tell yo' mama that she needs to take you and your sister and get out of that house. This place wants to kill your family and destroy your souls. These spirits are thirsty. They want you and your family and won't stop until they have you. Tell your mom she needs to get out now! Don't wait until it's too late," she said. "But Grandma, what about my dad?" "When you tell your mama these things, your dad is not going to believe you and will not want to move. Make sure to tell your mama that Grandma Stella said to get out of that house and out of this state and tell her I love her," she said with a straight face. "Okay, Grandma, I will tell her exactly what you said." I gave her one last squeeze of a hug and walked back towards the entrance of the tent. When I opened the flap, I woke up.

I ran into the kitchen, where I already smelled breakfast. My mom was fixing plates for the family and setting the round kitchen table. "Good morning, baby. How did you sleep?" my mother asked me, giving me a side hug and kiss on the forehead. "Ma, I need to talk to y'all." My mother saw the serious look on my face and looked at my dad and then back at me. "What's wrong, Porsha?" she asked with deep concern. "Grandma Stella came to see me last night. She said to tell you that we need to leave this house and this state and move far away because there's spiritual warfare over our souls. She said they want to kill us," I said, hurrying the words.

My mother was silent for a minute and kept looking from my dad back to me. "Wait a minute, my mama visited you?" she asked. "Yes," I said. "Porsha, my mama...my mama came to see you...last night?" she asked. "Yes, ma. And she made me promise to tell you exactly what she said. "And what did she say again?" my mother asked. I repeated the same thing I'd said earlier. "Hmm. Duke, what you make of that?" my mother asked my dad.

I dreaded her asking for his input, but not nearly as much as I despised his answer. "Well, Carolyn. I don't know. I *do* know we not about to just pick up and move because of a dream." "Duke, Ma came to visit Porsha and told her to give us a warning about staying here. We can't just ignore that. What, you don't believe her?" my mother asked. "I never said I didn't believe her, baby, but it's a dream," he said, chuckling. "You really expect us to just up and move because of Porsha having a dream?" he asked. "I don't know, Duke. I'm just trying to say we should think about it more and not blow it off." "So, Grandma Stella actually told you to tell us that?" he asked me. "Actually, she told me to tell her Carolyn. She said that you wouldn't believe me and wouldn't take heed to the warning, so she told me to not even try to talk to you," I snarled. "Oh really, she told you that?" he asked, with a frustrated grin. "Yep," I answered.

My mother looked at my dad, folded her lips, and raised her eyebrows at the fact that my dad had reacted exactly how Grandma Stella said. "Carolyn, now I know she's lying. She's saying that because she wants us to believe her. Ma wouldn't have even said something like that," he said. "Well, Duke, she did know you and didn't always like you. She could have told Porsha that," my mother said. "Look, let's just eat breakfast, okay? Even if she said to move, we ain't movin' today, so the girls need to go to school, and we need to get ready for work," my dad ordered, dismissing my dream.

Though the warning wasn't heeded by either of my parents, they would soon realize what a tragic mistake it was to stay and not leave like Grandma Stella said in the not so far future.

I began seeing spirits that seemed to be good but weren't, and ones that seemed to be scary but were good. It was a challenge discerning between both types. Eventually, I concluded that if the spirit would sway or move excessively or tried to lure me near, it was evil. But when a spirit would be able to approach me where I stood, be still, and give off the energy of peace versus anxiousness, it was a Godly spirit.

I had many conversations with my spirit guide, prayed with it around, and I grew very fond of my spirit friend. I wouldn't develop a name for my guide until my teen years. I also became very envious of it and was persistent in figuring out why I couldn't be with God at that moment in time permanently instead of on earth with my earthly family.

I hated my life and didn't want to live here anymore. I felt this way because I'd been getting a world of unwanted, inappropriate attention from all sorts of people, mainly adult men. I had all kinds of questions for my guide, and while some would be answered almost immediately, some were answered much later, and some wouldn't be answered until I would be called up to be with Him.

Tug of War

"Stand on God's word or fall for anything the evil one presents to you.
~A. S. E.

THOUGH MY SPIRIT guide was my friend and loved me very much, it seems I was sought after by evil even more once I began talking with it. I was always finding myself in demeaning situations and harsh trials, almost like spiritual tests. I aced most but failed many.

I remember going to school one day and having to use the bathroom. When I entered, a girl was standing on a bathroom stool that was put there for shorter kids. She was tying a belt to the hook on the inside of the biggest bathroom stall door. She was crying and look dazed. I asked her what was wrong, and she wouldn't answer me. She just kept tying that belt and pulling it tight. When she was finished with her task, she turned to me and asked me would I help her. I said, "Sure, what do you need?" "I want you to pull this step from under my feet when I tell you to." I looked at her in confusion and asked why. "Because I wanna die," she said whimpering.

Panic took hold of every nerve in my body. Had this girl just asked me to help her kill herself? Immediately, I started saying the only thing that would come to my mind. I began to tell her about how much God loved her and that Satan wanted her to die so that she would never grow up. I told her that God sent me a spirit friend that talks to me and help me not wish to die. She looked confused but inquisitive. She looked like she didn't know what I was saying but was interested to hear more. I told her to hold on while I let my teacher know that I needed more time to use the bathroom so I wouldn't get a write-up. She agreed that she wouldn't do anything until I came back.

I walked out of the bathroom calmly, but as soon as I made it to the hallway, I frantically went to go find help. I ran straight to the office and told the front desk lady to send a teacher or an assistant to the bathroom because a girl asked me to help her kill herself. The woman immediately got on the phone, and the next thing I knew, the principal was coming out of her office and asking me what happened. I explained everything to her, and she knelt down and hugged me and told me that she was so proud of what I'd done. She told me that the office lady would write me a note to get back to class and that everything would be alright.

I couldn't stop thinking about that girl, wondering what happened to her and what would have happened if I hadn't gone to the bathroom. It was tough to focus on my work for the rest of the day, and I was pretty zoned out at recess. When I got home, I told my parents all about it, but I left out the part about my spirit friend.

As the year went by, I ended up befriending a girl who was always sad and crying at school. We'll call her Shelly. I was in fifth grade, and she'd been struggling with losing a close relative, feeling alone and misunderstood by her family and feeling rejected by the popular kids at school. I never discovered what happened to her relative, but I comforted her by listening to her sorrows and praying with her. We began praying together often, and people would stare at us, but we didn't care.

We became best friends and did everything together. We studied, ate lunch, played, and even talked more in-depth about God. She gained the trust of my mother enough to come and spend the night at our home once. This panned out to be a great mistake. The moment Shelly entered my house, a tug of war in heavenly places began.

Shelly was hilarious and was always saying something to make me laugh. We played fun games like M.A.S.H. and Truth or Dare. When it came time to end the day and prepare for bed, we both bathed and changed into our pajamas. Shelly wore a collared button-down shirt and shorts set, and I wore a shimmery purple spaghetti strap top and pants set that I'd gotten as a gift for my 10th birthday.

When we laid our heads to rest, I felt a strange feeling that literally caused the hair on the back of my neck to rise. I was sleeping on the outside of the bed, and Shelly laid near the window on the inside. I was turned facing away from the window. I opened my eyes and felt the urge to turn over and face the window. I turned to meet Shelly's eyes, staring straight at me. Her expression seemed internally tortured, and she said nothing when our eyes met.

Being startled at the fact that she'd been watching me sleep for however long, I struggled to find the words to say. I immediately noticed something strange about her piercing glare. My gut almost audibly spoke to me and said, "This is not Shelly." I didn't know what was happening, but I felt an energy that seemed familiar to me. I felt the same uneasiness I would feel when I would see luring or anxious spirits. I also noticed that my bedroom appeared much darker than it would usually be during the night.

"What's wrong?" I asked. "Are you homesick?" "No," she answered. "Bad dream?" I asked, still trying to focus beyond Shelly's eyes. "No, just go back to sleep," she insisted. "Hey, whatever it is, we can pray about it. Okay?" She rushed to meet my lips and began kissing me. "No, stop! What are you doing? Really?" I screamed in the tone of a whisper, being careful not to wake my parents whose room was directly across the hall.

"Porsha, stop pretending like you don't feel the same way. You've even told me about you crying to your mom because you felt weird and didn't feel girly. It's okay, just..." she leaned in for another kiss. "I'm not pretending! Where is this coming from?" I asked bewildered.

Shelly didn't answer me. She kept her expression emotionless and turned over to face the window. "Shelly, when did you start feeling that way about me?" I asked. She didn't respond. "Look, I get it. I do. I promise. Sometimes, when you're used to being mistreated or invisible to people, you don't understand when someone shows you care. But I can promise you, my love comes from God, and this is not His way," I said in the most compassionate way I could.

Shelly turned back to face me, this time with an expression of fierce anger. "If this isn't God's way, why do I feel the way I do. You're saying I'm retarded or something's wrong with me for liking you?" she asked. "No, I don't think that at all. I think you like my personality, and that's fine. But, to want to be with me like that isn't...we don't fit each other," I said. "How do we not fit each other? We're best friends!"

"What about all the talks we've had? What about all the things I've told you about my cousins?" I scolded. "Porsha, I know! That's why I didn't want to tell you, but to be honest, this is really your fault." "My fault?" I screamed, still whispering. I couldn't believe what I'd just heard. "Porsha, my feelings didn't change *until* you told me about your cousins. Then, I started thinking about how I would like to do those things with you, too." "Shelly, I told you about those things, because that's something I'm not proud of. I was trying to tell you about God and how He helped me and my cousins to stop what was going on."

I tried to keep my emotions together, but I failed and began to cry. Shelly rushed to press against my privates with her hand. "You're wet," she said smirking. In that very moment, I felt betrayed by my body. I knew how my heart felt, and I knew that I was being completely honest with Shelly and myself. But somehow, my body, against my will, decided to prepare itself for something that I didn't want to happen. Those two words from Shelly made me feel small and not as in control of myself as I thought I was.

I started to feel a weak spell coming on but mustard up the strength to make one last declaration. "I don't know what else I can say to explain it to you. We have two forces in this world, and my mom says the enemy plays on people's weaknesses and opened wounds. Either way, that's between you and God. I'll pray with you if you want me to, but I can't...I can't do this, Shelly. It's not right."

I turned my back to her and tried to fall asleep again, but I couldn't. She was sobbing, and I didn't know what else to do or say. My heart broke for her. I definitely didn't want to tell my parents. My sister and I were never allowed to have company...ever. So, I didn't want to ruin my chances of being able to have friends over. This was a massive exception to the rules. If I'd told my mom about what was going on, it would have only confirmed her fears, and she would have never allowed future sleepovers or away visits with any other friends. Looking back on it, that wouldn't have been such a bad idea, considering everything that happened during many visits with many friends later in my life.

Considering the way my body had responded to what had just happened, I felt defeated. My heart, nor my spirit ever questioned my stand and never wavered concerning Shelly's proposal. But my flesh, the coat of my soul, enjoyed being desired by her and prepared itself to receive whatever she was offering. I cried in disgust with myself, because never once did I feel Shelly was the weird one. It was I.

I felt like there was some sign on my forehead, letting people know I was available to be used for their own pleasures, and I started to not even feel like a real person anymore. I felt more like an odd creature with some sort of luring scent that everyone was aware of but me. Just as I mentally condemned myself, I heard a voice say, *"Rest, my daughter. I am with you."*

I felt a warm embrace of light come over me, like a giant hug from Heaven. My room literally got so light that I could see everything in it. It was suddenly like having the light off during the daytime with the sun shining through curtained windows. I felt a sense of freedom and protection. The guilt rose, and the heaviness in my chest faded. I knew it was my spirit guide coming to let me know I'd made the right choice. Immediately, I began praying for my friend to be comforted. Eventually, we both fell back to sleep.

When we woke up for church service the next morning, I thought things would be weird, but the first words she said to me were, "I'm sorry." Her face appeared much different than it had the night before. She looked peaceful and like she'd found some type of joy. I hoped my prayers for her were heard and that she would be headed down a road of healing from the unintentional pain I had caused by trying to explain where I stood in my faith. We enjoyed church service and had a blast at the restaurant we went to eat in afterward. Then, it was time for her to return home and get ready for school in the morning. We said our goodbyes and she left.

Things were a bit strange between us at school, though. Any time I would try and approach her, she would noticeably scurry away. I was confused because I thought we ended the weekend on good terms, but she made it clear to me that I was very wrong.

Why was it that the only friends I seemed to be able to keep were spirits? I wanted at least one friend with a coat of flesh to be able to seek out God's heart with. It seemed like each time I would end an un-Godly soul-tie, someone else would come into my life with the exact same dilemma.

I withdrew and entered a deep depression because my best friend and I hadn't spoken to one another for about a week. Eventually, I caught up with Shelly in the bathroom one day and tried my best to explain myself to her. "Shelly, can we talk?" I asked. "Porsha, I have nothing to say to you," she said, washing her hands. As she started to leave, I grabbed her arm. "Shelly, wait! Please. At least tell me what I did," I said.

She turned to serve me with a glance that stabbed my heart. "You made me feel like I was less than you...like I was nothing. You made me feel like I wasn't normal. You led me on all this time and then made me feel like I was crazy for thinking you were into me," she said. "Shelly, I was only being a true friend. I swear, I didn't try to 'lead you on' or anything like that. I didn't even know you liked girls in that way." "See, there you go with your assumptions. I don't like girls. I like you," she said. "Shelly, what does that even mean?" "It means I don't like you because you're a girl, I like you because you're you. Porsha, you tell me you can't like me because of your faith, and your faith is the very reason I'm so attracted to you! How is that fair?" she asked.

"Shelly, I don't know. I'm not God, okay? I didn't make the rules. My guide says—" "Porsha, enough! I don't want to hear about no damned ghost!" Her words hurt deep and caused me to swallow hard before continuing. "All I know is that we can't always understand God's way, but we can trust it." "I have to get to class," she said, rolling her eyes. "Shelly, wait!"

She halted in her footsteps as I took a deep inhale to try and gather the words my heart wanted to speak. Can I tell you a secret?" I asked, flashing a warm smile through my tear-stained face. "What?" she asked uninterestedly. "I'm actually attracted to only three things, and you'll never guess what they are," I said. "Um, boys, old men, and your cousins?" she said, with a face of stone.

I clenched my teeth and closed my eyes in a failed attempt to will back the tears she'd pulled from my gut with that statement. "No. When I hear certain sounds of music, I start to feel like I want to kiss the music and be with the music. I feel like I want the music to come inside of me and explore me and me explore it with my body if that makes any sense."

"Um, no. It really doesn't." I contemplated for a moment about whether I should continue revealing those depths of myself. Shelly clearly had a wall up, and I wasn't sure if she was open to receive what I had to say. Against my gut, I continued, because I felt it was the only way to get Shelly to understand me as a person.

"Well, I'm also attracted to certain animals. I fantasize about being protected and honored by them," I explained. "Okay...sounds like you want a pet," Shelly said. "I can't really put it into words, but I feel like I want to be their mate...only, I think our spirits would be so strongly connected that we wouldn't need to have sex. We would be able to spend our lives together and be companions for each other until it was time to return to God."

By this time, Shelly was staring at me with her lips slightly parted, and her mind overworking, trying to process what I was telling her. Finally, she snapped out of her trance and asked, "Okay, what kind of animals? Like cows and pigs and dogs?"

I nervously laughed at the frustrated way she spat those choices out, hoping her asking the question was a sign of her actually trying to comprehend my confessions. "No, I like animals like panthers, lions, and tigers." "Okay, so you like big wild cats," she said, cutting me off. "Not only those. I like bears, big horses, gorillas, certain birds, wolves, buffalo, and dragons, too. If I was smaller, I'd probably like ants. They know what real teamwork looks like, and they're pretty strong."

I took notice of Shelly trying her hardest to keep the corners of her mouth from peeling back and smirked at her struggle. "Porsha, dragons ain't even real," she said, popping her neck forward and bucking her eyes. "Well, I've never seen one, but I feel like they are real. I think some of God's creatures are ones he made just for him, and I don't think he trusts humans to respect them. We don't really respect the animals we *do* know about. We kill them, eat them, mix them with other animals, decorate our homes with their dead bodies, and even try to have some as pets that don't belong near us or caged among us. Then, we whine about them taking a bite or killing us. Humans are dumb, selfish, entitled, and to be quite frank, I'm disgusted to be one," I said.

Shelly just stared at me in disbelief, trying not to laugh. "It's okay if you laugh. I know it sounds funny, but I can't explain it," I said. "So, you mean to tell me you want to actually be with these animals, like Princess Porsha and Prince...whatever animal you choose?" she asked. "Yes," I responded, smiling. "Porsha, so you want to like be in bed with animals?"

"Like I said before, I would think we wouldn't even need to have sex. The animal would just protect me and love me, and I would love it. I would know how it feels about me in my mind from the way it would treat me and take care of me."

Shelly burst into a laughter that brought tears to her eyes. I folded my lips inward and hung my head to allow her the time she needed to ridicule me, and she spared not the opportunity. "Porsha, to be honest, I feel crazy for even liking you," she said. "You should," I said, smiling. Her laughter halted, and she flashed me a look of disapproval. "No, I didn't mean it like that." She rolled her eyes and said, "Porsha, at this point, I'm scared to even ask, but go ahead and tell me what's the third thing you're attracted to."

"I'm strongly attracted to nature's elements; fire, the weather, the wind, the ground, the sky, and especially water. It's like when the wind blows, something's blowing on me, trying to convince me to let it in. The ground is always strong, letting me stand on it and carrying me wherever I want to go. Mountains are like kings to me or royal princes. The water carries me too, and sometimes, I feel like it tries to say things to me like it has a voice or something. Actually, I feel that way with the wind too. I can almost hear it speaking to me when it blows a certain way. But the water, it even lets me sink inside of it, and it's like a beautiful, big king that can be calm, but if something tried to hurt me, it would swallow them in anger or show it's feelings by making huge waves, which is why I'm jealous of Princess Ariel, the little mermaid. And sky sometimes feels like it's laying over me. Sometimes, when I look up, I feel like it gives me hugs. The power of hurricanes and tornados and twisters and storms, especially thunderstorms, makes me wish I could kiss the sky. Fire scares me a little, but only when it loses its temper. Other than that, it just warms you, and I get lost in watching it dance. Does any of this make sense to you?"

Shelly stood there, squinting one eye at me, trying to process the rant that had obviously made me excited. I hadn't realized how big I was smiling and how wide my eyes had gotten. My body had also started to feel warmer than usual.

Finally, she shook her head and said, "Porsha, everybody's turned on by things. That doesn't mean you're *actually* attracted to the things that turn you on." "Shelly, I'm not only turned on. I want to be a part of these things. I feel about these things the way you claim to feel about me. I don't know why, and sometimes I cry because I feel weird. I know I'm not like anyone I know, and that bothers me a little because I feel like I have no mate. I almost wish all of them would join together to make my perfect soulmate. Like, what if I was with a lion-dragon-horse-gorilla-bear made out of water, wind, fire, and ground that could make sounds in my ear with music that makes me cover my ears because of how it tingles my body to hear it?"

"Porsha, your cheeks are red!" she said, chuckling in disbelief. "I know, I'm excited just thinking about it," I exclaimed. I didn't know it then, but all this meant was that I was extremely in tune and attracted to The Creator. I heard His voice, and I saw His likeness and His hand and His pure, holy, sovereign love in everything that He'd made, except man.

It was tragically ironic because He made the species of man in His own image, yet I felt closer to God through the elements, animals, and music. This was because mankind had chosen another father and had begun to resemble him. The prince of darkness had convinced mankind that knowledge would make them like God, but knowledge made them wicked, greedy, sexually immoral, destructive, and selfish. They were nothing like God to me. God was sovereign, holy, pure, and above all, God and all His ways were love; not the lust, attraction, or feelings humans would define as love while using it to prey on young children or commit sexually immoral acts against themselves and others, but true love by God's definition. I would discover this in the latter part of my life through God's relentless pursuit of my heart.

I collected myself and my thoughts and tried to calm down. I had to remember why I was sharing with Shelly things I'd never told anyone. "Shelly, there's a method to the madness I just shared with you. While those are my truest feelings, God didn't make me an animal, and I could never be with one the way two mates are supposed to be with each other. I could never have a family with them, and I could never actually mate with the weather or music and have a family with them, either. God made me a human with a vagina, and the only way to pop babies out is to be with a boy. That's the way He made things work. Even if we don't understand *why* He made us the way He did, or *why* God allows us to feel certain things, we have to fight the urge to say that He's wrong and that He made a mistake. How would we know? We're not Him, and we don't always *understand* Him, but we can always *trust* Him. Our feelings are manipulated by Satan. We can't always trust *them*. That's why we pray and read His word because His word doesn't change. If we trust Him, He'll answer all of our questions when we get to Heaven. He didn't create you to like me in that way. If he wanted you to be the puzzle piece that fit me perfectly, He would have made you with a boy's privates, and you would be able to have babies with me, but He didn't. I don't believe He makes mistakes. God told me that sometimes the devil will make us think or feel something that's not true. You must pray about those feelings and ask God to show you what it is He wants you to do with being a girl. He has His own reasons and purpose for everything," I said.

Shelly stood there with a look of disappointment on her face. "But, Porsha, I feel—" "Shelly, if I lived only by the way I felt, I would die. Do you know I've actually tried to kill myself before?" "No, I didn't know that," she said. "Shelly, my feelings tell me that I don't belong in this world. My feelings tell me that I'm alone and will never even begin to be understood by anyone, not even my own family. I talk with spirits and see them. I have dreams that are always coming true. My feelings tell me that since I'm such an outcast, I should kill myself so that I can return to my heavenly family, the ones who understand exactly who, what, and why I am. But those feelings are wrong. They came to stop me from doing whatever it is I'm supposed to do on this earth."

Shelly just sat there in silence. "Do you think we could be friends again?" I asked. "Porsha, I don't think it's a good idea. We don't understand each other, and friends have to be on the same page," she said. "So, if we're different, we can't be friends?" I asked. "Porsha, you can't just be friends with someone you love." "What is love, Shelly? Is it caring about someone as long as they're who or what you want them to be? So what, I believe differently than you? What does it matter?" I asked. "I still don't think we should be friends," she said.

After a few moments of silence, I gave up the fight for our friendship. "I understand," I said, with tears welling up in my eyes.

Part of me felt like Shelly was doing the right thing for herself, and I was happy about that. But the other part of me was hoping that we could put our differences aside and just be 5th-grade 10-year-old besties. Shelly rejecting our friendship meant me returning to only speaking with my spirit guide. I enjoyed our talks, but it felt nice to feel normal for a while.

Off Guard

"The road less traveled is often a lonely one."
~A. S. E.

WEEKS WENT BY with me in complete isolation. Shelly had gone on to befriend the very girls who had rejected both of us when she and I were friends. I saw them in passing but never spoke. She even began looking my direction at lunch and recess with the other girls, giggling and pointing, just as the other girls had previously done.

I did the only thing I knew I could. I prayed my way through the sorrow. Sometimes, administration staff or teachers would see me sitting alone at recess and would offer to sit with me, but that did nothing but make matters worse with my taunting peers.

Eventually, I discovered a natural way to escape the scrutiny I was under. I would sing. I would steal away to the bathroom stall because of its beautiful echo effects and would sing quietly to God, at the beginning of almost every class after the tardy bell. My excuse would always be that I didn't have enough time to take care of business before the tardy bell, and the teachers would give me a bathroom pass.

Shelly and I shared a math class together, and one day, she decided to ask to go to the bathroom when I came back. The teacher agreed, but since I was taking my sweet time, Shelly conned the teacher into letting her go before I returned to class. I remember this day vividly. I was singing to The Creator with tears in my eyes, worshiping and trying to receive strength from the heavens to make it through the day when I heard footsteps entering the bathroom.

I immediately ceased my singing and was alarmed when the feet stopped right in front of my stall. I was sitting on the top of the toilet seat and hadn't really used the bathroom. I flushed anyways for effect and opened the stall door to find Shelly standing there with a smile. "Why did you stop singing?" she asked. "I didn't know who you were. I thought you might have been a teacher coming to accuse me of skipping class," I said, smiling.

Shelly chuckled, and then not only did her expression change but so did some of her facial features. Alarms went ballistic through my insides, but I kept the best poker face I could.

"Porsha, just let me do something this one time." "Shelly, no. I don't like *anyone* in that way, and probably never will. I never want a boyfriend; I don't want to get married or have kids. I just want to be alone! I want to be as far away from people as possible," I said with a straight, warning face. I immediately became aware of what was happening. This was another attack.

I felt as if I were met by an enemy clothed as a friend, and was caught without my armor, shield, or sword. It felt as if I wanted to desperately scramble to obtain protection but was ill-prepared and left to face the attack in all my vulnerability. I was already broken that day. I had been crying and worshiping for strength right before Shelly had entered the bathroom. The constant ridicule from Shelly and the other girls, along with many different mean cliques of school kids, had taken a toll on my spirit. I wasn't strong, nor was I ready. That didn't stop me from trying to stand.

I looked at Shelly with tears welled up in my eyes, still from worshiping. "It's not what I want, Shelly. It's not what I was made for," I said with a broken voice. She moved to wipe my tears with her hand, and I blocked her attempt by grabbing her arm. "Stop." I noticed the corners of her mouth, pulling back and realized Shelly was a shell. She wasn't even there.

"I'm sorry for making you cry, Porsha," she said. "I was crying before you came. I'm not crying for you. I'm going back to class," I said, trying to sound assertive. "Let me make it better," she said, pushing me backwards into the stall with her body. I pushed back, but not with all my strength. I kept willing myself to keep restraint, because Shelly was my friend, and I didn't want to hurt her, even if she was being used to hurt me. "Shelly, move!" I grunted, clenching my teeth. "Shh! Do you really want someone to walk in here, and we both get in trouble? They'll probably expel us! Just this one time, Porsha! And be quiet!" she yelled in a whispered tone.

Be quiet. The words shocked me back to the closet in my sister's room with my cousin. She knelt down and went under my skirt. I felt weak. My thoughts spun memories of the closet. I heard myself gasping, but saw myself crying, and eventually, the laughter turned into the sound of wailing and weeping. The bathroom seemed to turn red and move around. I didn't know what I was experiencing then but would later recognize it to be PTSD. I stood there frozen in shame and acceptance that this was all I'd been worth to anyone in my life.

As she moved my underwear to the side and orally stimulated me, I felt the blood draining from my face. This was sadly familiar to me. My body betrayed me the same way it had with my cousin when I was six. It felt good on the outside but hurt like hell on the inside, and the mixture of feelings was getting ready to make me have another weak spell. I wanted her to stop, but I didn't speak. I heard a voice say, *"The spirit is willing, but the flesh is weak. Fight, daughter of the Most High!"* But I didn't have an ounce of strength left, or at least it didn't *feel* like I did. I figured that maybe now, it'll be all over. Perhaps, since she's gotten what she desired from me, I won't be pursued by her any longer.

The tears just rolled down my face like a never-ending river, and I put my head back to the ceiling and decided at that moment to leave my body and Shelly to their own devices. I allowed my mind to take me someplace far away from that stall. Why had God made a slave out of me and allowed so many people to betray me, even after I'd prayed for Him to take it all away? The saddest part was that He had allowed two hurting people to come together to emotionally destroy each other. No matter what I said, I hurt Shelly, and she hurt me by what she consistently wanted to do.

I would later grow to understand that this selfish, sinful act was nothing short of a satanic attack on my value, my purpose, and self-worth as well as Shelly's. The enemy had made her believe that to fill the void she had in her heart, she had to be fulfilled sexually. And unfortunately, I was her out because I was a person she trusted and knew cared for her. Again, we were only in the 5th grade.

The incident seemed to last forever but couldn't have been any more than a minute or so. When Shelly was done, I was stoned faced, numb, and mentally absent. She was hurting, and now, so was I. We stared at each other for a long moment, and she looked as though she wanted to say something but didn't know where to start.

My face was straight, still stained with tears, and my eyes burned. "Happy?" I asked, barely above a whisper. Shelly stared at me with a heart-load of regret, and once again, it showed on her face that she felt rejected by me.

It seemed that as I forced myself to come back to my body and be completely present, myself (my spirit) and my body (my flesh) fought to remain apart from one another. I got nauseated and threw up where I barely stood. Shelly jumped back to miss the vomit. She left the bathroom and came back with a teacher, telling her that I was sick.

When the teacher arrived, I stood there and urinated on myself right in front of her and Shelly. "The toilet's right behind you, La'Porsha!" she said in disbelief. I couldn't move and couldn't respond. She instructed Shelly to get back to class, while I was guided to the office to call home so that I could leave school early.

When I got home that day, my mom knew something more was wrong. She always knew. Every single time that I've ever been violated or experienced something I shouldn't have, without fail, my mother knew. It was like she felt it. Unfortunately, even with all her keen motherly intuition, she could never have imagined how right she was about something being majorly wrong. Though everything happened in secret, it felt like everyone who met my eyes knew all my dark secrets.

I would typically tell you to rest here, but if we stay too long, this cave may swallow us alive. We should keep moving. There's a garden of hope not too much further ahead. Follow me.

Aftershock

"When you find yourself drowning in quicksand in the heart of a valley, look to hills from which cometh your help."
~A. S. E.

SOMETIMES, IN MOMENTS when my faith came under grave attack, I would ask my mother a random question about God just to get a rant about the heavens started, because hearing about that always seemed to be of great comfort. But this day...this day was different. My faith was just about completely replaced with a deep, tortured resentment.

Why? Why hadn't God protected me? Why hadn't God protected Shelly from her own flesh? Why was I, once again, served on a platter as the sacrificial lamb for someone's darkest fantasy. Hadn't He heard my heart's cry? Hadn't He watched from His mighty throne, what was happening?

I was a child, yet I was told to fight! Who was fighting for me?! My praying ceased to extinction. When I saw my guide, I would turn the other way. We didn't fellowship. My heart rebelled against God.

A questionable discharge began to flow from my 10-year old body that I, nor my mother, understood. "Porsha, are you playing with yourself?" she asked me one day on the escalator in J.C. Penny's. "What? What does that even mean?" I asked. "It's when you touch yourself down there with your fingers," she explained. I grew angry that she would ask me something like that. "No, why would you ask me something like that?" I asked. "Baby, Mommy's not trying to hurt your feelings or make you upset, okay, baby? I'm just trying to figure out why you discharging the way you are."

My mother eventually talked to my dad about my little lady issue, but this was a huge mistake. He would indirectly make me feel horrible because he would say things like, "What's that smell? I don't know. It's so strong like...I don't know." My mother would clench her teeth and say his name to try and gesture for him to be quiet since we all knew he'd be talking about me. I hadn't gotten into douching or wearing liners yet, either, which probably made things worse. So, if I would leak a little while pushing to get to the bathroom or if I had one of my sneeze attacks from my allergies, my underwear would be wet until my nightly bath. Eventually, we linked the strong scent to fish sandwiches from a fast-food chain. They went right through me.

My mother was so concerned with my 'lady issues' that she decided to schedule an appointment to see a female gynecologist. I was supposed to go in and receive a pap-smear, but I'm still not sure how my mother figured I'd be strong enough to take a pair of vaginal, duck-beaked tongs when I wasn't even able to withstand a small, straight tampon!

This doctor's visit was one for the records. The lady doctor came in and told me to open my legs. I wouldn't even let her touch me. So then, my mother decides to bribe me with none other than...food! "Porsha, if you do well with this, I promise we can get some Burger King or Subway afterward, okay?" she bribed. Fast food was always a bribe for my sister and me because our dad was such a cheapskate that we rarely ever got offered any. It was so bad that my sister and I could have just finished eating, and one of my parents would surprise us with an offer for fast food by asking, "Y'all hungry?" That would be the question, meaning, "Are y'all hungry for fast food." As full and satisfied as we'd be, we never failed to say, "Yeah!"

"You promise if I do this, we can get some Subway?" I asked, full-out crying. "Yes, I promise," my mother said, bursting into laughter. "It's not funny, Ma!" I cried. "I'm sorry, baby, you right, you right," she said, patting my hand she was holding.

After many attempts, the doctor failed to be able to perform the procedure, so I promise, you'll never guess what happened next! They put me to sleep! Yes! You heard me correctly. They gave me anesthesia to perform my pap-smear. My mother was so tickled when they suggested it that she told anyone who would listen about it.

They gave me a room and started talking to me and putting something in a tube they had connected to me. Before I knew it, I was waking up from a 'nap,' fussing at a man with a mask. "Y'all ain't done yet? Gyaaalee!" I said. The man was beyond tickled. "Sweetheart, we're all done. Now you get to go and see your mom." I passed back out, and when I woke up again, I was in a room with my mother on my right side.

When she saw my eyes open, she greeted me with none other than laughter! "Hey, baby! How you feelin'?" she asked through her chuckles. "Good. Where's my Burger King?" I asked. "They're gonna bring you some jello, and we'll get Burger King later, okay?" she asked. "Okay," I agreed.

Now, here's when you find out exactly when, where, and how my phobia of trees came to be. Yep, for those of you who don't know, I'm terribly afraid of/have mad respect for trees. It all started with a conversation between my mother and I about the coming of Christ. I'm not sure why, but my mother and I always ended up discussing the end times of the world and heaven and hell, things like that. In fact, it was a discussion about that very topic that triggered my first faint spell in the third grade.

Anyways, my mother started talking about the fact that there will be many people trying to run and hide from God, but they'll have nowhere to go and will have to face Him with all their accountability. She started singing this song that she used to sing as a child. I think she made it up. It goes;

"What you gon' do when the sky starts fallin', where you gonna run, where you gonna run?

What you gon' do when the rocks start cryin', where you gonna run, where you gonna run?

What you gon' do when the wind starts blowin', where you gonna run, where you gonna run?

What you gon' do when the trees start runnin', where you gonna run, where you gonna run?

Nowhere, nowhere, you can hide..."

This was the scariest song I ever heard my mother sing. She knew it scared me and would laugh when I asked her to stop singing it. Of all the lines in the song, the trees runnin' was what stood out to me. "Ma, so the trees actually gonna get up and run?" I asked. "Yep, they're not gonna let you hide from God behind them. They're gonna move straight out of the way," she said, smiling. "And the rocks?" I asked. "Oh yeah... they're gonna cry out praise to God for every person who didn't praise Him," she said.

I was deeply disturbed by what my mother was saying, and from that day, I could never view trees in the same light. They went from being just plants to beings that are waiting to be commanded by God to move, just as I believe the mountains are.

After awaiting the results of my pap-smear, doctors finally informed my mother of what was going on. "So, what it looks like to us is this may be a case of her having an imbalanced PH level. This is normal for lots of women and can be caused by certain things you eat, certain products you use, and a change in sexual activity, but I know that's not the case with her. I'm just naming all the things this stems from."

The doctor continued to speak, but my mind went back to what had taken place between Shelly and I. Hearing what the doctor said suddenly made the room feel like that dreadful bathroom stall. Now,

I understood the discharge in my underwear. It was my body's way of trying to testify to my mother, even if my mouth wouldn't.

My mother couldn't have imagined sexual activity being a factor, so she concluded it was the fish meals from the fast-food restaurant.

I soon learned about *everything* lady-part friendly. I learned about panty liners, pads, douches, sprays, deodorants, oils, and worse than anything, training bras!

I still remember when my breast began to rapidly grow. I immediately cried and told my mother I wanted God to cut them off. She scolded me, saying, "Baby, don't say things like that. Be careful when asking God things, because sometimes He'll give you exactly what you want. There are actual women who get their breast cut off because of breast cancer. Be thankful and grateful that you're growing the way you're supposed to.

Hearing that was fine and dandy at the time, and I understood what my mother was trying to say. But, to me, my breast was just another attention-getter, and I *hated* wearing bras! My shirts felt better without them. And since my mother had joked about me touching my breasts, which I never did, and that being a probable cause of them growing as fast as they were, I was just ready for them to be gone. I didn't want to be conscious of anything more than I already had been. Sometimes, without knowing it, my mother had a crude sense of humor.

Back then, I could never understand why entering and experiencing young womanhood was such an unpleasant experience for me. But now I recognize that it was because I hadn't had a lot of time to just be a girl. Inappropriate adult situations were basically tearing my virgin walls down and claiming the innocence that was meant to last a lot longer than it did. In a lot of ways, I related to Peter Pan. I remember watching that movie and wishing there was some sort of Neverland for girls like me. I wanted to go back in time to a moment when I was still considered pure and unknowing and stay there forever.

I truly felt yucky from the inside out. I began taking multiple wash-ups a day before my nightly bath and started being conscious of keeping distance between my dad and me since he'd been so vocal about my body's pheromones. My genitals, my breast, my light pigmented skin, my luring hazel color-changing eyes, they were all my enemies. In essence, the evil one told me I was my own enemy because of those things, and I believed him over the One who created me.

My mother's words kept playing back to me about 'playing with myself,' and I started wondering how it would feel, so I tried it. Note to parents. I get that you want to be the first to introduce or warn or teach your children about things, but try to keep them innocent for as long as you can. Sometimes, if the information is presented prematurely, you can introduce your children to ideas and knowledge they aren't quite ready to properly process.

It was a bit of a scary experience for me. From my body's dramatic reactions, I was so nervous and thought I had broken something. I wasn't expecting that outcome...the waters of my body went everywhere...all over my walls and dresser mirrors and ceiling. I thought my body was possessed or something. It was a while before I tried anything like that again.

Before we move along, I want to take a moment to bring awareness to signs of sexual abuse or trauma. Parents, if your children are experiencing a discharge in their underwear or have an intense and unusual odor, this may be an indication that he or she may be being sexually abused or sexually active. Boys and girls, if you see discharge or have a hard time controlling your bladder, you may be experiencing the aftermath of sexual abuse or activity.

Either way, no matter who you are, if you're reading this, please take a moment to contemplate a way to open up communication if anything like what I've experienced is going on with you or someone you know. It's the only true way to begin a path to healing and receiving the help you need. Know that you're not alone.

Okay, let's continue. You're doing well. It looks like I see a light spot ahead. I think we may be approaching pleasant gardens.

Hope Comes Knocking

"Light is most welcomed in the depths of darkness."
~A. S. E.

EVEN THOUGH MY heart had been broken for what I thought was God's lack of concern for me, I was still visited by my spirit guide. There were spells when I wouldn't come out of my room for anything but to eat and bathe. I'd just come home, tell my mother how my classes went for the day, and spend the afternoon writing and talking to my spirit guide in my room.

Sometimes, my mother would urge me to come out and spend family time with her and my sister by watching a movie and having a snack like ice-cream and teddy grahams. I would come out but wouldn't always be in the mood. Sometimes, I took the choice to go back to my room, but other times, my mother insisted I stay out of the room, at least for a couple hours.

I knew deep down that God still loved me, but I just couldn't understand why He wouldn't just take me away from everything that hurt. Well, God decided He wasn't accepting my quitting with ease. He began chasing me and used interesting people to do it.

Soon after that incident, I met a girl named after a season. We'll call her Krill. Krill was adorable. She was the sweetest person I'd ever known and was so nice to everyone, despite her being physically abused by her dad. Krill always talked with me about it and asked me to pray with her before going home for the day. At first, I didn't want to pray, but she told me that she knew if I prayed with her, it would help her be okay at home. Krill was also mentally challenged. I began befriending her and defending her against bullies because of her challenges. My mother had always taught me that you never know when you're entertaining one of God's angels, and she believed that people like Krill were his angels sent to earth to see how people would treat them.

As I began hanging with her, I made two more friends who were in the special-ed class. One was a girl who strikingly resembled Goldilocks (we'll call her Nudi) and would have screaming, crying tantrums. Another was a boy who loved dinosaurs (we'll call him Ling). I started playing with them on the playground and sitting at their lunch table. The special-ed teacher loved me and would always thank me for visiting with her children, but I'd shrug my shoulders and tell her that they were my friends and that it was nothing to thank me for.

She was impressed with how I handled being their friend. When Nudi would scream and cry, I would try to sing a happy song to her, and sometimes, she'd quiet down and listen. She'd then start trying to smile and wipe her tears. This was around the time I started trying to mimic my favorite Disney princess, Ariel. So, I'd sing to Nudi because I felt it was something Ariel would do to make someone feel better.

Singing inspirational songs became such an outlet for me that I couldn't stop. I even joined the school talent show and sang *Hero* by Mariah Carey. From the time my mother heard me singing *Fallin'* by Alicia Keys in the bathroom of her beauty shop until now, my parents had been doing everything they could to encourage me to develop my gift. Entering talent shows was one way they did that.

Krill wasn't as challenged as Nudi and Ling, but she was a little behind the rest of the kids in her grade. She appreciated my friendship so much that she started bringing me chocolate Rice Krispies every day for lunch. I felt extremely bad for her. She would talk about how her dad would beat her just for trying to get her medicine out of his bedroom and accidentally waking him up from his nap. "What does your mom say when he gets all mad like that," I asked. "Nothing, because if she says something to him, he gets mad at her, too," she explained. "Sounds like you need my mom to come over there and teach him a lesson. One thing my mom can't stand is to see someone mistreating children. She would fight him, you know." Krill laughed, and we finished our lunch.

"La'Porsha, I just wished that I could pray to God like you," she said. "You can! Anyone can pray to Him." "But you have spirits that protect you and visit you." "Well, they protect me sometimes, but sometimes bad things happen to me, too," I said. "I just think God's mean. It feels good to pray, but why would he let my daddy hurt me in the first place?" she asked. I could tell she was starting to get a little emotional, so I chose my words carefully.

"Krill, my mother says bad things happen because God gave the gift of free will to humans. Some use that gift to be good people, and some use the gift to do bad things to people and be mean. Either way, she says it's not God's fault." The words seemed to warm my heart, and I started wanting to be friends with God again and wanting to rid myself of the resentment that had grown in my heart towards Him.

My battered faith in God started to regain its strength the more I talked to Krill. It just made me realize that I wasn't the only kid with a not so perfect home and stressful life. I eventually went home and told God that I was sorry for being mad at Him and that I knew He really loved me, even if people around me didn't show love all the time. What had been a dark mood since the fight I had with Shelly had suddenly started getting lighter, and I became interested in being and determined to act like God's little princess again.

I'll never forget the day Ling bit my hand for trying to fix his dinosaur sticker that was coming off of his shirt. I didn't get angry or even upset, but the teacher kept apologizing to me and was about to give him a time out from the swings. I told her that it was my fault and that I should have respected his space, and I pleaded with her to let him continue swinging. She smiled at me and gave me a big hug and told me that I was an incredibly special young lady. I was glad to hear that because I felt like I was pure-hearted and kind, just like Princess Ariel.

One day, a boy that I'd never talked to before walked up to me and said hi. I smiled and said hello. He told me I was cute and that he liked the way I was so nice to the special-ed class. I told him that God tells us to be that way. He smiled and said that I was different from other girls there at school. He also told me that he believed in God, too. The bell rang, so our conversation had been short. We bid our goodbyes and went to class.

He was one of the most popular boys in school, was very handsome and had the deepest dimples I'd ever seen. We'll call him Landon. I found myself daydreaming about what he told me and how he smiled at me. For the very first time, I think I developed a school crush. He started choosing to hang with the special-ed class and me at recess instead of playing with the other boys. We talked about everything! We had so much in common, I wished he'd come over to speak with me sooner.

He was easily tickled by Ling and Nudi. On their good days, those two angels were hilarious and fun to be around. When I talked to Landon about my friendship with God, his eyes seemed to light up, and his dimples would grow so deep, I wondered if he was somehow swallowing his own jaws. "You're special, La'Porsha," he randomly told me one day at recess.

I could have kissed him at that moment just from the way he said my name. He was always winking at me and giving me mature compliments like calling me "beautiful" and "my princess". I was surprised at myself that I'd taken such a strong liking to him, despite my efforts to ignore my feelings. What if he was using me or had other reasons for being my friend? Each day, those skepticisms faded a little more until they were almost completely gone from my thoughts.

He did things for me that I'd only seen done in cartoon fairytales like open the door for me and let me walk in first or kiss my hand because I refused to let him hug me. He always had money to buy me concessions at recess and would buy my favorite snacks even though I'd forever turn down his generosity. My mother had always taught me not to let a boy pay for anything for me because they would feel like I owed them something. He would boldly and very publicly hold my hand on Fun Fridays in the schoolyard, no matter who saw him. He didn't care.

I'd become so passionate about the special-ed class and so close with Landon that I'd almost completely blotched out the incident with Shelly from my mind. I started to feel like myself again. I was happy and bright, artsy, and excited about God, and most of all, Landon completely respected me. He never even tried to touch me inappropriately or anything.

There's a current ahead, so be careful and stay near the rocks. Random question, which would you prefer to swim next to you; an eel or a stingray? Another question, which would you prefer to carry you through the water; a dolphin or a whale? One more question, which would you prefer to approach; a giant octopus or a giant squid? Interesting, let's continue.

Last Round

"The enemy is nothing short of predictable
if you learn the names of your demons."
~A. S. E.

I DIDN'T SEE IT coming, but my bubble of joy would soon be popped by none other than my ex-best friend.

I didn't realize this until one very awful day when everything came to a head. We were in math class, and I'd asked to be excused. While I was in the bathroom, I'd heard someone come in, and from looking at the space under my stall, I could see it was Shelly. I knew her shoes.

"Hey, Porsha." I knew that voice, and hearing it made my nerves uncontrollable. I mentally prepared myself for a blood bath. There was no way I was returning to the dungeon I'd recently been pulled out of.

I finished up in the stall and opened the door. Shelly stood there with a stoned look and tears welling up in her eyes. "I'm not doing this," I said. "So, you become my friend, and then you just leave? Porsha, you are so selfish, ignoring our friendship for some stupid boy!" she screamed at me. "What friendship? Whatever the twisted meaning of friendship you have in your head has nothing to do with friendship." "What's funny is you're not the only one who likes him, and he's playing with both of y'all! I'm right here! But I'm invisible to you," she said, breaking down. "I already told you what I felt about you, and I won't repeat myself. Not again. Not *ever* again. And I mean that" I said, trying to compose the rage I felt rising in myself from our last incident.

As I spoke, I could almost feel smoke coming from my nostrils and flames hanging from the words coming out of my mouth. "And as far as Landon goes, we're not together, even though that's none of your business." "Well, that's not what he's telling everyone," she said, rolling her neck.

I was extremely frustrated that we were even having this conversation. Just then, two more girls who she'd become 'fake' friends with entered the bathroom. We'll call one Tuna and one Amberjack. "The teacher sent us to see what's taking y'all so long," Tuna said. I knew by the look on their faces that they knew exactly what was going on.

Amberjack began trying to explain how Shelly and Tuna felt. "Porsha, you've been spending a lot of time with Landon when Shelly is supposed to be your friend. She's been upset for a while now but didn't want to say anything to you since you seem happy. But you don't have to make other people unhappy to be happy," Amberjack explained. "I can't help it if me hanging out with someone makes someone else unhappy, so just stay out of it," I yelled.

Tuna chimed in and said, "Well, to me, both of y'all crazy. Shelly crazy for wanting to be your friend and you crazy for thinking that Landon likes you because he's *my* boyfriend."

I must have flashed a look of disappointment because my reaction to her words sent Shelly over the top. "So, you *do* like him? I can't believe this! You know what, fine, whatever let him play you. I don't care," she ranted.

"That's enough! What the heck y'all think this is, Jerry Springer?" I shouted. "All of you need to get out of my face. I don't know what the heck this is, but I'm done with it." I turned to Tuna and said, "If he's your boyfriend, you can have him. Just tell him to stop flirting with me and trying to hang out with me all the time." Then I turned to Shelly, "As for you, I'm sick of this. You want to make it seem like me hanging with other people is the problem, but it's not, and you know exactly what I'm talking about." "You know what, Porsha? Gone and get ya heart

broken and run cryin' to ya daddy! You deserve whatever happens!" Shelly yelled. "Well, at least he's alive to run to!" I snarled back. The three girls gasped, and honestly, I almost gasped at myself. I couldn't believe I'd brought Shelly's dead relative into this argument.

The words seemed to cut my own lips as they departed, and Shelly stood there in shock with tears rolling down her face. I immediately regretted the *way* I'd told her my true feelings, but not *what* I said except the part hinting at her dead relative.

A teacher that had been pretty cool amongst the school kids heard the commotion in the bathroom and stormed inside. "I don't know what's going on in here, but if you all don't get back in class, you're all getting write-ups and phone calls to your parents. Got it?" We all shook our heads and started back to class.

But she held Shelly and me back. Because of the looks on our faces, she asked us what was going on. She'd been one of my favorite teachers to talk to, and I wanted to pour my heart out and tell her everything. But out of respect for Shelly's privacy, I said nothing. "We can't be friends anymore. That's what she's upset about," I said to the teacher. "May I please go back to class?" I asked.

"Hold on just a sec. Why can't you be Shelly's friend?" she asked. "I just can't, and it's not my place to tell you why not. We just can't get along, that's all," I said. When she turned to Shelly, they exchanged looks, and she expressed a sympathetic smile to Shelly. It almost seemed as if Shelly had already talked to her about how she felt. She tried to get Shelly to speak, but all she did was cry and coil her arms up like she was internally tortured by someone or something.

It scared me to stand there, watching her twist and cry in silence. After the teacher and I kept glancing from each other to Shelly, she allowed me to go back to class.

On my way back to class, Landon was just coming out of his class to go to the bathroom. He tried to stop me and talk to me, but I rushed past him, saying, "I can't talk right now. Just leave me alone." When I made it back to my seat, I told Tuna, "Your boyfriend is out there now."

She immediately got Amberjack to ask to go to the bathroom again. Then she told Amberjack to ask if he and I were together and if he really liked me. "After a few minutes, Amberjack returned and was silent. We had about fifteen minutes left of class, and this was usually when the teacher would tell us to study for the next class. At that moment, Amberjack came over where love-struck Tuna and I were sitting.

"So, what happened?" Tuna asked. Amberjack explained with a look of disappointment, "I asked him did he know you and Porsha. He said he knew Porsha. I told him that you liked him and thought he liked you too. He said that he never said that. He also said that he likes Porsha and is her boyfriend. Then I asked him if that were true, why did Porsha say that they weren't together. And he said that he thought they were but was going to talk to her today about it." Then, Tuna turned to me and said, "Well, I was wrong. He likes you and not me. And the sad part is he likes someone that doesn't even like him back."

Before I could respond, the teacher asked if someone would take a note to the teacher across the hall, which was the class Landon was in. I volunteered to go. The teacher instructed me to come straight back to class afterward. I knocked on the door, and the teacher told me to come in. Landon looked back and sat erect when he saw me. I passed through his row to get to the teacher, who was sitting in the back of the classroom. I gave her the note, and while waiting for her to write a response on the note, I noticed Landon writing a letter of his own.

The teacher took forever in writing her note, so he finished writing his before she gave me hers. I started back down the same row I walked through before. He smiled at me and grabbed my hand to provide me with the letter he'd written. I smoothly took the note and kept walking to the classroom door. Once I stepped outside, I turned to pull the door closed and got another glimpse of him winking at me.

When I returned to class, the teacher thanked me for making my trip quick. I was terrified of reading the note, especially sitting beside the girl who liked him. I opened my Tweety Bird zipped binder and opened the letter to read it. I held one side of the binder up to block the girl from being able to look on my desk.

The letter read,

"Hey my princess. Our class heard the argument in the bathroom from down the hall, and from what someone just told me, I know it was about me. I'm sorry you had to go through that. I want you to know that I really like you a lot. I know I haven't asked you to be my girlfriend yet, but I'm asking now. I think you like me, too, even though you try to act like you don't. You will make me the happiest guy in school if you say yes. Meet me in the hallway after class. You can give me your answer while I walk you to your next class."

I tried not to, but my heart fluttered, and I felt my face grow hot. Had Landon really been that interested in me to want me to be his girlfriend? What about all the much prettier girls in school? I had to admit, I was about as weird as they came. Why would he choose me over all of them? Anyway, I couldn't deny that I liked him too, so I met him after class like he asked me to. He greeted me with a smile and started to ask me a question but noticed the other girls from my class staring at us. "Let's walk and talk," he said.

He walked me to class and sat in an empty desk beside mine. "What are you doing? This isn't even your class," I said. "I know, but I want an answer first. Will you be my girlfriend?" "I can't. I'm not allowed to date, and besides, the other girls already hate me because of you," I said. "We don't have to tell your parents. We can just know that we're together but call each other friends until you're old enough to date. And don't worry about those girls. They're just jealous of you." "Why would you want to date a girl everybody picks on? You're popular. Don't you want a popular girlfriend?" I asked. "No, I want a smart and nice girlfriend. Those girls wouldn't last two minutes if my mom met them. They don't know how to talk to people or treat people, but I see the way you are. Please, just give me a chance." He smiled at me, and I nodded my head to say yes. He kissed me on my forehead and ran to his next class.

Can you see that massive kelp forest just ahead us? Be careful...

Prophecy Starts to Fulfill Itself

"You need not understand wisdom to heed it. The understanding usually comes after the opportunity to heed it has long passed."
~A. S. E.

FOR ABOUT THREE weeks, I was on cloud nine at school, but my home had become a living hell. My parents had been arguing and fighting over stupid things in front of my sister and me, but I suspected the fights were stemmed from greater problems behind closed doors.

One argument had been about our neighbor. Our neighbor and his wife requested some baked peanut butter cookies from us in exchange for some of his gumbo. He could really throw down in the kitchen. He'd often offer us seafood dishes he'd cooked up for gatherings or just because it was Sunday.

We liked my mom's peanut butter cookies, too. So, she made two batches. One of the batches she made was a little crisper than the other bunch. The cookies were a bit scorched on the bottom, but they were still yummy and very much edible.

My mother was the type of woman that wanted strangers to have her best. She was very self-conscious about anything she presented to a stranger that had her name and reputation tied to it. Because of this, she decided our neighbors would get the better batch of cookies, and we'd settle for the crispy ones. It didn't matter to my sister and me because the cookies would soften when dipped in milk anyway. But my dad expressed major jealously, and dismay for my mother's choice. He started making wild accusations of my mother desiring the neighbor in another way, and that sent my mother over the top. Forks and spoons started flying all over the kitchen. I decided to move from the kitchen to the living room.

My dad was upset and jealous because he knew he'd been doing wrong. My mother took such great offense because in all my dad's years of infidelity and foolery, up to this point, she had remained faithful.

Anytime my parents would argue, my mother would take us to the bookstore, the mall, the movies, and out to eat at our favorite restaurant. My sister and I grew familiar with this routine and would sometimes verbally voice our dismay for our dad to speed up the process of my mother snatching us up for a girls' day out.

One awful day, our lives would begin to change forever, and my Grandma Stella's prophecy would fulfill itself. My sister and I were in the library at our school, learning about the Native American constellations under a huge, beautiful starry tent the school had set up for the kids. It was also the day of the book fair when we'd be allowed to choose a few books at incredibly cheap prices to take home with us and keep.

I remember the principal coming into the tent and asking for my sister and me to follow her. When we came out, a few police officers were standing around, and confusion clouded our faces while anxiety filled our guts. My sister and I both looked at each other in fright and disbelief that the police could be here for us.

The principal kneeled to my sister and me and said, "You girls know that if there is *anything* at all wrong, you can talk to me, right?" "Yes, ma'am," we replied in unison. "Okay, well, these police officers want to ask you some questions, and I'll be right outside of the door waiting for each of you, okay?" "Okay," we answered.

The officers took us in different rooms at the same time. Everything happened so fast, and we were both trying to figure out why we were being questioned by the police. I couldn't hear what they asked my sister, but I found the questions they were asking me insulting and began catching an attitude with the police. Following questioning, we were given permission to spend the rest of the afternoon in the library, away from the other kids.

When the school day finally came to an end, my sister and I caught the bus home because our parents weren't able to come and pick us up. Just as we walked in the door, the phone rang, and we answered it. It was our mother. "Porsha, are you and your sister alright?" she asked in a panic. "Yeah, Ma. We're okay. But some police officers came by the school and took us out of activity time to ask us some questions. What's going on?" I asked. "Oh, my God. The police went to the school asking them questions," she said, relaying the news to someone who was with her. "Porsha, I need you to listen to me carefully." Before she could finish, an aggressive knock came to the door. "Is someone knocking?" she asked. "Don't answer that. Take your sister, be very quiet and hide behind the couch. Don't make any noise and don't let them know you're there. Do it now."

I gestured to my sister to be quiet, and we slid behind the couch. "Police! Open up!" the knocker sounded. My sister and I were kind of enjoying ourselves because we felt like we were in a movie or something. We were smiling wide-eyed at each other but being very sure to keep quiet until we heard the car leave the driveway. "They're gone. Ma, what's going on?" I asked. "Porsha, hurry up and hang up the phone. We'll talk when I get there and do not answer the door for *anyone*. Not even if you know the person. "So, do you want us to stay behind the couch?" I asked. "No, but no tv and don't make a lot of noise. Just quietly do your homework until I get there, and don't talk too much," she said.

We had absolutely no idea what was happening. Sooner than later, my mom arrived and took us to a park. She asked us how we would feel about her divorcing my dad. I was all for it and thought it was about time. My sister, of course, started to whine and cry about how she wants her daddy and wanted them to stay together. I told her that she would be more than welcome to visit him whenever she wanted to.

When my mother's sister came to live with us a few years prior to this day, there was an incident where my aunt was banging on my mother and dad's bedroom door, yelling, and crying, telling my mother to get out of there because she was sleeping with the devil. We'd all find out soon enough that she was right. My dad had become a willing vessel for the enemy in the foulest of ways. I don't know whose love was stronger; Grandma Stella, a mother who tried to protect her child from the grave, or my mother's sister, who with vigorous love and urgency, tried to tell her to leave my dad.

My aunt was fidgety to leave our home because of the spirit she'd recognized in my dad. She began drinking to try to deal with her inner turmoil.

My aunt had continuously called out to my mother, wanting her to come out to meet her. "Come here! Come here, Carolyn," my aunt would say. My mother ignored her because she knew my aunt had started drinking and she hoped she would fall asleep. Eventually, my mother decided to go and see what my aunt wanted.

My aunt had been sleeping on the couch every night in our living room. My mother came into the living room to find my aunt sitting on the couch in a puddle of her own urine and monthly flow, staring down the hallway at the bedroom door of my parents. "What do you want? Why you calling me?" my mother asked. "I need you in here with me. I need you to sleep with me," my aunt replied. "I can't do that! I got a whole husband in there. You keepin' him up, and he got to go to work. Look at you, you're drunk. Let me help you clean yourself off so you can rest," my mother replied. "Duke is the devil. You can't be in there with him," my aunt said. "Stop talkin' like that, you're drunk," my mother insisted.

My mother sat in the living room with my aunt, trying to convince her to stop drinking and to think about her kids. My aunt repeatedly said, "Carolyn, I ain't drunk." After a while, my dad came out of the room to see what was taking my mother so long. At that moment, my aunt sharply directed her attention to him. "Duke, you the devil! You the devil!" she yelled at him. "Carolyn, you need to handle that, or I'll put her out. She can't stay here like that!" my dad said.

My mother became angry with my dad, saying that he of all people had no right to demand she put her sister and her sister's children out after all the grace she'd shown to him. But my aunt had already begun putting all her belongings in garbage bags, and she left.

My mother had no idea where my aunt had gone, and she became restless in her efforts to find her. My mother eventually saw my aunt's car at a hotel, so she went back home to tell my dad she'd found the place my aunt had gone. She'd been driving and searching for about two days and two nights. My cousins had missed school, and it was coming up to the weekend. "Well, that's good. At least she's not in the streets," my dad said.

For the next week, my mother remained restless because my cousins continued to miss school. My mother decided to stake outside my aunt's hotel room and listen every day. One day, my mother gushed up the nerve to knock on the door, and my aunt opened it slightly. My mother recalls a strong stench of alcohol, and the smell of urine gushing from the door and immediately realized things with my aunt had gotten worse.

My mother went back home and told my dad that she needed to plan an intervention to get her sister some help without involving the authorities and to help my cousins out of their current predicament. She called the rest of her sisters, and they traveled from their homes to meet my mother at our house. My mother tried to brief them on my aunt's state of being, but no one cared to know anything. They were just anxious to see her for themselves.

My mother took my other aunts to her sister's room. "Sis, I got all of our sisters out there. We came to see you. We want to help," my mother said. "Get away from here. I don't need help from devils!" my aunt exclaimed. After much convincing, my mother's sister decided to gradually allow some of her sisters into her room, along with some of my cousins. "Come on in here. Hurry up! Come on if you comin'. She can't come in! She' the devil. Carolyn can't come in 'cause she' with Duke and he the devil!" my aunt said.

My aunt eventually decided to let another one of her sisters and her husband into the room. Five minutes later, that same sister was heard screaming, "I'm the devil! Let me out, I'm the devil!" Suddenly, the door opened, and my mother's sister pushed the scared sister out of the cheap hotel room into the parking lot where my mother and another sister were still standing. It was later discovered my mother's twin was 'anointing' all her guests with oil, and this frightened the sister that denounced her faith to get out of the room.

After about an hour, my mother's sister decided to allow help to come and transport her to a hospital, where she was held in isolation and eventually transported to the psych ward. She stayed there for two weeks before being released. My mother says my aunt seemed like a zombie because of the medication she was on. My aunt had low energy and slept quite often, not giving her a chance to engage much with her children. My aunt eventually stopped taking medicine but didn't return to drinking alcohol. She simply continued chewing her tobacco and reading her books.

My aunt went on to enroll and attend Nicholls State University, and she held the second-highest grade in her class. My aunt had always been extraordinarily intellectual and very interested in expanding her knowledge by way of books. Sometimes, her knowledge opened her eyes to things she probably should have left to rest.

Despite everything my aunt went through, she remained my favorite because I related to her most out of all my aunts. She pulled me to the side one day and asked me with a mouth full of chewing tobacco, "Baby, do you know where you come from?" "Um, heaven?" I answered. She laughed a slow jolly laugh. "I mean, do you know what people you come from." "Africa?" I asked. "You come from a tiny native tribe, [I can't remember what she called it] that's known for being really special. Your great grandma was a native. She was redbone just like you and had hair all the way down her back. You see things...spirits, don't you?" she asked. "Sometimes," I said, being a little frightened by our conversation. "So do I. I can see every spirit in your house, so don't think you're crazy," she said. "You can?" I asked. "Yep, and I can see that spirit in your dad, too. Be careful, baby. It's that spirit that wants to destroy you. All them spats and stuff you be havin' with your dad, don't think that's just normal quarreling," she said. "I'm scared," I said, wishing she would stop the conversation. "Oh, no, baby. Don't be scared. God will protect you if you stay with him. Whatever you do, don't let nothing tear you away from God. He loves you, baby, and I love you too," she said.

It's weird, but I was able to feel the truth in what my aunt was telling me, and it seized every nerve in my body. I tried to remain vigilant and watchful.

Since the happening of these terrible events, my mother has lamented her decision to ignore the advice of her mother and sister. She wishes she could travel back in time and leave my dad at the very moments her mother and sister warned her to.

Fresh Start?

"Sometimes traps come disguised as freedom." ~A. S. E.

I HAD SECRETLY FELT reservations about moving away because of Landon, but my disdain for my dad and every sexually immoral spirit that had been pursuing me with a vengeance was far more significant than any school crush. Maybe this was my chance to escape. I'd been bound by something I couldn't see but could feel. I hated the very thought of sex, but it seemed to be everywhere; on the minds of all my friends, my dad and his whores, and not to mention all the older men who had nicknamed me "pretty eyes." The entire environment just felt like a foul place, and our family was suffocating in the thick evil that consumed our home.

After deep contemplation, my mother made the decision to leave my dad. It was the first time she'd left him since I was a baby. I rejoiced, and every bone in my body was ready for the fresh start. I couldn't finish out the school year, so when we moved, I was still in 5th grade. School life was difficult, but it was better than my old school experiences had been. I didn't have any problems with kids being sexual towards me or anything, but I still got bullied pretty bad for being the new girl who could sing.

I hadn't broadcasted my voice to anyone, but many of the students attended the same worship place as we did with my aunt, uncle, and cousins. My cousins, my sister, and I were always breaking out into quartet songs, each assuming their respectful parts, and we were extraordinary. That's no exaggeration.

People started asking us to sing all the time, and my big cousins encouraged me to participate in programs like plays and praise groups in the church. We all envied the other's voices and appreciated the fact that we were able to be together so often.

My cousins were all grown up now, so it was a little tough at first to make sure we weren't getting in the way of them hanging out with their friends, but they both were extremely protective of my sister and me and they made us feel more than welcome to be in their home.

Since I'd been in the band back home, I thought I'd continue playing my alto saxophone at the new school. I really hadn't been used to a school being predominately people of color. My old school had been well diversified. To my surprise, I made two friends very quickly here. We'll call them Wally and Mahi. Wally was the absolute funniest guy I'd ever met, and he was extremely short. Mahi had been the most beautiful girl I'd ever seen. Her hair was thick and long like Pocahontas. She was a true friend of mine. Her heart was even more beautiful than her hair.

On my first day, Wally came up to me and tried to flirt. He was such a character that I just assumed he was joking. It didn't take him long to be content my friendship. Besides, his true love was for Mahi.

Mahi offered to sit with me at lunch and offered me the desks beside her in all our classes. We were quite the clan. We were always laughing, and the two of them would always warn me to stay clear of certain people. We took every class together; choir, science, reading, math, and my least favorite subject, but favorite class, history. I hated history. All it ever did was make me angry and depressed. But our teacher was a woman who was a little blind, and she was the absolute favorite teacher of the entire school. Of course, at recess, I'd stick under her. I noticed the other teachers didn't associate with her much.

We'll call her Miss Manta. Miss Manta had an interesting way of teaching. She always kept her students intrigued by her enthusiasm, and she was one of those teachers that we knew cared about us. Students who were called names and declared 'destined to fail' were the same ones she took extra time with and showed deep love to. She made us all feel like we were queens and kings and that we could do anything. She also paid very close attention to each student. If you were having an off day, don't expect her not to notice like the other teachers. Miss Manta would not only notice, but she made it her number one priority to get to the bottom of your issue and to help you start to rise above it the same day.

Miss Manta had one more exceptional quality about herself. She taught the Bible. She understood that there were many kids at home who weren't educated in God, not because their parents didn't believe, but because their parents were preoccupied with work and other stresses of life.

About fifteen minutes before the bell would ring, signaling the end of class, Miss Manta would cover the window on the teacher's door with a piece of construction paper. Then, she would play Bible games with us like who could find the books in the bible the fastest and who could tell her a critical event that happened in that book when they found it.

I'd never really zoomed my attention into the Word of God until then, and I must say, I became fascinated, to say the very least. I was so intrigued by what I'd been reading that I began copying bible stories from my Children's Bible Storybook word for word in a notebook.

Copying the words didn't really make much sense. It just felt like an urge was there for me to do it. It became a very calming therapy for me, especially in times of anger or depression. The more I copied, the more I learned and memorized the stories. Then I noticed that I began seeing the very same trials and tests in my own life. Whenever I'd have a bad day or things seemed to go wrong in the day, I'd reflect on my stories and try to react the way the prophets and other men and women of God did in the bible. I became a more caring, happier person, but that sometimes backfired.

As mentioned before, there were bullies at this school, and I don't mean bullies like the last school I'd gone to. These bullies were huge! They were like tall Amazons; they all seemed to be full-grown adults. In fact, most of them were taller than our teachers. Although I'd been picked on and verbally taunted by many of them, there was only one I was truly afraid of. Her name sounded like a 'murderous' name, literally. We'll call her Sharky.

Sharky was tall and beautiful. She kind of resembled one of my cousins mixed with a little Queen Latifah, who's always been one of my favorite celebs. I liked Sharky because she was hilarious. She would have the class laughing so hard at stupid things. She made everything funny.

One day, the school announced to us that we were beginning a sex education class. I remember feeling sick and sad because up until this point of being in our new place and a new school, sex had been nowhere in the picture for me. It wasn't as bad as I thought, though. Maybe the fact that I spaced out for most of the class and chose to keep copying my bible stories had something to do with that.

The teacher began talking to us about STD's and showing us pictures of how the diseases looked. It was awful, and I solidified in my mind the decision to never get married or have sex. The teacher stepped out of the class for a second. When she did, Sharky had a blast making jokes about the pics being shown and comments about never catching an STD. I can't recall precisely what she was saying, but I remember laughing just as hard as the rest of the class at her.

Sharky's desk was on the left side of mine, and she had her legs turned towards my desk. In the middle of her ranting and jokes, she turned her face to me and said, "B*, why you laughing? You probably got one of dem' diseases, ole' ugly self." I felt so ashamed and embarrassed. No one knew about my past or anything that I'd been through, but the words seemed personal when she said them. My laugh stopped, my smile faded, and I stared at her with tears in my eyes.

The rest of the class burst into laughter at my broken expression. I wanted to go back to writing my bible stories, but I couldn't. I just stared at her. It was almost like I noticed familiar energy. I was mixed between feeling both hurt and perplexed at her sudden attack all at once. "Get ya eyes off me, ole' yellow," she barked. She was taunting the light pigment of my skin. My gaze wouldn't leave her, and the tears continued rolling down my cheeks. In a moment, she kicked my shin so hard, my desk moved sideways from the force of the kick. My leg started bleeding and immediately formed a huge dark oval on it.

I was silent the rest of the day, and once again ran to the escape of writing the bible stories. When I got home that day, my mother was there. She didn't have to work or had just gotten off early, I can't remember which it was. When she asked me how my day was at school, I told her I was having so much fun at our new school. I bragged on how Miss Manta was always sneaking to teach us a thing or two from the Bible.

My mother was so thrilled to hear about Miss Manta. She was glad I had a teacher who cared enough to do that. It wasn't until it was time for my bath that my mother discovered the giant bruise on my leg. "La'Porsha! Girl, what is this?" she asked with the deepest frown on her face. I told her what happened at school and she was furious, so furious that she took off work the very next day to come up to my school.

The next morning when my mother and I arrived at school a little after the first bell rang, it was just my luck that Sharky was late, and she was about to walk into the office to get a pass to class. I pointed her out to my mom, and we approached her.

My mom walked up to her, pointing and asking, "Young lady, are you the girl that kicked my daughter yesterday?" Sharky was lost for words at first, but eventually said, "Yes, ma'am." "Why?" my mother asked. "I just did," Sharky said in a regretful tone with a cloud of fear on her face. "Well, let me tell you what I'm about to do. I'm going in to this office and reporting you to your principal, I'm going to have him call your mother up here so that she knows what you did to my daughter, and if I'm not happy with your punishment, I'm filing a police report against you. Oh yeah, since you wanna act big and tough and be a big bully, I'm gonna make sure you end up with all the other big bullies...in jail."

My mother took my hand and went into the office to do everything she said she'd do. Sharky's mom came to the school and, to my surprise, looked just like Sharky and was even taller than she was! But she seemed to have a gentle spirit. At least that's what I got from her. Sharky was scolded by her mom and told that when she got home at the end of the school day, she'd be getting a whipping. Sharky cried, and I remember feeling bad for her and wishing that I'd never told on her. Sharky and I were sent to class with a tardy excuse note, while our mothers stayed in the office with the principal.

Sharky didn't bother me that day and kept her head down throughout all the classes. I kept wishing there was something I could say to make her feel better. Wally kept trying to rub her back and tell her that everything was going to be okay. Then he came to me and asked, "Man, why Porsha? Why you had to be a tattle?" "Um, it's not my fault! Look at my leg! It's not something I could hide. I didn't even tattle when I got home. My mom saw it when I was taking my bath. What was I supposed to do? I did nothing to her but laughed at her jokes like the rest of the class. I shouldn't have gotten kicked," I said. "I feel bad for her, but it's really her own fault, not mine," I continued.

Although Sharky acted like it was the end of the world, the day for me had been peaceful with her head down. I did miss the jokes, and it seemed that since she was sad, so was everyone else. I got evil glares all day, but it didn't bother me because at least I knew I didn't have to worry about being picked on by her anymore. The other bullies were just loud mouthpieces, but they weren't real threats.

When I got home, I found my dinner and my mother waiting for me. "How was the rest of your day?" she asked. With the biggest smile, I said, "It was good." My mother started checking my body. "You don't have any more bruises, do you?" she said playfully. I shook my head 'no' and started laughing. She gave me a hug, and we ate.

It was very seldom that I was able to spend time with my mother because of her work schedule. She hated having to be away from my sister and me so much. But as a single mother, she had to do what she had to do for us. When she was home, though, she made sure that no matter how tired she was, she engaged with us to the fullest capacity.

The bullying at school died down for the most part, but the problems at home started up just as quickly. My aunt was a rather structured woman. She was big on impressions and appearances. She was a strong-driven woman who had to seem like everything about her life was perfectly intact. She had a warmness about her, but it would only show some of the time. Most of the time, she was trying to juggle the aspects of her life while still trying to make it appear to others that the juggling came easy to her.

When my sister and I first arrived, things were pretty awesome. But after my mom began working, things started to change and become hostile. One morning when my sister and I woke up and came into the kitchen to eat breakfast with my older cousins as we always did, my aunt stopped us in our tracks and told us that we had to wait until they finished eating, and then we could eat. She claimed that it was because she didn't want my sister and me distracting my older cousins from eating, because their school bus came earlier than ours. While that made some sense, my gut felt uneasy about it, but my sister and I quietly went into the living room to watch early morning SpongeBob while waiting on my cousins to finish their breakfast.

When the school days would end, my sister and I would make it home a little earlier than my older cousins did, which meant we would finish our homework a hair earlier than they did.

When we finished the homework, we would go to the living room to watch our favorite shows, which were usually kiddy shows that didn't appease my older cousins. They would come right behind us and want to change the channel, but we would insist that they didn't.

One day, my aunt heard me yelling about how unfair my oldest cousin was being and how selfish I thought he was for hogging the tv. She came in and had my oldest cousin to explain the situation to her. "They wanna watch baby shows, and we wanna watch our shows. Simple as that," he said. "We were watching our show first! That's not fair for him to just come and change the channel!" I said. "La'Porsha! Did I give you permission to speak? I asked *him* to explain the situation to me. Only speak when spoken to, understand?" she barked. I nodded my head. "Yes, ma'am?" she urged. I stared at her. "La'Porsha, you want a belt? I suggest you stop looking at me like that and say yes ma'am," she said, bucking her eyes.

Finally, I reluctantly agreed. "Now, you and your sister are more than welcomed to stay here, but you do need to understand that this is *their* home, and this is *their* tv. They usually watch tv when they finish their homework, so you can't expect them to change that just because y'all are here. I'm sure they won't mind letting y'all watch your shows after they're done.

After this conversation, I began to realize where my sister and I stood in the dynamic of her home. We were on the brink of a charity case. The last straw for me was when my aunt compared me to my dad.

My older cousin and I were really close. He was the younger brother and always felt misunderstood by his parents, much like I did by my dad. He had the same feisty fire inside of himself that I had, and was extremely protective of me. He would also often advocate for my sister and me when my oldest cousin would slip into one of his selfish moods. He was mean and would get carried away in the depth of his thoughts just as I would with my own thoughts.

He and I would often talk about a certain girl that he was head over heels for. He *loved* this girl but felt that she was more attracted to my oldest cousin than him. He would vent to me about her and ask my advice on ways to attract her. I would come up with extraordinary schemes, and eventually, one of them worked enough for her to agree to be his girlfriend.

My aunt seemed to despise the closeness between my cousin and me. She would often interrupt our private conversations about his girlfriend and demand we tell her what we were talking about. In any other case (or if my aunt was a mother like my own mother) I would count this as normal motherly nosiness. However, my aunt was big on giving her boys their privacy and freedom, so I knew that her inquisitiveness was directed at me.

Other things would give me this idea as well. For instance, one day, my oldest cousin was in his room, playing video games, and my younger sister was in our room. My older cousin and I were the only two in the living room, and we were trying to watch a scary movie that we had seen before to build up my courage. My cousins were really like mentors of mine. They even taught me how to play basketball in their front yard. They praised me for getting good, and their approval meant the world to me.

We weren't sitting close enough to touch each other, but we weren't on opposite sides of the sectional either. When my aunt came in and noticed we were the only ones watching tv, she attacked. "What are y'all doing?" "Nothing. Just watchin' a movie," my cousin replied. "La'Porsha, I'm not sure what you tryin' to prove, but y'all are sitting way too close to each other to watch a movie," she said. "Ma, what you talkin' 'bout? We not even close," my cousin said. "Are you talking back to me?" she asked. "No, ma'am," he said. "In fact, come on and take your bath so you can go to bed," she barked at my cousin just before walking off down the hallway. "I don't know what I did, but sorry for getting you in trouble," I told him. "You didn't do nothin', Porsha. Ma just being Ma," he said, rolling his eyes.

He was oblivious to what was going on, so I explained my theory to him. "I think your mom thinks that I view you in a way I shouldn't. I think she thinks I have a crush on you." "What? Naw, man, that's crazy. Why would she think that?" he asked. "I think she sees my dad when she looks at me, and she thinks I'm like him in corruptive ways." My cousin tried to reassure me that I was wrong, but I knew better.

I was furious inside! I can't remember the exact thing it was that she said to make things crystal clear to me, but I soon discovered that I reminded her of my dad, whom she despised because of his sexual demons and indiscretions.

Once I discovered that truth, I brought it straight to my mother. I cried and told her about all the changes that were going on while she was at work. My mother consoled me and said that she would talk to my aunt about everything, but I told her that I didn't want her to because I didn't want my aunt to know that I even told her anything. "I know it hasn't been easy for any of us, Porsha, but can you just hang in there a little longer for mommy until I can get us our own place? I promise I'm working hard to make that happen, okay?" "Okay, Ma," I said, trying to force out a piece of a smile.

I promised my mother I would lay low for a while and try to stay out of my aunt's way with her rules and skepticisms. I continued losing myself in copying my textbooks and practicing my alto saxophone in the front yard for the band. I'd gotten really good with my instrument, so good that I began playing by ear and learning some of my favorite old school slow jams. I grew to love the work of Kenny G. and had decided that I wanted to possibly grow to be a female version of him with my saxophone.

This dream halted when my mother came to me about complaints from my aunt that my practice in the front yard was aggravating her stuck-up neighbors. With nowhere to practice, I eventually had to quit the band and lay down my instrument. My mother promised that I could pick it back up as soon as we got our own place.

The only thing I was left with was my excessive writing, so that's what I did all day every day. My aunt didn't understand the purpose of what I was doing, so she would try to make me stop writing to go outside and play with my sister and my cousins, but I would refuse and let her know that my mother gave me permission to write whenever I felt like it. "Well, your mother is not here right now, I am. And I'm telling you to get outside and play with the other kids. When your mother's not here, I'm the adult in charge, La'Porsha. You understand?" she barked, once again. "I'm listening to my mother." "Okay, and you about to get a whipping for being smart-mouthed," she said. "I'm not smart, I'm telling you what my mother told me. You're picking on me!" I yelled at her. "La'Porsha, I am very fair to you and your sister!" "You don't even want us here, and to be honest, we don't wanna be here!" I yelled. "Well, ya here. And as long as you are, you do what I say you do. Now get outside, and leave that book and that paper in here," she ordered.

As if matters couldn't be coming to an explosive head any faster, my older cousin had become quite the 'wise guy' being caught up with his new girlfriend and all. He didn't hang with me as much as he did before because his new girlfriend became a priority, but that wasn't the worst part. He had started treating me like I was some weird outcast now that he was a part of his girlfriend's circle of somewhat popular friends at the church.

That night, we attended bible study. Both my cousins gathered with the older teenagers in the sanctuary while the adults stood conversing in the foyer. One of the older girls began making fun of me for copying my school textbooks. To my unfortunate surprise, my older cousin didn't take up for me since his girlfriend was also chuckling at the jokes. This hurt me to my core.

"I guess I should expect you to be nosey. Horses have long noses and can't help it if they poke in someone else's business," I said, directing my insult to both joking girls, one of them being my cousin's girlfriend. "Porsha, you done lost yo' mind. You know you don't talk about nobody like that," my older cousin chimed in. "Oh, shut up, cock-eyes. You didn't say nothin' when they teased me, now you wanna talk?" I snapped.

The small crowd of teens ooed and chuckled at my insult to my cousin. I felt a little bad for saying what I did because I knew my cousin had a laser in his eye, and it was something he was self-conscious about. But my guilt fled just as quickly as it came. He chose to be on the side of the enemy, so it served him right. "Who you calling cock-eyed, white cracker!" he shouted. His friends erupted with laughter. I was always being teased about my lighter complexion, and he knew it. "I'd rather be a white half-done cracker than a burnt one. You should slap yo' mama for leaving you in the oven too long." I responded. My cousin stood in shock, and his friends laughed even harder. They viewed it as my victory, but I ran out of the sanctuary into the foyer crying hysterically because I felt I'd lost my very best friend.

My aunt saw me and asked me what was wrong, but I couldn't answer her. I just kept crying. She eventually went into the sanctuary to ask my cousins what happened, and they told her. She summoned us to get in her truck, and we headed home. She told us that she was ashamed of our behavior and that we were going to both get a whipping when we got home. I tried to explain to her that it wasn't my fault, but she insisted that I should have come to tell her instead of carrying on the way that I did.

If she had been anyone else, I would have agreed with her. But I didn't feel like she was someone I could have come to about her own son. I was enraged after she finished trying to whip me. For a long while, I said nothing after the attempted whipping. I just sat on the bed, silently staring at the wall with tears of anger rushing down my face.

My aunt attempted to come in and talk to me. She sat down right next to me on the bed, but I refused to acknowledge her and kept my gaze straight ahead on the wall. "La'Porsha. La'Porsha, look at me. Auntie loves you, but you must learn to control that temper of yours. You know you should have come and told me about anything that was going on," she said. I turned to deadlock my gaze onto her eyes. "I told you it wasn't my fault, but it didn't matter to you." Then, I told her something that I'll choose not to repeat, in a voice as cold and vengeful as a sharp wind in a desert night.

My aunt stared at me in disbelief of what I said. I think she temporarily checked out. She was expressionless and she quietly got up and left me sitting on the bed. After a few more moments of staring at the wall, I decided to lay down while waiting for my mom to come home. My aunt was a stickler for time schedules, and her entire family would always be asleep by 9 o'clock every night, no exceptions...except for tonight. I watched her pace back and forth up and down her hallway. She was restless. I knew it was from what I'd said. She wouldn't even look towards my room.

Later that night, my mother arrived from work during the wee hours. My aunt was still awake and told her about what happened at the worship place. My mother was disappointed and furious with my behavior. She came into my room and talked to me. "Porsha, what's going on?" she asked. "She already told you, I'm sure," I said. "I'm asking you because I know that there are two sides to every story," she said with a warm smile. She was letting me know that my voice mattered to her.

I began spilling my heart out. I told my mother about the exchange between my cousin and me and told her how betrayed I felt. I also told her how my aunt had handled things and how that made me feel as well. I even told her what happened earlier that day when my aunt forced me to lay down my writing and expressed how everyone had been attacking the one thing that keeps my mind calm. She understood completely. After all, she was the one that told me to use it as an escape whenever I was uncomfortable or needed something relaxing to do since I loved doing it so much.

"Porsha, I completely understand how you're feeling. You and your cousin have been close, and for him not to take up for you when other people teased something so important to you was hurtful, but you have to control your emotions. You allowed him and the other kids to control you and make you act like someone you're not. I know he's older than you, but you're wise, and you should have chosen to be the bigger person. Now, although I understand your reaction, it doesn't make it right. I love you, but you still have to be punished for the way you acted. Understand?" she said. "I understand. I'm sorry. I'm not trying to be trouble for you while you're working," I said sobbing.

Although I was crying, I felt delighted and a little confused. I was happy that my mother understood me. It didn't matter to me that I was still going to get in trouble. I welcomed her rod of correction. The fact that she understood me, that she saw invisible me through the anger and past my actions, made it all worth it. I never doubted my mother's love for me, ever. But with her absence, with the hostility between my aunt and I growing steadily, and with my cousin being preoccupied with his new girlfriend to the point of no longer protecting me from the sneers of the popular kids, it felt good to be heard. It felt nice to be reminded that even if no other person in the entire world knew me, understood me, or even merely accepted me regardless of misunderstanding certain parts of me, my mother was that person. She would never not be that person in my life, come what may.

My confusion peaked from the fact that my mother hadn't mentioned anything about what I had told my aunt. That led me to believe my aunt hadn't even revealed that to her. After whipping me, my mother brought me out of the room to apologize to my aunt and cousin for my behavior. But as if she wasn't already my superhero of a mother, she did something I was not expecting. She addressed my aunt about my writing in front of my cousin and me. "From now on, if Porsha wants to write, let her write. She's not hurting anyone by doing that. Porsha is a very, very special child. She different, and that's okay. If she doesn't want to play or wants to be alone and write, give her that space. You don't have to understand it. Just leave her be," she said with a sternness. "Okay. I'll do that, Carolyn."

My mother made me hug my cousin and then sent me to bed. He apologized for hurting my feelings and reassured me that we were still friends and that I was still important to him. I accepted my cousin's apologies with a full heart, but the seed of reservation had already been planted. I totally checked out of my surroundings, especially since my mother had promised me on that night that no matter what she had to do, we weren't going to be staying there much longer.

My cousin really tried his best to include me in the group hangouts with the other kids, but I was no longer interested. Although my aunt and I often clashed because of her boujee ways and my fierce attitude, we weren't always on bad terms. I believe that after that night, she really began observing me and trying to see me in a different light. I think she pondered on the words of my mother and started to view my ways less rebellious and more individualized and mysteriously artistic.

My aunt was incredibly proud of my singing. The more I went into my shell of isolation, the more confident I grew. The other kids, even my cousins, started to notice how much I didn't care about what others thought of me anymore. When my voice was discovered by my cousin's friends and by the church members, I was asked to join a singing group and would often participate in many programs for holidays and plays put on by the church. My aunt would always be very proud, and it was in my singing that I discovered her vulnerability. Anytime I sang a song, her eyes would tear up, and her smile would grow big.

I loved seeing my aunt that way, and she doesn't know this, but seeing that from her pushed me to sing any chance I got.

My aunt must have been extremely hurt and even frightened by my evil words on that troubled night of events. When asked about the situation during my young adult years by another aunt, she denied remembering anything ever being said. I reckon that particular memory is best forgotten. I wish my memory was as gracious to me as hers. There are many memories I'd love to never remember for the rest of my time on earth.

Not long after the promise my mother had made to me, my sister and I came home from school to find our mother and aunt standing in the kitchen, having a quiet discussion. When I went through the door, my mother greeted my sister and me and told us to go to the living room and watch tv.

When I gazed at my aunt, she had tears in her eyes. "What about the girls, Carolyn?" she asked my mother. "We don't have any other choice," my mother said. "You know my door is always open. You do have a choice," my aunt said. "It's not working here. I appreciate everything you've done, but it's just not working. He's their dad. He's not going to hurt them. I know what I'm doing," my mother said.

I didn't hear anything after that, and my stomach turned in knots. "At least let them say bye to the boys," my aunt pleaded. "I don't think that's best," my mother said. My mother told my sister and me to come with her outside so she can talk to us. She brought us in the driveway and told us that our dad would be coming soon to help us move back with him.

My eyes quickly welled with tears, but before I could object, my mother started explaining that things were only temporary. I knew that wasn't true. I knew that when she returned to him, he would do and say anything he could think of to get her to stay for good. "What about my friends at school or our cousins. Can we at least wait until they get home to say goodbye?" I asked. "You won't be going back to school. We're leaving just as soon as your dad gets here. He's on his way. And you're going to have to trust me, but we should leave before your cousins get here."

I was devastated. I didn't know it at the time, but my mom couldn't get an apartment without having a cosigner, and the only person she knew to do that was my dad. She didn't want him financially supporting her at all. And since she still had rights to the home in Louisiana, and since she still insisted on us having a relationship with our dad, she felt this was the only sensible move for us at that time.

When we went back inside to retrieve the rest of our things, we bid our goodbyes to my aunt and uncle. My aunt was broken-hearted to see us go, and I never had quite witnessed her so emotional. I almost thought that maybe I'd misjudged her actions while we had been living there with her. One thing I was sure of was that things were about to go from not-so-good to all bad very quickly.

I must say, I'm quite impressed with how well you've been able to keep up! Let's keep swimming. I see a garden a few miles ahead that seems to be echoing laughter. Let's go!

Back Again

"Do you know what it's like to have to decide between two hells to live in?"
~ A. S. E.

WHEN WE ARRIVED back at the yellow house on Ayo St. in Louisiana, my dad tried to compose his excitement, but it beamed through his proud face. Finally, he gave in. "Well, I can't help but be glad that y'all are back. Make yourselves at home, no pun intended." My mother and I both looked at each other and back at him. She gave him a perk of her mouth while I flashed him a harsh look of disgust and disapproval. Of course, my younger sister gave him a big hug and said, "I'll miss my friends, but I'm glad to be back, too."

My dad played 'Mr. Nice Guy' for a while and was extremely patient and understanding of respecting my mother's space. It wasn't long before my dad sat us down with my mother at his side and gave us his "I'll do better, and I'm sorry" speech. I'll admit that it was nice to see my dad again, but I didn't want to stay. I would have much preferred a visitation-type relationship with him if any at all. The moment my mother agreed to give him another chance, my dad's humility and the act of humbleness flew out of the window. He was back to being 'Mr. I'm the head of the house, and you will respect me, even if you don't like me.'

My issue with my dad was always the fact that he would appeal to my mother for her forgiveness, but when it came to my sister and me, we had no choice but to accept him back. At least, that's what he thought. My sister fell into that spectrum, but me? I *took* the choice that wasn't given to me by my dad nor my mother. *I* decided when and if I forgave him and whether I showed him any respect.

I didn't care that he was my dad. I didn't care that, according to the law and my earthly years, I was considered but a child. In my eyes, my dad forfeited the child in me and forced me to become a woman. *I* was the shoulder my mother would cry on. *My* ears were the receptors of her grief and sorrow. *I* was my sister's protector and keeper while my mother worked. Therefore, *I* shared the headspace of the household, in my mind.

My mother never required him to earn back my respect. I was always told that "he was still my dad, and his transgressions didn't give me the right to disrespect him." My relationship with him had already been strained. But when my eyes became opened to the colors of his portrait behind the masked veil, I declared war against my dad.

Every chance that I got to defy him, I did. My dad had a habit of being ignorantly sarcastic. He appeared to be a child himself in many ways, and I rejected that. I didn't hold my tongue's lashings back from him one bit, and would often gnaw at his cloak to make him reveal his genuine ignorance to my mother and sister. Most of these quarrels would happen at the eating table over a meal.

We were a family to discuss our days and experiences and concerns with one another at mealtime. It was around this time that most of my dad's comments were either found offensive or just plain unnecessary to me. My mother would beg me to try and 'make nice,' but I wouldn't adhere. It wasn't until she pulled to me to the side and appealed to my heart for her that I would back off from my attack on my dad and try my best to fall back into a "child's place" with him.

I don't know, it was just tough to have respect for someone who would literally argue with dogs. My mother had a chihuahua named Fancy. Fancy was tan and feisty, and she loved everyone, but...my dad. She hated him, and he hated her. We used to think it was because she knew his spirit and didn't like it.

Fancy had a habit of barking, as ferociously as a mini- chihuahua could, at my dad every time he came home. One day, he decided he had enough and hear me good when I say this, got on the floor on all fours, and started a barking war with Fancy under the kitchen table. My mother was shocked, and we laughed until we cried *and* peed. It was unreal. And I know what some of you are thinking. You're thinking maybe he was just playing, but you had to be there to believe me when I say my dad was dead serious. In between him barking and growling at her, he would say, "This my house! You ain't 'bout to be barking at me every time I come to my house."

My dad and I had some good moments, but unfortunately, there were so many bad moments that the good ones are hard to recollect. He was always making me feel like he preferred my other two sisters over me, and I thought it was because I knew too much about him and held him to a standard of respect. If he didn't respect my mother, I didn't respect him. That was a huge problem because he thought being a dad and being a husband were separate. But they weren't, and later on, in life, he'd understand that. He never served as a blueprint on what a husband should be like or how I should be treated by a man. He always made me feel disposable, and like he just didn't like me as a person, even though my "attitude" and "disrespect" came from witnessing how he treated my mother.

My dad also wasn't a fan of my singing. He continuously voiced how much he preferred my sister's voice over mine. He said that my loud delivery was obnoxious and used to ask me why I couldn't sing soft and sweet like my younger sister. My delivery had always been more like a Tina Turner-Whitney Houston-Celine Dion mix, while my sister's voice was more like a Disney princess with a country twang.

My dad also referenced my weight often. He and my mother were having a discussion one day and he called me big-boned. My mother scolded him for describing me in that way, but he insisted he didn't say it to be mean. When I look back on photos of my younger self, I realize my parents compared me to the stick figure my younger sister had always been. She had not come into her womanly full figure yet, so standing beside her made me appear overweight. The funny thing is, because I started to believe it, I actually started becoming overweight.

Once, while we were experiencing a hurricane, my mother asked my dad if he could only save one of his daughters, which one would he rescue. She expected him to say that he wouldn't be able to even think about choosing one over the other, but he chose my younger sister. He tried to say it was because I was two years older, and he would deem me to be strong enough to survive on my own. Well, I'd work extremely hard to eventually become just that. A woman who didn't need or want anything from him.

I remember when my dad decided to take all his known children, my mother, and two of my cousins to Disney World. My two sisters were having a blast with my dad while I hung back with my mother to avoid friction with him or with my older sister, who I always felt tried to act like my mother at times.

I remember my mother saying to me, "Go ahead and go over there, Porsha. Go spend some time with your dad." "Ma, I don't fit in, and we don't like each other. You know that," I said. "Baby, look. Ree has her special place in your dad's heart and so does Keisha. Now, you've got to find *your* special place in his heart." "Ma, I don't even like him enough to care. So, if I don't have a place, that's fine, because he doesn't have a place in my heart, either," I said, meaning every single word. "Baby, I would love to see you and your dad grow closer. If you won't do it for him, will you do it for me?" she asked. With extreme dread, I agreed to join my sisters and dad on the wet rocks, where they were taking pictures.

During these trying times is when I found my comfort in writing poetry and pretending to teach a classroom full of students. I would often climb a tree or sit under the trampoline in the back yard and write poems to God. It was a way for me to feel close to Him since my spirit guide hadn't come to see me in a while. When we returned to the house, my spirit guide wasn't there or at least didn't make itself known to me. So, I wrote poems and songs to God almost all day every day.

I didn't have long left in 5th grade by the time we returned to Ayo St. I looked for Landon, but I was told he moved away. My heart was broken. I was back at this school without a single friend.

I kept my head in the clouds of heaven and remained occupied with my words and songs clean throughout the remainder of the school year.

My dad took notice of my addiction to copying textbooks and he also realized I loved pretending to teach. So he went to my school during the last school week and requested that he be allowed to gather any old reading and math textbooks. Then, he bought some school desks at an auction and brought them home.

He converted my bedroom into a classroom with about seven school desks and countless textbooks. He bought me expo markers, and I was allowed to use my giant dresser mirror as an "overhead projector." I would turn my room light off and turn on a desk light and point it to the mirror in an attempt to make the same effect the projectors from my teachers' classrooms would make.

I mimicked my teachers' every move. There was one teacher who had thin, almost invisible lips but would somehow manage to draw lips on with red lipstick. I would fold my lips in and put some of my mother's red lipstick on the rims of my lips while trying to talk with my mouth that way. I would beg and sometimes even bribe my little sister to sit in one of the desks and be one of my students.

This turned out to be a hilarious disaster because my sister was a clown. She would always pretend to have trouble with the other students (my stuffed animals), and I would always send her to the principal's office (my mother's room). She would stay there for about fifteen minutes and come back.

My dad had made this summer one of the best one's I'd ever had. I spent every minute I could teaching my classroom. It kept me sharp on my studies, too. My sister and I rode bikes together on Greenville St. and played outside when I wasn't busy teaching. My dad even helped me pick my saxophone skills back up.

I think we can rest a little here, but only for a moment. Thank our Heavenly Father for allowing us to make it this far! I must tell you, I've never had better company, besides Elohim, on a journey like this than you. Thanks for coming along. It means more to me than you'll probably ever know.

Church Chirpin'

"True praise dances to the beat of God's heart, not to the excitement of an organ. ~A. S. E.

THINGS SEEMED TO be getting better for a while. My dad and I still had our spats, but they became less frequent, and I actually started to like him again. He urged my sister and me to be more active in the church's choir. My sister and I stood out from amongst most of the other members of the children's choir, so we were allowed to join the adult REC choir. I still don't know what REC stands for, but it was the 'Motown' of choirs at our worship home.

We had many good times with that choir, and we traveled with them as well. My dad was very present around this time, and often was the one making sure my sister and I attended choir rehearsals and praise dance rehearsals. My dad was so dedicated to our singing that he even brought us to rehearsal when he was sick as a dog.

He had taken lots of medicine and was feeling groggy. He ended up stretching out on the very front pew during choir rehearsal. While our choir director gave instructions on our parts, my dad let out a huge fart that echoed in the nearly empty sanctuary, and the entire choir burst into laughter. His release woke him up, and he profusely apologized in between chuckles. When we made it back home, we couldn't wait to tell my mother what happened. She was extremely embarrassed and kept telling my dad how ashamed he should have been.

Our choir director was sent from heaven. We'll call him Shepherd. He was in his early twenties but seemed like a 'Moses' or 'Elijah' to me. God's spirit was undoubtedly shut up in his bones, and he was unapologetically a child of God. Although I was young, I recognized his spirit as one like my spirit guide and one like God's servants in the bible stories I'd read. I grew to be very fond of him and thought to myself that one day when I was old enough, I would make him my husband.

It wasn't so much of me being sexually attracted to him. In fact, I couldn't imagine him in that way at all. He seemed sincere and safe. He was amusing in the way he delivered his direction to the choir. He had a large gap in between his front teeth and would smile unusually big when he felt the choir was on fire for the Lord. He sweated relentlessly and would always have big spots of perspiration under his armpits and across his entire back. It amazed me seeing someone so dedicated to God without the slightest reservation or care about what anyone was thinking about him during the time of his praise to his God, who was clearly his everything.

He adored my sister and me. He often complimented my parents on our excitement to sing for the Lord. He would also brag in front of the other choir members that we, the young children, were singing stronger and louder and more enthusiastically than they, the adults, were.

There was a song he was adamant about me and my sister learning because he wanted us to sing lead backed by the REC choir. We practiced it a few times, but before we could fulfill Shepherd's wish, our parents summoned us to their bedroom to inform us that he had passed away. He had been sick for a long time, but hardly anyone knew about it. My parents swore that God must have taken him so young because God was pleased with Shepherd's righteousness. Even my dad acknowledged that Shepherd was different than any man he'd ever known. Strange enough, my dad revealed that Shepherd would have been the type of man he would have wanted to promise his daughters to in marriage.

Another director stepped in Shepherd's place, and while he knew his music, things just weren't the same without Shepherd. Things went from being sort of anointed to more technical. I liked our new director, though. He was always pushing me to lead more songs and encouraging my sister to step into her own. But...he wasn't Shepherd.

Another person of significant influence on me and my sister was a woman we'll call Miss Irukandji. This woman was shorter than my mother, even with heels on. My mother is only 5'1". Both her eyebrows were extremely pointed and often made her make expressions she wasn't necessarily trying to make. She became one of my mother's most respected friends, and that was extremely hard to do with my mother's private and reserved nature.

Miss Irukandji wasn't a very traditional person. She was always pushing for young people to take the lead on things. Miss Irukandji was probably the most invested person at our church home concerning the youth. She had a short, fierce hairstyle that she often wore in spikes slanted and flipped upwards. But the thing she was most known for was her wardrobe. I can honestly say I don't ever remember her wearing one outfit twice. And they all matched so well, I could have sworn she made them all herself.

She invited me, my sister, and my mother to her home once and showed us a room of shoes. She had so many, she gave a bunch of them to my mother and boy, did I regret not having tiny feet that day. She was a woman with a kind heart, but if you ever disrespected her or her God for that matter, she'd put you in your place with a sternness you would remember every time you laid eyes on her.

She wore her nails red most of the time and loved wearing extravagant jewelry. She was literally fashion goals, and the one time I witnessed her wearing a t-shirt, jeans, and a ball cap, it felt like the world was coming to an end. She was such an encourager and didn't stand for much drama at all.

She and mother would both shake their heads at one woman in the church who made me and my sister laugh. I can't disclose her name, but she, too, was a fashionista. Her clothing, however, was much more fitted, and she was much bigger than Miss Irukandji. She dressed to impress, only she wasn't trying to impress God.

Every time the music would get 'happy,' this lady would get up and start her 'holy ghost' dancing. She would go all the way from the mothers' side of the church to the right side where the deacons sat. She was unmarried and thirsty! She would stop right in front of them and dance, and would even bend over to the front while waving her hands in the air.

It was one of those terrible elephants in the room that everyone knew about, but no one would dare point out. Sometimes, I would catch the musicians purposely speeding up the tempo of music just to make her dance. My mother would just shake her head in disgust and roll her eyes, and Miss Irukandji would mostly ignore it. Yet sometimes I would catch her exchanging disapproving glares with some of the other choir members.

It almost became a sort of hobby to try and see if she would ever dance without heading over to the deacons, but that never happened. I knew her praise wasn't genuine because every time the music died down and got slower or completed stopped, so would her dancing. She was well aware of what she was doing and wasn't at all 'taken' by the Holy Spirit of God.

While the dancing lady was one of the most colorful characters at the worship place, she wasn't the only one that could make my sister and me laugh. Our pastor was pretty predictable with his sermon endings. He never changed things up and would always say the same exact exit speech at the end of each sermon every single Sunday morning.

One morning, my sister and I were sitting beside my mother in the middle of a pew and decided that we would be little pastors ourselves that day. My mother wasn't one for showboating, but would often reluctantly stand and applaud when everyone else did. When the pastor was finishing his sermon, my sister and I began mocking him and said the very exact words he did and moved our body the same way he did. "He walks with me! He talks with me! He tells me! I am! I am! I—" the pastor would shout, swiftly turning around to his deacons for confirmed approval of his sermon's ending.

We thought no one would notice us, but we were wrong. An older lady seated behind us saw what we were doing and became tickled pink.

The lady began laughing so hard, she drew my mother's attention. When my mother looked down and saw what we were doing, she looked back and realized the lady was laughing at us. We hadn't noticed because we were keeping up with the pastor. My mother tapped us on our shoulders and told us to stop, but couldn't help but laugh herself. She leaned over to tell my dad, seated on the other side of her, what we had been doing, and he laughed just as hard as the lady behind us. She tried telling him that it was no laughing matter, but he simply peaked around her at us and began laughing again, with tears welling up in his eyes from his tickled bones.

We'll call our pastor Ross. I used to think the dancing lady had a special admiration for him, but who knows. Anyway, my dad found me and my sister's impersonation of him so amusing, he decided to share what we had done with the reverend. He took the news with a surprisingly light heart saying, "Leave it to the youngins to let ya' know when ya' gettin' too comfortable." He released a jolly laugh and gave my sister and me a huge hug.

Our worship place did something I really liked. Before service every Sunday morning, the entire congregation would be able to purchase breakfast plates for low prices, and when my mother hadn't had a chance to cook before service, we would eat their breakfast. I loved their grits because they were chunky, and the eggs were seasoned to perfection.

We would sometimes break off into youth groups and meet with Sunday school teachers. One of my teachers intrigued me by the way she ate her bowl of grits in front of us. I rarely paid any attention to what she taught because her lips were big and lush and would always have faded red lipstick on them, and there would always be grains of grits all over her lips. When she spoke, the grains would pop on some of us students, which I found to be exciting and amusing.

That was the one worship place I can say operated much like any family I knew. There was always plenty of drama, but when disaster struck or when something terrible happened to any member, we would all band together for the greater good.

But there came a time when there was a great drama within the church that resulted in my parents deciding to find us a different church home.

Joe Jackson of '67

"I've realized the power and detriment of a man's thoughts, because it's a man's thoughts that define him."
~A. S. E.

My dad went through a stage of being a little local manager for my sister and me. Any church home that wanted us to sing, he took us there. We admired our dad for believing in us so much, and he seemed to be so proud to express it. Every moment we got on someone's stage, his smile would exceed his face's capacity.

Rehearsals were interesting. My dad really pushed my younger sister to reach extremely high-pitched notes, because she was a soprano. My sister never failed to cry and whine through rehearsals, saying that the notes were too high. My dad even resorted to threatening her with a belt, saying that he knew she could reach them because she would always go higher than the requirements during live performances.

It was true. My sister would start two or three whole keys above what we would practice. Then, she would nervously dig her thumb's fingernail into her index finger and look at me while singing. She would know that she began the song too high, but because she feared cracking notes and public embarrassment, her adrenaline would kick in, and she would reach the notes seemingly with ease.

Maybe that was the missing element in rehearsals. My sister was a funny performer. She was always messing up, and I could never hold my laugh in. If she wasn't starting too high, she was forgetting the words.

I guess what was so funny about this was when my parents discovered I could sing at the age of six, they became heavily invested. I had karaoke machines, and mics and songbooks...anything you could think of that would help cultivate a young singer into a great artist with a unique sound.

My sister took note of all the attention I received and asked, 'what about her.' She wanted in on the action, but I don't think she realized what that entailed. Still, my parents let her join me in singing, and my solo act quickly became a duo act named 'The Mays Sisters'.

While learning new lyrics and hitting the right notes came somewhat easy for me, my sister struggled big time. She was also not as confident with singing as I was, but this was because I practiced longer and harder than she did. I breathed music, while she just liked to sort of dabble in it.

I was always the one singing around the house and listening to my favorite artists around the clock, teaching myself new vocal tricks and techniques. When we weren't singing together, my sister would rather spend her time enjoying the outdoors and eating.

I guess it's fair to say the difference between our voices was passion. I enjoyed singing with my sister, though. She brought an essence to our music that was light and sweet. My voice was more seasoned and aggressive at times.

I had been singing just as high as she was until my voice decided it was going to do a puberty change. My voice became low and deep. I was between a second alto and tenor by the time I was twelve, and I hated it. All the high notes I was used to hitting were no longer an option. I had to dig deeper.

As I'm writing this, I realize that this has always been God's message to me. I've still held myself to a highness; high standards, high goals, high notes. But God says to me, "Stop trying to get high! Go deep!" When my voice got deeper, it was a perfect opportunity to find some other compelling aspect of delivering a song besides hitting high notes.

This change wasn't just meant to deepen my vocals, but to deepen the connection and spiritual power behind my vocals.

Our dad began taking rehearsals to a whole other level, and we taunted him about them. One day, the family sat down together to watch the infamous movie called *The Jackson Five*. While watching the film, my sister and I couldn't stop ourselves from comparing our own dad to Joe Jackson. We voiced the fact that we felt Joe took things too far at times.

He defended himself, but we insisted that the two were one of a kind. My dad had even tried to pick up the habit of whipping us with a switch from the movie. He said that's how he was raised, and he thought it would work better than a belt. He whipped me with a switch only once and welted my legs so badly, my mother forbade him to ever use a switch again.

He became infuriated, and my mother had to step in. He started taking up for Joe, saying that his boys should have been more grateful to him for his sacrifices. My mother told my dad that we were allowed to have opinions and that he couldn't control what we thought.

It was a pretty intense moment, but hilarious to my sister and me! How could he get so mad about our opinions of Joe Jackson? While my mother ripped him apart for being a hothead, my sister and I laughed until our guts hurt and retreated to our room.

Sometimes, our parents' arguments were terrifying, but most of the time, they were humorous. I remember there was one fight they had about money. They were always having those kinds of arguments. "Carolyn, something's gonna have to change around here! We've got more money going out than we have coming in!" my dad screamed. "Well, Duke, maybe if you wouldn't be so clenched fisted, God could bless you with somethin'! You are selfish!" my mother accused. "Selfish?! How am I selfish, Carolyn? I just gave your family 200 dollars last week!" "Yeah, grudgingly! The Lord likes a *cheerful* giver, Duke! You know how to be *cheerful*, don't ya?" my mother would say in her high-pitched, screaming voice. She sounded like a barking Chihuahua. "Cheerful or not, I did it! The Lord knows I'm broke, Carolyn! What's cheerful about that, huh?" my dad barked, with his nose flared out.

If you've ever watched the character called James from the tv show *Good Times*, you'll know exactly how my dad looked when he was upset.

"Duke, I'm not doing this with you. Come on, girls!" my mother beckoned. "And where you think you goin'?" my dad asked. "I don't *think*, I *know* I'm taking my girls for a girls' day out!" "Oh, no, you're not!" "Oh, yes, I am, buddy!" my mother reassured.

At that moment, my dad did something that had my sister and I laughing so hard, we wet our pants! My mother's purse was lying on the arm of the couch that was closest to where my dad stood. He reached down, snatched her purse, and tucked it under his armpit with a vengeance! We were shocked! My mother's mouth flew open at his attempt to stop her from being able to spend money, and she laughed herself to the ground. We all did, except my dad.

"Wow! Duke, we don't need yo' money to have a good time! You are ridiculous and pathetic! Keep yo' money, man!" she said, laughing. She beckoned for us to come with her once more, and we left. I can't remember if my mother had money elsewhere or if her spending card hadn't been in her purse, but she took us to all of our hot spots, and we had a blast.

My dad could always smell two things; money and fame, just like Joe Jackson. My dad had good intentions, I guess. He liked financial stability and wanted to make sure we set ourselves up for success. But my mother always acknowledged God as being the one to set someone up for success. She felt self-made moves were a waste if your steps weren't being directed by God.

This didn't stop my dad from chasing his fame and glory. When Hurricane Katrina hit, we lived in Raceland, which was about an hour away from New Orleans. My mother wanted so badly for us to evacuate, but my dad was insistent on us staying behind to catch footage of the storm.

He felt that if he could just get newsworthy pictures and videos of storm damage, he could get his big break. He got plenty of footage, but by the time he did, that same footage was already showing on the news channels. We laughed hysterically at his efforts, but we enjoyed being little news anchors for my dad.

He literally had me and my sister put on some rain boots and stand in our flooded back yard to report the aftermath of the storm. The flood-waters were full of eels and other creatures that my dad had to behead with the garden shovel.

We were without power for three weeks, but it all felt like a movie to my sister and me, so we didn't care. We never got famous for our news reporting gig with my dad, but boy did we have fun in our efforts.

There was a time my dad's heroic effort could have made the news if someone had been there to watch. We were all riding with my dad when he suddenly slammed on breaks and jumped out of his truck! My mother was shocked and confused, and so were we. He ran faster than I'd ever seen him run and jumped into the massive body of water that sat to the left of us.

My dad had just seen a vehicle veer off the road and plunge into the water, and we had somehow missed it. He was able to save the man from the drowning vehicle and swim him to the bank. It all happened so fast, we all just sat there with our mouths open and our hearts anxious to know if the man my dad saved was alright. We were so proud, but my mother had to be the proudest. She couldn't keep her hands off my dad for about two weeks, rubbing his neck and giving him random kisses. That was big because she usually wanted to slap him for something or another.

If only my dad had the same integrity for a wreck we saw on our way to visit family in the delta. A car was turned over, and a crowd of people was trying to turn the car back over. My dad pulls over, and we think he's about to join in to help. But my dad, still wanting his news fame, pulled out his camera and started recording. "You idiot! What do you think you're doin'?" a man screamed. "I'm recordin' the news, what ya thank I'm doin'?" my dad yelled back.

The man started walking towards my dad, waving his hand. "Put that camera away! If you're not gonna help, leave!" he yelled. My mother saw things getting ready to heat up, so she tried intervening. "Duke, get back in this car! You don't know if somebody's hurt or not! Get back in here. It would have been different if you asked them if they needed help first, at least," she said.

My dad looked back at the man walking towards him, not wanting to back down from a confrontation, but he took my mother's advice and got in the car with his nose flared. My sister and I laughed so hard. Then, my mother joined in with the laughter, repeating what the man had screamed to my dad.

That was the last time he tried to end up on the news or submit material. Funny enough, later, something happened that landed my dad on the news and the front page, but the circumstances weren't at all favorable to my dad.

I guess we should really be careful what we ask for or what our hearts desire.

Killer Caterpillars

"I'd say respect and fear go hand in hand. Wouldn't you?"
~A. S. E.

UNFORTUNATELY, HURRICANES WEREN'T the only natural disasters we would face at the yellow house on Ayo St. It's time I told you about the 'Killer Caterpillars.' Oh yes. We had big, black, spiky, stinging caterpillars that would attack our home every year.

You see, our backyard had a big tree that greeted you as soon as you came out of the back door. That tree would appear to be moving because the caterpillars would do formations and cover every single inch of the bark of the tree. Any part of the tree that was brown was covered with a crawling, black caterpillar.

When they would grow to be all fat and spiky, they would come down from the tree and cover every inch of our huge yard, every inch of our house, and every inch of our vehicles. It would be a takeover!

When my mother was doing hair in her beauty shop, my sister and I would make it home from school and spend about an hour standing at the backdoor, psyching ourselves up to make a run for it to my mother's shop.

Once we would finally build up the nerve to run, we ran across the big yard like we were running from an invasion of aliens! This tactic worked pretty well for us, until one funny day.

My younger sister was much more tolerant of nature's creatures and wasn't as frightened about crawling things taking over the yard as I was. One day, Ree and my younger cousin had been playing outside together. Then they came inside the house to rest.

My younger cousin asked, "Ree, what's that on your sock?" My younger sister had a t-shirt, shorts, socks and tennis shoes on. We all looked down to catch a glance at whatever it was that my cousin was seeing. It was a stinging killer caterpillar!

My sister jumped around, screaming and crying, and we were all crying and laughing! My aunt tried knocking the worm off with a broom, but it coiled up and starting pulsing like it was trying to sting my sister in its defense. We were terrified and disgusted at watching that caterpillar attack my sister's sock. She wanted to faint but couldn't, because her foot was being taken over by the stinging worm.

My aunt was finally able to somehow pry the caterpillar from its firm grip on my sister's sock, and my sister cried, still reeling from the traumatic battle that had just taken place between her and one of the killer caterpillars.

From that moment on, my sister was much more conscious about the killer caterpillar season, and no longer thought of herself to be immune to them or safe from their grasp. She joined me inside the house every time they emerged and waited for them to disappear before resuming her outside activities every year after that day.

After our adventurous summer, it was time for school again.

Bye-Bye, Big Pink School

"I've always been one to look more forward to saying goodbye than saying hello."
~A. S. E.

ONCE SCHOOL STARTED back, I felt nervous because I was now in the 6th grade, which meant I would be moving from my beloved 'Big Pink School' to the middle school. My very first day couldn't have gone any more wrong than it did. I had some engaging teachers, but their names were unheard of. My math teacher's name was Mrs. Barracuda. She was a gruff woman and came off as mean and harsh, but that was the furthest thing from the truth. She was hard on the outside but had a heart of gold, and I grew to love her.

However, on the first day of school, all the teachers were made to read the handbook to us students, the entire thing. We would all go from class to class, where the teachers would briefly introduce themselves and begin reading where the last class was supposed to have left off. Mrs. Barracuda read me straight to sleep! I didn't realize this until I was awakened with a huge smack of a ruler on my desk. I jolted up so hard, and the side of my face was full of slobber! "Huh!" I said. The entire class burst into laughter, and though Mrs. Barracuda tried not to laugh, she couldn't resist. "Miss Mays! Wipe the slob off my desk and wake up!" she scolded. "Yes ma'am," I said, flashing her a grateful smile for not writing me up.

Later that day, I would meet a teacher named after a popular flower and another one with a name I couldn't pronounce to save my life, but my history teacher took the cake. We'll call her Miss Flounder, but the children called her Miss 'Freaky.' It took about a month of saying her name before the class would stop laughing every time a student called on her. She was one of the most enthusiastic teachers I'd ever known and made learning history exciting and fun. She loved cakes, too. So she would find any reason to celebrate about and then have one of her students bring a cake that we would all share if we were on our best behavior.

That year, I befriended a boy we'll call Croc. He was shorter than me and had bucked teeth, but he was cute and funny. All the white girls liked him because of his crude humor, and the brown girls disliked him for the same reason. He almost reminded me of Shia LaBeouf's character from Even Stevens, the tv show. He would even make some of the same facial expressions. He and I were friends for a while, but I never really liked him because the only reason he wanted me was that I showed up to a school dance looking 'not so nerdy.'

A friend girl told me I should ask him to stop asking me out because she knew he was flirting with just about every girl in school, so I did. "Croc, I'm not interested in you in that way. I'm not allowed to officially date anyway, so..." "That's okay, I just asked another girl out like fifteen minutes ago. What? You thought I actually wanted you? Ha. I played you like a video game," he taunted.

His words stung, but not as bad as what my friend had to say to him. She was a girl who was a bit reserved unless she felt the need to put someone in their place, and this was one of those times. She literally made up a song about his bucked teeth on the spot called 'Beaver Heaven.' This song grew so popular that every time he came to class, the class would begin to sing it. It went,

"Chuck, chuck, chuck,
Chuck, chuck, chuck
One, two, three, four, five, six, seven
Chuck, chuck, chuck
Chuck, chuck, chuck
Let's all go to Beaver Heaven!

Then, the class would put both their hands together in front of them like a beaver and make sounds with their front teeth and bottom lips. Croc was such a clown that he would laugh at the song himself. Eventually, he apologized for treating me the way he did, and we became perfect friends.

My mother decided that she didn't want to work in her beauty shop and wanted to do something that would have her closer to my sister and me. She began substitute teaching and excelled! There wasn't one child who didn't want to be in her class or who didn't acknowledge her in the hallways. She was beloved by all children and even by the principal.

The principal took notice of the respect she had from some of the most troubled children of the school and wanted her to take a test to become a permanent teacher at the school. My mother declined the offer because she doubted she could pass the test. After all, she struggled in school as a kid herself and she also like the flexibility of being a substitute for different grades.

On the days my mother would be assigned to one of my classes, I took full advantage. She would sometimes scold me and tell me to get to my rightful class, but other times would allow me and two of my other companions, which included Croc, to come and be 'helpers' for her class as long as we weren't testing or something.

My mother loved Croc. She thought he was a mess and was often tickled by his sense of humor. Croc respected her and had begun to appreciate me as a friend as well, so she didn't really worry about his crush on me. He eventually hinted at wanting us to be more than friends, but I wasn't into dating anyone, so I regularly turned him down.

In my teen years, while visiting my dad during his and my mother's separation, my dad took me to a church home where I ran into Croc once again. It was the first time I'd seen him since the 6th grade, and he'd sprouted up to be taller than I was. He recognized me first, and we caught up. He was quite handsome and asked me for my number, but I didn't have a cell phone at the time and was still not allowed to speak with boys on the phone, so there was no way to keep in touch after that time.

My 6th-grade year was when I met two very special people and gained two of the most special friendships I would ever have. We'll call them Seahorse and Coral. Tay was a little skinny white girl who was infatuated with horses and could even make herself sound like one. People were always asking her to make the sound, but I told her to stop and I explained they were only asking to make fun of her.

Seahorse and I spent every recess together, and her mother and little sister treated me like I was part of their family. I was allowed to go spend time at their house and attend church programs with them sometimes. Seahorse's mom was beautiful inside and out, and she really loved Seahorse and her little sister. Her spirit was kind and gentle. Seahorse was a bit on the goofy side, and our relationship was much like the Raven and Chelsea characters from *That's So Raven*, the tv show.

With Seahorse, my life was great, but when I met Coral, my spirit leaped. Coral wasn't allowed to watch Harry Potter or any movie dealing with witchcraft or magic. Her family was extremely dedicated to their faith, and Coral was a lot like Shepherd. She said her grace before eating every meal at lunch and would treat even the meanest of people with the utmost kindness. She had a Godly strength about her character that made anyone who noticed want to be more like her.

I came home ranting and raving to my mother about an exciting conversation Coral had engaged me in about God and asked my mother if I could go spend the night with Coral one day and attend her church. My mother agreed, and that day changed my perspective on faith practices. Coral praised God without shame, and the entire church kneeled and prayed on their pews, crying out to God in the place of someone they knew to be hurting or struggling. Coral prayed for me that day, and I heard every word.

She prayed for me as if she knew the depths of my heart, but Coral knew nothing about me in that way. Her words wrapped me up like a thick quilt, and the warmth of her voice was like a fire kindled with the purest love. I remember opening my eyes to look at her while she prayed, and what I saw pulled all emotion to the middle of my throat. She was crying. She cried...for me. She barely knew me at this point, but she cried and begged God to keep me near Him and to show me the way back to Him.

It was as if her tears recharged my faith and inner spiritual strength. When I returned to school after that weekend, jokes that I used to find funny among some of my associates were no longer humorous. I could no longer hang around people who spoke ill or derogatorily. She reminded me of who and whose I was. She seemed like a pure spirit. I couldn't imagine her being disobedient or getting angry or doing anything other than what Jesus would do. I know that's high praise, but that's how I saw her.

She was one of the witnesses to the fight I told you about earlier with the girl who threw a pencil sharpener at my head. I remember the look of horror on her face when my eyes met hers while I was being taken out of the classroom by an administrator.

When I got back to school after my one-day suspension, I ran straight to her asking her to forgive my actions and telling her that I would understand her not wanting to be friends with me anymore. She welcomed me back with open arms and showed me compassion, but over the next couple of weeks, I realized how different our realities were. If she ever found out details about who I was and where I came from, our friendship would be over quicker than it began. So, I took it upon myself to stop hanging with her. Part of me felt like that's what she secretly wanted after the fight, and the other part of me felt like it was inevitable.

Maybe I was wrong about her, but things just didn't feel the same after that. Once again, I felt like evil won. It was somehow always able to squeeze out any glimmer of light or hope out of my grasp. Apparently, I wasn't the only kid in school battling darkness. The influences around me were just as dark as I'd felt I was.

We're coming up on some twisty vines. Don't let yourself become entrapped. We've still got a long way to go.

Be 'Watchful' of the Evil One

"Never fail to guard the gateways to your soul;
your eyes, your ears, and your genitals."
~A. S. E.

ONE DAY, WHILE we were in class, I noticed a small crowd gathered near the back of the classroom. "What are y'all lookin' at?" I asked. "Shh! You're gonna get us in trouble. It's pornography," one of the boys said. "*Pornography*?" I asked. I had never heard of that word. "Shh! You know what? Get away from us. We gonna get kicked out of school 'cause of yo' big mouth," the boy said. They kept hiding the computer screen from me, so I wasn't able to see anything.

When I made it home that day, I asked my mother what the word 'pornography' meant. "La'Porsha, you know what that is!" "No, I don't, Ma. We've never talked about that," I said. "Yes, we have! And why are you asking about that word, anyway?" she asked, frustratedly. "Well, some boys were looking at something called pornography on a computer in the classroom, but wouldn't let me see what it was," I explained.

My mother was highly disturbed at what I'd shared with her and had a good mind to pay the school a visit, but I begged her not to. "I know one thing, I'd better not ever catch you looking at that," she told me after informing me that it was something I didn't need to be concerning myself with.

I took heed to my mother's words, but while I was on the computer playing games and researching animals like I would often do in my spare time, a pornographic pop-up appeared. I clicked out of it in a hurry, but every time I clicked the 'x' button, another window would pop-up. Finally, curiosity got the best of me, and I decided to go ahead and explore the websites that were popping up.

I became intrigued by what I saw, but strange enough, the more videos I watched, the more I hated sex and men. I thought it was the most disgusting thing and couldn't imagine letting a man do those things to me. I definitely couldn't imagine any of it being as enjoyable as the women in the videos made it seem.

I became enraged with what God had made me once again. I was furious that I was a girl. The process looked painful and disgusting and demeaning, and degrading. Nothing about it seemed welcoming or loving or romantic. The worst part of all the videos was watching the way men received 'pleasure' from women in the most degrading and rude ways.

They seemed to treat women like dogs and had no respect for any part of their bodies. While I was exploring the very thing I'd decided to never take part in at any time in my future with a man, my mother and sister had crept up behind me to spook me and see what I was doing. My mother's sneaky smile quickly turned into a frown of disbelief when she discovered what I'd been viewing on the computer.

"Porsha! You looking at this stuff?! Really? Are you looking at this, Porsha?" she asked. She snatched me from the computer chair and pushed me all the way down the hallway to her bedroom. "What she do?" my dad asked. "Your daughter...go ahead. Tell your dad what you were doing!" she screamed. "Some videos popped up on the computer, and I looked at them," I said, whimpering. "They just popped up! I didn't try to go to them, and every time I tried to close out, another came up." "If that was the case, you know how to come back here and get one of us and tell us, but you didn't! You decided you gonna just sit there and watch all of that!" my mom screamed.

My dad's face was compassionate and regretful. "Carolyn, I have been on the computer, and those websites have just popped up, and they do keep popping up after you try to close them," he said. "She still knows how to come and get us, Duke!" my mother yelled.

My dad looked at me with disappointment, but he was more compassionate and sorrowful in his glance. I didn't think about it then, but he probably looked that way because those were websites he'd been visiting every now and then and knew that he was perhaps the reason they were popping up. I don't know that for sure, but it's possible.

Either way, I got one of the worst whippings of my life that day by my mother. I was angry with myself because I knew I didn't want to look at the videos, and my mother was right. I should have come and told her. I didn't even like what I saw, and I was in deep trouble for something that wasn't at all worth the trouble.

The images were now recorded in my brain, and I couldn't discard them. Resentment and self-hatred set in hard. I hated how God had designed us humans and thought we'd all be better off if He either killed us all or got rid of sex altogether. I'd had crushes before but didn't need sex to feel close to them or feel like we were an item. Their time and company were enough.

Dancing With Death

"To live is to die, and to die is to live." ~*A. S. E.*

To make matters worse, 6th grade was when I began having seizures. My body would experience temporary paralysis, and while not being able to speak, I would still be able to see and hear what was going on around me. The first time this ever happened to me, my mother and I were standing in the front doorway, watching for my school bus to arrive. She and I were engaged in an in-depth conversation about heaven and hell. Around this time, we always talked about things like what God expected from me as His royal daughter.

I was eating a peanut butter and jelly sandwich, and suddenly, I felt fragile and debilitated. I ran to the bathroom and sat on the toilet, thinking that maybe I just needed to relieve myself. But when I sat on the toilet, my body gave out, and I went limp. I tried to call for my mother but couldn't speak. Luckily enough, my mother came to the bathroom not long after me. She called my name repeatedly but couldn't get a response from me. "Porsha! Porsha, baby! Come on, Porsha! Porsha! Oh my God!" she screamed.

Tears began rolling down my cheeks from me trying so hard to respond to her and seeing her so frantic. I didn't know what she saw on my face, but I saw the complete and utter fear on hers. I knew it had to be bad. I've always felt like I was the rock for the mother, besides God, and I remember not really feeling scared but feeling ultimately betrayed by my body when it wouldn't allow me to respond to her, making her scream and cry. She was my queen, and I, her knight of a daughter.

My mother carried me to the car and told my sister to get in the car as well. She rushed me to the hospital. The doctors gave me some kind of liquid, and eventually, I was alright again. But my body was exhausted. It felt like I had been in a wrestling match with a giant animal or something. I was exhausted and fell asleep. When I woke up, the staff had brought me a coloring book and crayons. Shortly after I awoke, I was discharged, and we left the hospital. Needless to say, my sister and I missed school that day. My mother was adamant about me taking it easy.

When my dad got home from his welding job that day, my mother eagerly told him what happened. She couldn't tell the story without tears welling up in her eyes. She kept saying, "Duke, she looked like Ma. She looked like Ma in the face. Her face was white, Duke! All her color left." She went on and on about how much I'd looked just like my grandmother looked. She said I was just as pale as my Grandma Stella had been before she passed.

Over the years, I was given numerous explanations and many complex diagnoses. One doctor said it was a lack of electricity from my heart to my brain that would cause me to have a seizure. Another doctor said it was Epilepsy. And another said it was severe anxiety mixed with the fact that I had a heart that beat slower than it should.

Finally, after many indecisive explanations, my dad concluded in his mind that I was faking my attacks to get attention and to get out of trouble. My spells would often happen before or during a whipping or while being in the sun for too long. My body would just give way, but not without a few seconds of warning. It was always the same routine. My face would turn pale, and I'd try to mutter to whoever was nearby that I was growing weak and to help me. Then I'd slowly kneel to the ground and eventually lay my own body down, unable to move or speak.

They didn't only happen amid trouble. Once, I had an episode during a 5k walk/run for my diabetic cousin. My mother thinks the heat played a role in that one. Another time, I was dancing at my cousin's wedding reception and just passed out on the floor. From that point on, the rest of my childhood were tests and ambulance rides, which I absolutely hated. Sometimes, I would even try to refuse the trip because they would get me to come to before I would even enter the ambulance.

Doctors discovered that I had low blood pressure, which explained why my episodes would often happen around my monthly cycle. The medication they tried to prescribe me made things much worse, so it wasn't long at all before my parents gave me permission to stop taking it.

I became truly convinced that my body was a recycled coat from some old person because of all the issues affiliated with it. This was another thing added to the unexplainable cards I'd been dealt.

Looking back, I feel comfortable in saying that maybe my episodes made me a lot more comfortable with the idea of dying. I'd be lying if I said I didn't wonder about God's reasons for never letting me completely leave my body and move on from this world.

He would bring me back every episode or suicide attempt. Why?

Almost Normal

"Almost does count...against you." ~A. S. E.

THINGS WERE BEGINNING to slip back into the way things were before my parents' separation. They were starting to argue a little more than usual, but the main topic was money. My mother was a kindred spirit and had a very free and giving heart, while my dad was more practical and logical and had a tightly clenched fist. This was one thing I always felt they were both right and both wrong on.

My mother's argument was that my dad didn't understand the concept of sowing seeds of giving to receive an even greater reward than what was sown. My dad's case was that poor management of sowing seeds leaves everyone blessed and financially comfortable, but the person doing all the sowing. Like I said, they were both right. They were also both wrong because they were both on an extreme side.

I'll never forget the one day God decided to side with my mother. My parents had been invited to another church home that my sister and I grew fond of. We came to know of the church through a creole woman who initially wanted me to be her godchild, but I had too bad of an attitude for her, so she took my little sister instead. I preferred things that way and didn't mind one bit.

She was a great woman, but her daughter and I didn't quite see eye-to-eye at the time. Her daughter was much older than I, and she also had a bad attitude, so we were continually clashing about stupid things and misunderstandings. This church home was extremely active in miming and praise dancing. My sister and I took a strong liking to these activities and began traveling with the church to perform at different conferences.

They were very much invested in their youth, much like our previous church home.

One trip ended up costing the family five hundred dollars to sign up, and my dad was furious that my mother insisted on him paying the fee. She would say things like, "There's no price too high for the betterment of our children," and my dad would respond with something like, "Carolyn, they can't get no better than they already are." My sister and I would laugh at my dad being so passionate about not spending money, but also at the fact that we knew his argument was senseless and that my mother would always win, no matter what my dad thought to say.

Well, one day, my mother's substitution check came in the mail just a week after my dad had been made to pay the fee, and the paycheck read $499.99. She waved the paycheck in my dad's face and did a happy dance, jumping around and laughing like Rumpelstiltskin, and my dad just stood there watching with a corny smile on his face. My sister and I were tickled pink at my mother's 'victory' dance. "See, this is how my God works!" my mother boasted. "Oh ye of little faith!" she said. We couldn't stop laughing, and she couldn't stop dancing.

That was one of the first times I'd seen God take my mother's side, but there were many more instances that my mother proved to us that she walked with God's favor. Those times will be revealed later throughout this book. My mother's faith and favor made me grow uncontrollably thirsty for God's love and favor over my own life. I wanted God to love and care for me just as He did my mother.

My mother was not one to worry much about anything. When trouble would arise, she would have long, quiet moments in deep thought and meditation with God. When she would need uplifting, she would turn on her favorite gospel songs and start an enthusiastic praise all by herself.

If she got a little too excited, she would start screaming, "Yeah, yeah, yeah! Say that, say that!" and would tap you on your arm as an expression of overwhelming excitement. My mother's taps would be the same reason my sister and I fought to avoid sitting beside her during a good movie.

Anyway, my mother set the bar for being an enthusiast about serving God, and God never failed to reciprocate the love and favor. This would prove to be truest when my mother decided to allow God to carry her to a better place than what my dad had provided her.

Somehow, I miscalculated our route! Brace yourself for the black pit ahead! Don't fight against it. Save your energy and allow yourself to be sucked in. That way we can use our strength to continue swimming when the suction lets up.

Parasite

"The most dangerous enemy is one that will lay dormant for as long as it needs to in order to finish the destruction it started."
~A. S. E.

FOR A WHILE, things seemed to be going well for my family. We were all about as close as we were going to get, and we seemed to be headed in the right direction. But my Grandma Stella's prophecy was destined to completely fulfill itself.

My dad had been unfaithful to my mother yet again. My dad and mother had disagreements about something severe enough to make my mother begin sleeping on the living room couch. She slept there for about two or three days, expecting my dad to increase his efforts to make things right between them, but my mother was devastated when she, my sister, and I came home to find my dad racing off in his truck with another woman from her backyard beauty shop. He wasn't expecting us, but we returned home early from our outing because the movie we wanted to see wasn't playing that night.

When my dad returned home, my mother confronted him and revealed that she saw him leaving with the woman and asked him to confess what was going on. My dad confessed everything to my mother and then asked her, "So what? You wanna hit me?" "Na, I'll let God handle you. You're not worth it, and the kids been through enough. The girls and I will be out of your way," my mother replied.

The thing about masked people is that they eventually get tired of wearing masks and pull them off. A person can only fake real change for so long, but if they're not genuine, you'll see redundant failures, and you begin to notice bits and pieces of their true colors shining through face paint.

Within the next two weeks, my mother moved us back to Flora, Mississippi, where she was approached by an old man who came to her out of the blue at the gas station. The man appeared to be in his sixties. "You going through a divorce, ain't ya?" he asked my mother. "Yeah," my mother hesitated. "I know, the enemy wants yo' family and want to kill and destroy yo' whole family. He got a real stronghold on ya husband, and when he comes in, he comes in like that. He goes after the weakest one. And every time he leaves, he comes back stronger 'cause he mad. You have children, don't you?" he asked. "I got two daughters," my mother replied. "I know. Since he got yo' husband, he comin' for yo' oldest next. He ain't bothering you 'cause you strong, but he wants yo' daughter. He gon' try real' hard, but when he can't get her, he gon' go for the baby girl. The enemy ain't gon' stop until he kill ya whole family. But don't worry, you gon be alright 'cause you strong. This is what I want you to do with your kids. Draw a circle around them, and pray over their heads every night. He can't break that circle, ya hear? He can't break through that circle," he said.

My sister and I watched through the car windows as my mother talked to the man. We were fidgety and perplexed because my mother stopped to talk to no one. She trusted no one. But she spoke with this man.

This time when we moved, she made sure we were under our own roof. She found a rental property on Renfroe Dr. that all three of us adored. It was probably one of the coziest homes we'd lived in, and at night, she would take my sister and me to see a grove of fireflies.

Our new home was an upscale trailer home rental in a beautiful trailer park. These trailers were adorable. Our house had three bedrooms, one full kitchen, two full bathrooms, and a full living room area. The bathroom in my mother's room had a wide round jacuzzi tub with jets in it.

The first thing my mother did when we arrived was to make sure that every room in the house felt as homey as possible, but she completely neglected her own room. My mother didn't even focus on getting a bed for her room. Instead, she slept on the living room couch.

My mother pretty much allowed my sister and me to decorate our rooms the way we wanted them. I had a beautiful day bed in my room. She took us to Kirkland's and told us to pick out any decorations we wanted. I acquired many glowing lava lamps, mini waterfalls, fog pots, and best of all, I had an angel whose wings slowly flapped and changed colors. With the serene sound of constant flowing water and the wide variety of glowing colors, my room became extremely heavenly and tropical. She even allowed me to buy a nature sounds CD, and I played it faithfully every night while I slept.

My cousins were happy to see my sister and me back in Flora. We immediately began singing together again, and we even hung out at their home and attended worship with them sometimes. Things were different and better since we would only visit them and didn't live with them.

My mother was once again working the night shift at Wal-Mart and wanted to find a daycare that we could stay in, but we told her she could trust us to stay home alone. With hesitation, my mother agreed but warned us not to do anything to cause her not to trust us, or she would have to make other plans.

My sister and I held to our word for a long while, but as time went on, I began desiring companionship. My sister and I didn't really have anything in common. We would both come home and do our homework and eat whatever my mother left in the oven for us. Then, I would go to my room, and my sister would go to hers. I would write in my journals and listen to music while my sister did whatever she would do in her own room.

I can't remember how I ended up meeting this guy, but we'll call him Devin. Devin and I became close and talked on the house phone often. One day, while we were on the phone, he told me to come outside. My sister and I went to the door to see what was going on, and there he sat on a majestic white horse right outside our front door.

My sister and I couldn't believe our eyes! "Porsha! It's just like out of a fairytale!" my sister exclaimed. "I know!" I said, smiling from ear to ear. "Would you like to ride with me?" he asked. "I can't ride a horse! And I can't leave the house, you know that. My mother would kill me if she even knew I was talking with you," I said. "Too bad. Well, I want to hang out with you, so I'll go and put the horse up and have someone drop me back off here, deal?" he asked. "Deal," I answered.

It was only a few minutes before Devin knocked on the back door, and I let him in. He was only about a year older than I was, and my sister loved him. In fact, she loved him too much. My little sister grew envious and developed a crush on him. He took her to the side and said that if she was older, he would have probably seen her first. He winked at me when he said it, and I knew he was trying to make her feel better. He told her to not worry about guys and love right now, and that when she became old enough, someone special would come for her on an even prettier horse than he had ridden.

Devin enjoyed my conversation and would often tell me how different I seemed from other girls he knew. We would talk about things he said he never thought of until I'd mention them. Once, Devin kissed me and asked me to lay down on my bed. I did, but after he kissed me again, I knew I had to put a stop to where things were heading.

I told him that if we had sex, it would disgrace my family and that I wanted to please God with my body. He completely understood and kissed me on the cheek. He said that moment made him admire me even more than before. We continued to enjoy each other's company and watch movies together.

My mother found out about him through a letter I was writing to one of my friends at school and she came down so hard on me that when she whipped me, I turned around, and she accidentally slashed my eye with the belt. It grew purple and bruised, and she immediately felt horrible. She treated my eye but didn't want to keep me from going to school too long, so she held me home for a day and let me return to my classes the day after that.

The mark was still visible, and I'd grown a resentment towards my mother for marking my face, so I reported her to the school office. She explained the situation to them and was furious with me. I had done it out of anger, so I felt horrible about it afterward. The school told her they had an eye on her, and that if anything else were to happen, she would be in deep trouble.

I can't imagine how my mother must have felt, but I regret doing that to this day. I'd done something that deserved punishment and had I stood in place and not wiggled around so much, the belt would have never missed my bottom and hit my eye.

My mother seemed to enter a depression after that incident, and I felt horrible about severing my mother's trusting relationship with me. I knew that things were already stressful for her with raising my sister and me on her own and having to work the night shift. I felt I should have been more of a help to her than a rebellious burden.

Double Trouble

"Don't you just hate it when the egg you throw ends up on your own face?"
~A. S. E.

BY THIS TIME, I was entering 7th grade, and things were a little different from the first time I'd been to the school in East Flora. I adored every one of my teachers, but the principal gave me the creeps. Nevertheless, the students were cliqued up much like high school. The same two associates I had the first time we'd moved to Flora were the same two who befriended me this time.

I was less concealing about my singing voice and was often asked by my peers to sing them a song. There was another 'singer' in my grade we'll call Abalone. Abalone was very thin, petite, and very girly. She came off as a snob to me and appeared to be very cliquey. She was, by far, the most popular girl in school, and it was because of her singing voice. I'd unknowingly become quite popular myself for the same exact reason.

I don't think she wanted to be snobby, but instead became that way towards me as a result of our peers pitting us against one another. They always tried to get me to participate in sing-offs with her, but I would always refuse. Eventually, we both ended up entering a local gospel competition, and I won. That pretty much laid our 'unofficial' competition with one another to rest.

After that victory, she seemed to have a respect for me. She was still snobby but not as much as she had been. She was also madly in love with my oldest cousin and would always try to get me to ask him to take her out. I would lie and say I did, but I didn't want my cousin dating her. Things were too weird and uneasy between us. Besides, my cousin was one of the sweetest guys you would ever meet at that time, and he was considered good-looking. I wanted some princess to come along and steal his heart, not my middle school rival.

I hadn't been attending school long before catching the eye of many of the young men there for many different reasons. I didn't give most of them the slightest time of day because I'd been trying to gain my mother's trust back and remain on the 'straight and narrow' with my behavior. But my longing for intimate companionship remained, and there was one guy that I found to be relentlessly charming.

Our school offered a Christian gathering at the beginning of every Thursday morning for believers. The class would start an hour before the first school bell, and they would provide us donuts and juice. We would spend that hour discussing our faith and specific topics some of us may have been struggling with in our everyday school lives.

I had never taken notice that I had many admirers in the class, but one day someone called my name as I was leaving the class. "La'Porsha! Well, hello," he said. His smile was beautiful, and his dimples were deep enough for me to dive into. "Um, hi," I responded nervously. "I've seen you in class a few times, but never get a chance to catch up to you." "Well, you caught me. What's up?" I asked. "Um, nothing...I just...wanted to say hi," he said, smirking. "Okay, bye," I said, and I turned to walk away.

As I walked away, I looked back to find him standing there, watching me walk away. When he saw me glance back, he smiled and threw up his hand. I quickly turned back around and sped up my walking.

When I made it to class, I couldn't wait to ask Mahi about him. She'd gone ahead of me leaving the faith class, but I knew she saw the entire exchange. "So, tell me, who was I talking to? He didn't even tell me his name," I said. "That was Samson. And from the way he was talking to you, I think he may like you. He doesn't usually talk to people he doesn't know. To be honest, he's kind of mean, but he has a sweet side," she said. "Mean? Please, the boy almost wet himself just trying to say hi to me," I said. "Well, he's not mean unless you give him a reason to be. He's nice to girls and mean to boys." "He looks like a grown man!" I said. "He's fine, ain't he?" Mahi teased. "Girl, yeah, but usually that means they're no good." "I think you might like him. I could actually see y'all together," she said. "Whatever," I said, dismissing our conversation.

The next week after bible class, Samson ran up to me again. "Hey, listen. I have something I want to tell you. I just don't know how you're gonna take it," he said. "Okay, shoot," I said. "Um, I think.... you're beautiful..." My eyes grew wide, and I was entirely caught off guard by his forwardness. "...and I would love to take you out sometime," he finished. "Oh, wow, take me out? Um, well, I'm not actually allowed to date, so I wouldn't be able to go out with you anywhere," I explained. "Well, we don't have to go anywhere. How about we just start meeting up by the band hall in the morning so that I can get to know you?" "Um, okay. Sure," I agreed. We bid our goodbyes, and I rushed off to my first class to share the tea with Mahi.

I couldn't concentrate for the rest of the day. I was in such a daze that I blocked out my lessons and doodled on my paper the entire day. The next day, I arrived at school reasonably early to find Samson standing by the band hall, waiting for me. He looked like a strong, chocolate prince, and his eyes were deep and mysterious. The way he'd glare at me almost cast him to be forbidden.

He greeted me with a full hug that seemed to linger, and I melted into his strong arms. What was this *man* doing at my school? He was taller and more built than any guy I'd seen there. "Hi," he greeted me, smiling. "Hi." We took our seat next to one another on the bench. "So, you look beautiful today. Well, you look beautiful every day, but I really like the way you look today. Ah, I'm nervous, I'm sorry," he said, chuckling.

He was nervous? Seriously? If only he'd been able to see past my poker face. I felt like my stomach was in knots. I didn't even know what to say. "Don't be nervous. I'm a nerd. I'm no one to be nervous in front of," I laughed. "Well, I like your nerdiness. I think it's cute. In fact, it's part of why I'm attracted to you. You just stand out from the rest of the girls here. So, a little birdy told me you can sing. Would you mind singing me a song?"

I was completely caught off guard with his request. "Sing you a song? I'm too shy to do something like that." "I can look away if you want me to," he offered. "No, if I sing to you, I should look you in the eye when I do it. Otherwise, there's no connection between the singer and the audience. I'll tell you what. Let's keep getting to know each other, and if I fall for you or gift you my heart, I'll sing you a song as a sign of our relationship moving to a more serious level. Deal?" I asked. "When," he replied. "Excuse me?" I asked. "*When* you fall for me...and it's a deal. I look forward to that day," he said, smiling.

He had a way of making me smile so hard, and long, my jaws would begin to ache. The more we talked and hung out with one another, the more I fell for him. He was funny when he wasn't trying to be. He was actually a serious person and could even come off as cold or stern, but he was only that way with some of the guys he hung with. He was always gentle with me and kind. His embrace would be mighty with passion but strained and reserved out of an attempt to show me how much respect he had for me.

We grew fond of each other rapidly over a series of poems we'd write to each other. Samson would write me a poem expressing how he was feeling that day, and I would write a response in the format of a poem also. We wrote about deep things to one another. He would try and pry me to speak with him about matters of my heart in person, but I could never build up the courage. His aura was intense and passionate. He always had a way of making me feel safe.

After a few weeks of talking, my mother discovered a church with a babysitting program. After speaking with the pastor of the church, he assured my mother there would be someone available to watch us until she got off work. Flora's such a small place so I shouldn't have been surprised, but I was shocked to discover Samson went to this church. One night, he came to the childcare side of the church and saw me there. From then on, he made it a point to see me every night.

The sitter was completely fine with us seeing one another because she trusted Samson to be a gentleman, and he was. He would bring me into the sanctuary to teach me how to play the piano or just try to play a song for me. He would often even try singing to me. Sometimes, he would ask me to keep him company while he worked out in a small gym room the church had. I remember watching him and thinking, "*Wow... his strength is something I've never witnessed from any other guy our age.*" It was awe-inspiring.

"Come and work out with me," he said. "I can't do half the things you're doing, and I don't need to make you laugh." "I would never laugh at you, and you don't need to work out. I just wanted us to do something together. Trust me, you're fine the way you are," he said. "Hm, that's not really what I think you think about me. I think you're a wooer with a smooth tongue," I replied.

He immediately halted his work out and gave me the most serious gaze. He got up and walked towards me, and because of his non-smiling stare, I stepped backward as a natural reflex until I found my back pressed against a wall. "Let me show you just how smooth my tongue can be," he said. He gently pulled me from the wall and rested his back in my place, stretching his legs out so that he'd be face level with me in all of my shortness. He then pulled me to himself slowly and laid my hands to rest around his neck, and he kissed me. I'd never been kissed like that before. He kissed me long and passionately, but it wasn't wet or sloppy. It was like something out of a dream.

He took his time with me, and with every stroke of his tongue, his hands caressed the small of my back, never daring to go any lower or any higher. He wrapped his arms around me entirely, and his hands squeezed me when he started to feel his body reacting to my closeness.

Slowly, the kiss grew more urgent until finally, with his strong arms, he picked me up and placed my back against the wall with my legs wrapped around his waist. Suddenly he pulled away and shook his head, smiling. "What's wrong?" I asked. "We have to stop," he said, still smiling. "Yeah, I kind of feel bad for kissing you in a church. I agree,"

I said. "Oh no, I'd kiss you anywhere, anytime. What I feel for you is in no way dishonorable. But, you're worth more than...this. I stopped because the last thing I would ever want to do is disrespect my queen," he explained.

I was lost for words. Samson took my hand, kissed the back of it, and led me back to the childcare room. He kissed my cheek and bid me goodnight. I shared all the juicy details with the sitter and my sister, and we rejoiced like teenagers at a sleepover.

The next day at school, I saw him, but when I waved at him, he wouldn't respond. He didn't meet me at our usual spot, either. I spent the entire day on edge. When the day finally ended, I couldn't wait to get to the church because it was Wednesday, which meant bible study. I'd never attended the bible study class until tonight because I was desperate to see him.

I sat at the end of the table where I'd seen him and other teenagers sitting. He was flirting with a girl across from him, and I was invisible. Finally, I couldn't take it anymore. "Really? So you're gonna act like you don't see me sitting here?" I asked. The entire table grew silent. "Um, I don't know who you talking to, but it's not me," he said. "Wow, that's not how you were acting last night!"

Immediately, I could see the girl he'd been flirting with grow uncomfortable and a bit upset, but I didn't even care about her or the rest of the people at the table. "Look, um, can we just drop this? How about we talk after class?" he suggested. "Don't bother!" I said and ran out of the classroom back to my childcare room. I heard the entire table laughing. I cried myself to sleep that night.

When I arrived at school the next day, he tried to speak to me. I was appalled. "Get out of my face, Samson. I have absolutely nothing to say to you!" I yelled just before storming off. He appeared to have been taken back and confused. I didn't see him for the rest of that day.

The next day, he found me before class and profusely apologized for 'how he'd acted' the other night and asked that I give him one more chance. As much as I wanted to say no, he'd already snatched my heart, so I agreed.

When I saw him later that day, he was wearing different clothes. We started meeting by the glass display right in front of the main office before each class. "Why do you keep changing your shirt? I never knew you to be so high maintenance," I snared. He'd started to really annoy me with his changing clothes throughout the day and his laughter at every question I'd confront him with. It began to seem like suddenly, I was a joke to him. This continued for about a week, and finally, one day, I went to meet him at the bookshelf, and he wasn't there.

I was confused and ready to call the entire relationship off at this point. Samson had been acting strange, laughing all the time, constantly changing clothes, and being elusive. I'd even tried to kiss him a couple times, and he pulled away. I was done.

A short time after I'd been waiting by the glass case, two tall, dark figures turned the corner and began walking towards me. I thought I'd gone crazy from the confusion of the past week because I saw double! But behold, there were two tall, dark, handsome young men standing in front of me with huge smiles on their faces, wearing the same exact clothing. Samson was a twin!

I stood there with my mouth gasped open, and they both laughed hysterically. "Hey, Porsha!" one said. "Hey, Porsha!" said the other. "What the heck is this!?" I asked. "Seriously? You're a twin? Wow." I placed my hand over my mouth, and I felt my face growing hot. "So, I've been dating both of you?" I asked. "Yeah," one said. "We hope you're not mad, but we decided to play this little trick as a funny way to show you we're twins," the other said.

I couldn't stop staring at each of them, and to make matters a whole lot worse, there was no way I could tell them apart from each other. "Okay, so which one did I kiss?" I asked. "Both of us, one said." "You'd better be kidding," said the other. "And what if I'm not?" one asked the other. They stared at each other for a second and burst into laughter. "Okay, guys, which one of you is Samson?" I asked nervously. "I'm

Samson, and this is my brother, Samuel," one said. "Oh, you're more than brothers! You're twins! Don't leave that part out. And how do I know you're telling the truth?" I asked. One of them stepped forward and said, "Nothing I feel about you is in any way dishonorable, believe that." "Oh my gosh, Samson! It's you!" I exclaimed, laughing and relieved.

I hugged him and then turned to his brother. "So, the other night at the church for bible study?" I asked, with one eyebrow raised. "That was me, Samuel, and the girl sitting across from me that you probably saw looking at you crazy is my girlfriend." "Oh my gosh, I am so sorry," I said. "It's okay. When you left, someone said you might have thought I was Samson, and that made sense of everything. She found it funny. When I went back home, I told Samson what had happened and described you to him. That's when we decided to try this. The times I pulled away from you, I did it because I didn't want to kiss my brother's girlfriend." "Wow, well, we have a problem, because I can't tell you guys apart…at all!" I said. "Don't worry, you'll only be meeting one from now on," said Samson.

I was blown away by the fact that my boyfriend had a whole other face and body of himself. It was the strangest thing to see. But I was even more blown away that the two pulled this on me, successfully! When I went to class and told Mahi everything I'd discovered, her mouth flew open in disbelief that I had no idea Samson was a twin. "Girl, you didn't know? I thought you saw them; they're always passing you in the hall!" she said. "Yeah! But not together! While you were telling me all about Samson, wouldn't it be natural for you to say, 'oh and he's a twin, by the way' or something?" I asked. All Mahi could do was laugh.

Samson begged me to try going to bible study one more time, but I was too embarrassed about the way I acted last time I was there, so I didn't. I just agreed to meet him afterward. When I went into the classroom to meet him after the class had been dismissed, I saw a twin. "Samson?" I asked. He smiled at me with a mischievous grin and shook his head. "No, I'm Samuel," he said. "Samson should be back in a minute. He's just helping the pastor out with something," he said. "Oh okay."

I noticed something was wrong with Samuel, but I couldn't put my finger on what. "You mind if I stay and wait for him here?" I asked. "Be my guest," he answered. "What's wrong? Why the long face?" I asked. "It's nothing," he said. "Wow, if you died within the next few seconds, I'm pretty sure you'd go to hell for that lie," I said, smiling. He chuckled and smiled big, but then his smile faded, and his face grew sad again.

After a few moments of staring at him with an expecting gaze, he rolled his eyes and began spilling his heart. "I don't know, it's just a lot of things all at once. Between my family and my brother and my girlfriend, I don't know. Sometimes I don't feel like they understand me. I feel like I'm almost invisible. I'm always doing for everyone else, but nobody cares to ask what I want or what I need," he said. "Well, you and Samson are close, right? Try telling him how you feel," I suggested.

He chuckled. "Samson and I love each other very much, but we're not the same person. If you pay close attention, we don't really have the same face," he laughed. "Samson is very serious, and he can be mean and selfish sometimes. He probably hasn't shown you that because you're his girlfriend, and come on, only an idiot would be mean to you. You're so sweet. You know, I don't even know why I'm talking to you. I literally *never* open up to anyone; I almost feel tricked," he said, smiling. "Well, I guess that makes us even," I replied.

He laughed a goofy laugh that made me laugh. "What about your girlfriend? Can you talk to her about what you're feeling?" I asked. "She's not... It's.... complicated. She only cares about what I can give her and what I can do for her. She doesn't really care about my feelings, and I don't want to come off as weak. People see my brother and say he's manly and not a punk because he's mean. I'm called sensitive and childish because I'm nice," he said. "Well, maybe you're too nice. I actually think being able to be nice and sensitive is just as important as being able to be selfish sometimes and mean enough not to let people walk all over you. I know you call me sweet, but I never let someone make me feel like their servant, at least not anymore. I tell them about whatever it is their draining from me, give them a little time to fix it, and move the heck on if they don't."

Samuel laughed and looked at me with admiration. "Can I tell you a secret?" he asked. "You can tell me anything." "I really hate we tricked you, not just because it was mean on our part, but because when I was meeting up with you, you showed me your heart in a lot of our conversations, thinking I was Samson. I honestly began wishing I had been the twin to find you first. I kind of accidentally fell for you," he admitted. "But don't let Samson know I told you that. He'd kill me," he laughed. "Wow, I wasn't expecting that, but don't worry, I won't," I said.

Just then, Samson finally made it back to the room we were in. "Speaking of the devil," I said. "Well, they do say opposites attract," he replied with a smile. He was too smooth for me. "On that note, I'm gonna go," Samuel said. Samson whisked me off to a more private place, and our evening of romantic and intriguing conversation began. I was always amazed that he never ran out of new compliments to give me or new flattering comebacks to say. Samson was indeed like a prince out of a fairy tale. However, I should have known this fairytale would be short-lived, but he had been so devoted to me that I didn't see it coming.

The twins hadn't been my only admirers at the school. There was another guy we'll call Oar, and a girl we'll call Grouper that wanted a chance to be with me. The girl had approached me on the school bus one morning. "Hey, La'Porsha, let me talk to you for a minute." She sat down behind me, and since I would always sit by the window, she slid to the window in the seat behind me to speak through the crack. "You know, I could do you better than that goofy twin you think you dating," she said. "No disrespect, but I don't fly that way. And I don't *think* we're dating, we're dating," I responded. "Whatever, you'll learn," she said and returned to the back of the bus where she and other rowdy kids liked to ride.

The guy that was interested in me took one of my last classes with me, and would always make it his business to sit next to me. This was around the time my mom allowed me to get my first sew in weave, and I chose to get a long bouncy bob. No one was used to seeing me so dolled up, so I caught a lot of attention from jealous girls and horny boys. It fascinated me with how much they drooled over hair they *knew* wasn't my own.

Oar really shot his shot the day I walked into class late from my hair appointment. A lady named Renae had done my hair. It had been so fun because she and my mother had been laughing hysterically at how much I sounded like Prince when I sang his songs.

By the time I arrived at school, I was on cloud nine, but was brought down a little when Oar wouldn't stop trying to ask me out. Some girl that will remain nameless liked Oar and was extremely upset that he was flirting with me. As soon as the bell rang, the girl ran straight to Grouper, who was standing in the hall in the middle of a group of girls. I couldn't make out what they were saying because they were far away, but I knew by the looks on their faces that whatever it was, it was messy and would be causing trouble somehow.

About a week after that day, everything changed. Up until now, Samson had been the perfect gentleman to me. He was always finding some kind of way to make me feel good throughout the day. He would even pop in on some of my classes, pretending like he wanted to speak with the teachers when all he was really interested in was seeing me or passing me one of his poem letters. He was amongst the teachers' favorite students, so even though they were aware of what he was doing, they allowed it and eventually scolded him jokingly to get to his own class.

Now, he was seemingly avoiding me and was less interested in conversing with me between classes. He even started missing our morning meetings before school started. His poem letters slowed down to almost one every three days.

The entire 7th-grade class had gone on a field trip to a water park, but I hadn't been allowed to go because I had a D in my history class. My mother didn't know it at that time, but my history teacher was an extremely unreasonable man who seemed to want to fail many undeserving students. He absolutely hated his job, and it showed.

When everyone came back from the trip, rumors were circling around about Samson kissing some girl at the water park. When my friend came back, I decided to ask her about it. She told me he kissed the same girl who tried to ask me out. When I asked Grouper about it, she began laughing, saying it was a dare and that she and Samson are just cool and don't even like each other. Then she went on to say she told me so about Samson not being serious about me.

I started crying to Mahi, asking her why he had done that to me after all the letters he wrote to me. Mahi said that somehow, a rumor got to him about me kissing Oar near the girls' bathroom. It all made sense. I was furious that Samson would believe some gossip and not even ask me about it. The only reason I hadn't shared with him about Oar asking me out was because I knew Samson and Oar. They were both hotheads, and I didn't think it was necessary to tell Samson about something I'd already handled myself.

While Mahi and I were talking, a girl sitting beside us heard what we were talking about. She was a hushed girl and hardly said anything ever. She was known by the fact that she was "heavy topped" and "well-endowed" in the chest area. "Wait, you're Samson's girlfriend?" she asked. "Thought I was," I answered. "He just wrote me a love letter. See?"

Mahi and I read the letter. It was surely Samson's because the poetry was like the tone of my letters. He even used some of the same compliments he would give me every day. I'd never been so hurt by a boy I liked in my life. I thought we really had a serious connection. He'd put me on a pedestal fit for a princess just to tear me down and make me feel like the dirt under his shoe. My heart grew hard and cold, and the only flavor I could taste in the mouth was the taste of vengeance.

In all of Samson's letters to me, he'd revealed secrets and insecurities about himself, and I would tell him all about mine in my notes. The only difference between him and me was I'd grown thick skin and didn't care what anyone thought about me anymore. I didn't mind people knowing my secrets, but I knew he wouldn't feel the same way.

When the dismissal bell rang, I headed to my bus with my best friend, and there Samson stood, waiting for me like he did every afternoon. He stood there greeting me with a smile, but I felt my face have such an icy stare, it could have broken into a million pieces. I threw the papers painted with our intimate exchange of poetry right on his face and let them spill on the ground in front of him and all around him.

People oohed and laughed at Samson, and I went flat foot off on him. "Son of a b*! How could you?" I screamed. "Baby, what's this? What are you talking about?" I noticed Grouper out of the corner of my eye, laughing. "Don't worry, La'Porsha. I'm always right here for you. I ain't gon' do you like he did," she hackled. "That? That is what you let come between us?" I asked.

Samson flashed a look of realizing that I had found out about his water park indiscretions. "Well? You don't have anything you wanna say to me? Nothing at all?" I asked. "How about you? You have something you want to say to me?" he asked. "Wow. You're talking about Oar, right? He's been asking me out and flirting with me, and like a fool, I turned him down out of respect for what I thought we had! It was as simple as asking me about it or even Mahi! But out of some sick revenge, you go and randomly kiss the dike that's been trying to get at me? Na, you wanted this. You wanted your freedom and didn't have the balls to tell me. Well, now you got it," I snarled. "La'Porsha, let's go somewhere and talk in private, please," he said, with a face load of regret. "Na, you can talk to my a* while I walk up outta here," I said, throwing my hand in his face. "Samson, man, you gonna let her talk to you like that, bruh?" one of his friends asked. He said nothing and was deadlocked on my furious eyes.

The crowd of students around us couldn't believe what they had heard come out of my mouth, as I was known to be classy and quiet, a good girl. I was sure to strut the fiercest walk to my school bus. I wanted him and everyone standing around to see what he'd given up.

I heard the comments as I left. Grouper and the other kids joked about how much of a fool he was to have lost me the way he did. I didn't even look back. I walked fierce and fast. His brother saw the tears streaming down my face, and had missed the entire commotion. "La'Porsha? "La'Porsha? What's wrong? Wait! Please!"" he yelled.

I held up my hand without stopping to let him know not to even try and speak with me at that moment. "What did you do?!" I heard him yell to his brother in anger. I didn't wait for the response. I kept racing to the bus.

I got on the bus and sat in the very front seat near the window, as I always did. When I sat down, I inhaled and exhaled the deepest, most painful breath. It felt as if I'd been holding it in the entire time I strutted to the bus. I put my head down and began to cry.

Knock, knock, knock.

It was Samuel knocking on the window. "La'Porsha? What happened? Please talk to me. What did my brother do to you?" he asked.

I looked up at him with a tear-stained face but said nothing. "La'Porsha, please don't cry. I can't...I can't see you cry," he said. I couldn't speak. I could barely breathe. "La'Porsha, I'm coming to see you tonight. I'll be there, I promise," Samuel said. He stepped back as the bus drove away.

That night, Samuel kept his promise. When he arrived, he led me to the sanctuary, and we sat on the piano where Samson and I used to sit. There was a long moment of silence before we talked. "My brother told me everything," he said. "I'll be okay. I've gone through worse than this, so..." I shrugged. "You didn't deserve that, La'Porsha. You're by far the best girlfriend my brother has ever had and probably better than any he'll have in the future," he said. "Thanks, that means a lot coming from you."

He gave me one of the most genuine smiles. I never told him, but his aura reminded me of Michael Jackson. There was an innocence and a sincerity about him. "I've got an idea. How about you sing a song," he suggested. "You want me to sing you a song?" "Well, I've never heard you sing, and Samson says you have a beautiful voice." "Hmm, I'll sing if you sing to me first," I said. "I can't sing!" "You can try," I teased. "Okay, but only because I'm trying to make you feel better," he said.

I can't remember the song he chose to sing, but it made me smile so big because he was very obviously singing despite him being extremely bashful in front of me. I appreciated that. Before I could repay the favor, we were warned that my mother had shown up to pick me and my sister up. After this night, I wasn't able to continue going to the church sitter for much longer because Samson and I had gotten caught playing the piano in the sanctuary by the pastor a couple weeks earlier. He was furious because he'd promised my mother that we were in great hands.

I respected the fact that Samuel was still in a relationship, but eventually we ended up together. It was tricky because Samson still wanted me and had even told me that while I dated his 'prince' of a brother, he would always see me as his queen and himself as my king. He made things difficult for us for a while, but eventually he wished us both the best.

My relationship with Samuel was short lived due to another relocation that we'll talk about a little later. We tried to make long distance work, but we eventually fell off from each other. Things were too difficult with me not being able to actually date someone and having to sneak phone calls to him.

Sharky's Payback

"Sometimes, revenge is so 'sweet,' it's unbelievable."
~A. S. E.

WHEN THINGS WERE good, they were good, but when it rained, it poured. Sharky had been taunting me all year verbally, but she hadn't been physical. For some reason, she decided she was in an extra bad mood one day. I made the mistake of glancing her way in class, and it just set her off. "What the heck you lookin' at, Butterfinger?" she barked. The remark was aimed at my light skin pigment, so I returned the favor. Usually, I wouldn't have responded, but today was a bad day for me too, and I was just over school and over life. "I don't know. You tell me, Snicker," I said, smiling.

The entire class oohed and laughed. I guess Sharky was too embarrassed for an immediate response. Later that day, she and I were approaching one another in passing, right in front of the front office. "Well, look at this. I told you I would get ya," she said, pointing her finger. "Sharky, what's your problem? You're really gonna fight me over candy bar names. That's dumb, ignorant and shallow. You ain't got nothin' better to do? Would it have been better if I called you skittles?" I snarked. "I'll let you get the first lick," she said. "I'm not fighting you over something this dumb. In fact, I can't stop laughing in my head about how stupid this is," I chuckled. "Oh, so now I'm stupid?" she said.

That was all she wrote. She charged at me, knocking me down with a tackle. My tickle box was beyond activated because I was still astonished at how mad she was over the silly names we'd called each other. She punched me repeatedly, and the other kids all gathered around and watched. For some reason, her punches tickled me. She couldn't get any good ones in because of how I guarded myself in a rolled-up fetal position. "Sharky, man, get off her! She won't even fight you back," Wally screamed.

This was the strangest fight I'd been in. I was literally too tickled to even throw one punch. When a teacher finally pulled her off me, I was crying laughing. The teacher sent both of us to the office, and we had to wait in separate rooms. I waited at the front of the office sitting right by the big glass that separated the office from the hallway, and Sharky was sent to wait in the Principal's office.

The Principal decided to call me in to another part of the office to speak with me alone. "La'Porsha, what are you doing?" he asked. "It wasn't my fault. She's hated me since I moved here. Ain't nothin' I could do about that," I said rolling my eyes. "I know you're a good girl and I would hate for you to get in trouble, so I'll make a deal with you. Take a paddling or I call your mother," he said.

I had never been paddled before, but I also didn't want to stress my mother. So I opted for the paddling. He was an old, brown man and remained seated in his office chair while reaching for his paddle out of one of his drawers. He told me to bend over in front of him while he was still seated, and paddled me...softly. I felt my bottom jiggle and after two licks, things felt COMPLETELY off. "Just call my mom. I change my mind," I rushed to say. "Are you sure?" he asked. "Yeah," I said.

He sent me back out into the main part of the office.

My mother was called up to the school, and when she arrived, the Principal told her that he was suspending me for six days. "My daughter tells me she didn't even get one lick in! She didn't hit the girl, not once. How is she suspended for six days? What about the girl? What's her punishment?" my mother yelled. "I'm suspending her for six days as well," he said. "So my daughter gets the same punishment, even though she was attacked and didn't participate?" my mother asked. "I purposely didn't hit her so that I wouldn't get in trouble. Now I'm in trouble anyway? This isn't fair! You can ask any of the other kids, and they'll tell you I didn't touch her!" I chimed in.

The Principal called in a few students, and after speaking with them, he informed my mother and me that he was sticking to his punishment because he saw where the fight could have been avoided on both sides. I was scheduled to take part in a program where I'd been asked to host and sing by my choir teacher, but the Principal said that I was banned from attending the program and that the suspension was effective immediately.

When we got home, my dad had driven to Flora to watch me in the program. My mother furiously told him that I'd been suspended and didn't even get a lick off the girl I was fighting. My mother seemed angrier at me for not fighting back. She scolded me about how I should have taken a stand for myself and fought since I'm suspended anyway. I told her I had no idea I would get suspended regardless if I participated in the fight or not. My dad chimed in and showed his disappointment in me, too.

I remember feeling so confused. My parents were actually angry that I didn't fight! They decided to rub it in my face and go to the program anyway. I remember screaming at them and crying because I knew exactly what they were doing. I wasn't performing at the program, and there was no other reason for them to go. But they went and left me to wait in the car until the program was over. This was their way of punishing me.

I had a mental breakdown alone in the heated car and yelled every curse word I could think of. My parents didn't realize it at the time, but they were building a monster.

It wasn't the only time my parents had made me feel like an outcast in my own family. My dad came and visited a second time. I can't remember the reason why, but the school was getting ready to go on break, and this was a week of testing. My dad wanted to take the family out to eat to catch up on how things were going. I called my mother to ask if she could come and get me from school early since I thought

I was finished with all my testing. My mother asked me, "Are you sure you don't have any more tests?" "Yes, Ma. I'm sure. I'm all done. My teachers told me so."

After I got off the phone with my mother who had agreed to come and pick me up, my history teacher came and told me I needed to do an extra credit assignment for him to bring my grade up to a passing grade. By the time my mother arrived at school, the office had called for me over the intercom. I ran to the office and tried to explain to my mom what was going on. "Hey! I thought I was done testing, but there's one more small thing I'm working on for history. I'll be quick, I promise!" I said. "So you lied. Get back to class, Porsha! I'm not waiting for you. Me, your sister, and your dad are going out to eat without you. You're just such a little liar, I'm tired of playing your games. Go!" she yelled.

I cried like a baby and didn't care what office administrators saw me. I watched my mother walk out of the office, out of the school, get in her car and pull off in immense anger. I couldn't believe she didn't believe me! I didn't know it at the time, but my mother had just gotten fed up with what appeared to be my constant misbehavior. She was angry about the fight with Sharky, me getting caught in the church with Samson and me getting caught kissing him by the band hall at one of our morning meetings.

She had all those disappointments built up, and she finally exploded. Having my dad in town probably brought extra frustration because of how she felt things might have looked to him. When I would misbehave or disobey her, it made her look like she didn't have things under control as a single mother and made it seem like she struggled to make things work without my dad. I wasn't trying to be a fast girl or anything by dating. But I enjoyed having someone, a guy, to care about me. I was always respectful to my body and to God. Even when things were close to going too far, I would still have a conscience and stop before committing a mistake.

My suspension was long and tough. My mother made sure that every chore around the house was taken care of by me. I didn't understand my mother's reaction to me getting suspended for doing nothing but getting 'beat up.' I'd revealed to her why I didn't fight back. I told her that I was too busy laughing and couldn't get over how silly it was. So, me getting beat up and suspended for six days for laughing instead of for taking up for myself was a hard pill for lady Rambo to swallow.

Alright, get ready to put in some work. I need you to swim as fast as you can through this tunnel. If we move too slowly, we might be tempted to give up and stall here. Let's go.

Back to Darkness

"If anyone will kick you when you're already down, it's the enemy."
~A. S. E.

NOT LONG AFTER that, things started getting interesting. Our family began attending a church of Christ and met a pastor with a rather unusual name, but for the sake of privacy, we'll call him Mr. Tulip. Mr. Tulip was one of the kindest men we'd ever met, and his heart was huge and gentle. His wife was beautiful and even more kind than he was.

While my mother worked at Walmart, Mr. Tulip brought up a job opportunity at the post office in Jackson and told her she should try to apply. My mother explained to him that she would love to, but she was struggling to find a safe place for her children to stay while she worked.

Mr. Tulip then suggested that my mother give his wife a chance to babysit my sister and me since she didn't work and would be available. My mother talked it over with his wife and agreed to allow her to babysit us. Mr. Tulip was a chill guy, but I remember wondering how a pastor could come home to alcohol every day. He never got drunk, at least not to my knowledge, but I would always see him laid back on the couch, drinking. He was a man of little words and would just stay to himself in his zone in front of the television.

Mrs. Tulip offered for me to get on the computer in the back and play games. She noticed that I wasn't much of a talker and preferred to be alone. I went straight to Disney games. My favorite game to play was *Kim Possible's Sitch in Time*. I would spend hours trying to beat that game. Other ones I loved were *That's So Raven's Frog Toss* and *Corey's Piggy Bank or Corey's Money*...something like that.

Things were very comfortable. Mrs. Tulip would come back there to check on me and make sure I had something to eat or snack on. One day, I decided to lay off the games and research my favorite artists. I learned the entire lives of Whitney Houston, Celine Dion, Prince, and Michael Jackson. To me, they were the Fantastic Four, and I took a unique characteristic from each one.

My mother would always tell me to sing using my diaphragm and to think 'Whitney Houston' to command my voice without stretching my neck and tilting my head backward. I took the aspect of a graceful, classy command from her. My mother had me learn every single song recorded by Whitney, and I studied her. I studied her command, her confidence, her grace, her attitude, and I watched every concert she ever performed, and every music video she ever made.

From Celine Dion, I took her individuality. She stood out...on purpose and didn't care much what the world thought about her weirdness. She had an angelic spirit about her. Her voice was able to execute heavenly tones that I wasn't used to hearing. Her stage presence was one of a kind, never copied from, or by anyone.

Prince made me want to master the art of instruments. He also gave me the 'okay' to become someone or something most people wouldn't understand. I admired songs like 'Controversy' and 'Diamonds and Pearls.' But it didn't take me long to also begin admiring songs I shouldn't have at my age. We'll keep those nameless.

Last, but certainly not least, I adored Michael Jackson. His humanity was unparalleled to any artist I'd ever seen. I studied every single one of his songs carefully to discover their true meanings and watched all his videos, much like I did with Whitney Houston. I couldn't get enough of the Jackson Five movie, and I even promised myself I'd have a home zoo or 'animal observatory' just as he was portrayed to have done in the film, for the sake of genuinely protecting the animals from ignorant, selfish humans.

I researched these four artists extensively. I learned about their families and childhoods. I studied the positive and the negative and took unique qualities from each of them to shape myself into the artist I am today. This is what I chose to indulge in every single day of being on that computer in the backroom, until one day, unexpected pop-ups kept interfering with my searches.

This had been all too familiar. This time, I knew what was on the websites and had no interest in viewing them. When I tried to exit out of them, they only opened more windows and became worse. I was able to close out of most of the windows, but then something strange appeared on the screen. It was cartoon pornography. I had never even thought of cartoons having images and videos like that. The concept of inappropriate animations rattled my brain, and it almost seemed unreal and unbelievable. Still, I chose to close the window. But the image had been pressing on my thoughts since I'd seen it.

One day, I decided to indulge and see what I would discover in a cartoon world of pornography. What I found was disgustingly compelling. I know that sounds like an oxymoron, but it's true. I would begin to watch these things and feel horrible. I'd even cry from some of them, but it didn't keep me from looking. Maybe I was just amazed at the fact that something like that existed. It hurt because some of the cartoons were characters I aspired to be like when I grew up. To see them in such a derogatory way was shocking and cruel to me.

I think, in a way, any hope I'd clung to about sexual purity died that day. The world had literally tainted everything with vulgarity and depreciating sex, and there was nothing left for innocent minds or pure hearts, nothing left for children...not even cartoons. This evil world had taken the innocence out of everything I ever knew to be innocent, but it was no wonder to me that sex ruled mankind. It had become like a god and was worshiped in literally everything everywhere.

The really depressing thing was that they were called 'Adult Cartoons.' I remember thinking, 'Why is everything foul, perverted, wicked and sexually immoral labeled 'Adult', as if to equivalate being an adult with those things. It honestly made me not even want to grow up. Was that what I had to look forward to?

I eventually had enough discouragement and returned to playing my Disney games and researching my favorite artists and their music.

Finally! Gardens of bliss is what we've come to! If you don't mind, I'd like to hang here for a spell. It's one of my favorite places to visit. Come, let me show you around.

Divine Promotion

"When God deems you qualified,
the world's requirements become irrelevant."
~A. S. E.

WHILE WE WERE being kept by Mrs. Tulip, my mother was being Superwoman. She wasn't confident that she could land such a privileged job at the post office since it was a government job that was often handed to veterans, but she decided to do what always worked for her. She prayed and meditated to God and asked Him to make a way out of no way. She petitioned Him for His favor and thanked Him for the favor He'd already shown her. My mother went in for her interview and came back with the job! We were so happy; she took us out to celebrate.

My mother met this wonderful woman at her new job. We'll call her Miss De. Miss De was the only woman that could possibly hold a candle to my mother, besides Angela Basset. She was one of the sweetest people and had the same conservative views as my mother, not to mention they shared the same pear-shaped body build with extremely protruding hips. Miss De and my mother became the best of friends and grew very fond of each other since they were so much alike. This was very rare because my mother had no friends, and she liked it that way.

One day while my mother and Miss De were working, Miss De approached my mother with a message from an admirer my mother didn't know she had. "First of all, I want to apologize because I said I wouldn't do this, but he won't leave me alone. There's this guy named Greg that wants me to ask you if he could get your number," said Miss De. My mother was mad and disgusted with the request. "I don't give out my number," she replied with a frown. "That's what I figured, so I told him it was really something he needs to do himself," Miss De said.

About a week later, my mother had been assigned to Greg's section in the post office. "They sent me over here to help you out, but I'm not quite sure of what I'm supposed to do. Could you help me?" she asked Greg.

At first, Greg simply ignored her and continued working. "Do I sense an attitude?" my mother asked. "I don't take too kindly to rejections. All I wanted was a number. What does that hurt?" he answered. "Well, excuse me if you were offended, but I didn't come here to make friends. I'm here to work, and if it meant that much to you, you should have come and asked me yourself," my mother replied.

Greg grew silent and had no response. "Obviously, you don't need or want help, so I'm going back over here to my station," my mother said. Then Greg decided to go ahead and show my mother what to do.

The next day during lunch break, my mother decided to approach Greg about the elephant in the room. "We don't have to be enemies because we are working together, so let's start over. My name is Carolyn. Do you mind if I sit with you for lunch?" my mother asked.

Greg motioned my mother to have a seat with his hand but remained verbally silent. "What's your name?" my mother asked. "Gregory Sutton," he said. "Okay, Gregory Sutton. Tell me a little about yourself. You married? How long you been working here?" my mother quizzed. "I'm going through a divorce, and I've been working here for over 14 years. I came here straight out of the military. I have custody of my children, my two daughters," he said.

My mother became intrigued by the idea of a man raising his two daughters and gleamed at the fact that she also had two daughters. "Wow, that must be hard. You have any help? I've never known a man to be a single parent and with two girls." "I have my mother helping me sometimes," he said. "Oh okay, that's nice. So what do you do outside of the workplace?" my mother asked. "I'm very involved in my community. I especially care about the youth. I even run a little league football team," he said.

Greg asked my mother the same questions she'd asked him. "Yes, I am married but separated. I've filed for divorce, and I'm not looking for nobody and don't want nobody," my mother said.

By this time, lunch was ending. "That's really nice. Children are our future. Well, thank you for allowing me to sit with you and get to know you. Nice smile, by the way," my mother said.

A couple days later, Greg asked my mother for her number since they'd gotten to know a little more about one another. "I don't give my number out. We can talk at work," my mother said.

Greg and my mother continued talking at work until finally, she was comfortable enough to give him the digits. My mother wanted to be respectful of the fact that she was still legally married to my dad. However, she'd begun to grow an attraction to Greg, so she came home and asked my sister and me what we thought about her dating again.

"There's this guy that likes me. What do y'all think? Should I give him a chance?" she asked. My sister and I were beyond excited for her. "Ma, yeah! You ain't doin' nothing wrong. You deserve it! You deserve to be happy!" we shouted. "Well, how does he look?" I asked. "Well, he's extremely dark. He's got a bit of a potbelly. He's got a kind of block-shaped head and super white teeth. His teeth are kind of big, too. They're big and pretty. Oh, and he has hazel eyes," my mom said. "Um, you just described a funny-eyed, pregnant, cheesin' chocolate sponge bob to me," I said. "Porsha! He's good lookin'," my mother chuckled. "Well, I need you to do better 'cause what I'm hearing ain't good lookin'," I said.

My sister and I just laughed harder as my mother continued trying to accurately describe him to us. "Okay, off the looks. What about his personality, 'cause so far I'm not impressed," I said. "Well, he is extremely humble and loves to smile. He seems like a great dad. He has two daughters..." "Yay!" Ree exclaimed. "Uh oh," I said, rolling my eyes.

I was not looking forward to where this was headed. I struggled to get along with the one sister I was already being raised with. "Well, he wants to meet y'all, and he invited us to come and have a home-cooked dinner at his house," my mom said.

My sister and I glanced at each other and smiled. "At first, he was kind of shy about it because he describes his home as humble, and he's not really flashy or wealthy. He's more of a simple kind of guy," my mother continued. "We'll see," I said.

The evening came that we were to meet up with Greg and follow him to his home. My mother arranged for us to drive to a parking lot and follow him from there so that he wouldn't know where we lived. We didn't really catch a good glimpse of him there, but when we finally arrived at Greg's home, and he got out of the car, both my sister's mouth and mine dropped. Greg was fine! Heck, he even looked better than my dad to me. All the things my mother described him as were true, but it all worked together for his good and glory.

When we got out of the car, Greg greeted us with a proper-sounding hello and led us into his home. Greg had one of the humblest homes, and it wasn't anything fancy at all, but it was so homey and filled with love. His daughters were beautiful. One was older than I, and the other was younger than Ree. They were so welcoming to us. We all laughed and talked at this dinner and bonded so quickly, that it didn't take long for us girls to refer to one another as sisters.

Our visits to Greg's house grew frequent, and we eagerly got to know his daughters. The oldest one was extremely popular throughout the town and knew everyone. She was a cheerleader and had the cutest braces; I really admired and looked up to her. She was a little risky, but hey, she was a teenager. She had the biggest heart for me and was always trying to give me lessons on self-confidence, self-esteem, and guys.

One day, my cycle came on, and I asked if she had any pads. She asked me why I didn't use tampons, and I explained to her the terrible first experience that had me scarred. She tried to demonstrate to me an easy way to use one, and I attempted to insert one, but it just became a hilarious joke because once again, I felt faint. "Porsha, wow. Well, I know you still a virgin, huh?" she said, laughing.

She quickly became a big sister to me, but the younger sister and I struggled to get along. I think it was simply because of our age difference. She was more sensitive and childlike because she was young. But all four of us girls had a blast being sisters. We were always finding new ways to have fun with one another. We were all ecstatic at how well we all meshed as a family.

One day, we were all in Greg's living room watching television, and he whispered something to my mother with his arms wrapped around her shoulders as they sat snuggled up together on the couch. "I don't know. Ask them?" my mother said smirking.

Greg smirked at us with bashful hesitation and said, "How would you girls feel about calling me, Diddy?" We laughed and asked, "Diddy?" "Well, I don't want y'all to have to say daddy because I know you guys still love your dad, and I'm not trying to take his place or step on any toes," he said. "Alright, Diddy, it is!" we said. He showed all those pretty white teeth with a giant smile and said, "Thank you, girls. That means a lot to me that y'all are comfortable with me like that."

Greg was such a considerate man. He was very proud and protective of my mother. I remember one night, my mother decided we should go out and get burgers when she got off work. She was extremely spontaneous that way. There weren't really any restaurants in Flora, so she decided to drive us to Jackson.

When Greg called and found out we were basically joy-riding in Jackson for some burgers, he was furious. He kept telling my mother how unsafe it was for us to be out at night in a city like Jackson, where the crime rate was stupidly high.

My mother, however, was a woman who believed God was wherever she was, and no matter the circumstance, she was protected because she was always walking with Him. She remained fearless in our quest to find some tasty burgers, but she admitted to us that Greg made her feel important and desired with his concern. We were glad to see our mother so happy.

Greg was always looking for a new way to court my mother because he was just as spontaneous as she was. I remember once we were in his living room, and he randomly began dancing off some music he had playing on the radio. He even pulled my mother up to step with him. Then, we started talking about nicknames, and he said that in his early years, he was called 'Co-Chise' (pronounced co-cheese). I can't remember his exact explanation of that name, but I think it had something to do with his way of protecting himself from opposing boys who would want to fight him. He was magical, and my mother was falling for him, hard.

Though I liked the way Greg made my mother feel, I despised him for 'taking her away from me.' I reacted to him the way an oldest son would, I guess. He was very kind and patient with me, even when I showed him anger and ultimate disrespect. He was always trying to hold my mother back from disciplining me whenever I'd express my frustration about their time spent together. Eventually, he found a way to connect with me, and it was none other than the love of music that allowed us to find common ground with one another.

Greg was the master of music in my eyes. He took me, my mother, and sister out to a house in the country he was trying to make his home and showed me his entire music collection. He really won me over when he showed me every single album Prince ever made. He knew my mother didn't like me listening to Prince, so he would play the CDs a little bit while he worked on his house. He even let me take a few to download to my computer and warned me not to tell my mother, or he'd be in hot water with her. I swore myself to secrecy and basked in the unlimited music collection of his. He had everything from Alexander O'Neal to Anita Baker to Michael Bolton.

Welp, I never said the garden was without weeds. Let's chop through them together, shall we?

Blast to the Past

"Be careful of where your ties are made;
they bind you to them no matter how far or long you run from them.
~A. S. E.

EVERYTHING WAS PRETTY much going perfectly. In fact, things were so well that when the school year ended, we moved to Monticello for yet another new start and so that my mother could be closer to Greg. Greg helped my mother find an apartment that was almost as cozy as our luxury trailer had been.

The apartment owner had to be an angel because after engaging in a conversation with my mother and finding out a little about her, she allowed my mother to stay in that apartment rent-free for an entire year. She empathized with the fact that my mother was a single mother and would always compliment her on how well-behaved we were.

I finished out the school year in Flora, and summer came. I had a strange dream about my dad. I woke up in a graveyard that was sunny and bright. A faceless man of light started talking to me. "Look," he said, pointing to my dad. I looked and saw my dad's disproportionate body walking in the strangest way. One leg was on top of the ground, and the other was deep inside the earth. He was limping from the different ground levels. "He needs you," the man said.

Then the man went to speak with my dad and said, "Look," pointing to me staring from a distance. "She needs you, but you're already half dead. What good are you to her below the ground? Rise up and walk with her before she ends up walking like you are now," he said.

Then, I woke up. I told my mother about the dream and how sad it made me. I didn't know what it meant, but I knew enough to know it was a warning to both my dad and me.

My mother thought it would be good if my dad kept us for the summer. I told her I had no interest in visiting with him, but she told me to 'do it for her' and for Ree, my young sister. Ree missed our dad, and still loved him dearly. I agreed to it, knowing that I didn't really have a choice.

When my sister and I arrived at the yellow house on Ayo St., the territory was eerily familiar. I remember thinking, "Alright…Let the war begin…again."

My dad seemed excited to have us there and really tried to be the best dad he could be that summer. He was terrible in the food area, though. He had a cabinet full of stale cereal and was determined not to buy anymore until those old boxes were eaten up. "Well, I guess we won't be eating cereal then," I snarked.

My dad owned a car dealership and often took us to auctions with him so that we could see his buying process. My favorite thing about the sale was seeing how fast the auctioneer could speak. It was beyond amazing to me.

My dad had hired a woman to be his secretary at his shop, and right from the start, I knew there was something strange about her. She had no eyebrows and would draw thick black ones on her face every day. She had a couple gold teeth and always wore jet black weave.

She was kind to my sister and me, and would often try and spark up a conversation with us. My sister thought she was the nicest woman in the world, and I thought she was 'nice' too, but I always felt there was something more to her than I could put my finger on at the moment. She and my dad would often speak to one another with smirks and smiles that seemed a bit too flirty for my taste, and I let my dad know about it. In fact, both my sister and I did.

One day, my dad and I got into a light spat about my mother. "How is she?" he asked. "She's fine. She and Greg are as happy as they want to be," I said. "Well, we're not divorced yet," he said. He was referring to the fact that on paper, he and my mother were still legally married. But that was only because the lawyers were taking their sweet time with things. My mother had been hounding them about finalizing the paperwork for months.

"Y'all got divorced as soon as you took ya lil' 'man-man' and stuck it somewhere else," I said. "Alright...you tapping on being disrespectful, here?" my dad said with an expression of warning. "Well, you're being disrespectful by making a comment like that. Why can't you just let her be happy? She is never coming back to you and has no interest in leaving Greg. We like him...no, we LOVE him! So just leave her alone," I ranted.

My dad grabbed a portrait of my mother in a frame and pulled it close to his chest. "Well, I still got hope," he said. "You're fooling yourself. There is no hope! But go ahead with your lil' false hope. Don't choke when you hear wedding bells and get the invitation," I said. "Porsha! Why you being so mean?" Ree asked. "Girl, I'm *being* honest. That's it."

"Well, how would y'all feel if *I* started dating somebody else?" my dad asked. "You better take some cold showers. You done had enough partners and 'dates' for the whole family! This is the first man other than you Ma has been with, so we're happy for her. You, on the other hand? You need to cool down from being so hot all these years with all the hookers you done had," I said.

My dad started laughing and turned to my little sister. "You feel the same way?" he asked. "Well, yeah, she has a point. You should be tired by now and just kinda cool off. But I guess I wouldn't mind if you dated somebody else," she said. "Well, if I see you dating somebody else, I'm cuttin' it off!" I said, directing my eyes to his groin area. "Porsha!" Ree exclaimed. My dad laughed, and eventually, she did too. "Ooooo, Porsha. You so wrong," she said. "I'm dead serious. Try me. Put it up and keep it in," I said.

Ironically enough, we bonded over the crude conversation, but I couldn't help but think about the woman he had hired. I didn't say anything about her to him, but I remained observant of their interactions.

One day, he invited her to eat with us. I thought that to be a bit strange, but I figured he was just casually asking her to dine with us since she was so 'weird.' Maybe she needed friends or company or something. Before the food was done, she and I were sitting in the living room watching a show about breast implant surgery. "Um, I don't think we can watch this," I said. "Oh, it's medical and educational. I don't think your dad will mind. If he tries to say something, I'll take the blame," she said with a wink.

As we sat and watched the show, I couldn't help but feel like this was an awkward thing for us to be watching, so I tried to think of something else. I could have joined my sister, who was outside with my dad in his shop doing 'dad jr.' things, but I decided to stay and be company for the woman. "Would you ever do something like that?" I asked. "Girl, I'm terrified of knives! But I would love to have breasts like that. What about you?" she asked. "I'm fine with what I've got. I don't even want what I have, but it is what it is," I said. "I think you would look cute with some bigger breast," she said, briefly poking at my chest. "Well, if God wants me to have them, they'll grow," I said. "Well, either way, you're cute, so you're right. You don't need to have surgery. You're fine just the way you are," she said, smiling. "Thanks," I said.

Just then, Ree and my dad came in. "Uh, I don't think this is a channel y'all should be watching," he said with a cheesy grin. "It's educational! It's doctors and medicine," she said. "Uh-huh, find another 'educational' channel. As a matter of fact, come on, it's time to eat," he said. She smiled and winked at me, and I chuckled at her and my dad's exchange.

We all ate and talked and laughed. The woman seemed nice, and she was beginning to grow on me. When she left for the night, my dad asked, "So, what y'all think about her?" "Um, I know you not thinking about dating her. How can you get passed the eyebrows?" I asked. "Porsha!" my sister said, laughing. "I like her," Ree said. "She's nice, but I already told you about trying to date," I warned. "I'm not asking for that, I'm just thinking of companionship...not so much dating," he said. "Mmhm," I mumbled.

The woman worked for my dad as his secretary for a short while before she just disappeared. "Where's your secretary?" I asked. "Yeah, we haven't seen her in a while. Did she quit?" Ree asked. "Well, it was kind of a mutual decision," my dad said. We had no idea what happened, and my dad was very vague about the reason they had decided to no longer work together. I do remember him mentioning that there was some drama with her and some other people, and he revealed that she dated women and men. I wasn't sure how that information had been acquired, but I didn't question it. Her aura now made a lot more sense to me, though.

When she left the office, my dad 'hired' me in as a replacement. I didn't do much paperwork or anything related to the business, and I knew he just hired me on to basically babysit the office while he ran errands to make me feel relevant and useful. My sister and I volunteered to paint the office for him, and we had a blast doing it.

I didn't know it at the time, but I was being watched by nosey men who knew my dad. I walked with him next door to a gas station and received strange stares from the men that were hanging out inside. With my dad being such a long-winded person, I ended up leaving him to his boring conversation and going back to the office on the car lot to join my sister.

When my dad finally returned, he was laughing about something the men had told him. "Girl, dem nuts come to me talking about 'we see that new chick you be having over there, she a lil' young, ain't it?' I told 'em man get y'all minds out the gutter! That's my daughter!" he said. "Wow, if they would have been paying more attention to my face, they would see I'm your twin!" I said, laughing. "Exactly," he said.

My dad and I had many instances where people thought I was his wife because of my mature build and curvy nature, not to mention how much older I sounded when speaking to people. Even with my mother in our company, most would assume *me* to be the wife and mother and my *mother* to be my daughter. My mother is a very petite woman, and I've always had my fair share of curves and baby fat, so I guess their assumptions were understandable, but that didn't make them any less annoying and downright insulting to me.

There was even one Caucasian man who had missing teeth right in the front of his mouth that made a sexual gesture to me, asking me to come and have sex with him right on my dad's car lot while my dad was next door. When my dad returned, I told him what had happened, and he immediately went out and threatened the guy and told him he'd better not catch him on his lot again.

I witnessed the whole thing and, for some reason, started to feel guilty or shameful that I had been approached. I began to cry silently. "What's wrong?" my dad asked. "I don't know, I'm not trying to cause trouble," I said. "You didn't do anything wrong, baby. You're supposed to tell me when someone comes to you like that. There's nothing to cry over. Don't even worry about him. That's the last time you'll be seeing him, I can promise you that." My sister hugged me and wiped my tears to try and make me feel better.

When I think back on it, I guess I was angrier that in the moment of being approached, because I felt helpless and weak, I froze and couldn't even respond to the man, and that upset me. As snappy and feisty as I was, I couldn't think of anything to say. I just stood there until he walked away. I'd pissed myself off. I also wasn't too thrilled about going and crying to my dad, either. Though it's probably what I was supposed to do, it felt like going against my nature, in a way.

While my sister and I were in Louisiana with my dad, he tried to show us love and even tried to impress us at times. There was one instance that my dad had us dress up a little semi-formally and took us to New Orleans. When we pulled up to this enormous building, my dad said, "Hm...I wonder what's going on in there." The way he asked the question implied that this wasn't the initial place he was taking us. I think my mother had already told me that my dad planned to take us out to eat or something.

"Let's go and see what's going on in there right quick," he said. My sister was all game for it, but I remember being extremely annoyed. I wasn't really ever in the mood to just hang out with my dad, and I definitely hated spontaneous acts. "Come on, and let's go where you were trying to take us! It's already late, and I don't even like being out at night. Why are we going in here? It's probably something we're not interested in or can't afford anyway!" I barked. "Awe, don't be a party pooper! Come on, and let's just see. Then we'll go to the surprise, okay?" my dad reasoned.

I've always been the child that was utterly oblivious to surprises and tricks, so my parents were always able to surprise me with events and gifts. I was never expecting anything and didn't have a romanticized imagination for possible scenarios of a special occasion. I might have made things a little more difficult for them if I were one to ask questions or pry, but I always went straight to complaining and shooting down spontaneous suggestions.

My sister was also easy to surprise because she was extraordinarily spontaneous and never asked any questions, either. My dad, my sister, and I walked up to the building and made our way to the entrance. We saw a massive poster of Chris Brown on the wall, and I grew angry. My sister and I loved the young Chris Breezy, and we knew all his teen bopping songs. "See! Why the heck did we get out of the car to be nosey? Now, I'm mad. It's not like we can go in and see him!"

Just then, my dad flashed three tickets in front of our faces. My sister screamed, and I was lost for words. My eyes began to water, and I asked, "Really? You for real?" My dad simply smiled and said, "You are really something, Porsha. Why else would I press so hard for us to come and see this place?" "Because you're nosey!" I said, wiping my tears and chuckling. Within moments, I joined my sister in screaming, and we ran inside the building.

My dad had gotten us some middle floor seats, but my sister and I couldn't see a thing. So he had us stand on the chairs, and we still couldn't see. Finally, he asked one of the workers if he could move my sister and me a little closer to the front. I don't know what he said to the worker, but we were allowed to do just that. We were screaming even past losing our voices.

I kept thinking, '*Wow, our dad must really love us and want us to be happy because this is completely out of his element*'. My dad had called my mother and asked her what my sister and I were into these days, and she gave him the whole 'they love Chris Brown' scoop.

After the night ended, we called our mom and stayed on an absolute high for the next two weeks. We helped our dad any way we could around the house, and we got along. We had many amusing times with my dad after that, like the time he cooked us breakfast and accidentally fed us spoiled sausage or the times we would laugh at his arthritis, making him drop his utensils before he could get food up to his mouth.

I think one of the funniest times was when he and my sister decided to help me stay in shape and signed us up for a gym membership and entered us in an aerobics class that was taught by my first-grade teacher, Mrs. Beauty. She looked terrific and was thrilled to have us be a part of her class, but she was a beast. Her energy was unmatched, and she pushed us to the limits.

My sister, my dad, and I did the classes faithfully together, and my sister and I became warriors while my dad sucked. Still, he didn't let that deter him. He came to every class and made a fool of himself just because it was something he knew I wanted to do.

The other women in the class admitted to us after class that they were trying extra hard to keep up because they thought he was the famous Martin Lawrence; someone my dad has always been compared to. I think height is a significant factor. But what was even more hilarious was that even when he revealed to them, he wasn't Martin, some of them still wanted pictures with him and still fanned over him like he was actually famous, and they were all older Caucasian women!

My sister and I were tickled because we knew my dad ate the attention up and couldn't help but be ultimately flattered.

My dad began acting weird during the last month of summer. One morning, we woke to find him in an unusually happy mood. That same day, we went to the delta to visit the family. My mom called and told me to go somewhere private so that she could talk to me. "Are y'all alright, Porsha?" she asked. "Yeah, we're fine. Why? What's wrong?" I asked.

My mother held the phone for a minute, but I could have never imagined what she would say next. "Your dad was here, Porsha." "What? What do you mean?" I asked. "He was here at the apartment this morning," she said. "In Monticello?" I asked. "Yes." She proceeded to tell me exactly what had happened while my sister and I were still asleep.

"I had just gotten off work. You know I get off late, so when I pulled up, it was dark. When I got out of the car, I took a minute to view my surroundings like I do every night to make sure I can safely get into the house. As I got halfway up the sidewalk, I started to feel a strange negative energy. It was so strong, I jumped back and started saying, "Whoo! What in the world is this? Somethin' ain't right." I kept shaking my head and frowning and couldn't make my feet keep walking. I hurried up and turned around and went back to sit in the car. Then I asked myself, "Who's watching me? Why do I feel stupid right now?" I sat there for a minute and then tried to approach the apartment a second time. I made it all the way to the doorknob, and I stuck the key in but noticed the door was already opened, and I know I locked it, so I ran back to the car and called Greg. "Something ain't right. It feels like somebody in the house or watching me. I feel a strong, crazy energy," I told Greg. He said to me if I feel unsafe, to call the police. Then I started second-guessing myself and said to myself that maybe it was just my mind playing tricks on me, so I hung up the phone and went on in the house. When I popped the living room light on and turned to the kitchen, your dad is standing there with the balloon I kept that Greg gave me for Valentine's Day, which he had stabbed and a pair of my cute underwear and threw them on the floor. He also had a newspaper under his arm with a story of a boyfriend who killed his longtime girlfriend and told me, "I can understand how people can get to this point," like he wanted to scare me. Then I told him, "Is that what you here to do? You better do it now, 'cause I'm about to call the police." He didn't say anything. He just stood there staring at me. "Where are the kids?" I asked. "They're at home," he

said. "Are you serious. You left my babies all alone in another whole state in the middle of the night!? Have you lost your mind?" "They were sleeping when I left. They don't even know I'm gone," he said. Greg called, and I decided to answer. "Hey, you okay?" he asked. "No." "What's wrong?" he asked. "No," I said. I wasn't trying to really talk with your dad just standing there staring at me. "Is someone in the house?" he asked. "Yes." "Is it your ex-husband?" he asked. "Yes." "You need to call the police and get him to leave. Please call the police now, Carolyn," he said. I noticed his hand stayed in his pocket and asked him did he have something in his pocket, but he told me he didn't. I asked him how he even got in the apartment, and he said, "Don't worry about that." Then the shock started to wear off, and I became full of rage! I got mad because while he was here looking all stupid in my face, y'all were still in Louisiana by y'all selves, and all I wanted him to do was leave and get back to y'all, and that's what I told him to do. I told him that I wasn't afraid of him because God has been with me through all his crap, is still with me and will continue to be with me. I told him to get his skank butt back to my kids because jail ain't what he want. Then he threw the paper down and left."

"Wow, Ma! That's crazy! He woke up this morning in such a happy mood, I thought he was finally getting over you!" I said. "Really? Happy?" she asked. "Yeah, he was all giddy and jolly, and Ree and I even asked him why he was in such a good mood 'cause as always, he been cranky and mean. I knew the nice guy act wouldn't last for long. He even tried to get mad at me for almost having a faint spell, and Ree had to let him know that when I'm startled out of my sleep, my body reacts by getting weak. He was fussing about not turning the faucet all the way off or something...I can't even remember," I said. "Well, I know y'all have another week and a half down there, but do you want me to come and get you early?" she asked. "I mean, I would love to come home, but I think he's taking us to the water park for my birthday, and I don't wanna ruin that for Ree," I said.

"Porsha, are you sure 'cause I was coming today, but since y'all in the delta, maybe that will do him some good being around family," she said.

"Ma, I ain't scared of him. I was born crazy. If he wanna go off on the deep end, I'll go straight for them balls he think he got," I said.

My mother laughed and trusted that I felt comfortable enough to stay with my dad for the remainder of the summer. "Don't tell your sister. I don't want to ruin her visit. She's been looking forward to spending time with your jughead dad, and I'm not trying to upset her. I am so sorry for making y'all go down there to visit that fool. If you don't wanna visit again after this time, y'all won't have to go. I'll let that be y'all choice from now on." "I won't tell her. Now, I gotta try and be around him without laughing at his stupid face. Wow, that negro done went plum crazy! I mean, the way he's been acting around here, I would have never known anything like this ever happened." I said.

After ending the phone conversation with my mother, I carried on as if I knew nothing, and my dad never even suspected my mother had told me anything. My sister and I enjoyed our extended family's company, and when we returned to Louisiana the next day, my mother was sitting on the steps, waiting on us. She looked like a beautiful angel, and I was so excited to see her. She put on one heck of a poker face and didn't give off the slightest hint to my sister that there was anything to be alarmed about. She just wanted to see us and make sure we didn't wish to come back with her.

Since becoming an adult, I've informed my dad that my mother told me about his visit in the middle of the night and asked him to tell me his side of the story. He was extremely embarrassed and ashamed because, since then, he's changed and regretted that night ever happened. Either way, he agreed to tell me.

He said that when he and I had been arguing about my mother's happiness with Greg, and when I had been placing Greg on this pedestal, it ate away at him. He said that my mother put Greg on a pedestal, too, and he felt like Greg stood in the way of any chance of reconciliation with my mother.

Here's his recollection of that night.

I waited until y'all fell asleep and just started thinking about all the wonderful things that had been said about Greg. I just suddenly felt the urge to pay your mom and him a visit. I drove for about 3 hours to get there and looking back on it, I think God may have been warning me or trying to tell me not to go through with what I was thinking. I say that because I'd pulled over right near the exit and just sat there for a minute. A police officer or state trooper put his lights on behind me, and I remember thinking that things could be about to get real ugly real fast because I had a gun. It was completely empty, and I had it empty on purpose. But with me being a convicted felon, I'm not supposed to have any weapon at all. I can't remember what I told the police about me being pulled over, but whatever I told him, he bought it. When he left, I thought about turning around, but I'd already come so far, I figured I wanted to go through with my plan. Now, my plan was never to physically hurt anyone at all. I wanted Greg to have to either stand up or sit down...man up or show his cowardness. With all the praises that you and your mama gave him, I wanted to see what kind of man he really was and whether or not he was actually worthy of being the placeholder husband and father to my family. This is something I've never told your mama, but I planned to act like I was going to shoot her. I wanted to see if Greg would have gotten in front of her. I was going to ask him, "Are you prepared to lay your life down for her?", and if he was, I was prepared to shake his hand and walk away from her forever. I saw your mama when she pulled up to the apartment and noticed how fidgety she was. I watched her go back and forth, and finally, when she arrived alone, I was extremely disappointed. I figured they would be coming home together. I remember your mama asking me did I have something in my pocket because I kept my hand there. I never revealed to her that I actually had a gun. Nothing went the way I planned, so..."

"Porsha, does this particular story really have to go in your book?" my dad asked after telling his side. My mother had asked me the same thing when she told me her side. She said this story made her look like a bad mother to still trust my dad to keep us after his little showdown with her. I laughed and told her how funny it was that some people don't see how toxic their lives are until they see it on paper. But I assured her that telling this story would bring awareness to the toxic relationships others are allowing themselves to stay in.

"Dad, let me explain something. We, as God's people aren't serving Him justice. This story and all the other horrific tales of our past are critical to the testament of the blood of Christ and the power of a man submitting his heart to God. I hear preachers say all the time, 'We are new creatures in Christ,' but no one's wearing their dirt on their sleeve to prove it. How would we have known about the incredible transformation of Saul to Paul if we didn't first learn about him being a murderer of Christians? How would women know about Christ's grace and God's mercy in the renewing of Mary Magdalene if we didn't first learn about the seven demons that Christ cast out of her and her promiscuity? I know your past, mine, and everyone who has one makes us look bad, but that's just the thing. We need to look bad because that's how we truly look and truly are without Christ. I want people to stop focusing on the 'people war' and focus on the 'spiritual war.' You were a pawn for the enemy many times as was I and anyone else who's committed evil acts against others or even against themselves. But the way the enemy has our people captive is that he makes this war about people against people instead of evil against God's holy, sovereign, and righteous will. To truly testify about God's grace and mercy and about His unmatched power to transform a person, we must know what the person used to be and contrast it to what the person is now. It's time out for being cute in Christ. That's why we have people out here thinking there's such a thing as being too far or too low to be reached by God. Truth not only sets *us* free but our lost brothers and sisters as well. I'm not worried about our image. I'm concerned about salvation and being a witness to the power of God. See, people think that I came from this polished background with stability and guidance. I'm successful and renewed in Christ because that's what I chose to be, despite all I was put through. I'm demolishing excuses. I want people to know it doesn't matter where they come from; it matters where they choose to go. I want people to know the only formula for success is being reborn. My upbringing, my scars, my battles don't define me. My choices define me. I have the power of choice in every single aspect of my life. I can choose to be materialistically rich or chase after real prosperity and store my riches in heaven. I can choose to conform to the ways of this world and try to fit in and be liked. Or I can set my eyes to the new heaven and earth and spend my days, not as a citizen of this world tainted by evil and deception, but a citizen of the Kingdom of God that is near; a citizen of the new world that is to come. Our light shines brightest in darkness. People must know and see our pure darkness to understand and appreciate our light which was only acquired through the unmatched power of The Creator."

When I finished my rant of an explanation, my dad simply said, "I see God working, and I'm with you, baby. You're absolutely right."

As the summer drew to a close, my dad's birthday came up, and my sister and I decided to bake my dad a chocolate birthday cake. That evening when we all sat down to eat dinner, my dad seemed tense and irritated. When dinner was over, my sister and I brought out the cake and sang happy birthday to him. We then cut a big piece for each of us, but my dad refused his share.

"I don't think I'll have cake tonight. Thank y'all, but I'm full," he said. "Oh no, buddy. You're eating this cake. We worked hard on this cake," I said, smiling. "No, I'll have a piece tomorrow," he said. "Tomorrow is not your birthday. Here," I said, trying to feed him the cake. My sister and I both pushed for him to eat the cake, and finally, he snapped. "Stop! I don't want any cake! I will eat it tomorrow. Now, thank y'all, but no, thank you. I'm full."

My sister and I both stood in shock and didn't know what to say or do. "You can come back next summer, but I promise you this is my last summer coming here," I told my sister. "Honestly, I don't wanna come back either," my sister said. "Really, y'all? Over some cake?" my dad barked. "No! Over your attitude that came out of nowhere. Forgive us for trying to celebrate your birthday! We made that cake out of love, not because we had to! I don't know what your problem is, but you need to fix it! I didn't wanna come down here in the first place! And Ree did, and this whole cake idea was her idea, and this how you say thanks? Please." I said.

I took my cake and went to my room and shut the door, and my sister followed...with her cake. In a matter of minutes, my dad came to our room with tears in his eyes and said, "I'm sorry, y'all. I don't know what it is. I think it's because the time for y'all to leave is coming soon, and it's bothering me to see y'all go. I...I miss my family."

We suddenly understood my dad's sudden mood change. He was sad and hurting on the inside. We gave him a hug and tried to comfort him. My birthday was four days later, and we all went to the Blue Bayou water park, and then came the time for us to go back with my mother.

I will admit, for a moment, I felt a deep sadness come over me from leaving my dad in all his loneliness and inner torment. But I also understood that he needed to be alone for God to take him through the ringers. It was the path my dad had chosen, instead of taking heed to The Father's warnings. I was more sad knowing that I was leaving my dad behind in the middle of the brutal warfare he hadn't believed to even exist.

I know the military teaches the 'no partner left behind' concept, but in the heavenly war of spirits, one must learn to physically leave someone behind while continuing to fight for them through prayer. It's one of the hardest tactics used in this war with the best outcome.

When someone's alone, it creates the perfect opportunity for God to meet them where they are; whether it's to administer a chastening rod or to approach them gently about their shortcomings. Either way, most times we remain as stumbling blocks to those we care about out of selfishness or fear of them never returning to us.

Think about someone you may be causing to stumble by being their crutch. If you truly love them like you say you do, you'll let them go so they may experience a 'talk' with God.

Finally, welcome to the colorful corals! Its beauty fills my heart with so much joy!

Middle School

"The best feeling is always returning to wherever 'home' is."
~A. S. E.

ONCE SCHOOL STARTED back, I was devastated from being held back a grade because of that unreasonable history teacher I mentioned before. I passed every class with flying colors except his. My mother was extremely disappointed in me as well, but she gave me a pep talk and told me to try and see the situation differently. She told me to be the best repeat 7th grader I could be, which wasn't much comfort, but I knew what she meant. She wanted me to take the unfortunate circumstances head-on and excel. So I did. I spent the first few weeks at our new school in the 7th grade, but my teachers quickly noticed how bored and unchallenged I was with the curriculum. I wasn't even paying attention and could answer all of their questions and passed my tests with no effort at all. One day the principal called my mother and me into her office.

She looked over my transcript from my last school and said, "La'Porsha, your grades are all good except this one class, and you know what that tells me? That tells me that you don't belong in 7th grade. So I'm gonna bump you up a grade only if you promise to work hard and not make me regret it," she said with a stern smirk.

My mother and I looked at one another, overjoyed and excited. I agreed and entered my eighth-grade class that very same day. When I got home that day, my mother was thrilled and told me that God had shown me grace and favor and that I should be thankful to Him for that, and I was. I prayed a prayer of thanks to my Creator because I recognized that the same God that I'd witnessed carrying my mother in ultimate favor had the same big heart for me, too.

I did exceptionally well in 8th grade and was interested in all my classes. I had a unique group of teachers, too. Miss Ray was my science teacher. She found the most disgusting things exciting and had an unusually strong stomach. She could literally eat her lunch and teach us about parasitic worms of the body at the same time, picture slides, and all. I loved her. She was always pushing me and encouraging me to do better. She was like an aunt to me and every other kid in her class. I remember she had to get gall stones removed, and I think she even brought them back to class in a jar to show them to us.

Another teacher that became a favorite of mine was Mr. Clam Chowder. "Just call me Clam," he would always say. He was a real laid-back character who talked very slow. He didn't start off as one of my favorite teachers, though. We had a heated disagreement about the class material.

We were going over a chapter in our textbooks about the 'discovery of America,' and I refused to accept the notion or idea that Christopher Columbus discovered the country. I even ranted about how stupid I thought it was to have a holiday named after him. I also grew angry about the fact that we could celebrate something like that when the natives were maltreated in the land they once tried to share with us.

He had asked the question 'who discovered America', and I answered, 'the natives.' After my ranting, he became frustrated with me and said, "Miss Mays! We study and learn what the textbook teaches! I know what you're saying, but Christopher Columbus still discovered America according to the textbook!" "That doesn't make sense, and if the textbook is teaching something that we know is not true, we should choose another textbook!" I responded.

I don't think it was what I was saying that was bothering him, but rather my stubbornness about reading what the textbook was saying without objections. I felt I couldn't help myself. The lies in that textbook made my blood boil. They were plain to see and yet, were expected to just be accepted. It seemed like unreal brainwashing to me, and I just wasn't having it.

Sure, Christopher Columbus discovered it for himself, but to emphasize his discovery and say that he 'discovered' America, as if to discount the people who were already here, is just downright insulting. I would have even been okay with 'he traveled to America' or 'he came to America' on that day.

Finally, after going back and forth with him on the matter, Mr. Clam had had enough. "Miss Mays, be quiet before I send you to the office! I'm the teacher, and you're the student!" he said. I sank back in my desk, humiliated and confused about why Mr. Clam wasn't proud of me for pointing out the obvious truth.

I was so upset about it, I went home and told my mother and Greg about the whole thing. Greg, whose nickname, Co-Chise, derived from a great Native Chief, was furious about the incident and decided to have a conference with Mr. Clam about it.

Greg and my mother visited the school to confront Mr. Clam in a meeting about what happened in class. "La'Porsha, you want to start?" Greg asked. "You know what, I'll start," Mr. Clam said. "La'Porsha was given instructions to answer the question being asked according to the textbook's information. Now, I understand that everyone has opinions, but in this class, I'm the teacher, and she's the student, and I felt she was out of line." "How was I out of line?" I asked.

Greg placed his hand on my shoulder to gesture me to stay calm and remind me to be respectful. "Mr. Clam, all I did was point out something that everyone knows, and I followed instructions. You said to answer the question, according to the textbook. Well, the textbook clearly states that the natives were here first. To say Christopher Columbus' discovered' America is ignorant. To say Christopher Columbus introduced America to other people of the world who didn't know about the land is factual and accurate, and whether or not the textbook words it that way, it's stated right there in the textbook," I said.

Before I knew it, tears were rolling down my cheeks. I think it was because, contrary to what Mr. Clam might have believed at that moment, I really wanted his approval and wanted him to be proud of my wisdom on the matter. Mr. Clam looked at me with his lips perked. "I think that everything La'Porsha's said is fair to say. What I'm confused about is why instead of patting her on the back, you chose to humiliate a child for speaking on what she believed to be the truth," Greg said. "La'Porsha could have waited until after class to bring up her view on the matter, but she chose to waste precious class time—" "What better time to bring something like that up than during class? See, it was that kind of thinking that made me hate school and eventually stop caring altogether. What's so wrong with asking questions and having discussions about what you're learning in class?" my mother chimed in.

Mr. Clam sat quietly and reassessed the situation. After a moment, he finally said, "I'll be more open to discussion during class about the lesson we're learning, and you're right, La'Porsha. You should ask questions and voice your opinions about the things we learn. You're also right about the material, but that's what I'm given to teach y'all," he said. "Well, why not make your own material for teaching in addition to what we already have? You know, just to make sure we're not learning one-sided history," I suggested. "I will surely take that into consideration, Miss Mays. I must say you have one special young lady right here. She's got a good head on her shoulders, got some of the prettiest eyes, and is actually one of my best students," he said.

I was pleasantly shocked to hear Mr. Clam praise me that way. He and Greg and my mother stood there and talked for a while longer, and then we bid our goodbyes and headed home. I pondered the conversation and pictured the expressions of Mr. Clam's face during the discussion. It became clear to me that Mr. Clam's pride was insulted when I stood up so adamantly against what he was teaching. It wasn't a matter of right or wrong to him, but a case of a child correcting an adult; at least that's how he took it. To me, it was a child correcting the textbook.

The next day, we continued learning about the events between 'explorers' and natives, and things went smoothly from then on. Mr. Clam began playfully picking on me every time someone read a portion of the textbook. "Any objections, Miss Mays?" he would ask. The class, including myself, would begin to laugh, and I'd answer, "The state rests." I became very fond of my history teacher and began to realize the earlier misunderstanding had been a mere result of an elder's pride vs. a youth's pride.

When February rolled around, Mr. Clam ushered our class into the room and said he had a surprise for us. He called on me to hand out permission slips to everyone asking if we could watch ROOTS, the miniseries about slavery coming to America, as well as some other hand-picked movies about the subject. I'd seen ROOTS once before with my parents, so I knew it would be alright for me to watch it again. I was so excited and wasn't expecting anything like this from Mr. Clam.

He patiently explained to us that we would be watching the series for educational purposes only and that he had high expectations of us to keep things appropriate and handle the information we'd learn with maturity. I don't remember a single parent saying 'no' to us watching the series, so we began on the very next day.

Mr. Clam was very protective of what our eyes witnessed. He allowed some of the whipping scenes to be shown, but would often stop the tape and fast forward through a long, extended whipping scene. He also caught any scene that looked like it was headed towards a white man mistreating a black woman sexually before the act would begin. He would get up, stop the tape, and fast forward that too, but he would also explain to us in the most censored way what was happening.

One day, while watching one of the other movies Mr. Clam had picked out, a scene came up with a little light-skinned girl and an old white man. He stopped the tape and fast-forwarded to the next scene. But he explained the sad truth about the scene; the slave master, who was married, raped the mother considered to be the 'house nigger' and was now trying to rape the mother's daughter. He informed us that he came close, but he was stopped. He went on to explain that the little girl was so light-skinned because that was his own daughter by the mother he'd raped.

The class began looking at all of the light-skinned people in the room, and a swarm of people pointed at the light-skinned brown people saying, "You got white in you, and you too, and you and you!" Mr. Clam quickly summoned the class back to control, but he also added that while the statements were insensitively brought to light, there could be truth in them and that some of us lighter-skinned brown people may have gotten our complexion from a not so pretty ancestral history.

That day, I grew bitter and angry. I'd suddenly felt like I was trapped in the past because of my skin color and eyes. I felt that looking in the mirror was a disgusting reminder of a part of my history I hadn't made connections with until now. I knew about slavery but didn't really let it sink in that my ancestors and my traits could have come from a slave master's foul and wicked sins.

Suddenly, I was more than ready for black history month to end. I didn't feel more knowledgeable or powerful, and I honestly felt like I could have done without the new information. Mr. Clam noticed my head down on my desk while the rest of the movie continued to play one day, and he asked me to raise my head and pay attention. When I raised my head, and he saw my tears, he gestured for me to follow him outside of the classroom to have a private conversation.

"What's wrong, Miss Mays?" he asked with a warm smile. "It's just hard not to look in the mirror and see all that. My skin, my eyes...it just feels like forced blood runs through my veins and I can't do anything about it," I said. I'll never forget the profound wisdom he shared with me that day. "Miss Mays? Salt by itself is bitter and nasty. It can't help that it is salt, but instead of being sad about how it tastes alone, we use it to accent and flavor most of our favorite foods and make them way more delicious than they would be without it. It's not about how you were made or what you're made of. It's about how you use what you're made of to bring flavor to this tasteless world," he said.

He brought me close for a hug, and I've never felt the closeness of a granddad the way I did that day. Mr. Clam became one of my most respected mentors. I was able to go back into that classroom and watch the painful aspects of my history with a purpose. I was able to not allow my pain to turn into rage or passion, but simply to acquire knowledge and develop a new desire to rise above it all in the most glorious, 'flavorful' victory.

Tensions were a little rustled that month, but one fantastic thing about the students, even the mad ones, was that they wanted to and were able to talk out their frustrations with each other as well as other teachers. It was a beautiful thing. Of course, you had those ignorant people who would have rather ignited hate between friends and cliques, but their agenda didn't get very far with the students of Rod Paige Middle School.

Last, but certainly not least, there was a teacher by the name of Mrs. Dot. She was one of the best math teachers I'd ever had. There was a particular project I enjoyed from her that required each student to have 'fake livelihoods' and balance our checkbooks. If you came to the correct balance of your checkbook by the end of the two school weeks, you received your passing grade. It was one of my favorite and most influential school projects to participate in.

I had other interesting teachers like my language arts teacher who would always make us write our vocabulary and spelling words once with our dominant hand and once with our other hand. He would always say, "You never know what could happen, so..."

Another one of my teachers was quite strange to me. Any time she would turn her head to address a student, her entire upper body would turn with her. It almost seemed to pain her to use her neck. She was also one of those teachers I thought to be inappropriately dressed most times. Though she wore long khaki pants and blouses, her clothes were revealing and would cause young male students to make sexually derogatory remarks about her. Her tops rarely showed cleavage, but she was big bottomed and wore her pants so tight, we could see the imprint of her too-small underwear. Sometimes we even saw her thong. It disgusted me because I thought she did it on purpose, and she would hear the boys' remarks sometimes and seemed to be flattered by them.

I can't remember much about my other teachers, but I know I liked them. Everything about this school I liked. There were a couple guys who claimed to 'like' me, but one stood out.

This guy was timid and always quiet. Every time I passed him going to my classes, he would speak to me with a soft voice, and I would smile and speak back. He would glance at me but never fully looked at me for more than a millisecond. One day, I was sitting on the steps outside, and he, with a gang of other boys, approached me.

At first, he stood his distance under the walkway with the other guys whispering in his ears. I noticed there was something strange going on because he was staring at me! This was the very first time I'd really seen his face in full. After a moment, he nodded his head and began singing to me! The name of the song was *Reasons* by Earth, Wind, and Fire.

I was in utter shock! He slowly walked closer to me and sang that song. The other guys were edging him and cheering him on. The girls stood around, giggling, and watching what was happening. And to my surprise, he sounded just like the record! I couldn't believe my eyes or ears! He suddenly became the most handsome creature in my view at the time.

I was so embarrassed because I blushed the entire time uncontrollably. No guy had ever been able to do that, and the other guys knew it. Some of them had previously tried with corny pick-up lines and insulting flirts. So, when they saw what this singing Casanova had accomplished, they high-fived him and called him 'the man.'

That day, I ran off the bus straight to my mother to tell her about the unusual event that had taken place at school that day. She laughed and oohed at the situation and told me I should go back and get to know the boy. Of course, she was only joking, because I still wasn't allowed to date at that time.

Take a moment and bask in the beauty of the corals. Try listening to I think I saw something pacing in that tunnel ahead. Let me go first, and you can follow in about 30 minutes. Okay? This way, you're strong enough for battle if need be.

Private Tiger

"You often think you're special in being a targeted prey for the enemy, until you meet someone with deeper battle wounds than yourself."
~A. S. E.

IN OUR NEW apartment complex is where I met a boy I became good friends with. We'll call him Tiger. Tiger had been through an awful lot, and because I could relate to him, we became best friends. Tiger liked the captain of the cheerleading team but was never given a chance because he was dead set on not being intimate with her before marriage.

For a while, I thought Tiger's gesture was one of religious obedience, but I soon found out things were deeper and much more complex than that. I would soon learn that Tiger struggled to even show affection to anyone, let alone physical intimacy with anyone.

Tiger's mother was a kind lady, but she was very mentally challenged, and Tiger more so took care of her than she did him. When my mother met Tiger and his mother, she felt comfortable enough to start allowing me to hang out at their home.

One day while I was there, we decided to watch a movie called *Antwone Fisher*. While watching the movie, there was a scene that depicted a little young boy being raped by the daughter of a mean old woman who was supposed to be his caretaker. I cringed at the scene and turned away in Tiger's direction, but when I looked at him, I saw him tearing up and wanting to say something.

I got up and turned the movie off. Tiger got up and went to his room. I followed him because I could tell he was upset. "Tiger? Hey. You okay?" I asked. "We shouldn't have watched that movie," he said, clenching his teeth. "Wow, I've never seen a guy cry from a movie, even if it's a sad one," I said. "La'Porsha, you...you don't understand," he said, looking at me with intense sorrow.

I sat quietly for a moment and tried to silently decode what he meant by that. Finally, I thought I'd figured it out. "Tiger, you can talk to me about anything. We're best friends. I promise not to judge you or tell anyone. Did the movie upset you because that happened to you?" I asked. "Something like that, except I would have rathered it happened like the movie. I was raped by my older male cousins," he said. "Oh my God! Tiger....wh...how? I mean, how can that even happen?" I asked. He knew what I was asking. "They penetrated me from the back, La'Porsha."

I was horrified. I had never heard of anything like that before. I had never heard of guys wanting to have sex with other guys. I definitely hadn't heard of guys *raping* other guys. I hadn't heard the term *rape* at all and knew very little about it. I cried and held him as tight as I could. "Oh my gosh, Tiger, I'm so sorry! I don't even know what to say," I whimpered. "La'Porsha, there's more. I...I like you. I mean, I really like you, but I knew you would never give someone like me a chance. I can't even kiss you, La'Porsha. I can't show you how I feel without thinking about my past. I don't even really know how to be with a girl, which is why I don't have a girlfriend now," he explained. "You ...like me. I had no idea. I mean, we're best friends. But, hey, I would have never turned you away for something like that. You're attractive and sweet and one of the kindest people I know, Tiger. I would never judge you or blame you for what happened," I said. "Well, you're different from any girl I know around here. It's almost like they sense that I'm not a whole man," he said. "Being violated and hurt by force when you were a boy doesn't make you any less of a man, Tiger." "Yeah? Tell that to my heart," he said, with fresh tears rolling down his face.

His pain pierced my soul like a sword from hell. I became furious with his cousins, people I didn't even know, and wanted to kill them for what they'd done to him. The more I thought about it, the sicker I felt. I started to feel nauseated, and he noticed. He got up and went to the kitchen and brought back a soda. "Here. I'm sorry for telling you all this. I didn't mean to spill out all my dirt. It's just that you're so easy to talk to. I've never felt this comfortable with a girl before. Actually, I've never felt this comfortable with anyone. What if...what if we did give it a shot? Would you ever consider being my girlfriend?" he said.

I took another sip of my soda and placed it on his desk beside his bed. "Tiger, I can honestly say I love everything about you, and there is nothing that would make me happier. But, you're vulnerable and hurting right now. There's a certain cheerleader you've been dead set on being with since I met you. I wouldn't be a true friend if I took advantage of how you're feeling right now. You know, I've never been raped, but I have been touched and pressured to do things and let things happen to me that I didn't want. I can't imagine going through what you have, but what's helped me deal with my past is my faith. Satan uses people to hurt people and do evil things. That's all he's ever been good for. But God loves us no matter what happens to us, and knowing that He loves me even if no one else does makes it easy for me to not live in the past," I said, grabbing his hand.

Tiger grew angry and yelled, "La'Porsha! God? That's what you want me to believe? God? Where the h* was God when they were f* me, huh?!" "Tiger! He..." "No! I don't want to hear about no God! He doesn't love me! What God would let somebody do that to a little boy with no choice, huh? He doesn't even love you! Tell me something. How many times have you been molested?" he asked. "Molested? What does that mea—""It means touched! How many times, La'Porsha?" "I... Tiger, calm down, please," I said, crying. "How many times?! Answer the question! Now!" he yelled.

I jumped back against the wall and cried because my friend was hurting and there was nothing I felt like I could say to help. "Tiger, I...I don't know. Too many to keep track of, but that doesn't matter!" I screamed. "Like h*, it doesn't. Where was your God then?" he asked. "He was there! God never left me! He was...there," I said with a broken tear-filled voice, almost as though to try and convince myself that what I was saying was true.

I stood there against the wall, staring at Tiger. Shaking. Crying. My rattled nerves helped heighten nausea, and I ran to the bathroom to throw up. Tiger ran after me, placed his hand on my back, and stood over me while I vomited. "I'm sorry," I said in between hurls. "Shh, it's okay. I'm sorry. You were just trying to help. I shouldn't have attacked you like that. Here." He reached under the bathroom sink and pulled out an extra toothbrush. I was thankful and brushed my tongue. He left me and went back to his room. When I was done, I went back to his room and sat on the bed with him.

I could see he was still in much pain after our conversation. "Tiger, I'm going to help you get the girl of your dreams. I promise. Everyone deserves a chance," I said. "La'Porsha, she's a cheerleader, wanted by every guy in school. She says she likes me but doesn't want to date me because I'm not like the other guys," he said. "Meaning, she's turned off because you won't kiss and touch her like they do. Right?" I asked. "Right." "Well, I agree with you not touching her, but you could at least kiss her once," I suggested. "La'Porsha, I told you. I don't know how."

I glanced around his room and then went to the living room to find a stuffed-animal rabbit his mom kept on the couch. I brought it back to the room with me. "Here. I'm going to help you. Kiss the rabbit," I said. Tiger burst into laughter. "What?" he asked. "Kiss the rabbit!" I said, smiling. "La'Porsha, baby girl, it's not the same thing. I can see why you think this would help. You're young," he said. "Tiger, I'm one grade lower than you are, and believe me, I know how to kiss," I said. "Then show me," he said. "I'm trying to," I said. "No," he said, guiding my hand, holding the rabbit down from his face to lay it on the bed. "I mean, *show* me," he said.

I'd always liked Tiger but never said anything because we were such good friends, not to mention my mother trusted him and his mom, and I wasn't about to mess that up by trying to date him. "Tiger, I can't ... we're friends," I said. "Yeah, but friends help each other. You promised me you'd help, and I'm telling you the only way she'll go for a guy like me is if—" "if you show her what she's worth to you," I said. "Exactly," he said. "Okay, but doesn't this go against that? I mean, if I were her and found out that my boyfriend's best friend kissed him to prepare him for me, I would flip." "I'm not her boyfriend yet. If she ever found out, she wouldn't even have a right to be upset because it would be something that would have happened before she and I were together. She wouldn't be able to say anything," he said.

I was nervous. I'd kiss a guy before, but only someone I was in a relationship with. It felt weird being the one to show a guy who was older than me and had never kissed before how to kiss. But he was my friend, so I agreed. "Okay. Close your eyes," I said. "I want to see you," he said. "I'm too nervous for you to look at me. There's enough pressure with you depending on me to teach you something like this," I said. "Just think of me as the boy you told me about from your old school," he said. "Um, I don't really think I should kiss you like I kissed him. That would be too much for your first time," I said.

After a few inhales and exhales, I leaned in and kissed him and closed my eyes. The kiss was gentle and sweet. His lips were soft and tender, and he looked at me with heated desire. Once I pulled away, he leaned in and kissed me again. He gently placed his hand on the small of my back and laid me down on his bed. He climbed on top of me and straddled my body with his legs. "La'Porsha, you are so beautiful and so special," he said. "Thank you," I said, smiling. "Although, I wouldn't suggest you get carried away and lay her down when you kiss her," I said, chuckling.

He looked at me with an intensity that told me all the words he wouldn't say. "Tiger, you want to go further, don't you?" I asked, yet more like a statement. "It's not that I just want to have sex, but I've never been that way with a girl before. I have a feeling she's going to want that, and I'll start withdrawing again," he said. "Well, we can't have sex because I'm a virgin, and I'm supposed to wait until marriage. But...you can touch me so that you start to feel comfortable with a girl if you want,"

I said. "You'd actually do that for me?" he asked. "We're best friends, remember? Sure I would," I said, simultaneously taking a deep breath.

He kissed me again and began squeezing my breast. Then he guided his hand from my chest down my stomach and stopped right before the button on my pants. "La'Porsha, I can't. Not because I'm scared. You make me so comfortable. But, the fact you're even willing to do something like this for me ...you're too special for this. I don't want to be just one more guy that used you for his own needs," he said. "You're not them, Tiger. They gave me no choice, but with you, I'm choosing this," I said. "La'Porsha, you're too beautiful for this. I think I'm comfortable enough to at least kiss her, but anything else would have to wait. And please don't take this as me rejecting you. Believe me, I want to keep going, but there's a light about you that won't let me," he said.

A light about me. God had done it again. He shined through me to keep me from making a mistake with my body. God placed it on Tiger's heart to want me to preserve myself and not offer myself to someone in an intimate way that wasn't my husband. At that moment, He'd used Tiger as a reminder of how much He valued me. It was ironic because the evil one had used Tiger earlier to make me begin to doubt that very truth.

From that day forward, Tiger and I had a new respect for one another that was even stronger than what we had before. Tiger eventually became the cheerleader's boyfriend, but he was miserable. He said she would try to make him be over affectionate in front of her friends and that he felt she was only dating him to show him off to the other girls. He didn't feel like he could talk with her or even have a genuine friendship with her. "Porsha, I wish you were able to date. I like and respect your mom too much to go against her wishes, but you're perfect for me," he told me one day. I promised him that I would ask my mother about us dating the next year when I made it to high school.

I'd made my mother so proud because I'd been the big little lady she had needed me to be for her and my sister. I wasn't getting into any trouble, and I wasn't needing or wanting any companionship other than Tiger. This would soon change, but not before something terrible happened.

I was visiting with Tiger and his mother one day, but I felt weak and had a faint spell. It was because my cycle was coming on that day, and almost anytime my monthly flow came on, without fail, I would have a weak spell. Tiger's mother told me to go and lay down in Tiger's room and take a nap for a little while. When I laid down, it was just the three of us in the house. But I woke up to my mother storming through the house into Tiger's room, yelling and screaming at me.

She was saying so much so loud, I couldn't understand her, and part of that was because she had awakened me out of my sleep, and I hadn't fully come to yet. She dragged me out of the room through the house, saying, "You determined to be fast? I'll show you what happens to fast little girls in my house!"

While she was dragging me through Tiger's living room, I didn't see him, but I saw about five tall guys standing in his kitchen. I had no idea what was going on. When my mother and I finally made it inside of our apartment, she screamed at me and slapped my face, shouting, "You're acting like a little whore, Porsha! That's all you seem to want to be!" "Ma! I promise I don't know what's going on! I got weak, Ma! I got weak and almost fainted, so Tiger and his mom told me to lay down, and they stayed in the living room. I don't know those guys and didn't even know they were there until we were leaving! That's my first time seeing them!" I screamed and sobbed.

My mother didn't believe me at all. "Pull your pants down!" she yelled. "What?" I was confused. "Pull 'em down, and let me see the inside of your underwear!" she said. I pulled my underwear down and showed my mother nothing was in them. I didn't really know what she was looking for, but whatever it was, she didn't see it. "Ma, go ask him! Go ask Tiger and his mom!" I screamed. "I didn't even see his mom over there, and I told you not to be over there when she's not there!" she screamed. "Well, she *was* over there when I laid down!"

My mother stormed out of the door and went over to speak with Tiger's mother, who had just returned home. I was so shocked that my mother had, in my mind, called me a whore that it didn't matter to me if she found out the truth or not. I thought for my mother to say something like that to me, she must have hated me. My mother wasn't even a woman who would use language like that, so her saying this to me was like being cursed out by her. I'd never even heard her say that word before, and her opinion of me was life or death to me. It never mattered to me what I felt about myself because my esteem was gaged on how my mother felt about me.

In an attempt to escape the tortured feeling of my heart breaking, I found a bottle of Motrin and downed the whole bottle. Tiger's mom told my mother everything.

When my mother came back inside, she apologized and said that she was wrong. She said his mom had told her exactly what I said, and explained that she left to run to the store. She said that Tiger was in the bathroom, and those guys were friends of Tiger's. I was blacking out, so I couldn't answer her or respond to what she was saying. She must have noticed the dazed look on my face, because she started panicking. "Porsha! Porsha, what did you do? Porsha! What did you do?" she screamed.

She looked down at my hand and saw the empty Motrin bottle. She kept screaming, but eventually, her voice faded out, and I couldn't hear or see her anymore. She rushed me to the hospital, and they gave me black charcoal to cleanse my system of the medicine I'd taken. The nurses asked me a bunch of questions, and I answered in a way that I knew would be less of a headache on my mother and would get them to discharge me.

My mother allowed me to stay home from school the next day, which was a Friday. I wasn't quite the same after that day, though. Something felt different between my mother and me. I didn't know it then, but I was becoming numb.

I started not caring about school or anything or anyone after that day. I think maybe it was because I'd tried so hard to do the right thing and be a good kid for my mother but had failed even though my efforts were at their peak. My mother's words to me that day killed something inside of me, and I couldn't change the feeling I had to save my life.

I grew distant from her and my sister. I hadn't written in a while, so I began losing myself in my writings once more the way I used to. I wrote poems and songs to God about love and life. There was a creek Greg used to take us to that had the most transparent water all around except a deep, dark spot in the creek where you couldn't see the bottom with your eyes, nor could you feel the bottom with your feet. I wrote my best material there. The dirt was like red clay, and there was nowhere else in Monticello like it.

Tiger and I would sit together on the school bus every day, even though he would get dropped off first since he was at the high school, and I was at the middle school. But the Monday after I had gotten chewed out by my mother and returned to school, he didn't get on the bus. I didn't see him outside later that day when the bus dropped me off, and when I went to his house, I got no answer. Something was wrong, but I couldn't figure it out.

The next day, Tiger's face was bruised, and when I asked him what happened, he said it was nothing for me to worry about. I left it alone and didn't ask anything else about it.

Tiger and I remained friends, but he noticed a difference in me since the day of our incident. Unfortunately, he was one of the people I began to distance myself from. I can't explain what I felt, but whatever it was, it made me feel dirty and wrong, still reeling from what my mother had called me. I think it was the first time I'd felt that way since my incident with Shelly.

I'd grown a bit stronger in spirit, so I was able to not direct my anger towards God. But my loyalty to Him was still a bit shaky. I'd equivalated me being a 'good girl' to me, not having to deal with as much adversity as I had when I was disobedient or rebellious. But when that didn't turn out to be the case, I questioned if it even mattered what I did or who I chose to be.

Unfortunately, there's no light to meet us at the end of this particular tunnel. Stay close and keep swimming.

FROZEN

"The battle on the outside only reflects the war on the inside."
~A. S. E.

MY MOTHER MUST have noticed a difference in me and decided that it'd be best for my sister and me to get plugged into a church home. Summer was here once again, and I firmly expressed my decision not to spend the summer with my dad. He was disappointed but said that he would make trips to come and visit with my sister and me, and he did.

The church members quickly discovered that my sister and I were singers and asked us to join the choir, so we did. My sister and I quickly became known as the up and rising 'Mary Mary' sisters, and there wasn't a Sunday that passed that we weren't asked to lead the choir in song along with a few independent duets of our own. We mainly performed songs by Mary-Mary since we were told we sounded so much like them.

My mother was in such a happy place that she even joined the choir. That was something we never dreamed she would do. My sister and I were beyond excited to be singing with my mother in the choir. We didn't care that her voice wasn't of a professional standard. We had never seen her like this, and we had never seen her coming out of her shell the way she was. The moment my mother joined the choir was the moment my sister's dreams and mine came true. Everything felt right. My hardness began to soften just a little.

But that high was short-lived because once we joined, it was brought to our attention that to serve as part of the choir, we had to wear skirts because ladies weren't allowed to wear pants in the choir stand. My mother was pretty much living paycheck to paycheck, and though we weren't poor, we didn't have any money to go on a shopping spree for some church skirts. My mother dropped right out of the choir and told the first lady she didn't have money for skirts so my sister and I wouldn't be singing with them any longer.

The first lady came the next Sunday with a bag full of skirts that looked like renaissance peasant costumes, and my mother was even more insulted. Finally, Greg's mother saved the day. We called her Maw-Maw. She was quite the old young woman. She was up in age but so full of life, you wouldn't even guess it. She was always grabbing Greg around the neck and handling him like a wrestler every time we visited her. She drove like a bat out of hell and had the most contagious laugh we'd ever heard. She almost sounded like a happy, friendly witch or something when she would hackle at her own jokes. She genuinely cared for my mother, my sister, and me, and she made the best tea cakes and home-made ice-cream.

When she found out about what happened with the choir, she took my sister and me to the store and told us to pick out any skirts we wanted. She waited patiently while we tried them on and complimented me on my hips. "Girl! You been hidin' dem thangs under all dem baggy clothes you be wearin'? You cute, chile! You got a lil shape to ya!" she exclaimed. I didn't realize it then, but she knew I had low self-esteem at the time because my mother had talked with her about me. She meant every word she said to me, but I think because of what she knew, she laid it on thick purposely.

When we came home, my mother was touched to see what Maw-Maw had done. She hadn't bought us cheap skirts either. She took us shopping at stores like Belk's and Cato and JCPenney's.

Greg and his mother seemed to have a really good relationship, but there was something Greg deeply regretted, and he wore the everlasting shame and guilt on his sleeve every day.

When he was younger, his mother had left him and his younger brother at home to go to the grocery store and told him not to leave the house. Greg got bored with himself and decided to take the horses out to the lake to swim even though the water was icy. Greg, his younger brother, and a friend of Greg's, went out together along with the family dog. I can't remember how old Greg said he was, but he was old enough to watch after himself and his brother until his mother's return.

While they were swimming, they ended up caught in a current that was too strong for either of them to handle. Greg was able to save his friend but wasn't able to save his little brother from the current. The family dog laid across Greg's chest to keep him warm, and when the authorities arrived, they said he would have died from hypothermia if it hadn't been for the dog.

When authorities were finally able to pull his little brother up, his brother had frozen in a position of reaching up with his arms and hands stretched upward and looking up with his eyes still opened, and head cocked backed.

Greg said that he felt his mother could never really forgive him for that awful day, and he often had nightmares about the tragedy. Then he said one night, his little brother came to visit him as if to tell him not to blame himself anymore for what happened and that he was safe and okay wherever he was.

When Greg shared his story with us, I asked Greg if he would mind me writing a movie about it, and he smiled at me with tears in his eyes and said, "That's fine by me." I told him how compelling his story was and how I believed it would touch the hearts of many.

I could tell that every time Greg spoke about what happened, he was reliving the experience all over again. He, too, was frozen.

Sometime after relocating to Monticello, my mom was laid off from the post office since they'd hired her due to a temporary increase in the need for workers. As God would have it, a new Family Dollar store was being built right down the street from the apartments we were staying in. My mother quickly landed a job when they opened and kept my sister and me in their newest apparel since, as a worker, she was always one of the first people to know about new inventory. She bought us the latest clothing almost quicker than it even reached the shelf. Everything there was extremely cheap, so she'd bring home the clothing in huge bundles every paycheck. She was pleased about being so close to us, and we would walk to her job just to say hello.

However, I was once approached by an older man on my way to the store. That deterred me from frequently walking. He slowed down while my sister and I were walking and called me pretty eyes, asking me if I wanted a ride. When I told my mother about the incident, she remembered a very similar situation happening to her when she was a young girl. She told my sister and me to stay inside the apartment with the door locked from then on, but it was okay because she always made sure to visit with us on her lunch breaks.

It took my mother a while to even agree to let us stay at home alone. At first, we were to stay at Greg's house with his oldest daughter in charge. But when his daughter became more social for the summer, my mother agreed that I was old enough to look after my sister and myself. I was twelve and a very mature twelve-year-old at that.

My dad had been having a hard time accepting Greg in our lives. He decided to visit with my sister and me once, and because we knew he was already tense, we played a dirty trick on my dad. We sang a song he knew nothing about. It was *SEX* by Lyfe Jennings, but the only part we would sing is '*Girl it's just yo' s.e.x. no secrets, daddy gon' go crazy when he finds out that his baby found s.e.x*' and it drove my dad mad. We didn't even have the lyrics all right.

He started huffing and puffing about us singing something like that. "I don't know what Greg's been allowing y'all and his daughters to listen to, but I know ya mama don't know about this!" he said. We couldn't stop laughing. After torturing him for about five minutes, we sang the rest of the song, and *he* couldn't stop laughing at how we'd tricked him.

Hug the Tree

"Forgiveness isn't a tax on your heart, it's a freedom for your soul."
~ A. S. E.

MY MOTHER DECIDED she wanted to do something kind for me, so she found a girl who did micro-braids and allowed her to do my hair. My mother asked if I would be okay to stay there while she went to visit my aunt in the neighboring town of Flora. The hair lady was in Jackson.

There was a man who was in his early twenties that rapped and knew how to change his voice to match Bugs Bunny. When he and the girl who worked on my hair discovered I could sing, we had jam sessions the entire time she worked on my hair.

All three of us bonded, and we began talking about different 'life' topics. When they heard the wisdom I had to offer concerning the issues, they started to express awe for me, saying that I had an old spirit and was 'wise beyond my years.' I excused myself briefly for a bathroom break, but when I returned, I found the young man and the hairdresser whispering amongst themselves.

I didn't ask what they were talking about because I didn't think it was any of my business. But soon after, the young man left to hang out with some friends and the hairdresser, who was also in her early twenties, told me what they were discussing. "He likes you," she said. "What do you mean?" I asked, already knowing what she was talking about. "He likes your mind, but I told him that I think you may be too young for him. How old are you? Sixteen?" she asked. "Actually, I'm twelve," I responded.

She halted her work on my hair and expressed utter disbelief at my answer. "Girl! You cannot be no twelve years old!" she said. I laughed and nodded my head 'yes' to reaffirm what I had told her. "Oh my gosh! I don't even wanna tell him that 'cause he's gonna feel bad and probably even embarrassed," she said. "You don't have to tell him my age. Even if I was sixteen, I still wouldn't be allowed to date, so just tell him I'm not allowed. I know I'm young in age, but I find him interesting, too. Maybe we could just remain 'friends' and talk," I said.

She made a face as to say, "Girl, you know your mama would flip!" and she was absolutely correct, so I planned not to tell my mom. I liked the young man, but not in a romantic way. I fancied the conversation we would have, and since she deemed me a whore anyway, I figured why not have someone to talk with.

I know in my heart I was being purposefully rebellious against my mother and hadn't quite forgiven her, but anger still festered inside of me from thinking of what she had said to me.

The young man and I began talking on the phone whenever my mother went to work. One day, he said he wanted to come by and have a conversation in person. I told him that I didn't think that would be such a good idea because my mother was at work and I wasn't allowed to have company, especially men. At first, he laid the thought to rest, but then persisted in asking me could he come and visit me.

I finally agreed but told him the visit would have to be quick. I didn't realize it at the time, but that situation could have been terrible because my sister and I were the only ones at the apartment. He came over, and we sat and talked in the living room. Then, he kissed me and wanted to take things further. "I really like our conversations, but I'm saving myself for marriage, and I'm not old enough," I said. "I mean, I know you're a couple years younger than me, but not that much. How old are you?" he asked. "It doesn't matter. I'm saving myself, and that's final," I said with a smirk.

He looked at me and smiled. "You know, all that does is make me respect you even more than I did before. I know you're not allowed to date now, but maybe our friendship will turn into something more in the future. Who knows?" he said. "Yeah, who knows?" I said. I wasn't physically attracted to him at all, but I enjoyed his company. We laughed and talked for a while longer, and then he left.

A couple weeks later, my mother came home furious, saying that someone came through her check-out line talking about me having boys coming in and out of the apartment. I told her about the one time I'd invited the young man over and told her that he wanted to have sex, but I stopped things before they went to that point.

My mother was furious and disgusted, as she should have been. She was so angry and disappointed with me, but for some reason, I couldn't feel as bad about things as I would usually feel. I felt terrible for hurting my mother, but I also felt...I don't know...crappy and numb. My mother decided to take my sister and I out to Greg's country home so that we could receive our punishment without disturbing the close neighbors of the apartments. My sister was being punished because she tried to cover for me.

A few minutes after we arrived there with my mother and Greg, my dad showed up in the driveway. My mother had called him down to administer punishment for what I had done. My sister got a whipping for not telling on me and being okay with me having company over, and I got a beating for what I'd done.

When I saw my dad show up, I was infuriated. The nerve of him! He couldn't be man enough or dad enough to 'dad' us when we lived with him, always chasing whatever street meat that presented themselves to him, but he could 'show up' for an occasion to discipline me? I was hot! I was so angry, I wanted to whip him! And the nerve of my mother! I remember thinking, "*How could you bring a man who didn't even want us or couldn't choose us over street hookers to whip me for finding companionship with a boy?*"

The young man's age didn't really register for me because of how advanced I was. It wasn't until Greg, and my mother told me they were going to pay him a visit and threaten to lock him up that I realized how much trouble our age difference really meant. "He didn't know my age! I didn't tell him, even though he asked," I explained. "Still, he knew you weren't allowed to date and that I wasn't home!" my mother said.

They paid him a visit later that week, and from what they told me, they scared the life out of him. "Come on! Hug that tree like you hugged that boy or that young man!" my mother said. She made me hug the giant tree in Greg's yard, and she whipped me and instructed me not to lift my hands from the tree. When she was finished, she gave the belt to Greg, and he whipped me. He was sorrowful about what he felt he had to do, but he went ahead and did it. Lastly, my dad was given the belt, and he whipped me.

After a few moments of getting licks from my dad, my eyes went black, and I lost my sight. "Ma! I can't see! I can't see, Ma!" I screamed. I started reaching my hands out, trying to feel for someone. My dad stopped whipping me, and I was led away from the tree to sit down and was given a bottle of water. After about a minute or two, my sight returned. It was blurry for a while but eventually became clear again.

When I look back on the situation, I respected the lashings of my mother and Greg. But I think the factor that created a monster of resentment in my heart was that my dad was allowed to come from his absence and whip me for something that may have not even been able to happen, had he been there.

My parents and I have discussed this situation since then, and my mother has apologized multiple times about how she handled everything. She said she needed the reinforcements of a man for the level of insolence I'd shown. At the time, she thought it was befitting for the man who would possibly become my dad in the future and my biological dad to discipline me to show a sense of 'togetherness' with their concern and care for my well-being.

I understand now what she was trying to do, but it took me years to move past that day. That was the day I began to become darker than night, and my heart was hardened. Everything I thought and did suddenly had an ulterior motive and my soul became a pit of secrecy. Satan had me in his grasp. And at this moment, I didn't want to be free from him. This new numbness made me feel protected and safe, though ironically, I was in more danger than I'd ever been in before.

I remember thinking, *Why would God place me with such a family*. My life made no sense any more, and I didn't fit in with any of my family members. Everyone seemed happy and content, but my blood boiled with every ounce of oxygen I breathed. I knew I'd entered a very dangerous zone in my thinking because my hatred calmed me on the outside. My hatred for life became my fuel. It had a weird effect on me. I no longer wanted to take my life, but I would rise and conquer. I wasn't even sure of what or who I wanted to conquer, I just knew that's what I wanted.

I began having thoughts about humans as if I wasn't one of them. I lived my life in the third person and checked out. I believe that God knew exactly where I was and what I was becoming, so He came to meet me. I began to have dreams about other realms and creatures that I couldn't describe aloud, even if I wanted to. I became hateful, calm, confused, lonely, and dark spirited. I no longer made sense to even myself.

We're almost to the clearing. Keep swimming. I know you may be tired, but we can't stop here. It's too dangerous.

Give and Take

"Mothers, beware. The powerful connection of someone you've been intimate with can sometimes take priority over protecting your own children."
~A. S. E.

TIME DANCED AND wouldn't allow me to catch up to it. The days meshed, and I lost track. My appetite decreased, drastically and I was more trapped inside myself than I'd previously ever been.

In a desperate attempt to reach me, my mother decided the only option she had to pull me from my dungeon was music. She bought herself, my sister, and me an mp3 player and had one of her ex-coworkers from her post office job to fill it with almost three hundred gospel songs.

It was filled with everything from Detrick Haddon to CeCe Winans to Lashun Pace to Mary Mary. It was a modern-day heavenly choir. My mother had hit the jackpot with this gift. There was a song of encouragement on there for every fear, every doubt, every hurt, and every other tactful negative emotion I may have been experiencing.

My spirit became lighter, and the weight on my soul lifted a little more with every Godly lyric. One of my favorite songs to hear was 'What is This' by Mary Mary. The music was incredible, the lyrics were relatable, and it had precisely the right amount of everything in it. From their harmonies to the violin work in that song, it never ceased to chill my bones and flood my heart with love and thanksgiving for my God. I loved the instrumentation so much, I learned to vocally mimic the violin and would switch from singing the words to singing the melody being played.

God and I became intimate partners once more. My dreams increased and became more vivid and urgent with each passing night. I ate with my mp3, bathed with it, and slept with it plugged into my ears.

One day, my sister and mother were taking a trip to Flora to visit my aunt. I opted out of going when my mother had asked me about it the day before. I was napping and dreamed my sister and mother were driving when they suddenly wrecked because of some colossal distraction and landed in the median.

It was a very short and precise dream. I jolted up from my sleep to find my mother and sister walking out of the apartment door at that very moment. "Bye, baby. I didn't want to wake you because I know you needed to rest with how much trouble you've been having with sleeping lately," my mother said. "Okay, see you later. Oh, and y'all be careful. Don't get distracted by anything. Don't let Juice (our dog) distract you, either. I had a dream y'all were in a wreck," I said.

My mother inched back inside the doorway a little more. "What? You did?" she asked. "Yeah, just now. That's why I jumped up. So, just be careful," I warned. "Wow, that's strange. Okay, baby. We'll be watchful," she said.

Not much longer after that, my mother called the house phone with a voice of panic. "Porsha! We got in a wreck!" she said. "What? Are you serious? What happened?" I asked. "Porsha! Oh my gosh, let me catch my breath! You knew! You knew this would happen! You told us before we left, Porsha! I can't believe it!" she exclaimed. "Ma, what happened?" I asked again.

"Porsha, it wasn't Juice. He's been okay for the ride, but there was this truck in front of us, and out of nowhere, like a tent or blimp thing flew off the back of it and landed right on our windshield! So, I swerved to the median, and the car just zoomed through and stopped right before we were about to run out of 'median space'! Porsha! All me and Ree could do was look at each other, huffing and puffing and say, 'Porsha!,'" she said.

"Wow...I can't believe that," I said. I was in shock. I didn't tell my mother right off, but I started feeling guilty at that moment, thinking that maybe if I hadn't actually *said* anything, it wouldn't have happened. After all, the church was always talking about how life and death were in the power of the tongue.

When my mother finally made it to my aunt's house, she told her everything. My mother said that my aunt got a little spooked and started thinking I was some kind of witch. My mother said that she immediately began to regret saying anything about my dream.

When my mother told me how my aunt had reacted, it pierced my heart. I hated that word. I didn't want to be referred to a witch, an oracle, or even a psychic because I wasn't. God just communicated to me through my dreams whenever he had something urgent he wanted to tell me or wanted me to tell someone else. It wasn't like I could summon answers from Him any time I wanted to, or at least that's what I thought at the time.

I'd later discover that I could very well do that, but God still had the last say in whether or not He wanted to reveal something to me. The bottom line was, I didn't have actual control of my dreams or visions. They happened when God said so.

I went through many peculiar changes, especially mentally, around this time. I started feeling an urgency to eat nothing but dry spinach, which was highly unusual for me because I hated anything healthy. I also drank water with strange desperation.

Every morning, I would wake up and fill about seven cups all the way to the rim with water. I would drink them back to back and repeat this routine every morning. I had an awareness about my health that wasn't there before and became very conscious about how active I was.

I almost entered some kind of robotic spiritual fasting. I wasn't at all prepared for what happened next. My mother came to me and said that my dad had been experiencing suicidal thoughts, and she requested that I give my dad... my mp3 player. Her mp3 player was still being programmed, and she didn't want to take Ree's because she was younger.

She said that she felt he needed it more than I did. I was heartbroken and refused at first. But then she got me with the same line she always did. "Porsha, do it for me. Please?" she said. "Your dad is really having a hard time about losing his family. I don't want you and Ree to grow up without him in your lives. We can't get back together, but we can at least do this for him," she said.

"Why can't you just buy him his own?" I asked. "I don't have the money to right now, and I'm supposed to be meeting him in a minute to talk. I don't want him to leave without having something like that. It could really be a matter of life and death. I wouldn't ask this of you if I really didn't think that." I agreed to her request, but then she said, "One more thing. Let this be our secret. Don't ever tell your dad I got this from you. He would feel so bad if he knew." Once more, I agreed to her request.

She didn't know it, but this mp3 player was the only light in my life. It sickened me that even though we were physically separated from my dad, he managed to still be a parasite and suck any joy I found. This wasn't the first time I felt my mother let him steal from me, and it wouldn't be the last.

My heart grew hard, and honestly, I didn't care if my dad committed suicide. It was a horrible way to feel, but at the time I felt that maybe if he did, it would be better for everyone. That's how I knew that I hated my dad. And because my mother kept trying to care for him, I began to hate her, too.

We're here. We've made it to the clearing, but be careful. Since we're out in the open, we're vulnerable. Keep watch of your surroundings.

Up Yonder

"Some prefer greener grass; I prefer a foundation of rock."
~ A. S. E.

WHEN THE SCHOOL year finally ended, my mother and I decided to go tour the high school to see what I had to look forward to for the next school year. My nerves were rattled about attending high school for two reasons. First, Tiger was there, and I'd severed our friendship through my period of withdrawal. Secondly, I had witnessed how ruthless the high school students were.

Before school had let out, I'd gotten quite close with a girl we'll call Sandy. Sandy was beautiful and looked like a grown woman. She was Caucasian and wore caked make-up to school every day and was always wearing her school uniform a little too tight for my liking. Yet, her heart was pure gold, and she became friends with me over my admiration of her make-up.

My mother had even allowed me to go and visit her house one evening. Her home was big and beautiful, and she was a bit spoiled. There was a football game going on that night, and Sandy had asked me if I wanted to go. I knew my mother wouldn't have wanted me going to a game, so I told her that I couldn't. But there had been this older guy texting her to come to see him at the game. She said he was one of her ex-boyfriends.

After constant nagging about how much she wanted to go and see him, I agreed that we could drop in for only a few minutes. I didn't know why she wanted to see him because she claimed to not like him anymore. She talked as if she hated his gut.

She lived right down the street from the high school, so we walked to the game. When we arrived, she asked me to leave them alone for a minute so that they could talk. I walked around the corner to the other side of the fence and waited for a few minutes.

I started hearing Sandy's voice grow louder, and when I tuned in to listen, she was yelling, "Stop!" I zoomed back around the corner and saw the high school boy pressing against her with his body. "Stop! Get off me!" she yelled. "Hey! If you know what's good for you, you'll move. Now!" I yelled.

Honestly, I hadn't even meant to say anything. It just came out of my mouth, and I regretted it the instant I said it. The boy turned to look at me and said, "Sandy, tell your friend to mind her business." I remember feeling so scared and helpless.

This huge guy that looked like a grown man was mashing my friend against the fence, and there was no one around to make him stop. "I could take you right here, right now, if I wanted to. You know that right?" he asked her. "Please, get off of me, please," she sobbed.

I thought he was going to do it. I started feeling my body give out. *Not now*! This was not the time to have a faint spell! But I felt it coming like a swelling tsunami. I had two choices; I could stand there and watch my friend be attacked while lying on the ground, unable to speak, or I could make a run for it and try to find help.

I ran. When I caught a glimpse of the boy lunging after me, my heart skipped all kinds of beats. Sandy grabbed his arm, yelling, "Leave her alone!" I had run right back around the corner I went to at first and bumped into the stomach of a tall, handsome boy that had been about to leave the game. "Whoa, I'm sorry," he said.

I couldn't speak. My chest had started to tighten up from running. To make my nerves even more uncontrollable, the boy had startled me. He must have seen the look of horror on my face. "Hey, you okay?" he asked. All I could do was shake my head 'no' and point in the direction I'd left Sandy and the boy.

He took off in that direction without hesitation, almost just as I'd pointed that way. I followed him, jogging, and he went straight in for the mean guy. "Dude! What you doin', man?" he said, clenching his teeth, grabbing Sandy's ex with both hands by the shirt.

Sandy was able to squeeze away from her ex. "La'Porsha, let's go! Come on, get up! We have to go, now," she said. I'd fallen to my knees because, by this point, my chest wasn't even allowing me to take full breaths.

We walked as fast as we could back to her house, but she had to help me along to keep me from collapsing. When we made it, she told me to go straight to her room, so I did. She came in a few moments later with a glass of water. I drank it, and my chest seemed to loosen up.

I sat there, traumatized and silent. "La'Porsha, I'm so sorry," she said. "Did you know he was like that?" I asked, with my nose flared. I was angry because something told me the answer was 'yes.' "No," she said. "Sandy, don't lie to me! Has he ever tried to do that to you before? You know what? No, answer this. Why did y'all break up?" I asked. "We broke up because of his anger problems. He was always getting mad and was extremely jealous of any other friends I would have." "Okay, he was mad and jealous. Was that not enough for you to stay away from him?" I asked. "La'Porsha, please stop screaming at me! I said I was sorry!" "That's not enough, Sandy! Do you realize what just happened? You were attacked, Sandy! You were attacked by some mad, jealous ex, and I couldn't do anything but watch!"

She sat there, staring at me and started crying. Usually, I wouldn't have been so upset, but something about this felt off. It seemed like she enjoyed the drama, and that made me want to drag her. "I'm going home, Sandy," I said. "La'Porsha, at least wait until you feel better. I mean, if you leave now like this, your mom will wanna know what happened. You don't want her to know we went to the game, right?"

I folded my lips so hard together, my face should have turned into mush from the pressure. Sandy was right, and at that moment, all I could do was be angry with myself. None of this would have happened if I had just been obedient. Unfortunately, this wouldn't be the last time I would think to myself *If I had only been obedient.*

This memory flooded my mind the moment my mother and I stepped foot in the hallway of the high school. She was so excited that she finally had a high schooler, and I was thrilled about being one step closer to being done with school altogether.

As soon as we walked inside, my allergies went crazy! There was thick, navy blue carpet covering every inch of the school's floor, except in the bathrooms. "Wow. Porsha, look at all this carpet! Your allergies gon' kill you!" my mother said in distress. "They already killin' me! What am I going to do? I won't be able to concentrate on anything. I'll be sick all the time!" I said.

My mother decided that we would go to the office and ask them if they were planning on uprooting the carpet before school started. When they said they weren't, my mother decided right then that I wouldn't be able to attend that school.

Immediately, my mother started scouting out another place for us to relocate and for me to go to school. She and my dad had always said that if they ever moved back to Mississippi from Louisiana, they would move to either Brookhaven or McComb since they didn't want to return to the Mississippi delta. They thought this would be a healthy distance between them and the extended family.

My mother remembered that discussion with my dad, so that's where she decided to try her luck. She took my sister and me with her to look for a place to live almost every week but found nothing satisfying. In our search for a home, we came across a church home one day and decided to go in. We had a blast and really enjoyed the choir. The pastor was also an instructor at one of the Pike County schools, so we asked him about the best area to try and relocate to.

He and others we spoke to swore that McComb was the best way to go. In driving around, we ended up riding through Summit and Magnolia. We seemed to have found a place that we thought would work perfectly for us, but staying there meant that we would have to attend South Pike. We knew nothing about the schools and their differences. All we knew was that we had ridden past McComb High and saw the huge building and its extensive campus. It resembled a mini college campus to us, and from that alone, I was determined to attend school there.

Greg was heartbroken about my mother moving away from Monticello. My mother says she didn't break up with him, but he didn't believe in long-distance relationships and decided to let things go when he discovered we were moving to McComb.

It was a bittersweet moment for us. We missed Greg and were sad things didn't work out between him and my mother. But we were also extremely used to starting over in new places because of my dad's infidelity, so we were strong-minded about it all.

Let me introduce you to my favorite clown fish! His name is Sphinx. Do you mind if he sticks around for a minute? He likes to join me for this part of the journey. It's rather amusing to him.

Humble Beginnings

"Struggle will show you what you're truly made of."
~A. S. E.

MY MOTHER HAD started attending this newly found church every Sunday morning. Our commute would involve leaving a little early so that we could hunt for a house before service. It should come as no surprise to you that it hadn't been long before this church realized my sister and I could sing. Before long, we were in the choir, leading songs the way we had done at just about any church home we went to.

When the school year started, my mother hadn't found us a home in the school district we wanted to be in, yet. We were allowed by one of the choir members to use their uncle's uninhabited address for me to enroll in McComb High School.

My very first day at school was so nerve-racking. The kids looked like tall adults towering over me. There were so many people, and they even had lockers like on the Lizzie McGuire tv show! I was overwhelmed by having to walk upstairs, downstairs, outside, and to different buildings of the school to get to my classes. I felt invisible; like the school in all its essence, just swallowed me up. The first week was the hardest, but not even because of my classes or the students. It was because of the detective man. We'll call him Mr. Bug.

Every morning, my mother woke up and drove me to school from our apartment in Monticello. We knew we weren't supposed to be attending the school without actually living in Pike county, but we were desperate and still hadn't found a place to live yet.

Well, Mr. Bug was the school's detective whose job was to make sure that every child attending McComb High actually lived in the proper county. He wouldn't have known about our little scheme except he lived right down the street from the house we'd listed as our address! It was a home no one had lived in for a while, and he knew it.

He had made a disturbing phone call to my mother, and she knew we had to think smart and fast. The man had requested, more like demanded that he come to see us living in our home. He said the process would be quick, but that he had to make sure we were living there. He asked my mother if that would be a problem, and she quickly said no.

We went back to the lady that had convinced her uncle to let us list his property as our home. The man agreed to let us stay there, but warned us that the house was unlivable and tore down on the inside. My mother had told him that we were accustomed to humble homes and didn't mind. She had no idea what she was saying.

When we arrived and walked inside of the home, there were insects and roaches and gunky canned goods all over the place. The house was indeed deserted, and we had precisely one day to clean it up before Mr. Bug would pay us a judge's visit.

We thought we would be able to work hard, clean the place up, and get a good night's rest back at home in Monticello, but things got even more interesting. While my sister had been outside playing, a boy walked up to her and started talking to her. He befriended her, and he even had a little crush on her. After a few moments of speaking with my sister, his dad came around the corner looking for him. It was Mr. Bug!

When the man saw my sister, she said he paused to study her for a minute and then began walking up to her. He ended up trying to speak with her, but she was baffled because she knew exactly who he was. So, he decided to come and knock on the door. When my mother opened it, she found Mr. Bug standing there and was in shock!

"I thought our meeting wasn't until tomorrow," she said. "Oh, it is, but my son was talking to your daughter, outside, and when I noticed her, I thought I'd come and see you as a neighbor," he said, with the creepiest smile.

My mother was careful to keep the door closed to not let Mr. Bug scan the front room in its current state. "Well, it's cleaning day for us, so I guess we'll get back to work," she said. "Welcome to the neighborhood," he said, with a straight face. "Thank you," my mother replied.

When the man left, my sister ran into the house, and all three of us went crazy! "Oh my gosh, it was him! He lives right down the street? This is not good," my mother said. "I know! And did you see the way he was talking to you, like some creepy serial killer or something?" I asked. "Yes!" my mother exclaimed. "I didn't even connect the dots, but I should have seen how much his son looked like him!" my sister said. "Y'all, we have to hurry with the cleaning, and from the looks of things, we have to spend the night here," my mother said. "What? Oh, heck, no! I ain't sleeping here! Ma, this is roach heaven! In fact, I think all the ones we've killed so far have died and risen! I can't, I'll die from running into a wall from one of them and not wake back up!" I shouted. "Well, Porsha, what are we gonna do? I mean, the man lives right down the street! If he sees us leave tonight and not come back until the morning, then all this was for nothing," she said. "Porsha, we are doing this so that you can go to that big nice high school. You think you can try and stick it out just for tonight?" my sister asked.

I couldn't believe what was happening! We stayed that night, but I didn't sleep. I watched roaches, and other crawlies travel the walls like it was their night out on the town. There was even one point when daylight started to break that I went and stretched out in the car. I got about an hour of sleep before my mother and sister woke up and joined me in the car.

Since we hadn't planned on staying, my mother had to drive to a nearby Walmart and buy Ree and me some cheap clothes to wear for school that day. We went in, and she bought me a brown Tweety Bird t-shirt and some jeans, and she let my sister pick out what she wanted.

My mother always picked out my clothes, because I wasn't the person who knew fashion, in her opinion.

My mother dropped us off at our schools and headed back to her job in Monticello. When she came to pick us up from school, she told us the most unexpected story. "Y'all will never guess what happened to me today!" "What?" my sister and I asked anxiously. "I was working the front register check outline, and a man came through and started talking to me. I kept thinking he was familiar lookin', but I didn't think nothin' of it after a while. Somehow, he ended up sayin' that he hadn't seen me around there and asked if I stayed there. Without thinkin', I was like 'yeah, right around the corner.' Then it was like, as soon as I said it, I recognized who he was! It was Mr. Bug!" she said. "Ma, no way! What? Dang, what is he, the mafia? It is not that serious!" I said. My sister started laughing and said, "Well, it is to him!" "I gotta hurry up and find us a real place," my mother said.

She ended up finding a place on 10th street, and we were so excited for our exodus out of that old roach shack! When we were leaving, the man who owned the house said, "Awe, y'all leaving? I had started liking the idea of y'all being here. Welp, I'll feel better if you let me take ya mama out," he said. We laughed so hard because he was such a character and old! "Out where?" I asked. "I can take all y'all to Red Lobster! How dat sound?" he asked. "Sounds good, but we'll pass. Thank you for everything," my mother said, chuckling.

When we arrived at our apartment on 10th street, we all walked inside and vigorously began cleaning the place up. When we were done, we were exhausted in every sense of the word. We all laid out on the floor, looked at each other, and laughed hysterically! "Oh my gosh! I can't believe what we've been through!" my mother said. "I know, shoot! Our life is a straight-up movie!" my sister said. "Well, Ima, write about it!" I said. "Go ahead and write baby, but leave that roach house out! They gon' ask what kind of mother I am to let us stay somewhere like that," my mother said. "You're the kind of mother that would do anything for her girls to have the best of everything," I said. "Aw, y'all really feel that way?" she asked. "Ma, yes. I know it was a crazy house, but with all of us together, it was actually kind of fun!" my sister said. "I wouldn't say all that, but we are a team," I said. And well, folks, here I am, writing about it.

No More Naptime

"Sometimes, life just makes you wanna take a nap."
~A. S. E.

So here I was, in 9th grade. What a journey it took to get here! But what a journey, still, that I was about to embark upon. Nothing could have prepared me for high school, nothing in the world. My teachers were all the most interesting teachers I had ever met.

We'll start with my world history teacher. We'll call him Coach Clark because he looked like a goofier version of Superman. Coach Clark was ...unusual. You know how some high school football players get up to speak, but they struggle to be articulate? That was him. His speech included lots of uh's and aight's. He didn't seem qualified to teach, but since this wasn't English class, I figured it didn't really matter all that much.

It wasn't until he got into an argument with a child in our class and decided to say, "Yo mama" that I reported him to the principal. His contract wasn't renewed with the school. I'm not sure if I had anything to do with that or not.

My Spanish teacher, we'll call Mr. Shrimp, was German, I think, and had a unique face to me. His children were both top students, and he had the most patience a teacher could have. He was kind, but strict and really pushed us to learn the language. Yeah, that never happened. I'm not bilingual at all. However, music is a universal language, and I was obsessed with J-Lo in 9th grade.

I was so obsessed, I bought her Spanish album, *Como Ama Una Mujer*, and check this out. I ate with it playing, bathed with it playing, slept with it playing so much that I learned the entire album. I didn't have a clue of what she was saying, but it sounded beautiful.

I had a Spanish test one day and was supposed to hold an entire conversation with my teacher for a grade. I didn't get past 'Como Estas?'. I failed with flying colors, but when my teacher heard me singing at my desk while walking past me, he noticed I was singing in Spanish. He expressed amazement at how well I articulated the language I didn't understand.

"Sing some more," he said. I sang my favorites from the album, which were Me Haces Falta, Por Arriesgarnos, Tu, and Sola. My teacher was beyond blown away, and so were the other kids! "La'Porsha! Are you... you're not...how are you singing those songs so perfectly?" he asked. "I love music, and I love JLo," I said. "You know what, you didn't have to sing. I'm giving you an A, that should bring you to a passing grade overall, at least," he said. I was ecstatic! Without that grade, I was failing Spanish that year with a F. "I'll give you another A if you can tell me what you're saying," he said. "I'll take the first A for 200, thank you," I said, causing him to almost break his sides, laughing at me. Yep, JLo helped me pass the 9th grade with a D.

My science teacher, who we'll call Ms. Bony, was a pretty sad case. She was always talking to me about her problems at home. She passed everyone, even if you slept through her entire class. She was going through so much at home that she never taught us. She just had us watch science videos and do busywork until our next class every day. She told me that her husband had just up and left her for the housemaid.

I remember trying not to let my face show whatever confusing feelings I had. I didn't understand why Ms. Bony felt so comfortable talking with me about those things, and I couldn't do anything but lay her head on my shoulders and let her spill her tears on my t-shirt. The students would just do and say whatever they wanted to every single day, and she'd be numb to the chaos.

Maybe she felt comfortable because of the mature old spirit I was always told I had. I appeared so 'mature' that one day I was trying to figure out where I was supposed to go for a particular period. I stopped and asked a teacher in the hallway, "Excuse me, where do we go during this period?" "Well, the kids usually go to the cafeteria, but you can come to the teacher's lounge with me. You new? Whose class you watchin'?" she asked. "Uh, I'm a student," I said. "Oh my gosh, I'm so sorry. You just come off so much older. The cafeteria is down the hall," she said, smiling. "Thank you," I said, laughing.

Another account of the staff thinking I was older was when my mother showed up to get my progress report from the cafeteria. "I've heard great things about your daughter. The teachers love her," the woman said, looking straight at me. Eventually, my mother realized that the woman thought I was the parent. "Uh, she's the child, I'm the parent," my mother said, smiling. The woman laughed hard at herself and apologized to my mother. My mother blushed and took no offense to it, while I started wondering if I would look forty when I turned twenty.

I decided to take up a two-year vocational class in fashion design. We'll call that teacher Miss Paper. Miss Paper was the youngest of all my teachers. She came off more as an older sister type teacher to all us girls. Her nonchalant way of teaching really made this elective class more like a break from school.

I spent most of my hours on the computer, searching and playing music. The girls in this class were all incredibly snobby and fashion-oriented. I only took the class because I thought it would be neat for me to learn how to sew. I would have chosen something dealing with culinary arts, but I literally couldn't stand the heat in the kitchen and had way too many faint spells for a class that required standing up for most of it.

Now, we get to my favorites; my English teacher, my JROTC instructor, and my math teacher. Let me tell you a little about each of them in no particular order.

My English teacher was the most energetic little old lady I'd ever met. She wasn't of this world. She was hip and elderly and loved making up songs that she thought may help us remember things like character plot and subject-verb-noun agreement.

Let's call her Miss Mackerel. Miss Mackerel had a small, petite frame and was shorter than most of her students. I think she and I probably stood neck to neck. One day, she decides she's going to rap to us in class as a means to help us learn her lesson. "I got a surprise for y'all," she said. "Are y'all ready?" she asked. "Yeah!" the class screamed.

She let us have it! She started rapping and got so into the song that she jumped onto a chair and then onto her desk and kept rapping! She had the sway and hand movements of most desperate wannabe rappers, and it tickled us 'til we hurt. But her rapping was actually very nice! Everything she said made sense, and we were anxious to learn her song. English wasn't my best subject, but I knew from the moment I met her that I would be in excellent hands.

My math teacher, we'll call her Coach Star, was...a...beast. I'd never met anyone like her in my life. From the way she carried herself to the way she taught to the way I had heard she coached, she was an ultimate threat to any other teacher lacking skill.

Coach Star was beautiful. She wore her hair a golden color, short and fanned to the back. It was almost like a throwback cut. She wore her collared shirts tucked into her pants with the collar flipped up and with the shirt pulled out enough not to show her abs. She wore long, khaki pants with a belt most of the time, with some high heeled boots.

Coach Star was extremely short, too. But she was a little taller than I was. During the open house, my mother, my sister, and I came to meet Coach Star. When I saw her, she seemed to glow with an unexplained radiance. She was wearing her usual get up, except this time, she had on an orange fitted long-sleeved turtleneck sweater. She had the prettiest smile with the coolest braces. The sweater accented her fit arms and cut abs. She was also extremely bow-legged. I wanted to be Coach Star.

Her methods for teaching played to many of my strengths and preferences. She knew math like I knew music. She would scan over your paper while walking through your isle and tell you that you were wrong before you even got your answer.

She was such a neat writer, and wrote corrections and notes tiny on our papers, being careful not to take away from any tidy efforts we'd made with our own writing. Every morning we came to her class, she would put inspirational, thought-provoking quotes on the board and ask us to write a journal entry during the first ten minutes of class.

She would take her time and read our entries for the next ten minutes of class while we reviewed the math we learned the previous day. Sometimes, if the entries were troubled, like many of mine were, she would write a response and put it on our desks.

She was always giving me gift cards and little trinkets, but my favorite gift from her was a mini tiger stuffed animal because it smell like her and she'd given it to me as a thank you token for singing at a teacher's surprise appreciation. The perfume she wore was uplifting and bright.

She walked swiftly and secure with unstoppable purpose, and she was a stickler for time. She hated tardiness with a passion. As if she hadn't already been an inspiration to me, she revealed at an assembly once that she was in her thirties and was still a virgin. She encouraged us to stand out and not succumb to the usual pressures of our peers. She helped us to value ourselves more than anyone else and to be the best version of ourselves we could be.

She reawakened my determination to be clean unto God. Without even knowing it, she renewed my faith and made me excited about saving myself for God's beau, despite everything I'd already experienced.

Above all these admirable things, she was one bad to the bone teacher. She was so diverse in her way of teaching and so successful with having students pass and understand the material that the school took the classes of the teachers who were failing their students and combined them with Coach Star's classes in the auditorium to let her teach their classes as well.

Yeah, she was a force to be reckoned with. I don't know much of anything about basketball, but I can tell you she had her girls right and was even colder on the courts than in the classroom. I was careful to stay in her good grace and favor. She taught me the importance of being *your* best and not trying to be *the* best.

Last but certainly not least, there's a man we'll call Sgt. Major Megalodon. He was the JROTC instructor and was one of a kind teacher. His appeared harsh when I first met him, but later I learned just how much he cared for each one of his pupils.

He was tall, dark, and bald-headed and walked with a notorious limp. I think it was from his time spent in the military, but he made it look so cool, I wanted a limp just like his. This man was a true Rambo and wasn't afraid of anyone or anything. He was unpredictable, and you never knew when he would approach you or what he would say when he did.

I didn't even want to join JROTC, because I've always despised the military. I've always had a problem with having to put a government entity before yourself, your family, and your faith. You'll understand this more in reading the story of my marriage. I hadn't been married yet, but I knew many people who were in the military, including my dad, and hated their mentality pertaining to certain aspects of morale and Godly honor.

My mother, however, thought that this would be a good way for me to explore the possibility of earning a military scholarship. She told me that even if it wasn't my will to join the military, there were still benefits of participating in the JROTC program, and she was right.

Before joining this class, I had signed up for the band. But there had been a boy who was extremely sexually charged and violent. One day, while I was putting my instrument back in its case in the storage room, the boy approached me while I was kneeled down.

When I looked up and noticed we were the only two in the room, I started feeling uneasy. His aura seemed off, and it alarmed something inside of me. "Hey, La'Porsha, right?" he asked. "Yeah," I said, smiling. "You have the most beautiful eyes I've ever seen," he said, biting his bottom lip. "Uh, thanks," I said, raising up and moving to walk past him with my instrument case in hand.

"Wait a minute," he said, placing his hand on my chest and pushing me backward. "Don't touch me. You got something to say, say it with your mouth, not your hands," I snarled. "Alright, La'Porsha. Girl, I want you," he said, moving closer to me. He looked like a horny worm someone forgot to lock up. Both his ears were pierced, and his hair was cut low and had deep waves. He dressed like he came from a good home, but the way he acted made me wonder exactly what he'd been exposed to there. As he walked towards me, I moved backward, eventually being cornered against the wall.

A girl we'll call Tam showed up in the nick of time and confronted the boy. "I can't believe you! Get back, nasty. You need some help, for real. Come on, La'Porsha," she said, pushing him out of the way and grabbing my hand. When we left the room, we headed to the outside seating area for lunch.

"Girl, you okay?" she asked. "Yeah, if push came to shove, I would have defended myself. I think I was just trying to gauge whether it was some kind of dark humor or something. I mean, we were in the band hall. It wasn't like there was much privacy. I didn't really think he was serious," I said. "Girl, you're not the first girl he's pushed up on like that. There's even a rumor going around that he actually attacked a girl. Just stay away from him, okay?" she asked. "Got it," I said.

"My name's Prawny if you didn't already know. Welcome to McComb High. Don't be afraid to let me know if there's anything you need," she said. Prawny was the very first girl to befriend me there. When I got home that day, I didn't tell my mother about the incident. I thought it wasn't enough to be considered a big deal and wasn't trying to make waves at my new school. I was determined to be as invisible as possible and just make it to graduation.

The next day, I came and took my seat in band class to find a letter on my music stand. It was from the boy. It was one of the most disgusting messages I'd ever read. My mouth dropped as I read all the vile things the boy admitted he wanted to do to me. It brought tears to my eyes, not because I was sad or hurt, but because I was unthinkably angry, and I wanted to beat him to death. I looked at the boy and saw him watching me read the letter. He winked at me when our eyes met, and I folded the letter and tried my best to focus on class.

After class, Prawny and I met for lunch again, and I showed her the letter. "Wow, La'Porsha, you need to report this. He seems pretty serious," she said. I was speechless and could only cry from all the anger that burned my insides. "Aw, La'Porsha, don't cry," Prawny said, hugging me. "You want me to walk with you to the office?" she asked. "I think I'm gonna wait. I want to show this to my mother first," I said.

When I made it home, I did just that. My mother was ready to go to jail. "Porsha, a boy, actually wrote this to you, girl?" she asked in utter shock. "Yep. I wanted to show you before I turned it in to the office," I said. "I'm coming up there with you, and we will definitely be talking with the principal."

My mother did just that. We showed the principal the letter, and she called the boy in the office to personally and directly apologize to me and my mother for what he had written. My mother, not being satisfied with his apology, told the boy she would be paying his parents a visit, and after school that day, she did.

It was this incident that made me tell my mother I was no longer interested in being part of the band and that I wanted to find a different elective class. I ended up in P.E. but got out because I hated sharing the gym with the guys. It was so uncomfortable. This is what then led me to join JROTC.

Very early in the program, we were given uniforms and tested on our abilities to dress in Class A properly. I always found it extremely hard to align my nametag because of my breasts and ended up not meeting the standards of Sgt. Major Megalodon.

I walked into class one day, dressed in Class A uniform, and in front of everyone, Sgt. Major Megalodon yelled, "Mays, what the h* is this? Naw, you can walk right back up outta here lookin' like a soup sandwich from hell!" I was mortified! I didn't walk out of there, I ran! I ran all the way to the front office and called my mother to come and pick me up!

I called her crying, telling her what Sgt. Major Megalodon had called me in front of everyone.

When my mother arrived at the school, I got in the car, and we sat for a minute to talk. I was infuriated because I could tell she was trying not to laugh at Sgt. Major Megalodon's remarks about my uniform. "Baby, do you think you're a soup sandwich?" my mother asked, trying to be as serious as possible. "Ma, I think ain't no man gonna sit there and talk to me that way. I'm going to the guidance counselor and getting out of this class before I catch a case," I told her. "But then what chance will you have to prove him wrong?" my mother asked.

She played on the one thing she knew I would never want to be defeated, and that was my pride. I was a lion, born July 28, and she knew how to make me roar. As I wiped my tears, she saw the look of a new determination on my face. "That's the lioness, I know. Girl, you done spent all these years choppin' ya daddy's head off, and you can't handle one limpin' Sgt. Major Megalodon?"

She and I shared a moment of laughter, and I agreed that she was right. I kissed my mother goodbye and told her that I was going back to class. I walked back in there, stood in front of the tall mirror that met me almost right at the entrance, fixed my suit to be as crisp as I could make it, and took my place in the platoon's formation.

When Sgt. Major Megalodon came to me to grade my uniform, he formed an upside-down smile with his mouth and examined every inch of my suit. "Hmph," he said, as he marked notes on his clipboard. He didn't say anything else to me until class was dismissed for the day. "Mays!" he yelled, "I need to you to stay behind for a minute."

I reluctantly did what he had requested. He walked up to me and showed me my grade besides my name on the clipboard. I'd passed inspection with flying colors. "One thing you need to know about me is I don't fuss at people I don't see potential in. I knew you could do it. Na, don't come to my class lookin' like no soup sandwich no more, aight Mays?" he said.

I tried to hide my smile, but it pushed its way through the tears I couldn't stop from rolling down my cheeks. "Okay," I said, smiling. "Alright, now get outta here, 'cause I ain't writing you no pass to ya next class. If ya late, ya late," he said. I laughed, grabbed my belongings, and left for my next class.

He followed me out of the door and took his post by the entrance to wait for his next class. He saw me walking and shouted, "You ain't gon' make it like that, Mays! You betta run, jog, somethin'!" he yelled. I looked back to see him full out laughin'. I laughed and began running to make it to my next class on time.

From that day forward, I saw the love shine through his toughness. Word had gotten around to him that I could sing. "Mays, I hear you got a big mouth. I could use that. I think I'll make you one of my officers," he said, and he did.

I worked extremely hard to stay in his favor, but had many dumb moments and eventually earned the nickname 'Cadet Kelly' from him, referencing the movie. My experience with JROTC was exactly fashioned like that movie. The class would laugh every time he would call me that, but it couldn't have been more accurate, so I'd laugh too.

I became one of his favorites, and it showed. He was always taking me aside and teaching me things to prepare me to be an officer. My mother grew to admire and look forward to the stories I would come home and tell her about him.

The thing Miss Mackerel, Coach Star and Sgt. Major Megalodon had in common was the fact that they exemplified something that I didn't feel many other teachers did. They paid attention to the weaknesses of their students and built strength around them. They pushed students to be a better version of themselves than anyone could have imagined. They all cared about their students far above and beyond the classroom.

They ignited purpose and ambition inside of myself that I didn't really know I had pertaining to my studies and growing into a better me. They made me look forward to going to school and made me never want to leave.

Okay, let's wave goodbye to Sphinx. He's got to get back home before the hunting creatures come. We should speed up a little ourselves.

Circles and Cliques

"Sometimes if you're not careful,
your 'circle of friends' becomes a 'web of enemies.'"
~ A. S. E.

As I mentioned earlier, Prawny was the first person to befriend me at the school. She was delightful and pretty much got along with everyone. There was a group of girls Prawny would always sit with at lunch. She introduced me to them, and they accepted me because of her.

Prawny loved and believed in Christ. She became someone that I could have conversations with about my faith. She literally introduced me to everyone who she considered to be cool people and warned me about people she thought I should stay away from.

For a while, Prawny and her group were the only people I hung around. One day, when I was gathering my belongings in JROTC, I started humming, and a girl noticed me. "Oh, wait a minute. Girl, you can *sang*, can't you?" she asked. I chuckled, and she continued, "Na, don't stop. See, I already heard you. We gon' be good friends," she said.

We'll call her Orca. Orca was fierce, and she was like a lady pimp. She had guys eating out of the palm of her hands. She could be the sweetest person, but could also flip at the drop of a hat and be the meanest person.

I remember her giving me a 'Orca lesson' one day about how to not get played by guys. "See, you gotta act just like these guys out here act. You need one for different thangs. Don't just be bein' all in love with just one. I got a man that I kinda really care about that's my main squeeze, a man for money, a man for cuddling, a man for eye candy, and a nice nerd to do my homework," she said. "Are you serious?" I asked. "As a heart attack!" she said, raising one eyebrow with a straight face.

I was tickled pink at what she was suggesting. "Orca, wouldn't that be like being as bad as the guys. I mean, just because that's what most of them do doesn't mean we should be that way, right? You can just wait for some respectable guy to come along. Maybe you think that way because you haven't met the right one," I suggested.

"Oh, okay. I see you still a little wet behind the ears. Porsha, I got news for ya. Fairytales is fake. They not real. You either take advantage or be taken advantage of in these streets. You all sweet and nice now because you ain't learned yet. But when that guy comes along and breaks your heart, you gon' come to me and tell me I was right. Me? I don't even give 'em a chance. By the time I catch them cheatin', I'll been and upped them by like six other dudes," she said, laughing.

I laughed at her ruthlessness, and though I appeared to shrug her comments off my shoulders, the conversation never left my mind. Is that really how things had to be for girls not to get hurt and to earn respect from guys? It all seemed counterproductive and senseless to me, but there was no real basis for what I was suggesting, either. I would have loved to think there was truth in what I told her about waiting for the right one, but I had never met anyone like that.

Orca ended up introducing me to a guy she considered to be like a brother. We'll call him Nar. Nar was charming and sweet. He was always so respectful of Orca and almost acted as one of her servants. She could ask him for anything, and he would get her whatever she required.

"Nar, come here. I want you to meet my new friend, Porsha," she said. "Hey, nice to meet you," he said. "Nice to meet you, too," I said. "Wow, your eyes are beautiful," he said. "Ain't they, though? I told her she cute!" Orca said. I hated being called cute, but I accepted the compliments.

The three of us started hanging out at a table in front of the JROTC building in the mornings, and I would hang with Prawny and her group during lunch. Orca had started hinting at Nar having a crush on me and how she felt we would be a cute couple.

Prawny revealed to me that I had another admirer and told me to be careful because his girlfriend was one of her friends. I began feeling annoyed with all the attention of guys, and all the conversations seemed to be directed towards hooking me up with someone. That was pretty much the meat of high school; being 'hooked up.' I expressed to them both that I wasn't looking for anyone in that way, and I wasn't allowed to date.

Prawny kind of accepted it, but Orca was adamant. I just learned to laugh and discount Orca's suggestive comments. I noticed the attention of many guys but ignored them all. Strange enough, it seemed like the more uninterested I showed myself to be, the more interested they became.

One funny day at lunch, Prawny and I were laughing and talking, and a unique person caught my eye. "Who's that?" I asked. Prawny looked at me and smiled, "Oh...you? Okay, I'll...um, stay right here," she said. Before I could stop her, she brought the person over to me to introduce us. "Hey, what's your name?" "Hi, I'm Porsha," I said, embarrassed. "You're the new girl, right?" "Yeah," I said. "Oh, okay, so what's up?" "Um, nothing. I was just asking Prawny about you, and she brought you over here," I said.

Prawny was as tickled as can be, but she didn't say why. "Well, can I have your number?" "Um, I can't really talk to boys on the phone," I said. Prawny laughed aloud. "What's so funny?" I asked. "Um, you don't know, do you?" "Know what?" I asked. "I'm a girl," the stranger said. "Oh my gosh. Wow! I mean, I'm so sorry I thought...you're handsome! Oh, that's terrible! I am so sorry...I don't know what to say!" "Yeah, the more you talked, I figured you didn't know and that you didn't swing that way. But no worries, it was cute. You're cool people," she said, laughing. "Thanks for not getting mad," I said. "Hey, we ain't like that here. Well, you do have some idiots here, but I ain't one of 'em," she said. She chuckled and chucked up the deuces and walked back to her crowd.

"Why did you do that?" I asked. "You seemed like you liked her, and I didn't want to judge if you were that way," she said. "You knew I didn't know," I said, perching my lips and smirking. "Yeah, you're right. I knew. But I needed that laugh, and I've known her forever. I knew she would be cool about it. I think she still likes you," she said. "Well, I think that's just too bad. I didn't even say I liked him, I mean her. I asked you who that was," I said. It was something that took her forever to live down.

I can honestly say I was off to a pretty good start at the new school. But then, the frequency of my weak spells picked back up. During my first week, I was found laid out on the sidewalk by a lady gym teacher. I woke up in the ambulance facing a crowd of students in the outside eating area. This could not be happening.

I was taken to the hospital and referred to a specialist to help conclude a diagnosis of my condition. I was placed on a heart monitor and had to wear sticky cords on my chest that connected to a loud beeper that would call the hospital if my heart got too slow or too fast.

The beeper was crazy. It would go off for no reason, causing students to overreact and laugh and tease. But there was a funny incident. I had a crush on a football player who invited me to hang with him at the top of the bleachers of a junior game.

"Would you mind getting me something to drink?" he asked. "Sure," I said. I had baby doll shoes on with no grip, and when I squeezed by him, I slipped. It had been raining, and the stairs were wet. I bumpily slid down each step on my behind all the way from the very top to the bottom.

Since most were aware of my heart monitor, including my crush, they didn't laugh. But as soon as someone came to meet me, asked if I was okay, and they saw me say yes, the entire side of the stands burst into thunderous laughter. It was the most embarrassing moment of my life. And yes, the heart monitor stayed as silent as a sleeping baby. Go figure.

Intimate Stranger

"Most sexual assaults happen by someone you know;
someone who's gained your trust."
~A. S. E.

I HAD BEEN INVITED to a church home one day. This was when I met someone we'll call Lamprey. He was handsome and had a way about himself that seemed well rounded and gentleman-like. Lamprey became attracted to me and asked if we could get to know one another. He seemed much like my older brother, Antuaine, and I think that's what attracted me to him. He made me feel utterly safe, no matter who we were around or where we were.

We started meeting up and hanging out while my mother was at work. Since moving to McComb, my mom had quit her job in Monticello, and gotten hired as a hairdresser at JC Penny's. My mother had spent all her money making sure my sister and I had clothes that wouldn't get us teased by the other kids, so she didn't have fancy clothes of her own.

Her boss confronted her about her clothes and insulted her in front of a shop full of clients. My mother was brought to tears, which was hard to do. She was embarrassed and quit that day. She began working as a cashier at Wal-Mart and was often not home until night time.

I invited Lamprey over to watch a movie with me, but he wanted more. When I stopped things from progressing, he respectfully honored my wishes and said that he wasn't the type of guy to pressure anyone.

We continued hanging out and getting to know one another after I'd get out of school. My mother had been so impressed with the way she *thought* I'd been carrying myself, that she allowed me to have a little more freedom when it came to hanging out with associates. Eventually, I spent the night at the house of a friend Prawny had introduced me to. Lamprey came to visit with another guy.

Prawny's friend had the biggest heart and sweetest attitude, but she was a bit "fast" and said she wanted us to have guy company over. When she asked me if I could think of anyone, my mind went to Lamprey because I'd grown comfortable with him. I called Lamprey and asked him if he wanted to come over, and he agreed. He asked if it would be okay to bring a friend, and since my friend wanted that anyway, I agreed.

When the two young men arrived, Lamprey's friend and my friend went to another room to 'get to know one another,' and Lamprey and I stayed in the room I was sleeping in. We sat on the bed and talked for hours until we both fell asleep. I felt so comfortable and so safe.

I woke up to Lamprey, gently climbing on top of me. I smiled and said, "What are you doing? I told you that's not an option," I said. He smiled back. "I know, but you turn me on. You're beautiful inside and out, and I want you," he said, kissing my neck. I giggled at the tickling of his chin hair. "I understand, but we can't. I'm sorry," I said, smiling.

My smile began to quickly fade when he didn't stop. In fact, he seemed he began to move faster in his efforts. When I realized he wasn't listening to me, I tried pushing him off of me. When I started showing force, he stopped and looked at me. "Really, you think you're strong enough to push me off? Why are you acting like I'm a monster? Who's hurt you in the past to make you not trust me?" he asked.

His eyes began to water, and I was taken back. Was he crying? What was this? Was I being unreasonable? "I' m..., I'm sorry. I wasn't trying to make you feel bad or anything, I just want to save myself for whoever I end up with in the future," I said. "La'Porsha, I love you. Do you hear me? I've never said that to anyone. I love you," he said. "Um, I mean, I... love you too?" I stated with a questioning tone.

He got off of me and sat at the edge of the bed. "Wow, I feel so stupid right now. I wish I would've known you didn't feel the same way before I came all the way here. I would have never even tried this if I knew," he said. "Lamprey, I didn't call you here for that. You're an amazing guy, and who knows, we may be together that way in the future. I'm just not ready now, but that doesn't mean I don't care for you. Come on, you're making me feel bad," I said, rubbing his back.

"I've got one question for you. Do you love me?" he asked. "I mean, I think that's a word that shouldn't just be thrown around. I don't know you well enough to say that," I said. "La'Porsha, we've spent every day together for the last few weeks. Look, I'm sexually active. I'm not a virgin. I really like you and think you're beautiful and I really want to be with you, but I can't just neglect my needs. I understand if you're not ready. I'll respect that, but that means we can't do this anymore. I have to find someone that's where I am in life. Understand?" he asked.

I was naïve, confused, and appalled. What was happening? "Lamprey, so are you telling me we can't be friends if I don't have sex with you?" I asked. "So that's what we are, friends? I thought we were more," he said. "Lamprey, the first time you asked me about this, I explained to you where I stood, and you accepted it and said you weren't the type to pressure anyone. I find that funny because now all I feel is pressure!" I said. "I said that and meant it, La'Porsha. But—" "Obviously not!" I said. "You know what, I'm leaving. It's cool," he said. "Lamprey, wait. Don't leave like this. What could I do other than that to show you I care?" I asked.

I should have let Lamprey leave like he said he would, but something in me felt guilty that I had, according to him, led him on and put him in this predicament. "Would you at least give me a kiss?" he asked. "I don't want to make things harder for you," I said. "So, what you're really saying is you don't trust me?" he asked.

Lamprey had a masterful way of turning everything I said around and putting words in my mouth to victimize himself. He had talked circles around me, and I fell for it. I felt horrible and thought I'd make the insults up to him by granting him his kiss.

Right before we kissed, his friend knocked on the door and entered the room. "Hey man, you ready to go. Don't look like I'm getting none tonight. Ole girl trippin'," he said. "Why did you and your friend invite us in the first place?" Lamprey asked. "Why not just to talk and hang out?" I asked.

Lamprey's friend laughed. "Man, come on. I told you about trying these lil' kids. They, not real women," he said. I shouldn't have allowed it to, but his comment offended me. Lamprey stared into my eyes and said, "Well, I don't know about her friend, but my girl *is* a woman, not a kid. Right, baby?" he asked, kissing me. My nerves seized me, and I hesitated to respond. "Right?" he asked a second time, kissing my neck. "Right," I said, on the verge of tears.

"Let's show him how much of woman you are," he said, guiding me to lay back on the bed and climbing on top of me. "Lamprey, I—" "La'Porsha, don't embarrass me. You said you're a woman, and you said you cared. Now prove it," he whispered in my ear.

His tone was stern and demanding, and his body tensed up. There was no trace of kindness in his voice, and I started to feel trapped. My body grew weak, and I started realizing I was in real trouble.

"Lamprey, I don't want to. I don't care anymore, please get off me," I cried. "Relax, or it'll really hurt," he said. "No! Stop, please!" I cried out.

I noticed Lamprey's friend take a seat on the soft bench that was located not too far from the foot of the bed. Thinking Lamprey would care enough to stop, I brought that to his attention. "Lamprey! Your friend!" "Don't worry about him, baby. Focus on me," he said. I grew sick. What was this? Was Lamprey actually allowing his friend to watch? When Lamprey wouldn't adhere to my cries, I turned to his friend. "What are you doing?! Why are you just sitting there?" I cried to Lamprey's friend. "I'm enjoying the view since I can't get none from your friend," he

said.

'My friend! Why hadn't she come back downstairs?' I thought. Just as soon as the thought entered my mind to call for her, Lamprey covered my mouth. I wiggled and wormed and wore myself out, trying to break loose. Breathing became a struggle from crying so hard, and because Lamprey's weight made it impossible to take a full breath.

I felt *him*. I panicked and tried fighting even harder. With a violent thrust and a sting, he'd done it. He had broken my beautiful gate...the gate that was intended to only be entered by someone who planned to spend the rest of his life with me, someone who would water my garden and create fruit for the both of us to nurture and submit back to our Creator.

Lamprey stated in vain that he loved me, and yet he, being the wicked thief he was, had taken my most sacred and treasured possession. Lamprey grunted and groaned while I screamed through my smothered mouth and cried. "Porsha, you feel so good," he kept repeating in my ear. Every word burned my ear like a scalding hot iron being pressed against it. When Lamprey went to kiss my neck, I lowered my eyes to catch a glance at his friend pleasing himself in the dark as he watched, biting his bottom lip. Since my eyes had adjusted to the darkness, I was able to see him clear as day.

I threw up and started choking on my vomit. Lamprey moved his hand when he felt the warmth on his palm and turned me over to throw up on the floor beside the bed. While I vomited, Lamprey, all of a sudden, *cared* for me again. "Baby, you alright?" he asked. I was in so much pain. My inside and outside simultaneously hurt. He asked me twice more, but I didn't answer. When I'd finished vomiting, he took the sheet off the bed and raised it to my mouth and wiped it. I guided my eyes to his lips and saw them moving but heard no sound.

I saw his friend get up and leave from the corner of my eye. For a long while, I heard nothing. But, then, my ears slowly opened to receive Lamprey's voice again. "Porsha...Porsha. Baby, say something," he said. "You..." I couldn't think of anything else to say other than that. With every effort to speak, my throat grew sore and heavy, trying to hold my dismantled self together.

"Porsha, I didn't do anything you really didn't want. You called me over here. When I tried to leave, you told me to stay. I said, I love you, and I mean that. I love you so much, I couldn't hold myself back. You've

...you've got sex appeal. It was torture not being able to show you how I felt about you. Do you understand what I'm saying?" he asked.

"You...I didn't wa—" I started. "You did. You just didn't know it. Porsha, I read your body language. Your eyes said you wanted it. You flirted with your lips. Everything but your mouth told me you wanted me. Guess what? You were *ready* for me when I entered," he said.

I whaled and moaned and let out soft, agonizing screams to his comment. My body! My body had prepared itself and, once again, betrayed me. If I'd had a gun, I would have shot myself. What I felt against Lamprey, against my body, and against all men was more agonizing than I thought death to be.

My privates felt like someone had been punching me down there, and I burned from the inside. I heard the bedroom door open, and it was my friend. "Porsha! You okay? It sounded like you were gagging or something. What's wrong?" "She's fine. Get her some water and bring a towel. She threw up," he said. She did as Lamprey asked and brought back a glass of water and a towel, and came around the bed to the side I'd been leaning over. "Oh! *That's* what I heard. Girl, why you sick? What's wrong? You missin' home?" she asked. "That's probably what it is," Lamprey chimed in before I could answer.

I laid down on my side in a fetal position with my head to the pillow, faced away from Lamprey. Lamprey took a blanket that had been folded at the foot of the bed and covered me with it. "Porsha... I'm gonna go now, but we'll talk tomorrow, okay?" he asked. I was silent. "The first time is always the hardest and the scariest, but I promise it wasn't as bad as you think," he leaned over and whispered. Before raising up, he kissed my forehead and left.

When my friend climbed on the bed from the other side, I laid on my stomach and buried my face in the pillow. She nonchalantly started talking about how horrible Lamprey's friend had been. "Girl, he was so ugly to me, I just couldn't. Wanted to though, but I needed somethin' better to work with. Porsha? Girl, you sleep?" she asked. "I just don't feel like talking," I said. "Aww, boo. Did something happen? Lamprey seemed kind of bothered when I came in? Did y'all have an argument?"

When I raised my head to meet her eyes, she knew something had happened. "Oh my God, Porsha. What happened? Tell me now," she said. I sat up in the bed and looked up to the ceiling. "I don't know," I said, dropping my head. She scooted near me and laid my head on her shoulders, wrapping her arm around me. "You know I'm here to talk, and you can tell me anything," she said.

I felt exhausted and wanted to just lay down and never wake up. What had I done? How had I allowed something like this to happen?

I remember not even being worried about what my mother would think, but being extremely desperate to know if I'd fallen out of God's favor. How did He feel about me now? I hadn't heard any voices or seen any spirit. *Am I still your daughter?* I thought to myself. *Of what value am I to You, now? Of what value am I to anyone who might have loved me or chosen me in the future? I'm a...a nothing.*

The night played over and over and over in my head again and again and again. I thought about all the moments I could have let Lamprey leave and stuck to my guns. I thought about how I could have not invited them in the first place. I thought about all the times my mother hadn't wanted me to spend nights at other people's homes. I wished she wouldn't have allowed me any freedoms. It seemed every time I was given freedom, I allowed myself to be bound by someone or something.

I had given away the only thing of value I had left. All the times I'd stopped things before going too far. All the people I'd turned down only to end up this way. I couldn't stand being in my own skin. Even though he was gone, I felt him for the rest of the night. I felt his wet tongue on my neck. I felt the thrusting, repeatedly. I felt the eyes of his friend watching me suffer.

When I came home the next day, I put on the best poker face I could, but my mother knew. She didn't know what she knew, but she knew. "Baby, are you okay? You look...different," she said. "I'm good, Ma," I lied. I rushed to my room to beat the tears welling up in my throat.

I checked out. I was hardly concerned with my classwork and had begun slacking, even in Coach Star's class. My teachers showed great concern for me, and almost all of them pulled me outside of the classroom to ask me if everything was okay. I wasn't even able to convince them that I was.

Coach Star, Sgt. Major Megalodon and Miss Flounder all told me the same exact thing on different days. "Baby girl, the Lord never puts more on you than you can bear," they said. But that was just it. I never blamed God for this. I blamed myself. I wasn't a complete fool. There were many opportunities I had to stop things before they spun out of control, but I didn't.

The only thing I had held against God was that He created me female and He had made me desirable. I withdrew from all my friends, and while some accepted it and didn't miss me, some took my withdrawal to heart.

I came to Spanish class one day, with Orca already seated and chatting it up with her usual clique of girls. Typically, I would've greeted her with a hug before taking my seat. But this day, I didn't feel like speaking to anyone, so I took my place and put my head down on my desk. "Uh, wait a minute. I know this b* didn't just sit her a* down without talking to me," she said.

Orca had a way about her that made it very difficult to tell whether she was joking or not, and she had a bit of a potty mouth. But she had never called me out of my name and knew how I felt about that. Today, I just wasn't up for being tolerant. "Who you callin' b*?" I asked. "Who you talkin' to like that?" she asked. "Don't answer my question with a question. In case you haven't noticed, I'm not in the mood today, Orca. Okay?" I warned.

She was baffled. The girls around her aroused her anger and urged her to not take my disrespect. "Look, I don't know what the heck happened to you, but check ya attitude 'cause I'm not the one," she said. "Orca, I don't know who you think you are, but if that's some kind of threat, I pray you know *I'm* not the one. I mean, all this over me not speaking to you when I walked in? You could have spoken to me! Orca, I don't ANSWER to you! I don't OWE you anything. I speak when I feel like it, and if I don't, you sit down, shut yo mouth and be cool with that."

Orca stood from her desk, and I rose from mine in response. "Y'all, come on. Y'all too good of friends for this," a girl said. "Na, we ain't friends. I better not catch this hoe by herself," Orca said. "Orca, for your sake, I agree," I said.

I took my seat, but she stood for a while longer before her clique convinced her to sit as well. I slept for the rest of the class and was awakened by the lunch bell. I didn't go through the line. My appetite had left me entirely. I sat at a table alone, but not even a minute later, Orca came to my table, ready to fight.

"What you got to say now, b*?" she asked. She was pretty loud, so most of the lunchroom heard her. "I ain't got nothin' at all to say. I'll let you have the first throw. Make it count, 'cause when I get you, I'm coming for blood," I said. The spectators tried to edge things along and were utterly shocked at what had come out of my mouth.

Before this time, I was known to be a quiet, introverted good girl. The janitor stepped in before anything could hit the ceiling and asked us to walk with him to the auditorium. He was a sweet, quiet guy that no one hardly noticed. However, I would always speak and give him hugs every day. His spirit was pure and kind, and gentle.

"Now, I know both of you. This isn't you? Don't give them what they want. You both are better than this. Please, stay in here away from everybody else and talk it out. Please," he said.

When he left Orca and me alone, Orca waited a long while before she said anything. "I wanna know why," she said. "Why what, Orca?" I asked. "Porsha, you've never talked to me like that. I really wanna know what's going on," she said. "Well, Orca, you've never called me out of my name," I said. "Okay, I get that, and I'm sorry. But I don't feel like that's it," she said.

I stubbornly tried to avoid her inquiry, but she just stood there, waiting for me to explain my hostility. "Orca, I'm...pissed...at mm...

myself," I struggled. The tears began to flow, and I broke down. "I was... hurt by a guy I trusted, and it was my fault," I whimpered. "Porsha, I know you. Ain't no guy got you this upset. You're not even attracted to dudes like that, so what's really going on?" she asked. "Orca, I was *hurt* by a guy I trusted, and it was my fault. He...he took me, Orca," I said.

Saying it aloud stirred up all the physical hurt from that awful night once again. Orca studied my face, with her lips departed and one eyebrow raised for a short moment. When she realized what I had told her, her tears flowed uncontrollably, and she grew angry. "Porsha! Who?" she asked, clenching her fists. "I can't say. Orca, promise not to tell anyone. With the way things happened, no one would believe me, anyway," I whimpered.

"Porsha, so you're not going to tell your mother?" she asked. "No, Orca. Telling her now would only inflate things and create a whole bunch of drama. I mean, she would get the police involved and my dad would probably come trying to blame me and send me off to boarding school or something. He's always the one suggesting my mother send me to a boot camp. It's happened. Just let it be," I said. "Porsha, but you shouldn't have to deal with it alone," she said. "I'm not, we're friends, right?" I asked, smiling through my tears. "Nope. We're sisters," she said, hugging me.

From that day on, Orca allowed me to have my space and time to personally deal with the trauma I'd gone through. Though we buried the hatchet, we were still not very close. She respected what I felt I needed, and that was to be a loner. I put on a happy made-up face every day, and though I continued to try to wear a smile, I had journeyed far, far away from myself. I was empty and lost, and would only show up to briefly interact with necessary individuals.

One day, while my mother and sister were gone, I was at home alone. As always, I was watching shows like 'Sister Sister' and 'Lizzie McGuire'.

There was a knock on the door. "Who is it?" I asked. "Lamprey." I opened the door. "What do you want? What are you doing here?" I asked. "I...I just wanted to see how you're doing," he said.

I stood there, contemplating on what to do or say next, but nothing came to me. "Can I come in?" he asked. "H* no." "Porsha, please. I just want to talk. When I left, you weren't doing well." "Well, I'm fine now. Bye," I said. "La'Porsha…" he said, with a sorrowful look. "You've got two minutes," I said.

I removed myself from blocking the doorway, and he walked in and sat on the couch. I sat on the floor, quite a distance from the couch he was sitting on. "Really?" he asked. "Say what you gotta say and leave, Lamprey." "La'Porsha, I'm sorry. I'm so sorry about how our first experience together went. I was so attracted to you and really thought you were just playing hard to get or something. When it was too late, I noticed how you acted afterward and realized what I had done. I never ever meant to hurt you, Porsha," he said.

I folded my lips, careful to calm my anger, and say the right things in response to what he was telling me. "How could you have never meant to hurt me? You said you're sexually active right? Then tell me this. How many of those girls cried and screamed for you to stop?" I asked. "Most of them," he answered. "Well, you stopped, right?" I asked. "Porsha, baby –" "Don't! Don't you dare call me that," I scolded, with a quiet, icy voice of warning.

"Okay, I'm sorry. La'Porsha, I know that you're not going to understand me when I say this because you're not sexually active. But, normally, when women say they want you to stop, they really don't. They're wanting me to love them through whatever fear they're feeling. Some even cry," he said. "Do they scream and fight? Do you cover their mouths? Do they throw up?" I asked. "I thought it was only harder for you because you were a virgin. I covered your mouth to stop you from waking your friend's parents up and scaring her and you didn't fight me." "I couldn't, Lamprey! You were pressed on top of me!" "Porsha, if I really wanted to hurt you and didn't care about you, then why would I have turned you over so that you wouldn't choke on your vomit? And even after that, why didn't I just leave?" he asked.

I took a moment to breathe. "Lamprey, if you cared or loved me, why did you allow your friend to watch?" "Baby, all I was focused on was you! He didn't matter. It was dark. He couldn't see anything anyway. I just wanted to focus...on you. At the time, you were all I saw and all I wanted and all I cared about," he said. "This may work on other dumb girls you screw, but I know better. You're a monster, Lamprey."

He gripped his hands together and looked down at them, clenching his teeth. For a long while, we said nothing to each other. "La'Porsha, come sit beside me." "Time for you to go," I said. "La'Porsha, I will not touch you. Please, come sit. I'm not leaving 'til you do," he said. "See, that's what I'm talking about. You like control. You don't know what love is. If you loved me, you'd do what I asked," I said.

"I do love you, but I'm not leaving with things like this between us. I need you to understand that I never wanted to hurt you," he said. "Me sitting on that couch isn't going to make me understand that. Leave," I said. Part of me felt like he wasn't going to budge, but he got up and walked out the door.

I sat there on the floor for a moment, thinking about everything he said. Had I overreacted? Was he right about what most girls wanted? Before now, I'd talked with a few women about sex, and they always told me it hurt starting off, but once I got used to it, it wouldn't hurt anymore. Could this be what they meant?

My thoughts put me in a boat and rowed me away from shore. I'd gotten so caught up in what Lamprey had told me that I completely smeared out the thought of being assaulted. Things started to look and feel like I was the bad guy; like I was the one who overreacted and made him out to be a monster when he was only treating me like the woman he thought I was.

I'd seen Lamprey a few days later, but when I passed right by him, he wouldn't even look my way. I called him, and he didn't answer the phone. Then a few minutes later, he called back. "Hey, I was running when you called. What's up? You okay?" he asked. I was surprised to hear the kind tone in his voice since he'd ignored me earlier. "Yeah, I'm okay. You mind if we talk?" I asked. "When and where?" he asked. "My place and as soon as you can come," I said. "On my way," he said.

My sister and mother hadn't been home again, and I can't remember why not. I would often opt out of going places with them; not because I planned to be mischievous, but I was just more of a home body. But I was there all by myself and had a lot of time to spare. Since I felt guilty about the way I acted with Lamprey, I decided I would cook us dinner and pick out a movie we could watch after talking. When he arrived, he had on a tight, black track shirt and some long, black loose shorts with tennis shoes. He was sweaty but still managed to smell good.

"Hey," he said. "Hey, come in." We sat on the couch. "What's this, Porsha?" he asked. "I just wanted to say I'm sorry," I said. "For what?" he asked. "For overreacting and being mad at you. It seems like we misunderstood each other," I said. "So, you don't think I'm a monster anymore?" he asked. "No, I don't. I think I was wrong to even invite you over," I said. "So, you regret being with me?" he asked. "I regret the way things happened," I said. "Well, that doesn't really make me feel any better," he said. "I'm sorry, it's just how I feel," I said. "So, where do we go from here?" he asked. "You tell me," I said. "Well, I kind of have a girlfriend now, so..." "A girlfriend? Are you serious?" I asked. "Porsha, what was I supposed to do? You told me you didn't want me...or this." "You're right. Well, I've said what I had to say," I said.

"Porsha, you're not being fair," he said. "Lamprey, you have a girlfriend. We don't have anything else to talk about. I accept what's happened. My apology still stands. There's nothing left to talk about," I said. "Stop doing that! Stop...stop saying everything but what you really want to say," he said. "It won't make a difference what I say, Lamprey." "Try me," he said. "When I called you over, I wanted to apologize because I thought about what you said. I thought maybe I did overreact, and maybe you did misunderstand me because of what you were used to. I then thought about the fact that I wanted this...I wanted to try and continue with us, especially now that you're the one I lost myself to. I can't even imagine being with anyone else at this point. You literally have all of me now, and I don't want to just throw that away," I said with tears streaming down my face.

He cupped my face in his hands and kissed me. "I'll figure something out, I promise. We'll get through this mess together, okay?" he said. "Okay," I said. "Are you cooking something?" he asked. "Yes, I thought we could eat and watch a movie," I said. "Really? You cooked for me? Wow, that makes me feel special," he said. "Yeah, well, it was my way of showing how sorry I was for everything," I said.

I raised up from the couch to go to the kitchen and fix our plates. As I started walking away, Lamprey grabbed my hand and kissed it, then released me. When I came back with our plates, we ate and laughed and talked. When we were done, Lamprey said, "We could watch a movie, or we could just stay like this and talk. I love talking to you, La'Porsha. I don't think I know anyone with the kind of mind you have," he said. "Yeah, well, my mind's not all that. It gets me into situations like ours," I said. "Hey, we're moving forward. Let's let the past be the past, okay?" he asked.

I looked at him and couldn't help myself. Tears began to swell, and my throat began to hurt. "I'm trying to be okay, I promise. But, it still hurts. I hate how things are and how things happened. I know I can't change anything or take it back, but I just feel so...empty," I said. He dried my tears with his hand. "How about...how about you let me make it up to you," he said. "How?" I asked. "Let me show you how things could have been if you hadn't panicked." "You mean, have sex?" I asked. "No, make love. Let me make love to you." "I...I can't. I honestly don't think I could ever let a man touch me in that way again," I said. "Let me fix it," he said.

He took my hand and led me from the couch to the floor. "Lay down," he said. He began preparing me to receive him and kissing me. Then, he began to rock steady. It was excruciating, and I couldn't help but cry. But he reminded me that my tears were 'normal' and to relax so that when he made the 'move' that would connect us, it wouldn't hurt as much as it did last time.

But the more he rocked and inched, the more I tensed up. Then something happened that I wasn't expecting. I started to feel like his hand was covering my mouth when it wasn't. I began hallucinating through my tears and could have sworn I saw his friend sitting on the couch watching us. I started shaking my head and telling him I couldn't go through with it. I started urgently apologizing and begging him to get off of me, but once again, he told me it didn't work that way. "Baby, a man can't just stop in the middle of things. We're too far, now. Just relax and trust me." "Lamprey, please, I feel sick again. I can't do it. I'm not a woman. I'm not. I thought I was, but I'm not. I'm sorry I ever made you think I was. Please, stop," I whimpered.

He stopped his movement and dropped his head, then raised up from me and held out his hand to help me stand up. "Thank you," I said, still crying. "You're welcome. Come here," he said, pulling my head to his chest. He held me for a long while, kissed my forehead, and left the apartment. I felt like crap. I felt like I was broken and didn't work right. It was at that moment that I decided I wasn't going to be with anyone, ever. I didn't want to lead anyone else on or hurt anyone with my brokenness.

I didn't realize how naïve and misled I was at the time. Lamprey was such a great manipulator that he actually made me believe everything he said about how sex was supposed to be between two people. Then again, it could have been that Lamprey's experiences with other women were exactly what he said. Either way, it was a tactic of the enemy to make me think that my expectations of holy, pure love wasn't meant to be a reality. I had really been duped into thinking that my willingness to be misused by Lamprey determined how much of a woman I was. And since I wasn't willing or even able, in my mind, I was not only not a woman, but I wasn't a properly functioning female. Therefore, I wished to be alone for the rest of my life to avoid hurting anyone else or making them feel like a monster the way I thought I'd done to Lamprey.

Please, those were rough waters to navigate. Let's rest a while to catch our breath before moving on to the next section. We've got a ways to go before reaching another breezy flow. I don't want you to give up before we reach the end of these ocean caves. It's not about how quickly we arrive to the next terrain, but that we make it there.

Put On Trial

"To believe, or not to believe is the real question."
~A. S. E.

About a week went by, and I began feeling extremely nauseated. My appetite completely went away, and I started having these bad cramps, but my monthly flow hadn't come on. It was past its due date, so I began to worry. I waited for about a week, but still no cycle. I confided in Prawny about all that had happened and what I thought was going on with my body.

"Wow, Porsha, I'm so sorry. So, you think you're pregnant?" she asked.

"I don't know what to think. I just know I'm not feeling right," I said.

I was walking home from school one day when someone who knew Lamprey pulled over and asked me to get in the car. I did as she asked. She took me to a parking lot to talk.

"Porsha, I'm going to ask you something and do not even try to lie to me. Are you pregnant?" she asked. "I—" "Porsha, before you open your mouth, choose your words very carefully," she said, slowly blinking her eyes and shaking her head. "I'm not sure," I said. "You're not sure. What the h* does that mean?" she asked. "All I know is that my cycle hasn't come on," I said. "Did you and Lamprey have sex?" "Um, well... yeah, I mean not really," I said nervously. "Little girl, don't play with me," she said. "It's complicated. It wasn't really—" "Did he release inside of you?" she asked, cutting me off. "I...I don't know," I said. "You know, for someone who don't know nothin' you sho' runnin' yo mouth to people like you know somethin'," she snapped.

I started to hyperventilate, and it became difficult to catch my breath through my tears. She took a deep breath and handed me a Kleenex tissue. "Porsha, I'm not gonna lie. I've heard rumors about some claims you've made against Lamprey. I'm only gonna ask this once. Did he force you?" she asked. "Well, I said no, and he didn't stop," I answered. "At what point did you say 'no'?" "When he started trying to have sex," I replied. "Were you guys already having sex? Was he already inside you?" she asked. "No. I cried and screamed, and he wouldn't stop," I said.

She put her head back and rolled her eyes while taking a deep breath. "Porsha, you're a bright girl; very intelligent and wise far beyond your years. What did you think someone at that age wanted with someone as young as you?" she asked. "I thought he wanted a relationship like he told me. He knew I was a virgin, and he knew I was waiting for marriage," I said. "No, Porsha, *you* knew. You knew what he wanted, didn't you?" she asked. "Yes, but I believed him when he told me—" "I don't care what he told you. You have to think for yourself. Men will do what you allow them to do. If you lay it out on the table, you better believe they gon' eat. Now, I want you to understand something. Lamprey is going to continue his career path, whether you're pregnant or not. If you are, you gon be the one held back here raisin' it, you hear me?" she scolded. "Yes," I said. She pulled over to let me out of the car and walk the rest of the way home.

As I turned to walk away, she called out to me. "Porsha! One more thing. Shut yo' mouth and stop talkin' about it, ya hear?" she said. "Yes," I said.

I remember feeling even more broken than the night of the happening. That day was no doubt my most ridiculously failed suicide attempt. I drank a bottle of perfume! All that happened was I was burping up some pleasant-smelling fragrance for two weeks.

I was more withdrawn than ever in school and usually sat alone. One day, I decided I would take a seat at a table with a girl who was known to be a tough stud. She was heavyset and hilarious to speak with. She could light up the saddest rooms with laughter. When I sat down, I placed my lunch tray in front of me and my Bible on the right side of my tray. "Porsha, I got a question," she said. "Shoot." "Why, did you come and sit at my table?" she asked. "Oh, I'm sorry. If you wanna be alone, I can leave," I said. "No, it's not that. I'm just trying to figure out why you would hang with someone like me. You know you're talked about a lot here, and I wouldn't be surprised if you sitting with me starts rumors," she said. "Well, let 'em talk. I don't care, and you shouldn't either. All that matters is what God thinks of us, anyway," I said.

She resumed to eat her lunch, but I noticed when I lifted my head from my plate, she was playing with her food, wading her fork around. "You okay?" I asked. When she looked up, I was shocked to find tears in her eyes. "Porsha, you carry that bible around like it's your life. I see you around here and how you carry yourself. You're one of the realest people here, which is probably why you get hated on so much. But what I guess I'm struggling with is you a child of God, right?" she asked. "Yeah," I said. "Then why would you hang with someone like me, knowing how I am?" she asked.

She was referring to the fact that she dated girls. "Are you human?" I asked. "Yeah," she chuckled. "You get hungry?" I asked. "Smh, man yeah, what you getting' at?" she asked. "You and I are the same. That's what I'm getting' at. Why would you find it so weird for me to sit and have lunch with you just because of that?" I asked. "Well, 'cause most 'church folk' I know wouldn't even speak to me," she said. "Well, that' sad and pathetic, and what that really means is they aren't even real 'church folk.' They're just pretending to be," I said. "Well, I can't say I believe in God. He's let too much happen to me for me to just trust Him like you do," she said. "I can understand that, but don't think I trust Him all the time. I have my weak moments. He's just always pulled me back to Him when I lose my way. So, I don't give up on Him because He never gives up on me, even when bad things happen to make me turn my face from Him," I said.

"Would you, like, do a bible study or something with me if I asked you to?" she asked. "Girl, heck yeah," I said, smiling big. "You alright, La'Porsha," she said. "Thanks," I said.

This conversation was one of the lamps of my dark high school years. It reminded me that I wasn't the only one with questions and doubts and fears. It also reminded me to never judge a book by its cover. The girl had been so jolly and jokey all the time. I never knew she felt the way she did until she spoke to me, and I never thought I'd see someone like her cry over a topic like that. Although we never actually started a bible study, I'd remind her that I was waiting for her every time I saw her. She'd laugh and say she would come one day.

Looking back, I don't think she was actually ready to walk through the door of faith, but she just wanted to know she had an invitation if ever she did want to in the future.

You're doing great. Remember to pace yourself. We've got time. In fact, how about we listen to some music to help our energies balance? Hm, I'm thinking we should hear *Psalm 23* by People & Songs. Go ahead and take a listen while we keep swimming.

WILL AND ME...AND SHE

"Everyone must have at least one friend who serves them a daily dose of laughter for the heart."
~A. S. E.

A TALL, DARK, GOOFY fella we'll call Will began sitting with me and befriending me out of the blue. He said the same thing everyone always said about me being different and exciting. His humor was unmatched, and he was always making me laugh until I cried. I knew he crushed me, but I kept our relationship strictly platonic. After Lamprey, I wasn't interested in anyone the least bit.

Will and I hung out and walked to every class together. He was a senior. He would do kind things for me like make me Tweety Bird clip arts and carry my books wherever I was going. He had the biggest heart and really cared for me the way any true friend would.

Unfortunately, I became part of a love triangle I didn't even know existed. Will had an admirer that we'll call Betty. Betty was a heavy-set girl who was friends with just about every girl in school. She was head over heels about Will to the point of being a stalker. On Valentine's Day that year, she decided to present him with some singing black and red underwear shorts. He brought them straight to me.

"Porsha! Look!" he said, showing them to me. I cried, laughing at what he didn't find funny at all. "Aw, Will, give her a chance. You never know, you might like her," I said. "Porsha, don't play with me." "Well, you said you like thick girls," I said. He gave me the coldest glare and squinted his already slanted eyes. The look made me laugh even harder.

"There's only one way I'll wear these underwear," he said. "And what's that?" "I'll wear them if I'm with you," he said.

I laughed even harder. "I'd kick you out of my house if I ever saw you in those," I hackled. I spent the rest of the day teasing him about the briefs. That afternoon, while he was getting ready to walk me home from school, Betty approached us. "Hey, baby!" she said, smiling. "You like the gift?" she asked.

Will flashed me a look, and I shot him a 'you better be nice' one right back. "Uh, this was...nice. Thank you, but don't you think underwear is a little personal?" he asked. "Well, duh. That's the whole point! Boy, you so silly!" she said. It took every inch of my being to stand there with a somewhat straight face. "Well, um, see me and Porsha are kind of dating, so this is inappropriate," he said.

I choked on my spit and bucked my eyes at him as he slid his arm around my waist. "Betty, baby, he's all yours if you want him, believe me," I said. "Baby, why you actin' like that. Just tell her the truth so she'll know, baby. Ain't no reason to be shy," he said with a corny lying smile. "How about *you* tell her the truth," I said. "I. Just. Did," he said, motioning for me to go along. "I gotta get home so, Betty, it was nice meeting you," I said. "I'm walking her there, so I gotta go, but again, thank you so much. Just, out of respect for my girlfriend, can we not... do this anymore? Thanks. Bye," he said.

I turned around in disbelief of what he was doing and felt horrible when I saw the angry look on Betty's face. She had been known for chasing him long before I'd arrived in McComb. "I can't believe you did that! What the heck is wrong with you? Now you gonna have her hating me!" I said. "Well, better her hating on you than trying to love on me!" he said. We laughed all the way home.

Will had been allowed to hang out with me since my mother had met him and liked him very much. She would even convince me to give him a chance and try to date him. But Will became my very best friend, and I didn't want to lose that over something stupid...like sex. Will was respectful, but I only knew him as a friend. I didn't know him as a boyfriend and didn't really want to find out what that meant or what that would entail. Things were perfect just the way they were.

Will and I had many adventures together, and many exciting moments arose during our friendship. I remember a time my mother decided she wanted to take Will and I out to eat and was planning to pick us up during the school lunch hour. Will and I had gone through the lunch line and taken our seats at an empty table. "Will, we're not eating our food today, okay?" I said. "Um, Porsha, I'm not even gonna try and figure out that statement," he said. "Will, I can't tell you why. It's a surprise. Just don't eat your food," I said.

Will flashed me a look like 'you crazy' and went to start eating his food, so I did something despicable. I spit in his food. Will was so upset, he got up without saying a word and walked outside. I followed him and found him propped up by the courtyard tree.

"Will! Hey, don't be mad. I have a surprise for you that I can't say, but it was important for you not to eat," I said. "Porsha, what the heck could you have for me that would possibly make up for what you just did. Tell me now, or our friendship is over," he said.

I laughed because I knew although he was dead serious and wanted to mean what he said, he could never walk away from our friendship. It was easy to surprise Will in this way because I was always turning down his quirky advances, and he had no idea that my strict mother would agree to something like taking us both out to eat.

My mother didn't initially plan it as a date or anything. She just told me she wanted to take me out and that I could invite one friend. I chose Will, knowing it would be the closest thing to him being on a date with me as he would get.

"Will, my mom is picking us up in a minute and taking us somewhere," I said. "If the *somewhere* ain't food, then Porsha, I ain't tryin' to—" he paused with his mouth open, and the expression on his face turned cheeky. "Hold on, did you just say your mom is taking *us*, as in me and you, somewhere?" he asked. "Yep," I said, smiling. "Porsha, since when is your mom okay with taking me and you somewhere together?"

he asked. "Since she likes you. She wanted to take me out and asked me who I wanted to bring. I chose you," I said. "Porsha, don't be playing with me." "I'm not! I'm serious!" I laughed. "I'm speechless...I feel so special right now," he said.

"That's why you couldn't eat anything," I said, feeling validated about what I'd done. "Oh, no, no. Let's talk about this. I'm still mad at you. Porsha, I'm a big boy, and I can eat. School lunch is about the only real food I get. My mama don't be cookin' like that! I was near 'bout suicidal. You had me thinking the next scrap of food wasn't coming for another four hours when school lets out," he fussed. All I could do was laugh. "Okay, how can I make it up to you? I'm sorry for spitting in your food," I said. "Na, I don't believe you." I smirked and beckoned for him to lean down as if I was about to whisper something in his ear and kissed him on the cheek. "I'll take that. You're forgiven," he said. "I would have been forgiven anyway," I said. "Yeah, you're right. But I had to milk it," he said, smiling. "Mmhm," I smirked.

There was another instance I wanted to hang out with Will at the apartment after school. Will did not want to come and refused me for a long time. He had mad respect for my mother and didn't want to be 'that guy,' but I was persistent, so he eventually folded. I didn't want my sister feeling like a third wheel, so I had her invite a guy she liked to come and hang with us. I liked the guy she crushed on and always referred to him as my future little brother in law.

We had so much fun together that day until my mother came home during her lunch break. Ree's friend was able to jump out of the side window, but Will struggled since he was so tall. We had no time for him to find a way to fit through the window, so my sister and I stuffed him in the closet.

We ran to meet my mother in the living room area and sat with her at the dining room table. We were laughing and talking slightly louder than usual to mask any noise Will may have made from the closet. Will had called a friend and said, "Bruh, man, she got me trapped in the closet!" The phone call dropped due to bad reception, but then his friend decided to call him back. The phone started vibrating, and the sound was loud. "What's that noise?" my mother asked. I had to think quickly. If my sister and I pretended not to hear anything, my mother would have been persistent and sniffed out that we were up to something. "Hmm, I hear it too," I said with an inquisitive look on my face. "Let me go check and see if I left my radio on or something," I said.

I went to my room and opened my closet door and told Will to remain quiet and get off the phone. Then I laughed and left. "No, nothing was left on. I don't know what that was," I said. My sister was sitting there, amazed, and scared at how good I was at covering up. Finally, my mother left to return to work, and Will was able to come out of the closet. "Porsha, I love you. It's been fun, but I'm out," he said. He threw up the deuces sign and walked out of the front door.

My sister and I couldn't stop laughing at how shaken up he was, so we decided to walk outside and make things even worse for him. "Will, run! Ma just called, and she left something! She's headed back!" I shouted. I was bent over laughing. "Yeah, Will! If she catch you, you going to jail!" my sister yelled. I've never seen Will run so hard and fast before. With his dreads slinging in the wind, he looked like a tall, dark mop running from the dust he was kicking up.

My platonic efforts didn't stop Will from flirting in between jokes every now and then, but I didn't mind. I'd just let them roll off my shoulder and keep trucking. I was able to talk to him about any and everything, and he always knew what to do or say when I'd be struggling with my faith. He was adamant about me staying true to who I was and not letting unfavorable circumstances change me. Our friendship stayed strictly platonic until one very eventful JROTC trip during the winter of my 9th-grade year.

We were headed down to New Orleans for an exhibition drill competition. Our JROTC class was pretty close to one another. We all kind of had mutual respect. But there was this girl I'd never seen before. She was some kind of special guest on the trip. We'll call her Carmen.

Carmen was beautiful and free-spirited. She liked to laugh a lot and had one of the sweetest personalities I'd ever known.

There were rumors about Carmen spreading throughout the company, but I paid no mind to them. The girls decided they would personally request not to be roommates with her, and when someone did end up as her roommate, they would just sleep in a friend's room for the night. I automatically drew to her because of what my mother had always taught me; befriend those who are outcasted.

We ended up getting into a conversation about the rumors flying around. "Why is everybody acting shady towards you?" I asked. "Girl, because I'm bi," she said. "What's bi?" I asked. "I like girls and boys," she explained. "Oh, I see. Well still, that's no reason to be ignorant," I said. "People gonna say what they say. At the end of the day, I just ignore them," she said.

I was intrigued by the weird terminology she'd just used to describe herself. I'd never heard of anything like that before. "So, what are all the other terms?" I asked. "Huh?" she asked. "I mean, you said you were bi. What are the other names for people like you?" I asked. "Girl, there's a whole bunch of names. Let's see, you've got bisexual, which means you like girls and boys; not at the same time, just whoever loves you at the time, you love them. Then, you've got studs and fems. Studs are girls that dress like boys, and fems are like the 'girl' of the relationship," she explained. "Okay...so what are you, a fem?" I asked. "Well, I ain't no stud!" she laughed.

"What are you?" she asked. "Huh?" I asked. "What are you? A fem?" she asked. "Oh, no, I'm not like that. I don't date girls," I answered. "Really? Then, why you asking all these questions?" she asked, smiling big. "Well, two reasons. I didn't want you to think I felt awkward talking to you, and I was curious about the different names when you said you were bi. I've never heard that word before; not used like that," I answered. "Oh, okay. I thought you were a little curious or something," she said. "No, been there, done that. Not my thing," I said. "Oh really? You?" she asked. "It's not something I'm proud of or wanna talk about," I said.

"Okay, so what made you join JROTC?" she asked. "I don't even know, really. It was just better than band and P.E." "I feel ya," she laughed. Shortly afterward, we arrived at the mall in New Orleans, and since it was the winter season, the mall was lit up so beautifully, it felt like a Winter Wonderland.

We all anxiously departed from the bus to get in as much shopping as we could. We all split into cliques, and since Carmen and I had become acquainted, she decided to stick with Nar and me. Nar had made his admiration of me known, but I'd been uninterested because of the past event. He said he was willing to wait until I was ready to try and date again, and agreed to us being just friends.

There was a store with a whole bunch of things I wasn't used to seeing. They were pretty vulgar, but they excited Carmen. "Well, I'll let you have fun in there while I go someone else," I told her. "Oh, you are such a square. We have to get you out of that shell, girl!" she said. "I just have standards of faith, that's all," I said. "Blah, blah, blah. Well come on then, since you're uncomfortable," she teased. We chuckled and left to a store with unlimited cute sleepwear.

I stumbled across these fuzzy bunny shorts I liked and wanted to try them on. I got a stall and went in with my shorts. Carmen followed me inside, while Nar sat right there in front of the door, waiting for me. Honestly, the thought did flash through my mind that maybe she shouldn't have been in there, but I didn't want to treat her any differently than a normal friend girl of mine, so I didn't say anything. I wasn't trying to make her feel like her way bothered me. Since the other girls had made such a big deal about her, I wanted her to feel comfortable with me.

I tried on the shorts and looked in the mirror. "Cute! Girl, you should definitely get those!" she said. "I don't know, I don't think they fit right. See? When I pull them down to cover everything, they're too low," I said. She started laughing so hard. "What?" I asked. "That's because you're wearing them wrong, girl! Do you know what boy-shorts are?" she asked. "Uh, no." "Pull them back up," she said. "I can't 'cause then they don't cover everything," I complained. "They're supposed to fit like that! Wow, you are so green!" she said. "You and these terms! I'm guessing that means I'm dumb?" I asked chuckling. "Only when it comes to stuff like this," she said. "Well, I normally just sleep in a t-shirt and pants. All this fancy stuff isn't really what I do. I just thought I'd treat myself," I said. "Oh, okay. Well, you should get those. They're cute," she said. "Hey! I wanna see! Y'all talkin' too much," Nar shouted from outside the door.

"Is that your boyfriend?" she whispered. "No, but he likes me," I said. "Do you like him?" she asked. "He's nice. I'm just not into dating anyone. I can't seem to be attracted to anyone. Just focusing on my books and being a nerd," I smirked. "Well, you got the nerd part down packed. You wanna open the door and let him see?" she asked. "Yeah, go ahead," I said.

She opened the door, and Nar's mouth dropped. "You are so beautiful," he said. "Aw, that's so sweet! Girl, he really likes you!" she said, laughing. "Thanks, Nar," I said with an embarrassed smile. "You say beautiful, I say sexy! Baby got back!" Carmen said, snapping her fingers. Nar and I laughed. "Yeah, she's that too," he said. "Wow, I can't stop smiling. My cheeks are hurting," he said. "Girl, let's get you out of these shorts before his face locks up," Carmen said. We all laughed, and I changed back into my regular clothes.

When I headed for the check-out counter, I began looking for my money, but couldn't find it. Turns out, I had accidentally left my money on the bus. I put the shorts back and walked out of the store. Carmen followed, but Nar lagged behind. When I noticed he wasn't with us, I decided to sit on a bench and wait for him.

Nar came out of the store with a bag in his hand and approached me. He had bought the fuzzy boy shorts! "Nar, you shouldn't have done that! I'll pay you back soon as we get on the bus, deal?" I asked. "Na, Merry Christmas," he said. The three of us continued going into different stores and shopping until it was finally time to head back to the bus. "Hey, Porsha. Can I talk to you in private real quick?" Nar asked. "Sure, what's up?"

Nar waited for Carmen to walk on ahead closer to the bus. "I think Carmen likes you." "Oh, come on, Nar. I thought you were better than the other ignorant kids on this trip. Just because she's that way doesn't mean she's thirsty for every girl she hangs out with. She can't just like hanging out with me?" I asked. "Porsha, I'm a dude, and I can pick up on certain things. When you left the store, she begged me to buy those shorts for you," he said. "Okay, and what? That's supposed to mean something?" I asked. "Porsha, she wanted me to buy those shorts for *her* to enjoy you in them...alone," he said. "You're being ridiculous. She saw how much I wanted those shorts and asked you to do me a favor. Period," I said. "Porsha, I've been patiently waiting for you to get back into the swing of dating. Promise me you won't let her turn you out. Promise?" he asked. "Turn me out? Like, make me like her?" I asked. "Yes." "Nar, I have my own mind. I'm not naïve or gullible." "Porsha, you're oblivious when it comes to catching signals. I can name about five guys off the top of my head that you don't even know like you, and they flirt with you every day," he said. "I promise I won't get turned out. Now, can we drop this annoying conversation?" I asked. "Okay, Porsha."

We went back to the bus, and I'd been so tired from walking the mall that I fell asleep. When I woke up, we were at the hotel. The entire company decided we were gonna all meet Orca in her room so that she could tell us the movie 'Friday.' The idea came when someone was talking about the film, and I told them I had never seen it before. Of course, everyone was shocked, and Orca said she would tell me the movie tonight.

Orca was so good at telling the movie and acting out the parts, I was able to know what actors were in the film without ever viewing the movie! She was a beast and had everyone cracked up. After our 'movie telling' time with Orca, we all dispersed to our rooms for the night. "Porsha, you know you welcome to come and stay with Terri and me, right?" she asked. "I know, but I'm good," I said. "You sure, 'cause ole girl is...you know..." "Orca, I don't think y'all are fair to her. She's not gonna attack you or something. She's capable of being friendly," I said. "Yeah, I know. That's the point. Look, all I'm saying is that she got a reputation for turning people out," she said. "Yeah, and I got many reputations at this school that ain't true. I'll be fine," I said. "Alright, goodnight, sis," she said. "Goodnight."

I couldn't wait to get back to my room. I was exhausted. I allowed Carmen to take her shower first because I wanted to take my time. When I came out of the shower, Carmen was wrapped in a towel, laying on her bed. "If this makes you uneasy, I can get dressed," she said. "Girl, be you. Be comfortable. You ain't got nothin' I ain't seen before."

She sat on her bed, and I sat on mine, and we talked for a long moment about life and people and family. "I like talking to you, Porsha," she said. "Yeah, I get that a lot. I like talking to you, too," I chuckled. "You wanna see something I bought?" she asked. "Sure."

She pulled out a bag that had a finger grip slip in it. It was in the shape of a bunny. It looked like something I had seen in that store that I didn't like. "Girl, why you go and buy something like that?" I asked. "I don't know, I thought it was cute," she said. "Mmhm," I mumbled.

We decided to watch a movie on my computer together. In a moment, Carmen just abruptly paused the video and looked at me, smiling. "What?" I said. She leaned over and kissed me. I was shocked because, at this time, I'd been feeling ugly and sexually checked out. I had no idea she liked me, even though I was adamantly warned! She was pretty and seemed to have been popular at her old school. Why would she be attracted to a straight nerd like me?

"So, Nar was right? You like me?" I asked. "I mean, I know you don't go that way, but you're cute and fun to be around." "Hmm, well, I really don't know what to say. I wasn't expecting that," I said. "You don't have to say anything." She kissed me again, and I didn't stop her. Before long, we were full-on intimate with one another.

The phone rang, but I ignored it. Then, it kept ringing like three times back to back. "Hello?" I answered. "Hey, what you doing?" It was Nar. It was almost like he sensed something was going on. "Uh, nothing just laying here," I said. "Can I come to see you?" he asked. "Um, I don't think Carmen would...I mean, she's trying to sleep," I lied.

Carmen didn't stop what she was doing and laughed at everything I said. "I'm headed there anyway. See you in a minute," he said. "Um, it looks like we have to stop. He's coming," I said. "Girl, let him stand at the door and knock. You told him not to come," she said. "I know, but that would just make things worse," I said.

We got up and rushed to clean ourselves off. When Nar knocked, we took a minute to answer but eventually did. "Porsha, what's going on?" he asked. "What are you talking about now, Nar?" I asked. "It's like I'm connected to you. I can feel it. Something happened. What did you do?" he asked, turning to face Carmen. "Whoa, stop Nar. Don't talk to her like that. She didn't do anything, and neither did I. Now, can you drop this and stop being paranoid? What I'm trying to understand is, why are you so concerned with me when we're not even together?" I asked. "' Cause I care about you, Porsha. I don't want you taken advantage of," he said. "Carmen's not a dude. She doesn't even have anything to take advantage of me with!" I laughed. "Go to bed, Nar. Please. I'm fine," I said. "Porsha, look me in my eyes and promise me nothing happened." "I promise," I said.

When he finally left, Carmen laughed. "That boy more than likes you, girl. I think he's in love," she said. "He don't even know what that is," I said. "So, do you want to finish what we started?" she asked. "Carmen, I think you're beautiful, but I'm not like that. What just happened felt good, but it was wrong. And my heart's not in it. I'm not attracted to anything or anybody. That's why I can't even give Nar the time of day. I don't want to use you or anything. I roomed with you to show you real friendship, not to get anything from you," I said. "You don't have to be bi to be curious," she said. "I'm not curious. I know about it already. My faith is more important to me. Heck, I have to repent for what just happened," I said. "Why would you be sorry for something you enjoyed?" she asked. "Everything that feels good ain't always right. You caught me off guard with the first kiss, and I guess because of how I've been feeling about myself lately, I didn't have a strong enough will to want to stop at that moment. But maybe Nar's urgency to contact me at the very moment we started was God trying to keep me from making a huge mistake in hurting you and me both," I said. "Nothing about that hurt me," she said. "So, you're okay with being used? You're okay with someone being with you even if they're heart's not in it?" I asked. "I mean, it is what it is," she said. "Well, it doesn't have to be. God and I both think you're worth more than that," I said. "Goodnight, Carmen." "Goodnight, Porsha," she said, smirking and tucking herself into bed. "You're still my boo," she said. "Lord, help us!" I said. We both laughed and went to sleep.

The next morning was literally all hell to pay. Nar had confided in some other guy about his heartbreaking suspicions, and the guy spread talk about Carmen and me being with each other the night before. Though from our brief encounter, it was true, no one else knew but us. I had all kinds of boys from the company coming up to me, asking me if I 'got down like that,' suggesting threesomes and all sorts of other demeaning things. I was pissed.

I can't count how many inquiries I got that day, but every time someone came up to me and asked me about the situation, I denied everything. My instructor even asked me if everything was okay, and I told him I was fine. About midday, someone who was cool with Carmen came to me and told me Carmen had been hurt and crying.

"Porsha, tell me the truth, did y'all do something?" she asked. "No," I answered. "Don't lie," she said. "Yea, but whose business is it? I'm tired of being asked that, and why is it my fault she's crying?" I asked. "Because you're denying the truth, and she feels like you're ashamed of her or something." "Look, even if she was a straight dude, I don't kiss and tell. And honestly, it didn't even last long enough to be anything to discuss or talk about. We started something, then stopped because Nar came to visit me. End of story," I said. "Well, I get where you coming from, but maybe you should just not say anything instead of just lying and denying everything." "Alright, fine. I'll keep my mouth shut," I said.

"Now, this ain't got nothing to do with the rumors, but I want to personally know. Are you bi?" "No." "Are you at least curious?" she asked. "No! I'm a straight weird nerd with problems," I said, laughing. She laughed with me. "I don't know what I am. I do know that I'm not attracted to girls, but I'm not attracted to guys either. I feel like if push came to shove, I could tolerate girls better than I could guys, but I still don't find them desirable. At least they don't make me wanna puke like the thought of being with a guy does. I mean, I hate every inch of their disgusting bodies. That's one design by God I rebuke on a daily!" I said. "Wow, you're crazy!" she said. "So I'm told," I said. "Well, you'll figure it out one day. Meanwhile, just ignore the nosey people, and you may want to check on Carmen," she said. "I will."

I found Carmen and tried to approach her, but she held out her hand and said she didn't want to talk to me. "She'll come around," her friend said. "Honestly, I don't care if she doesn't. I was clear about my intentions the entire time. She was the one scheming, so if she's hurt, she hurt herself," I said. "Wow, you know, to hate dudes so much, you sure do sound like one," Carmen said. The comment stung, but my face remained unphased. "Take care, Carmen," I said, walking away.

The ride home was lonely and quiet for me. I just lost myself in the music of my new mp3 player. When we got off the bus, I got my bags, and my mother was waiting there to pick me up. She asked me all about the trip, and I expressed how well we'd done in our competition and how much fun I had.

The next day was eventful. Nar was upset with me because he didn't believe I hadn't been intimate with Carmen. Orca was bothered and didn't trust our friendship anymore. "Porsha, let me find out you like girls. Ima beat the h* out of you 'cause I done got dressed in front of you and everythang!" she said, while we were hanging our uniforms. "Orca, I can promise you I've never looked at you in that way," I assured her. "So how does it feel?" she asked. "How does what feel?" "How does it feel to have guys and girls after you at the same time?" she asked. "Orca, heck, I don't know. Feels like I need to stick to my first mind and be alone...forever," I said.

When I made it home that day, a guy was snooping around the house. He kept peeking through my windows. My mother and sister weren't there, and I thought it was Will playing tricks on me, especially since he called me that very moment. "I see you outside, Will. Why you peeking through the windows?" I asked. "Porsha, I'm at home," he said. "Will, stop playing I'm looking dead at you," I chuckled. "Porsha, whoever is outside, it's not me," he said.

I grew quiet. All I could do was watch the guy move from window to window like he was trying to see inside, but couldn't. "Porsha, I called to ask you something, and don't you dare lie to me! Did you let Carmen turn you out?" he asked. "What? No, it wasn't like that, and I'm tired of everybody saying that" I barked. "Well, tell me what it was like, then, Porsha! I'm so...I don't even know what to say right now. You're better than that, Porsha! What about your faith? What about the high standards you be around here holding for yourself? You just give all that up to be turned out by a girl you don't even know?" he asked. "Will, why are you so upset? It's not like we're together, and no. I didn't give up my faith. It was a moment that didn't even last long enough to talk about. Drop it!" I said. "No, you should have dropped it!" he said. "So what? We're not friends anymore?" I said. *Bang, Bang, Bang*!

It was the man banging on the front door like some addict. "Who is it?" I yelled. He wouldn't even answer me and kept banging on the door! "Porsha, what's going on? Who is that banging on your door like that?" he asked. "I don't know, Will! That's what I was trying to tell you! Some man is outside and keeps peeping through the windows. I think he may be a stalker or something! Maybe he thinks I'm someone else." I said. "Porsha, stay on the phone."

All I heard was heavy breathing, and within about five minutes, Will was in my front yard. I'm not sure if the man saw him coming down the street, but when Will got there, the man had fled from around the windows. I unlocked the door, and Will just stood there and looked at me. His eyes showed a deep hurt.

I couldn't stand there and face him for long, so I took my seat in the armchair and buried my face in my hands. "Porsha..." Will came and kneeled in front of me. He gently pulled my hands from my face and held them sandwiched between his own hands. "Porsha...look at me." I looked up and said, "What you want me to say, Will. It happened. It's over. Hate me, I don't care." "Porsha, I could never hate you. I just hate that I feel like *you* hate you. I know you. What's going on? Speak your heart," he said.

I began to cry. "I don't know, Will. I feel empty and lost like I'm floating from day to day with no one or nothing trying to ground me. I haven't prayed in weeks...I'm just...not here anymore. And no one can find me because I can't even find me. Since what happened with Lamprey, I can't get back to myself. I don't know who I am or what I am," I rambled in tears.

"Are you attracted to Carmen?" he asked. "No, I'm not, which is why I stopped things. I'm not trying to use anyone. She's a nice person, and I feel bad that I even let things go as far as they did." "Are you attracted to me?" he asked. "Will, you're my friend. No, I'm not attracted to anyone at all. I want nothing." He cupped my face in his hands and kissed me. His kiss brought tears to my eyes. I tried pulling back, but he gently encouraged me not to. "What did that feel like to you?" he asked. "Feels like you care about me," I said, smiling through my tears. He kissed me again and held me for a long time. "What does this feel like?" he whispered in my ear. "Feels like you might...love me," I said.

I realized that God had used Will to remind me that despite what had happened to me, I was still loved and cared about. I had mentally shut off any sensuality about myself to stay safe and protect myself from being mistreated. "I'm gonna leave now. I think you've got some praying to do. I want to give you space to think about things," he said. "Will, thank you," I said. "Porsha, I'm rooting for you. You're my spiritual rock!

You can't lose faith. Your faith makes me stronger and inspires me to be better. I'll be a phone call away if you need me," he said. Then he left.

I thought about what Will had said to me. I couldn't understand why things had gotten so confusing for me. Ever since Lamprey, I felt like I was hanging on to my faith by a finger, but my heart wasn't there. No matter how hard I tried, I couldn't get back to my sacred space. My spirit had been broken. I was an empty shell trying to hold on to substance that was no longer there. A brief violent determination flashed across my mind that I would diligently start healing and getting back to being about my Heavenly Father's business.

My heart softened for a millisecond, but then grew harder and colder than it was before. I mentally divorced my faith and decided if God wanted me, He'd have to catch me.

AWOL

"Either you run because you can't hide, or you hide because you can't run."
~A. S. E.

"OKAY, PORSHA. YOU'VE been in the slumps way too long. It's time for you to open up again and date. Look around, pick out a cute guy, and I'll go talk to him for you," Prawny said. "Girl, ain't nobody cute here but me. Too bad I can't be with myself," I said. "Wow, Porsha... your head done grew ten sizes over the last couple of weeks," Prawny said. "No, I've just stopped letting my brain lay dormant. Ain't nobody here worth my energy," I said.

Just then, a light-skinned boy with glasses and a goofy forward-leaning walk approached me. "Um, hi," he said. "What do you want?" I asked. "Um, wow, okay. I wanted to ask you—" "Not interested. Move, I've got to get to class," I snapped. "My teacher sent me to ask you about singing in the talent show," he spat out faster than he could catch his breath. "What talent show?" I asked. "She wanted you to consider representing the 9th-grade class at the talent show," he said. "Tell her I'll think about it. I'm not really a fan of singing in front of people right now. I'll let her know," I said. "Okay, bye," he said. "Yeah," I said, walking away.

I eventually agreed to do it and won second place. I felt it was fair because the senior class had a hype presentation that had me rocking hard backstage. It was pretty fun, but I wasn't up for doing it again. I preferred being in the background during this time.

I seemed to lose genuine interest in all my classes, except for JROTC. I don't know if it was because of all the physically demanding exercises or what, but it was the one class I felt some sort of stress relief from. I didn't really find myself thinking about much of my personal problems in that class. I never had the time to. If I wasn't focused on passing my PT test, then I was focused on learning cadences and commands.

The JROTC exhibition drill team worked fervently to prepare for upcoming meets and Sgt. Major Megalodon trusted me to be a platoon leader. I worked extremely hard to perfect my assignment and strived to be the best. I was extremely disciplined and competitive. It was around this time that I started to feel like a sexual nomad. I deemed I no longer had a feminine or masculine sense about myself. I was neither he nor she, but an 'it' or a thing in my mind.

Halloween came around, and my sister and I were allowed to go out with a friend of ours to the town's haunted house. It was pretty scary but more so funny. We had a blast but was not expecting to come home to what we did.

My dad had come to visit us, and since we weren't there, he had visited with my mother. "Hey!" we said, walking up to him standing outside by his vehicle. "Uh, wow. What happened to you?" we asked. My dad was missing a whole piece of face, literally. It looked reattached but was still more detached. "Ya mama and I got into it," he said. "Okay... but what happened, though?" I asked. "Ya mama clunked my face with a high heel shoe," he said.

My sister and I burst into hard laughter! We could not believe what my dad had just said. Every time I tried to picture it, my body ached with laughter. I know that sounds mean, but we were immune to things like that. "What the heck did you do, man? Dang!" I said. "It's fine, don't worry about it. I'm getting ready to head back home. I came here to see y'all, anyway. I tried to give ya mama $400 for anything she might need, but she doesn't want it," he said. "We'll take it!" we both said, laughing.

My dad gave us two hundred dollars apiece and told us to go and shop for some new school outfits with it. "Why it's all shiny and stuff?" I asked, examining my dad's face. "I was able to have it glued back on at the hospital," he said. "Look, man, why don't you just stop coming. If she don't want you here, why you keep showin' up? Do you want the rest of yo face?" I asked. My sister burst into laughter. My dad just stood there lookin' all hurt and teary-eyed, so we forced ourselves to compose our tickle boxes and tried to reach way, way, way deep down inside to empathize with him. "Alright y'all, I'm gone. Be good. I'll be talkin' with y'all," he said, bidding his goodbyes.

We stood there to watch him drive away and then rushed inside to see our mother. "Ma! What happened?" I asked. She started crying, and our tickled boxes were momentarily killed. "Aw, Ma, don't cry. What he do?" I asked. My sister and I both held her until she was ready to talk. "He and I started arguing about y'all, and he started tryin' to act all aggressive with me. Since things were getting heated, I asked him to leave, but he had the nerve to tell me he wasn't going nowhere. I started trying to push him out of the door, and he grabbed me and called himself pinning me down. I was like, 'really negro, in *my* house!'" she said.

"So then, you dug a chunk of his face out with a high heel shoe?" I asked. My sister and I couldn't hold back the laughs, and my mother tried not to join us, but eventually laughed at us laughing. "Y'all are silly. It's not funny, it's sad. How he gonna come here and think he can run me in *my* house?" "I don't know, Ma, but I bet he won't think that no more," I screamed, and started hackling with my sister once again.

As I'm reflecting on this time of my life, I'm utterly bothered at how desensitized my sister and I were about a situation like that. I want to take the time out to say that although I do believe that some monsters are born, others are made. Let me explain.

There are children I've seen who have the exact evil characteristics of a parent or relative they've never even met. My ex-husband was one of them. But then, there are those who begin innocent and are only allowed to stay that way for a moment before the toxicities of their parents or guardians start to settle into their blood, creating a creature most regret making.

There are many instances where I was proudly evil against my dad, and I'm not at all proud of that today. I could try to justify it by saying he was a monster first, but it wouldn't be the full truth. He was a lost soul and a vessel for the enemy. If only I'd had the wisdom and Godly knowledge to be the life jacket he needed back then. Instead, all I could do was watch him struggle to keep his head above water...and laugh... laugh to keep from crying about the fact that the other half of who I was, was a dead man walking.

Cover Up

"Pay attention to the reason behind what your child does. Things are always deeper than the surface."
~A. S. E.

My sister and I took the money my dad had given us and went shopping for ourselves. My mother allowed us to split up in the store and meet back up at the cash register. We both went in different lines and were extremely excited to model the clothes we'd picked out for our mother.

My sister dressed in her hip teen clothing and had bought just about every outfit we'd seen the popular kids at school wearing. Her clothes were a little flashy and very colorful. My mother loved everything my sister picked out and told her that she'd done a remarkable job clothes- shopping.

When I modeled my clothes for my mother, she was shocked and appalled. "Porsha, what is that you got on, girl?" she asked. I had bought about three 'teacher' sets from the store. The pants were elastic around the waist and stretched as far as you wanted them to. The length stopped right at the ankle. All the pants had a matching blouse with a sweater attached to it.

"I like it. It makes me look like a teacher or something," I bragged. "Girl, you look like a grandma in those clothes, baby. You're young and beautiful! You should be dressing like your peers. Baby, mommy wouldn't even wear what you picked out," she said.

My feelings were hurt, but I just laughed her and my sister's taunting off. "Porsha, no ma'am. I'm taking you back to the store, and we're finding you some clothes fit for a fourteen-year-old high schooler," my mother said. She did just that. We went back to the store, returned all the outfits I'd picked out, and went on a shopping spree. I hated to depart from my picks, but my mother begged me to trust her.

She picked out Baby Phat shoes and bubble jackets and crop top tracksuits; all the latest fashion of teen girls that I really couldn't stand. What she didn't realize and could never have guessed was that I purposely picked those clothes out to shield myself from looking appealing to anyone. Those clothes made me feel protected. No one liked a square, and that's exactly what I looked like. The clothes she picked for me were bound to draw in a bunch of haters, and they did.

When I returned to school, everyone was saying how I'd amped my game up and that I got my groove back. Guys were shouting, "I see you, La'Porsha!" Even my best friend, Will, said, "Um, wow. You look amazing! What's the occasion? You left a nerd and came back dressed like a teen pop star or something."

I found myself subconsciously trying to match my personality with the clothes that my mother picked out for me, but I couldn't. The closest things we bought to my character were some dark denim blue jean bell bottoms with some black high heeled ankle boots and a black long-sleeved collared button-down shirt.

My mother was only trying to lift my self-esteem and put me in clothing that spoke 'confidence'. I'm sure if she had known my reasons behind the clothes I preferred, she would have been more accepting of them.

As I went on through the school week, I reflected back on my dad's incident with my mom and couldn't help but feel like maybe that fight was the very thing both of my parents needed to realize how toxic they were to one another. I was almost glad it happened the way it did. Surely now, my mother would stop allowing my dad to keep wiggling his way back into our lives.

Anyway, my thoughts couldn't have been more wrong. During drill practice one afternoon, my mother approached Sgt. Major Megalodon and asked me to be excused. "Ya Dad's house on fire, we gotta go," she said, rushing back to the car. We drove all the way to that yellow house on Ayo St. and sure enough, it had burned to the ground! My dad finally got his fame and [mis]fortune on the front page and in the news.

As I, my mother, my sister, my dad, and several officials stood there watching the firemen spray the house, all I could think was '*Grandma Stella warned you.*' As hard as I tried to feel some kind of sadness or sentimental sympathy for the burning house, I couldn't. All the dark swaying spirits I'd seen, all the evil sexual demons that had been lurking in all its rooms, and all the vicious attacks that had been assigned to my family made it impossible to even sigh a breath of sadness.

Instead, I stood there and watched it burn...with a smile on my face. '*Well, God...it's about time,*' I thought. An organization was able to put my dad up for the week until he figured out something else to do. We left after standing there with him for a couple hours and returned to McComb.

A couple weeks later, my mother broke the terrible news to my sister and me with my dad on speaker over the phone. "Ya dad is going to come and move in with us," she said. Angry tears welled my eyes. Why was she doing this again?! She took a chunk of his face off for being a jerk, and now, because his house burned down, she thinks it's some sort of sign from God for them to get back together?

I was beyond hurt and frustrated. I was silent and said nothing. "What they doing?" my dad asked on the phone. "Ree is smiling, and Porsha is crying. She's pretty upset," my mother said. "Baby, tell me what you feeling. Speak your mind," my dad said sympathetically. I didn't want his sympathy. "We don't get along. Things will get worse with you here. I don't want you moving with us," I said. "Baby, I don't think it's a coincidence the house burned down. I didn't belong there," he said. '*I know...you belonged on shishkibob fried in the fires of hell,*' I thought.

"Don't worry, baby. It won't be easy, but we'll be alright," he tried to reassure me. "Baby, I think that it's best for the whole family if your dad and I give it another shot," my mother said. "We don't need him!" I said. "Porsha, you around here misbehaving and sneaking people over...I mean, I need help! He's your dad; he's supposed to be helping me with y'all," she exclaimed.

She was referring to me getting caught sneaking two friends in the house while she was at work. There was a girl and a boy. The girl was such a goody-two-shoes, and the boy panned out to be one of my good friends. We were just hanging out and having fun. We ate, watched movies, and laughed and talked.

Then, my friend guy and I went to the back bedroom. He was struggling with sexuality and wanted to see if we could try to do something. Nothing happened, and we ended up just lying there and laughing and talking. Although he and I claimed to be an item, he admitted to me later that he was homosexual. Then, we heard my mother come home surprisingly early. We jumped up, and I came running out of the bedroom in my bra and some long pants. My little sister had taken the boy and hid him in our room. First, he hid under the bed and then in the closet.

My mother didn't know about the friend boy and had only seen the girl, so she assumed I was 'involved' with my friend. She called my dad on the phone and said, "Duke, I've caught your daughter together with some girl in my house!" "Ma, that's not true!" She slapped me. "Don't you raise your voice at me!" she screamed. "You hit me again, I'm calling the police," I said. "Call the police, Porsha!" she said. And I did. When the police answered, she snatched the phone from me and told them I was calling to avoid getting in trouble. They assured her that they understood and told her to give them a call back if she needed further assistance with anything.

After my friend girl left with her father, who came to pick her up, my mother questioned me about the shoe she saw on the floor. I kept lying about it, and my sister and I managed to keep the boy hidden for hours until my dad arrived from his hell hole once again to be the disciplinarian.

While he and my mother were screaming at me, we heard a thump coming from the back. "Porsha! Is somebody else here?" my mother asked. I lied, so my dad said, "You better speak now or forever hold your peace because I'm about to shoot!" He picked up the shotgun and walked towards the back. My sister and I both cried the boy's name out and told him to come out.

He came and sat beside me on the couch. He and I had a beautiful friendship, and since I wasn't allowed to have friends over, I decided I would hang with two of my favorite people from school that day. My parents called the police and his parents. Both he and I knew that my parents just wanted him to be humiliated, and we despised them for it.

When the police arrived, they were disrespecting my friend and laughing at him and teasing him because of his lack of masculinity. My dad joined in with the teasing and joked about being ready to shoot my friend. "Young lady, you should be ashamed of yourself! You don't care anything about him! You almost let your dad shoot him? Man, this is the girl you like? If I were you, I would get somebody better than that, man," the police officer said.

My dad just stood there and let the police down the both of us like we were not even human beings. How dare he? Didn't he and that dumb police officer know that children's actions are a significant reflection of the parents? I know many would disagree with that statement, but it's the truth.

"Well, do what you gotta do, man. You can whip her as long as you stay on her behind. And young lady, you better not call me trying to tell on your parents. I'm giving them permission to tear your behind up. In fact, I wish I could have the first licks," he said. "Hey, go ahead, man!" my dad said. "Yeah, go ahead since she think she grown," my mother said.

I stared at the police officer with a rage in my eye that could have killed. "What you staring at? You got something you wanna say to me?" he asked. In that moment, I could have made a statement that would have turned the laughs on my mother, my dad, and that smart-mouthed police officer, but I didn't. I kept silent. Because of my love for my mother, I took the insults and said nothing. "No," I answered. "Oh, okay. 'Cause I sho' was interested to hear what you possibly could have said to defend all this," he said.

"How about the fact that my dad isn't really a dad at all. In fact, he has some nerve, even showing up to discipline me."

That's what I wanted to say, and it lay eager on the tip of my tongue, but I held it back. I had done wrong, and unlike my dad, I was going to be bigger and better than he was by accepting and acknowledging my wrongs and dealing with the consequences...because I *was* grown.

I hadn't chosen to grow up before my time, but the fact was I no longer felt like a child or teenager. I'd witnessed grown folks stuff, I'd been in grown folks situations, I'd dealt with grown folks heartache and disappointment, and I'd even taken grown folks places in their times of weakness. So in my mind, I was grown...maybe not fully grown, but I definitely didn't feel like a child anymore.

Since that situation, my mother had been uneasy about raising us alone and didn't trust me to act responsibly, and so it had come to this. My dad was back in the family again.

Well, it sure didn't look like God was looking for me anymore. As far as I was concerned, he'd let yet another devil back into our lives.

When my dad arrived with his backpack and a few things from the burned house, he and all his belongings smelled horrible! '*So, this is what taking in a stray dog is like. No, it's worse than that, because at least strays come bearing the gift of genuine love.*' I thought.

Crowded

"Where two or more are gathered outside His name, run away!"
~A. S. E.

We were getting ready to be out for winter break in school, and I couldn't bear the thought of spending two weeks at home with my dad, so my mother agreed to go and let me stay with my older sister in Starkville.

My favorite cousin had been there attending college, so my sister allowed me to visit with her at the college first. I saw her for a little while, but she was so busy that our visit couldn't really last long. My sister couldn't come and pick me up from the college until she got off of work, so I told her I would hang around and just wait for her there.

I'd been on an adult friend website, and a married couple had come across my profile. They wanted to meet up with me for relations, and they lived in Starkville. I felt the same disgust towards sex, but I think I was looking for a rebellious escape from my current home circumstances. When I told them I had some free time to meet, they agreed to come and pick me up from the school. They arrived in an older-modeled car and told me to get in.

I used a nickname. A middle-aged Caucasian man was driving, and a middle-aged dark brown woman was sitting in the passenger's seat. I approached the car and told them, "I have to be honest. I'm not as old as my profile says. I'm only fourteen," I said. "It's alright, baby. We can teach you a few thangs. Get on in," the woman said. I got in the back of the car, and they drove me to a cheap hotel. When we went inside, the man asked me if I wanted to shower with him. I told him that I would prefer to wait on the bed with the woman.

His wife lit another cigarette. "So, have you ever done this before?" she asked me. "No, I've only had sex once," I said. "Wow, only once? Was it good?" she asked. "Not really," I said. "Well, don't worry. We'll be sure to be better than whoever it was," she said.

All of me started regretting being there, but I didn't think it would be a good idea to try and back out. The woman was smoking, and the man was in the shower, getting ready. When he came out of the shower, he dropped the towel that was around his waist and smiled. "Are you ready to be raped?" the woman asked me, smiling.

Terror struck my gut, but it was too late. The room became a demonic merry go round, and the married couple did what they pleased to me. The woman was who gave the man and me instructions. She had me do things to her while he did things to me. Then she had him do things to me while she did things to him. Eventually, she had the man have his way with me while she watched. When he was 'finished,' he wanted me to wait around for another round, but I told them someone would be looking for me soon, and that I needed to get back to the school. "Oh no, you're not going anywhere, sweetheart. I'm not done with you, and neither is he," he said, smiling and pointing to his privates. "Tim, she says she has to go. Hopefully, she'll keep in touch, and we can pick this back up at a later time, okay?" she asked.

He agreed, and they let me take a shower before heading back to the campus. When they dropped me off, they thanked me for a fantastic time and left. I sat on the sidewalk, waiting for my sister to arrive.

My mind involuntarily began playing back the hour I'd just spent with the couple. Tears began to flow from my eyes out of nowhere. I didn't think I was sad. I felt more numb than anything. I felt like I was finally operating the way I was designed to work. I no longer had to feel bad when receiving the wrong attention because it didn't register to me as faulty anymore. I no longer felt wrong about the wicked perversion of those who lusted after me because it wasn't me they wanted, but my body. Since I didn't like or want my body anymore, it was absolutely fine for them to treat it however they wanted to.

After about 15 minutes of sitting, my sister finally arrived. "Hey, girl! How was your visit?" she asked. "Interesting," I said. "Okay..." she said, looking confused. When I didn't say more, she said, "Okay...I guess we'll leave it there," she said.

My time visiting with my sister and my cousin was a nice escape from home for the most part, and I wasn't looking forward to it ending. It passed by so quickly that before I knew it, I was back in McComb... on the front line, ready to go to war once more.

Hm, do you smell that? Maybe it's just me. Let's keep going.

Oh Really?

"There's only one rule for playing with the devil, DON'T.
~A. S. E.

My dad and I argued almost every day from the time he moved in. The remainder of the school year was difficult, but I made it. My dad had bought us a fixer-upper house that had been burned. We spent the summer working as a family to make it livable and be settled in by the next school year. It was yellow…like the one that burned down on Ayo St.

"Why is every house we live in yellow?" I asked out of frustration. "Yellow is a happy color," my dad said. "Well, yellow stresses me out. Nothin' happy about that," I said. With much teamwork, sweat, and muscle ache, we managed to get our house ready in time for school.

My dad and I were still on very turbulent terms and hated each other's guts. My dislike for him grew more sinister with each passing day of the summer.

There was one day, I was being punished for something I'd done. I don't remember what I did, but I know my dad still had an attitude about it. While my mom was at work, he wanted to take my sister and me to Louisiana to rake the leaves of the property that had burned down as a punishment.

I was so upset about returning to that property. I voiced the fact that I didn't want to go, but my dad told me I didn't have a say in the matter. He asked me to do something, and I did it with a noticeable attitude. He grabbed me around my neck and pinned me to the shed door. "Little girl, lose the attitude, understand? I'm the adult around here, not you! I'm the head of this house, not you! You're gonna show me respect!" he screamed. "I'll show it when you earn it," I said. "Oh really? I'll show you how I'm gonna earn it," he said, snatching his belt from his waist.

In that moment, I started having one of my weak spells. I knelt to the ground, still showing determination to defy my dad but holding my gaze on his eyes. "Porsha, I don't have time for this. Get up and get in the truck. You're going to Louisiana." "Dad, I think she's really sick," my sister said. She went in the house and came back out with a cold towel. That did the trick and snapped me out of my weak spell.

"Good. Get in the truck," my dad barked. "I have to use the bathroom," I said. "Use it on yourself. Get in the truck. You done already wasted enough daylight today," he said. I went to get in the truck and tried letting my sister get in first so that she would be seated by my dad, and I would have the window seat. "Naw, you sit by me and let Ree have the window," he barked.

He was being vindictive and childish, but I decided that whatever game he thought he could play with me, I could play ten thousand times better. My mind turned wicked, and I did something my dad and sister never saw coming. Because my dad revoked my bathroom rights and forced me to sit beside him in the truck, I decided this was going to be the ride of his life.

We drove for about an hour before things started to get interesting. I silently watched both my dad and my sister crinkle their noses and sniff. Then they started frowning and looking around at each other. "What's that smell?" my dad said. "I don't know. You smell it too?" my sister said. "I been smellin' it for a while now, but it's getting stronger and stronger," my dad said. "Maybe it's coming from outside," my sister said. "Porsha, you smell that?" my sister asked. To them, it smelled horrible enough to gag them, but to me, it smelled like sweet revenge.

I looked at her with a sinister smile, said nothing, and turned back to focus on the road. "Porsha! Did you..." my sister started. I then looked at my dad and gave him the biggest devilish grin and turned back to focus on the road. "Girl! Porsha, did you...you didn't!" my dad scream.

I let out the witchiest laugh and said, "You told me to do it, so I was obedient." My sister held her mouth wide open in shock and covered it with her hand. "Girl! Porsha— yo— you didn't—" my dad spit out in between frowns and glances back and forth between my sister and me. My dad was speechless, just like I liked him to be. All he could do was look at my sister and me in disbelief, and all I could do was smile. I hadn't been able to bake him a pie, but I sure was able to make him *smell* my crap.

My dad pulled over to a store and allowed me to buy new clothes and clean myself up. He sent my sister to go in with me and make sure I didn't try anything else to avoid going to Louisiana.

My dad was never a person to believe that a place could be ruined by bad memories and experiences. Neither he nor my mother understood the mental detriment returning to those wretched grounds had on me. That was the last time I went there.

My dad told my mother about the incident when we returned to McComb, and she couldn't stop herself from laughing in disbelief of what I had done. "Girl, if I didn't birth my twin sister, I don't know what you are! She's the only other person I know crazy enough to do something like that! Wow!" she exclaimed.

I guess now you know what that smell was! Truly I tell you, anyone is capable of anything once evil rests in their minds and hearts. Moving along! Ooooo, another one of my favorite gardens lies just ahead! From colorful crystals to unique stones and lush grass beds, this place is probably the most beautiful paradise in this terrain.

Accidentally on Purpose

"The best feeling in the world is having fate reach out to you in the darkness and pull you out."
~A. S. E.

When my 10th grade year finally started, we were well settled into our new house. I reconnected with Orca and Nar, but my bestie Will had gone on to college, so I felt extremely lonely. We didn't keep in touch with one another because I still wasn't allowed to talk to guys on the phone.

This was my second year being in fashion design vocational school and I ended up being befriended by a fashionista we'll call Violet. Violet had the biggest dreamiest eyes and the widest smile you'd ever see. She wore braces and retainers most of our friendship. She'd approached me one day asking me why I always dressed like I didn't care. I told her it was because I didn't want the attention and didn't want to be like every other girl at the school. "I think it's because you just don't know how to dress," she said, laughing. I liked her straightforwardness. "Okay, maybe that's got a little something to do with it, too."

Violet and I became inseparable. We took every class but one together, and I was always making her laugh just by being the off weird girl I was. Violet had a gigantic crush on a boy in one of our classes. We'll call him Pilch. Pilch was skinny and nerdy, and I had no idea why in the world she would be attracted to him, but she was head over heels about him. No matter how many times she would ask him out, he would turn her down because he was utterly faithful to none other than Orca, the school playa.

Befriending both Orca and Violet proved to be a bit tricky because neither one of them appeared to like each other. Violet didn't like Orca because she was the enemy that had Pilch's heart, and Orca didn't like Violet because she thought she was whiny and extra.

Orca and I had remained friends through the summer, though not as close as we were the previous year. Our friendship had gone downhill after she and Nar accused me of trying to link up with a boy she liked. They literally told me that they were taking a break from being my friend and asked me to leave 'their' table. Since then, we'd kind of made up, but once scarred that deeply by people I considered friends, I could never really bounce back. So, Orca and I were cool, but not really close.

We were, however, close enough for me to approach her about Pilch. "Hey, are you and Pilch actually together?" I asked. "Girl, Porsha. Now you know how I roll. He cute and sweet and everything, but do you really see me with somebody like that?" she asked. "Well, no. That's why I thought I'd ask. Violet thinks that—" "Porsha, don't bring that hoe's name up to me," she warned. "Girl, listen. I'm trying to fix this 'cause it's childish and ridiculous. For some reason, Pilch seems to think y'all are in a relationship and he's been telling everyone that you're his girlfriend. Now, if that's not the case, do you really want him spreading that and messing up whatever else you got with whoever else? He also uses that as the reason he won't give Violet a chance," I said.

"Hm, this Violet done gone and made you soft. Since when you play matchmaker?" she asked. "Orca, I don't play anything. I'm not into games, I'm into truth. I don't like seeing people get hurt and from how loyal Pilch is to you, it looks like it's headed that way. It's better to go ahead and squash this, because once you hurt a dude, he decides not to be a good guy anymore and goes hurting other girls trying to retaliate against the way you made him feel," I explained. "Dang, Porsha. See, that's why we gotta be friends from a distance. You always gettin' deep," she said. "What can I say, wading in the *shallows* ain't really my thang," I shaded.

She cut me an under-eyed look and then smirked. "Alright, Porsha, fine. I ain't got no problem with talkin' to him this afternoon. Dang, I can't believe this dude still claiming me after a whole summer passed without us talking," she said. "You've never had a loyal dude before, huh?" I asked. "Not really!" she laughed. "Ever wanted to try and be in a real relationship?" I asked. "Porsha, go on with that. Do *you* want a real relationship?" she asked. "I mean—" "Oh, I see. Ole yellow done got you thinking about love and fairytales, huh?" she asked. She was referring to Pilch's best friend, Liam. She'd caught me staring at him longer than usual a couple times. "Anything's possible, that's all I'm saying," I said. Orca waved her hand and left the conversation, annoyed at even the thought of being with one guy.

I reported to Violet what Orca had told me about the supposed relationship between her and Pilch. Violet began crying her eyes out. "Porsha, I just don't understand! Why doesn't he like me? He's always telling me how his heart belongs to Orca and she don't even care about him. He wouldn't have to worry about me talkin' to other dudes if we were together," she cried. "Violet, find somebody else! Dang, I mean, he ain't even cute! You deserve better than that mosquito elf looking boy. But if you are so in love with him, just walk up to him and tell him exactly how you feel! No use in crying to me about it. I can't do anything," I said.

"Oh, so you think it's that easy to ask somebody out? Porsha, he sees all the signs. He knows how I feel about him." "See, why girls do that? Signs, Violet? Forget signs! Go talk to him. You playing games that ain't nobody got time for," I said. "And what if he turns me down?" she asked. "Then forget him! I think he got a lost screw, anyway. How you be in a relationship with somebody that don't even know y'all in a relationship?" I asked. "Porsha, she used him like she does everybody. He's loyal so he didn't know," she said. "Violet, this whole thing is a bad idea. Even if he gives you a chance, how do you know his heart won't still be with Orca?" I asked. "When he sees how I treat him, he'll know how bad she was," she said.

I rolled my eyes and shook my head. It was difficult trying to support someone through what I saw to be a huge mistake.

"So you wouldn't be hurt if you asked someone out and they turned you down?" she asked. "Violet, I've been through way worse than some boy who probably ain't even started growing pubic hair saying he don't wanna be my boyfriend," I said.

"Well, that's just it. You're different, Porsha. In your world, you don't care about anything. You don't care what nobody thinks about you, and you don't mind being turned down because you've never been in love," she said. "Girl, you call this love?" "Porsha! Stop doing that! Stop making me feel like a sad case," she said. "You *are* a sad case!" I said, laughing.

"Okay, go ask his friend out," she said. "Who? You talking about the light skinned nerd sitting right beside him?" I asked. "Yep." "Girl, no. I'm not the one 'in love'. Now you either go and spill your gut to Mosquito over there or quit talking about it," I said. "Porsha, why you so mean?" "I'm not mean, I'm a realist. Now, go on," I said. "Porsha, I promise I won't ever bring him up again if you ask his friend out." "The two tasks aren't even related, Violet. What's the point?" I asked. "I just wanna see if rejection really doesn't bother you," she said. "Violet..." "Porsha, I dare you," she said.

She knew exactly how to get me to do something. My pride was one thing that worked against me in situations like this one, so I agreed. I got a piece of paper and wrote, 'Do you want a girlfriend?'. "Porsha, what the heck are you doing?" she asked. "Hey, I'm asking a guy out the way I ask a guy out," I said. "Porsha that's childish." "Not nearly as childish as daring your friend to ask someone she doesn't even like out so that you can watch her get rejected and feel more confident about yourself," I said, raising my eyebrows. "You got a point, keep going," she said. "I thought so."

I folded the note up and passed it back to the boy we'll call Liam. He looked confused when he received the note and I watched him read it. He looked up at me and mouthed, "Are you serious?" "Yes," I mouthed back. He began writing something on the paper and passed it back to me. 'Sure.' What?! When I read the note, my mouth dropped open and Violet took the paper and read it, then looked at me and laughed. "Violet! This is all your fault! What the heck am I supposed to do now?" "Girl, I'm so proud of you! You got yourself a boyfriend!" "Violet, he was supposed to say 'no.'" "Well, he said yes. Blow a kiss to yo man," she giggled.

I was infuriated. Liam was one of the smartest kids in school, and I just knew that he'd heard about my reputation and had no interest in being with someone like me. I never thought in a million years he would say yes, but he did.

"Crap, now you got a man and I'm still single! Can you go and ask Pilch about me?" she asked. "Violet! Your cowardness has already gotten me in some crap I don't think I can get out of. I need you to boss up and go talk to him for yourself!" I barked. "Well, you leave me no choice. If you don't go and talk to him for me, I'll tell Liam it was only a dare and that'll hurt his feelings and he'll hate you," she said. "You wouldn't," I said. "Try me," she dared.

I was pretty cold and heartless during this time, but not to anyone who hadn't deserved it. "Pilch, um, can we talk?" I asked, approaching his desk. "Sure, what's up?" he asked. "Well, Violet wanted to know why you won't give her a fair chance," I said. "I've told her a million times, my heart belongs to Orca," he said. "Um, about that. I asked Orca today if you guys were together and she said no. Are you sure she knows your heart belongs to her?" I asked. "She said no?" he asked. "Yep. She said y'all were together before summer, but she didn't expect you to think y'all were still together now, after not speaking for the whole summer." "I mean, she didn't tell me nothing different so of course I thought we were still together," he said, his voice laced with heavy disappointment. "She's gonna talk to you about everything after school, okay? But meanwhile, you might consider giving Violet a chance. I mean, she wants you...bad. And she'll actually *know* y'all are together," I said. "I'll think about it. I have to talk to Orca first," he said. "Of course."

I walked back over to Violet who was sitting at her desk anxiously awaiting the verdict. "He says he's gonna talk to Orca about it first, and then he'll think about giving you a chance," I said. Violet's smile reached her ears and she hugged me. "Thank you, thank you, thank you!" she exclaimed. "Girl, he ain't said yes yet," I said. "He will. When Orca breaks his heart, I'll be there to pick up the pieces," she said. "Why you wanna be the clean-up woman, though? Forget left overs, I would want a *fresh* plate," I said. Violet rolled her eyes and heard nothing I said. She smiled long and big for the remainder of class.

When the bell rang, I jetted out of class to get as far away from Liam as possible; not because I didn't like him, but because I was trained and prepared on being rejected, not accepted. I didn't even have a clue of what to say, especially not to a top of the class scholar like Liam.

The next day, I was beyond mortified whenever I'd pass him in the hallway. He didn't look at me and I didn't look at him. When each bell rang, I ran from class to class without giving him the chance to speak to me. Because of this, he decided to outsmart me.

When we'd made it to history class, he'd left a note on my desk before class started. 'Hey, if you didn't mean to actually ask me out, we don't have to keep this up," he said. I felt horrible. Not only did I ask him out on a dare, but I'd been too much of a coward to simply greet him and now, he thinks it was all some cruel joke or something. I wrote back, 'No, it's not that. It's just that I'm actually pretty bashful. I'm not really used to having a boyfriend...especially one like you.' 'One like me?' he wrote. 'A smart guy.' 'Oh, wow. Well, you're pretty smart yourself,' he wrote. 'Thanks, but coming from you, that makes me feel worse.'

Just then, our history teacher decided to assign us to work in groups for something that I can't even remember, because any time there was a group project going on, I would check completely out. I was beyond embarrassed to be placed in a group with Liam, Pilch, another smart genius girl and a smart Asian boy. While they were all diligently working to figure out what it was we were supposed to be presenting, I was standing around cheering them on in the only deflective clownish way I knew how.

The teacher came by and noticed my lack of effort. "La'Porsha, if your group members say you didn't help them, I'm failing you for the day," he said. "I'll just make it up on the backend," I smiled. The teacher we'll call Mr. Crab just rolled his eyes at me and went back to his desk. I noticed Liam smirking at the exchange while still trying to focus on the project. "La'Porsha, find this one answer and we'll say you helped," Pilch said. I did as I was asked, but almost ended up getting into it with the smart girl in the group.

We'll call her Amy. Amy and I never got along. I didn't hate her because she was smart, I strongly disliked how she was always the kid to put down on others whenever she felt like they asked a stupid question. She learned to not do that one day, but we'll talk about that a little later. "La'Porsha, it's not that hard. We shouldn't have to beg you to participate," she said. "Hmm, I wonder if I would get a passing grade if I made your face my project," I said smiling. "Probably not," she snarled. "Probably is still not a no. Maybe I'll take my chances." "Alright, come on guys. We're a group, remember?" Pilch asked.

I continued half way trying to help. It wasn't that I was just not interested, but the kids who were all into their history moved a lot faster than I did at finding information. I didn't want them watching me slowly discover the answer. I always found smart, elite students to become fidgety when other students took longer to discover something they thought to be common sense.

We finished the group project that ended up not even being a grade. Mr. Crab had just told everyone that so we would participate. Mr. Crab was a big, short man. I don't really know what nationality he was, but he was a different kind of fella. He was very corny and easy to take advantage of by his favorite students, who were usually the girls he coached for soccer.

When the bell rang, I gathered my things and walked out the classroom door to find that Liam had decided to wait for me in the hall. "Um, hey. What's up?" I asked. "Nothing, I just thought I'd walk you to your next class," he said. "Why?" I asked. "Isn't that what boyfriends do?" he asked. "Right," I smirked.

When we made it downstairs to the double doors that led outside, Liam held the door open for me. "Um, thanks," I said, nervously. '*Pull yourself together, Porsha. You're a queen. He's supposed to do these things*,' I thought to myself. My mental pep talk didn't stop me from feeling any less awkward. "Um, can we exchange numbers? We don't get much time to talk here, and I'd like us to get to know one another," Liam said. "Uh, sure," I said.

By this time, I could talk with guys on the phone, but still not allowed to visit with them or have them come to my place. That afternoon, when I made it home, I waited for my flip cell phone to ring, but it never did. I kept looking at it and checking it, but there was nothing. This angered me. Why the heck would he ask for my number and then not call?

Then one of the scariest thoughts conjured up in my head. What if all of this was payback for me asking him out on a friend's dare. What if this entire time, he'd decided he was going to show me how it felt for someone's feelings to be played with. I couldn't honestly say that I wouldn't be deserving of such a cruel and humiliating fate, but nevertheless, I wasn't about to risk that being the case. The very next day, when I made it to history class, I broke things off with him in the name of me not being allowed to officially date anyone. He said he understood, and didn't really show any emotion about it.

About a week passed and it was Valentine's Day. Violet had come crying to me again because Pilch had bought a gigantic teddy bear for Orca, even though he was now dating Violet. He had agreed to date Violet, but warned her that his heart was still with Orca. She thought she could love him hard enough to change his mind. I tried to speak against her getting involved with him on those terms, but she didn't listen. Pilch had her heart, whether he'd earned it or not.

"Porsha, do you know how embarrassing it is to have your boyfriend buy some big butt teddy bear for a girl who don't even want him, and then turn around and give you some candy? He gave her the bear in front of everybody! He doesn't care about my heart!" she cried. "Did you honestly expect him to?" I asked. "Porsha, he could've even gave her the bear in private if it meant that much to him!" she screamed. "Do you hear yourself? Why would you lower yourself like that? What is it? You feel like no other guy here is better than him? I don't understand why you're determined to put up with this!" I said. "It's complicated," she said. "No, that's the excuse girls use when they know 'it's dumb'. You know what, I'm about to show you how to be in a real relationship, if he'll let me," I said.

She looked at me with water still sitting in her eyes. "You...you mean Liam?" she asked. "Yeah, I don't know. I know I'm a little messed up, but the short time spent with him made me feel things I hadn't felt in a while. I kind of felt like I wanted to be nice and happy. I wanted to smile and laugh and come out of my normal dark self," I said. "Aw, Porsha! Well, my relationship may be gone to hell, but if you and Liam end up getting married one day, it would all be worth it. I was the one to get y'all together, remember?" she asked, smiling and wiping her tears. "Yeah, I remember Violet."

I don't know what came over me, but I'd missed the little things about the way Liam had made me feel when we were together. I decided to take a real leap of faith and ask Liam out verbally, in front of the class. I walked in, presented him with a card, got on one knee with a sucker in my hand and said, "Liam, will you be my boyfriend?"

He smiled and looked back and forth from Pilch to me as if to ask Pilch what he should say. After a while, I began deflecting again and said, "So, unlike most girls at this school, I actually have bad knees and am not used to being down here. It's okay if you turn me down, you know. But please don't. Want me to beg?" I asked, playfully. He laughed and said, "Yes." "Wait a minute, say what now?" I asked. "I'm saying yes, I'll be your boyfriend, not yes to you begging me," he explained. "Oh!" I said, rolling my eyes and flashing Violet a warning look. "All her sweetness was about to go out the window," Violet said. "Yeah, bruh. You almost got got!" Pilch added.

We all laughed as Liam helped me back to my feet. When I made it home and had just finished dinner, my phone began to ring. It was Liam! "Um, hello?" I answered. "Hey, it's me, Liam. Is this a good time?" he asked. "Sure," I said, finding privacy in my room. "Well, I wasn't expecting your call," I said. "I don't know, I just thought I'd call you and ask you something," he said. "Okay, shoot." "What made you ask me out today? I mean, your parents still aren't allowing you to date, right?" he asked. "Well, no, they're not," I said. "So, what changed?" "Well, I broke up with you because there were some loose ends I needed to tie up and to be honest, I got kind of nervous with you. You're not really the type of guy I go for," I said. "Oh, then what type do you go for?" he asked. "The kind I don't need. They're usually jerks wrapped in jerk's clothing, so I don't even have an excuse," I said. "I see," he said.

There was a moment of silence. "So, I guess we can start with an ice-breaker conversation. Tell me your favorite color," I said. "Blue, what's yours?" "I like royal purple and lime green." "If you had to pick just one, which is it?" "Um, I think I'd pick lime green," I said. "Oh, okay. So what do you normally do after school?" he asked. "Well, normally I write." "What do you write?" he asked. "Poetry, songs and stuff like that." "I'd like to hear some of it. How about a song?" he asked. "Um, no. I can't sing for you, I'm too shy," I said. "Oh, you are definitely not shy. At least, you don't come off that way in class," he said. "Oh, and how do I come off?" "You come off as confident and like you know who you are and what you want," he said.

I went silent, contemplating what he just said. "Hello?" he asked. "Yeah, I'm just...I find it interesting that you see me that way. I'm actually very bashful. I guess the way I act at school is a cover up," I said. "Oh, and what are you hiding?" he asked. "Maybe you'll stick around long enough to find out. As for my writing, I can read you a couple poems, if you'd like," I said. "I'd love that. I'm interested to get inside your mind, since you've been covering up so much."

He is the Truth

"Never judge a book by its cover, the title page, or even the first chapter. Read its entirety to discover its hidden treasures."
~A. S. E.

I WENT AND FOUND my not so little black book filled with poems and songs I would often escape to. "So, what type of mood are you looking for?" I asked. "Give me you, whatever that means," he said. "Um, *I* can be pretty dark. I'm not trying to scare you," I said. "I'll be fine, just give me something you'd normally write." "Okay, here goes nothing," I said.

I read him a poem called *Illusions*. Then, I read him one called *Only For One Night*. "Wow, those are really good. And you're pretty deep, too," he said. "Yeah, I kind of can't help it. Trying to write about something light and fluffy is like me trying to fit in with the girls at school," I said. "That's actually what I like about you. You don't fit it. You're your own person, and you don't really come off as someone who cares about what other people think," he said. "You're right, I don't. Not anymore, at least. I used to before life taught me it was pointless," I said.

"So what type of music do you like?" he asked. "I listen to a lot of classical and movie soundtracks. I don't really listen to a lot of wordy songs, but I guess I'm an oldies baby," I said. "Oh, okay. I don't really like a lot of artists, but I do like John Legend and Alicia Keys," he said. "Okay, I'm gonna need you to name at least one old school artist," I said. "Um, okay. I like Kem," he said. "Nice! Okay, I guess you know a lil' something,'" I teased.

Our conversation continued until my mother told me it was a school night, and that I needed to be off the phone. We said goodnight to each other and looked forward to seeing one another at school the next day. Although we'd seen each other before, we both felt as if we'd actually just met one another through the phone that evening. Seeing one another, knowing the information we now knew about each other, would be a different experience.

When we entered the classroom, we couldn't help but flash a smile at one another. We were a little giddy and tried not to show it, but failed. "Um, what's this?" Violet asked. "What?" "You just sitting over here smiling and everything. Why you so happy?" she asked. "I can't be happy?" I asked. "Not without something being wrong, no. You're not a happy person," she said. "Just because I don't walk around here showing everybody the back of my throat like you do doesn't mean I'm not happy," I said. "You can sit there and pretend all you want, but I'm gonna find out what it is," she said. "You need to be finding out how we're gonna turn in homework we didn't do," I said.

Violet and I were horrible at completing our history homework. It was mainly because Mr. Crab was always having us create timelines and organize events. I hated world history. All we did was learn about things that creeped me out. Like how all the children's nursery rhymes were actually laced with all kinds of evil ancient rituals and hidden meanings; and how when someone wanted power or wanted an already taken woman, they would just kill the person or people who were in the way. I found it depressing.

With that being said, I always made sure to lighten things up a bit. I was a bit more of a class clown in the most subtle and classy of ways, of course. I got a kick out of challenging Mr. Crab on his knowledge of actual history versus his perception and gossip about what he thought might have taken place. I was probably the student he rolled his eyes at the most.

Violet and I started making it a habit to get our boyfriends' homework papers and copying them every morning before school. They didn't really mind. One day, Liam surprised me. "I'm not giving you my homework," he said. "And why the heck not," I asked, melodically. "Because I think you're better than that," he said. "So, what are you now, my life coach?" I asked. "No, I'm your boyfriend that really cares about you. I don't want you to be dependent on my mind when you have such a beautiful one of your own," he said. I won't describe what I felt in the moment, but I will say I became a 'Mrs.' in my heart.

Liam was always saying thoughtful things like that and pushing me to be a better me. We had started off trying to not make a big deal out of us being together, but we ended up becoming one of the school's most popular couples. Our dynamic worked. He was calm and gentle and smart. I was feisty, wild, and wise, even if I didn't apply the wisdom to myself.

The most important part of our relationship was music! Since we were both introverted to a certain degree, we decided to communicate through music. I made Liam a CD with songs telling him how I felt about him and our relationship, and he did the same for me.

Liam couldn't resist my persuasion, and I couldn't resist his gentle care for my heart. I ended up not wanting to depart from him at the bus stop and made him miss the bus just so that he could ride home with me. When my mother pulled up in her dark grey Chrysler Sebring, I asked her if it was okay to take Liam home because he had missed his bus. She looked him over and agreed with a smirk.

I took my seat in the back and allowed Liam to sit in the front with my mother. I knew she wouldn't be able to compose herself from drilling him about himself, and she didn't. She asked him everything she could possibly think of. I hadn't told her about any interest in him yet and I acted nonchalant about the questions she asked.

When we pulled up to his house, both my mother and I held our composure and waited for Liam to walk inside and shut the door. As soon as he did, we went ballistic! "Porsha! Do you see this house, girl! Wow!" she said. "Ma, I know! I should have expected him to live in something like that! It's beautiful!" I said.

You don't stand a chance. I don't even know why you're siking yourself up! He's out of your league, filthy girl. I remember being startled by the voice and jerking away from my window, then trying to play it off to not make my mother suspicious. What was that? It wasn't my spirit guide. I hadn't even talked to it in a while, and it definitely didn't give off any Godly aura, and I actually heard it! It was wickedly smooth.

That was the moment the demonic voices started. It was the first time I'd heard them, and the last time I'd be without them until Book 5 of this memoir series. I shook the horrid statement out of my mind and assumed it was my own conscious, getting nervous from seeing the house Liam stayed in.

When my mother and I arrived at our home and pulled into the driveway, she parked the car, turned it off, and turned to me, crossing her hands in her lap. "I like him!" she said. "What? Really?" I asked with excitement. "Yes! He's so respectful and gives off this positive energy about him. Now, with that being said, tell me the truth, do you like him?" she asked. "Are you trying to trick me?" I asked. "No, you can tell me, and you won't get in trouble. I know you're getting to that age, baby. Mommy wasn't born yesterday. So, do you?" she asked. "Yes, I do. I actually didn't expect to, but he's kind and smart and caring and... beautiful!" I said. "I didn't picture you'd like a guy like him," she said. "What, a nerd? Well, I'm a nerd, too. I'm just a deep, dark, weird nerd, and he's a light one," I said.

My mother laughed. "Well, with that being said, you know you're only fifteen, and you still have to wait until you're sixteen to start dating him, right?" she asked. "I mean, I know I have to wait to officially have a boyfriend, but dating is getting to know someone, right? Do I honestly have to wait a whole year to do that? I mean, we're friends now, and I think that's a great start. But waiting a year may just hinder natural progress," I said.

My mother sat there and thought for a minute. "I tell you what. Let me talk it over with your dad," she said. "Aw, Ma, really?" I asked. "Yes, we need to discuss things like this together. Trust me, your dad is more lenient than I am when it comes to things like this," she said.

We went inside the house, and my mother sent me to my room while she spoke with my dad in the kitchen. I didn't eavesdrop, but it wasn't much longer until they called me from my room and said, "We've decided that he can't be your boyfriend right now, but we will allow you to slowly get to know him as a friend and maybe hang out a little."

So basically, we can date, and since we're dating exclusively, that makes him my boyfriend, I thought. "Great! Can we have him over for dinner Sunday?" I asked. "Um, that's a no. Sunday is family day, " my dad said. "Well, what better way to meet someone and interact with them for the first time than in God's house? We can invite him to church service, and then he can eat with us afterward," I said.

My mother looked at my father, then they both looked at me, smiling. "She's got a point, Duke. I mean, does he even go to church?" my mother asked. "Um, I don't know. Let me go and ask him," I said, holding up my finger to call him on my cell phone.

I had Liam on speed dial since he was the only person I talked to on the phone, so I hurried and pressed the call button to dial his number. "Wait a minute, we haven't given an answer yet," my dad said, smirking. "Too late, I'm already calling. It's church and dinner, dad," I said, smiling.

"Hello?" "Hey, Liam." "Hey, what's up," he asked. " *Let me hear him!*" my mother whispered. "Shh," I said. "Um, I was wondering, do you go to church service?" I asked. "Yeah, I do," he said. "Would you like to come to service with me this Sunday?" I asked. "Um, let me ask my parents. Hold on," he said. "Okay," I said gleaming.

My parents stood there, shaking their heads at me and smiling. "You better be thinking about what you gonna cook!" my dad told my mother. "I know! I know! Oh my gosh! This is so exciting!" she said. I was shocked and extremely overjoyed that my parents were embracing the idea of me actually dating Liam.

"Hey, they said it's alright," he said. "Okay, we'll pick you up around...10. Sound good?" I asked. "Yeah, that works," he said. "Alright,

I'll call you back in a minute," I said. "Okay," he said. We hung up the phone, and my mother and I screamed and flapped our hands with each other's hands like little girls. "Y'all are some silly," my dad said, trying not to laugh.

"Wow, Porsha got a date?" Ree asked. "Now, don't you go getting no ideas," my dad warned, pointing his finger at her. We all laughed, and I went to my room to call Liam back. "Hello?" "Hey. So, you're coming to church with us. Wow," I said. "Yep, looks like it. I'm surprised your parents let you invite me," he said. "Me too. How did your parents act when you asked them?" I asked. "Oh, they just said okay. They're not really strict on me when it comes to things like that. They trust me," he said. "Oh, okay."

We talked and talked about everything from school to people to our parents. "I must warn you, my dad, and I don't really get along. He's kind of sarcastic and is always trying to belittle me," I said. "I'm not worried. I'll be too focused on us," he said inhaling. I could tell he wasn't used to saying sweet things like that. "That was corny," he said. "No…no, it wasn't. It was really sweet," I said, smiling.

Sunday morning finally came, and my family packed into my mother's car and drove to Liam's house. My dad and Ree had the same reaction my mother and I had when we first saw his home. "You wanna go knock on the door?" my dad asked. "No, just honk the horn," I said. "Aw, she's shy," my sister teased. "Shut up, Ree," I said, laughing.

My sister and I had been seated in the back seat. Liam came out looking *dressed*! He had a pair of black slacks on and a white long-sleeved dress shirt. "Wow," my mother said. She made me so nervous, I couldn't react. "Let me out so he can sit in the middle," I said. "Don't put him in the middle. Let him sit on the outside by the window," my mother said. "You're right," I said, scooting over towards my sister.

My mother got out and let him into the back of the two-door convertible. "Good morning," my dad said in his 'proving' voice. "Good morning," Liam said. "Huh?" my dad asked. "He said good morning,"

I said. "Oh, my bad, I didn't hear ya," my dad said. I flashed my dad a warning glance in the rearview mirror. "Duke, behave," my mother said.

I looked at Liam, and we exchanged looks acknowledging what I'd warned him about the other night on the phone about my dad. I was growing upset, but Liam leaned over and whispered, "Hey, don't worry about it. You look beautiful." "You look nice, too. It's weird seeing you so dressed up," I said.

We drove to the church, and every single person asked about who Liam was. If they didn't come up to my parents, they came up to me. "Porsha, who is that boy you're with?" "He's a friend," I said, winking.

Liam decided he would make me laugh during service because he could tell how nervous I was with him being there. "Have you ever noticed everyone claps, not because they know what they're clapping for, but because someone else is clapping?" he asked. I laughed. "No, they don't! Stop." "I'll prove it," he said. "You wouldn't," I said.

Liam waited until the pastor said an entire sentence that wasn't even something to clap from, and he started clapping! And low and behold, the rest of the congregation joined in with him, including my parents! I was so tickled! I passed my mother a note telling her what we'd just done, and she laughed at herself for participating. She showed my dad, and he whispered something to her. She wrote on the paper and passed it back to me. "Your dad says this is not the place and to pay attention," she said. I shot her a look, primping my lips, and she rolled her eyes and shook her head to dismiss my dad's hardness.

This was coming from the same man my mother used to have to stick with a stick pin every Sunday just to stay awake. I showed the note to Liam. "He's right," he whispered. He saw my mood change and grabbed my hand. The very touch of his soft, gentle hands soothed me.

After a while, service finally ended, but we were stuck introducing Liam to everyone, and it took us forever to leave. We finally were able to head home to my mother's Sunday dinner. She'd done a lot more than she usually would have, and my dad, of course, expressed jealously while my mother was preparing all of her best soul food dishes. "You ain't cooked like this in a minute," he said. "Duke, don't start. We have a guest. Of course, Ima put my best foot forward. This represents me!" she said. "I know, baby, I'm just kidding," he said. "Sure you are," I said.

When we pulled up in the driveway, we got out and went inside. My mother told my sister, Liam, and me to make ourselves comfortable on the couch in the den while she warmed the food up. "Your parents are really nice. Even your dad," he said. "If you say so," I said. "I mean, every family has it's issues, right?" he asked. "I guess," I said.

I didn't really want to get into a conversation about my family. I didn't want to scare him away. Liam appeared to have the perfect family and perfect home and an ideal upbringing. He had told me he only got one whipping when he was younger and said that was all it took. He had freedoms I only heard about on tv shows, his parents trusted him, and he was actually a good kid. I had no idea what that felt like. But I wasn't about to tell him that.

My mother called us to dinner, and my dad said grace over the food. We ate and talked and laughed. My dad and I kept butting heads over little stupid comments he would make, but that was the norm. When we finished eating, my mother asked Liam if he wanted more food. "No, ma'am, I'm good," he said. "Don't be shy now. Do you want anything? Some more tea. Want more sweet tea? Sure you do, you choking over there with that empty cup. Porsha, go fix him some more tea," she said.

I took his cup to the kitchen, and filled it up to the top with more tea. "Why'd you fill it up?" he whispered. "You didn't want it full?" I asked. "I'm pretty full," he said, smiling. I chuckled. "Oops, well, you don't have to drink it all if you don't want it," I said. "And waste your mama's sweet tea, I don't think so," he said.

He forced himself to finish the cup and then started rubbing his chest and clearing his throat. "You aight, man?" my dad asked. "Yeah, I um..." he began. Liam placed the top of his closed fist to his mouth and held it there for a moment. Then he excused himself from the table and speed-walked outside onto the back deck. My mother watched through the screen door and said, "Oh my gosh, he's throwing up. Porsha go get him a towel from the bathroom and wet it."

I rushed to the bathroom to wet a face towel and headed outside. "Calm down, y'all acting like he's dying or something. He's just throwing up," my dad said. "Duke hush, you so insensitive. I feel bad. He was trying to tell me he was full, and I pushed that last cup of sweet tea on him," my mother said. "You didn't *force* him to drink it. He could have said no," my dad shrugged. "Duke!" "Okay, okay," he said, throwing his hands up.

Liam stood bent over with spit on his lips and vomit hanging from his nose. "Wow, it even came through your nose, huh?" I asked. "Go back inside, I don't want you to see this," he said. "Hey, if we're gonna be together, I'm gonna end up seeing more than this. I may even have to wipe your behind one day when we're old," I said, laughing.

He stood upright and looked down at me. I took the towel and began wiping his nose. He tried to take the towel and do it himself, but I was thoroughly enjoying taking care of this beautiful creature I'd grown to care about. "Uh uh, let me," I said. "Wow," he said. "What?" I asked. "You love me," he said. I paused and smiled, then kept at my task. "What makes you say that?" I asked. "Why else would you want to wipe the vomit from my nose and spit from my mouth? Or, maybe I could just be reading too much into it. You're just nice," he said.

For a moment, I forgot my mother was standing in the doorway until I glanced her way. She was standing there, smiling. When I held my stare with her, she walked away from the door knowing I didn't want her just standing there watching us. "Come on, let's get out of the mosquitoes," I said.

I took Liam's hand and stepped up a stair higher than where he stood and briefly kissed him on the lips. "You're right, I do love you. Vomit and all," I said. He smiled as I walked him back inside. Liam and I sat on the couch snuggled together, while my mother, dad, and sister took their own seats. We watched a movie and then took Liam home.

"So what you think?" my mother asked my dad. "I think he appears to be a nice young man," my dad said. Liam's visits became frequent, and it didn't take him long to be considered a part of my family. Although my parents tried to hold fast to their 'waiting until I was sixteen to date' rule, even they couldn't stop the beautiful music being made between Liam and me. Towards the winter months, they had begun to accept that he was indeed, my boyfriend.

Rock Steady

"Your first love is usually the truest,
the hardest, the most painful, and the most fulfilling."
~A. S. E.

LIAM AND I had talked about everything, but the main topic was God. Liam struggled with his faith in God and often feared oblivion. He feared the thought of not remembering himself or anyone else when he passed on. He didn't understand or even know how to trust God with his life and his heart.

I found myself wanting to defend God's love for him and trying to tell him that God is who He is, and we were not Him, but with each testament that left my tongue, I felt an overwhelming sense of hypocrisy. I hadn't wanted anything to do with God for a while. I played the part and went to church service, clapping my hands, and singing exciting music. I would even cry every now and then when the energy in service would be charged on days like Easter and Christmas. But my heart was far from Him.

I didn't know it at the time, but Liam was God's love for me. I brought him out of his shell, and he covered my heart in his hands and protected and cherished it. Our chemistry was so strong, no one dared question it or speak against it. They admired our union and didn't even quite know why. We weren't exactly the couple everyone would expect.

I heard many of our mutual associates say things like, "Liam, how the heck did you snag the girl with the most beautiful voice in school?" Liam would smile and shrug the comments off. But all I thought in my mind was, *How on earth did this beautiful creature enter my world...my dark and troubled world, my confusing and depressing world. He doesn't belong here.*

One day, while Liam was outside waiting on me to come out of the house, he and my dad got into a conversation. It was later revealed to me by Liam that my dad basically hinted warnings to Liam about me. He told Liam that he thought I might not really be good for Liam because of my attitude and emotional baggage.

To this day, I don't know the exact words that were said. All I know is hearing about my dad trying to sway Liam away from me was one of the most hurtful moments of my life. But what my mother said to me took the cake. "Porsha, Liam is a nice guy, and I like him a lot. But he's a book worm, and well, you're a...a special girl," she said. "Ma, what are you trying to say? There's nothing wrong with Liam. I like him that way," I barked. "I'm not really talking about him, baby. I'm saying, have you talked to him about what he wants to do after school? Is he going to college? I'm just saying I see you and his life going in different directions. I just don't want you to get so hooked on him and then get your heart broken if he pushes you aside to pursue his life," she said.

I can't remember exactly why, but I missed school the next day. But the day after that, I went to my homeroom and wrote one of the saddest letters I'd ever written. It basically said,

> *Dear Liam,*
> *My parents seem to think you're too good for me. From what my dad told you and what my mom told me, that's what I gather, and they're right. You don't know me at all. You really don't know anything about my family or my past, and I fear if you knew or ever found out, you would hate me and never want to even look at me again. I'm calling things off before both of us get hurt. I hope you can understand, and I'm sorry for even bringing you this far with me.*

Liam and I had a habit of passing each other notes and letters between classes. I gave him this note and wouldn't even speak to him. I looked at him with tears in my eyes. "What's wrong?" he asked. I just walked away. I just knew that me breaking things off a second time with him would have made him never speak to me again, but I was wrong.

Liam caught up to me while I was on the way to my vocational class and passed me a return letter. I won't say what he wrote, though, 'til this very day, I still have that letter locked away in a safe. Just know the words he sketched onto that sheet of paper validated me to new heights, and I never questioned his love for me again. He'd even addressed the pessimistic warnings of my dad in a way that made me want to marry him right then and there.

Liam had later expressed to me that he missed me the day before. "You did?" I asked. "You're the whole light of that class. You're funny and unpredictable, especially when dealing with Mr. Crab," he said.

He was right. Mr. Crab showed favoritism, and that's something I didn't tolerate too well.

After Liam and I had been together a minute, there was an incident in our class that shook things up a bit amongst the students. Three girls were talking, but not to each other. They were laughing and talking and not doing their work. Two of the girls were dark brown girls, and one was Caucasian. "That's it! Get out!" he said to the brown girls. They pleaded with him to not write them up, but he wouldn't listen. I didn't feel bad for them because they picked on me nearly every day.

But then, the other girl that had been talking asked, "You're writing me up, too?" I watched him slightly shake his head 'no' to her and put his finger to his mouth to motion her to be quiet. I couldn't believe it. "Did you see that?" I asked Liam. "Yeah," he said. I couldn't help myself.

I stood up and addressed Mr. Crab in front of the class. "Um, why isn't she getting a write-up, too?" I asked. "La'Porsha, sit down and mind your business before you follow them out of that door," he said, raising his eyebrows. "I'm not going anywhere. And you've got two seconds to make a decision. You either write this lil' white girl up with the two brown ones you just sent out of here, or you get on that phone and call them back in here," I said.

The class was shocked at the showdown and sat quietly and anxiously awaiting the outcome. "Why don't you mind your own business? Especially for girls who don't like you. I see how they act every day," he said. "First of all, racial injustice is my business, and second of all, I'm mature enough to separate my personal feelings for the greater good," I said. "La'Porsha, that's enough! Sit down, now!" he screamed. "What punishment will this girl receive," I asked. "I don't owe you anything," he said. "Um, actually, Mr. Crab, she has a point. I mean, I feel some type of way about it, too. If all three girls were talking and playing, then all three should be sent out," D.C. said. D.C. was one of my best acquaintances.

Other students of color chimed in and agreed. "I was making her run laps after school! I'm her coach," he said. "Run laps? You kidding me? She may like running. That ain't good enough. So, you make her run while the other two get permanent write-ups on their record?" I asked. "You know what, that's enough. I'm calling the principal," he said, storming to the class phone. "Please do," I said. "Hey, Dr. Spells, I got a student who is causing disruption in my class and won't take her seat," he said. "He's being racist!" I screamed, loud enough for her to hear me from the other side of the phone. "She wants to talk to you," he said, passing me the phone.

"Hey, what's your name?" she asked. "La'Porsha Mays," I answered. "Oh okay, now what's the problem?" she asked. "Mr. Crab decides to send the two girls that are in your office down with write-ups while a white girl that was talking the same as they were gets to stay in class. I simply told him that either all girls should be allowed to stay in class, or all girls should get write-ups," I said. "I see, okay. Give the phone back to Mr. Crab," she said. I handed the phone over, Mr. Crab placed the phone on the hook, and the principal spoke to Mr. Crab through the intercom for the class to hear, instructing him that I was correct in what I was saying. Within minutes, the two girls were back in class.

They came in laughing like they'd won something. "Take your seats and hush! If it weren't for your friend you're always teasing over here, you wouldn't be in here," he said, pointing at me sitting next to a proud Liam. "Girl, La'Porsha! Thank ya, girl! We won't mess witcha no mo!" they said, trying to dab my hands. "I didn't do it for you, I did it for me," I said. "Well, thank ya anyway," they laughed.

"You are so beautiful," Liam whispered. "High five," I said, raising my hand. "I want to kiss you, but this will have to do," he said.

Though both our parents seemed to want to discount what we felt for one another as puppy love, neither set could deny that Liam and I were having significant impacts on each other. My mother ran into his mother at a clothing store she worked at. My mother said that his mother bragged on how much Liam had started to come out of his shell. His mother said she noticed her son was in a much different light than he had been before.

My mother then told his mom about the changes in me, as well. "My daughter's been through a lot, so it's exciting and scary to see someone change her so much," my mother said.

My family had started teasing me about the fact that they deemed me to be a much nicer and much sweeter person with Liam in my life. "You smile more than I've ever seen you smile," my dad said. "Well, that's what happens when you've got something to smile about," I said…smiling.

I noticed the hurt looks on my parents' faces and tried to butter up my statement. "It's just different. Y'all know I love y'all, but it's…different," I said. "We know, baby," my mother said. There wasn't a moment that went by that I wasn't writing Liam, or thinking of Liam, or planning my future with Liam, or being with Liam. Things were almost too perfect.

Liam loved my singing and believed in me. I'll never forget how proud he felt to witness me performing in a local hall in town. Having Liam there really brought me out of my shell, and I will admit it was one of my best performances.

Wounds in the Way

"Sometimes, the fire overwhelms the firefighter, but then sometimes the firefighter conquers the fire."
~A. S. E.

I WAS SO HAPPY with Liam that I began feeling guilty about the joy I felt. I almost felt like it was wrong to feel this way with someone as unique as he was. He'd loved me past nearly everything; the nightmares, the insecurities, depression, insomnia, and yes, even the suicidal thoughts. The incredible thing was that he didn't know about any of the things he was helping me deal with.

I had made it a point to be extremely elusive with him to not scare him away. But one day, he felt a distance between us and asked me to talk about whatever was on my mind. "I just wonder about our future," I said. "What about it?" he asked. "Well, you're going to be a doctor, and well, I'm...I want to sing. I don't plan on even going to college," I said. "And?" he asked. "What will your parents think of me when they find out I'm choosing singing over going to college?" I asked. "They'll probably think it's not the smartest decision, but they won't judge you for it. And they know that it's up to me of who I want to be with," he said.

I remember looking up to the sun and tears falling down my face. "I have to tell you some things. If I don't tell you now, I never will, and that's not fair to you," I said. "Okay," he said. "I'm not...clean. I've been... touched many times by many people. I've done...things that you would never imagine, and I'm...I'm not a virgin. I got...hurt," I told him. "None of those things change how I feel about you, Renae. And most of what you just told me if not all of it isn't even your fault. Is that really why you're nervous about our future?" he asked. "Well, yeah. I mean, if we're serious, eventually we'll have to actually be together, and I don't really know how I'd handle that. Sometimes, I have flashbacks about things that aren't even related to anything that's going on at the moment. They just come and change my mood and leave," I said. "I'm here, and I'm not going anywhere," he said.

Some of our teachers noticed how close Liam and I had become and started telling me how much they liked and approved of our union. His friends and my friends didn't really understand us but liked us being together. "Porsha, what makes you like him?" Orca asked. "He's just perfect for me. We do well together and balance each other out," I said. "But he's so...quiet," she said. "He's only quiet around people he doesn't know," I said. "Yeah, but he's always got that look in his eye!" "Girl, what look are you talking about?" I asked. "Ima be honest, and please don't get mad when I say this, but he looks like he wanna kill any and everybody around you. He looks like a serial killer, and he so dang quiet with it," she said.

I laughed until I cried. I knew the look she'd been talking about. Liam had a habit of not wanting to look people straight in the eye when he wasn't invited to, so his eyes would dance back and forth between looking at a person and away from them. He was just very observant. He was very protective of me, too.

There were some rough guys in our JROTC. Since I had grown cold and hard, sometimes they looked at me as one of the guys and would rough play with me. One afternoon, while I was waiting with Liam to catch his bus to go home, a boy walked up on me like he wanted to fight. He was hype, but that was the way he always played with everyone. Liam didn't get the memo, and snatched me out of the way and nosed up with the boy. "Porsha, get ya boy," the boy said.

I stood there shocked for a moment and then pulled Liam back and told him that it was okay and that the guy was just playing. "Well, I don't like that way of playing. You don't play with a woman like that," he said. I was speechless and didn't really know what to say.

From that day forward, the guys teased about no one messing with me if they didn't want 'Serial Killer' coming for them. Eventually, we were all able to laugh about it, but that was a while after the incident.

Liam and I had many kinks to work through in our relationship. He was always trying to be the old school chivalrous gentleman he was taught to be, while I was still being the independent firecracker I was taught to be. One incident that stands out to me is when my mother took Liam, my younger sister and I to the mall in Hattiesburg one day. My mother and sister went their way to give Liam and I some time to ourselves to walk the mall.

We got hungry and decided to get something to eat. When it came time for me to pay for my food, Liam insisted that he pay for it, and I wouldn't let him. We got into an argument about this that hampered our trip. "Renae, why are you like this? Are you telling me I can't buy a meal for my girlfriend? What could it hurt for you to just let me do something like this for you, even if it's just one time?" he asked. "I was taught never to let a guy do anything for you," I said. "And I get that, but your boyfriend? Doesn't the rule change a bit under these circumstances?" he asked.

I told you so. There was that voice again! "Why are you so passionate about wanting to buy my food? All that makes it seem like is you have other motives. Most guys would happily accept the fact that I want to carry my own tab," I said. "Are you dating most guys, or are you dating me?" he asked. "You know what, I don't like your tone," I said. "Well, we're even, 'cause right now, I don't like your attitude," he said.

I was shocked! This was the first time I'd seen him upset with me. Was he really getting this frustrated with me not wanting him to pay for my food? On the ride home, my mother and sister sat up front and gave Liam and I the back seat.

But when they saw we were silent, they knew something was wrong. "What's going on? Y'all so quiet back there," my mother said. "Ma, didn't you tell me not to let a guy buy me things or pay for my food?" I asked. "Well, yeah, but I was only talking about random guys. If you're friends with someone and you trust them, you could let them do that if they really want to," she said. "That's not what you told me. You told me never to do it because they would feel like you owe them something," I said. "Well, some guys would feel that way," she said. "Okay, so how do you know when and when not to let them?" I asked. "Well, that just depends on how comfortable you are with the person. You have to trust them to let them do things like that, so it's really up to you," she said.

I remember feeling a little salty because my mother was adamant and demanded us never to let anybody do anything for us, not even some family members. Now, it seemed like she was softening her views. Even with her very correct explanation of things, my heart was hardened, and I didn't want to give up my independence. I wanted Liam to know that I was with him because I *wanted* him, not because I *needed* him.

Liam was notably frustrated and hurt at my stubbornness. When we made it home, he held me outside in the car to talk while my mother and sister went in. "Renae, I don't want our relationship to be like this. If I wanna do something for you, I want you to trust me enough to do it. It was just a meal this time, but what about your birthday? I don't want to have to beg you to accept a gift from me," he said. "I understand, but I don't want to be forced to accept your offer, either. Can we just—" "Can we just be *together*?" he asked. He kissed me long and deep, and I agreed. That was a cheat move from him, but it worked.

He had some of the biggest, softest lips and the most amazing sensual instincts. There were countless times he drove me wild, but we'll get to that later.

It took me a while to get used to his kindness and not think anything of it. He was always opening the door for me and throwing away my lunch tray. One night I asked him why he was always doing things like that, and he told me, "It's nothing special. It's what any man is supposed to do for his woman. It's sad you're not used to that."

He was right. My dad didn't open car doors for us or anything. And he was never serving my mother at the kitchen table or us. She was always the one cooking his food and serving all three of us while saving herself for last. She even cooked for him when he made her angry. I didn't even understand that concept. I knew I could never do that without some malicious intent being behind it. A man heats me up with his attitude and then expects me to deal with the heat of the kitchen too? It wasn't about to happen.

We grew to be the best of friends and had some hilarious moments as well. The time that stands out to me was when we were eating in the cafeteria with Violet and Pilch. Liam was always funny without trying to be. He said something hilarious right after I had taken a swig of some chocolate milk, and I spit it out right on him by accident. This happened about two weeks after we started dating. I was so sorry and embarrassed, and he smiled and wiped his shirt, saying, "You better be glad I like you."

I rushed to get napkins to help dry him, but he kept saying he was alright. When the winter months came around, things changed between Liam and me. We were madly in love with one another and decided we would try to take things to the next step. He made sure his number one priority was to 'serve' me and make me comfortable. I enjoyed and loved him so much that all reservations went out the door.

I asked him to make love to me. "Are you sure?" he asked. "Yes," I said, drunk off the waltz of his tongue and the pressing of his lips against mine. He raised to meet my eyes and repositioned to give himself to me. It was intimate and magical, and wonderful until... *Baby, it feels so good.* "What did you say?" I asked. "I didn't say anything, relax, baby," he said.

He must have felt me tense up. *This is all he wanted from you. It's all you're worth, slut!* The voices! They were back, and they were loud. The room turned a strange reddish color, and my head began to hurt.

"Wait, baby. Get off, get off," I rushed. My mind had succumbed to the violent flashbacks of Lamprey. Why, after all this time, had his face appeared? Though the process was the same, Liam felt nothing like Lamprey, and I loved him. "Are you okay?" he asked. "Uh, no. I need...I don't know, let me up, please," I panicked.

I hid my face with both hands and cried. I didn't even cry for me, I cried for Liam. I knew I'd hurt him deeply and that he was trying to be strong for me in the moment, and I felt horrible for it. Was I really too broken to give myself to a person I actually loved? "Hey, come on. Let's get some fresh air," he said. He drove me to a drive-through to get some sweet tea, and we talked about what had happened.

"I'm so sorry, Liam. I don't know what happened. I was fine one minute and then started seeing and hearing things," I said. "It's okay. I love you, Renae. We can work through this, I promise," he said. "I appreciate that, but tell me the truth. How did I make you feel?" I asked. "You're beautiful. And the look you gave me when you asked for me is one I will forever vividly remember. It was the sexiest thing I'd ever seen," he said. "But then?" I asked. "Well, when you had your flashback, I saw it happening before you said something, and I felt like...a monster," he said.

Tears gushed from my eyes. "Baby, don't do that. I know you weren't rejecting me. I know your mind took you to another place. Don't cry. Our love is strong and will grow stronger. Eventually, you won't even have to worry about that happening. It's going to take time for you to get used to being with someone in that way again. But I'm not going anywhere," he said.

About a month later, I told Liam, "I want to try again." We'd been in my upstairs attic rooms with lime green walls and a day bed. Liam had helped me put my computer desk together and was researching something with me on my computer. "Right now?" he asked. "Yes," I said.

First, he laid me down in my day bed and served me the same dance he'd done a month ago. Then, as he raised to give himself to me, he said, "You know what, come here." He guided me to the computer chair. "What are you doing?" I asked, smiling. He took a seat on the chair and guided me to straddle him. In between long, passionate kisses, he said, "I want you to have your way. I don't want you to ever feel helpless again. You're in control."

We started slow, but as things began reaching a climax, my dad started walking up the stairs. We were able to hurry up and reposition ourselves to look like nothing was going on. "What y'all doing up here?" my dad asked. "Nothing, just researching stuff on the computer," I said.

I called my dad over to show him the window I'd left open. "Oh, okay, sounded like I heard some thumping," he said. "No, we're just sitting searching the internet," I said.

My dad looked at Liam and me inquisitively and headed back downstairs. When he left, we laughed and hugged one another. Liam gave me a long kiss once again. "You're beautiful," he said. "I wish you would stop saying that," I smiled. "You are," he said. "I've gained so much weight, it's not funny. There was even a woman at church who asked my mother if I was pregnant," I said.

Liam took my hand and guided me to the long mirror that was perched up by my window. He raised my shirt up from behind and said, "One day, this belly will give us children. I want you to start embracing everything about yourself, Renae. See yourself the way I do," he said. "You know what, you're even more beautiful than I am," I said, turning around to face him in his arms. "Not even possible," he said, kissing me once more.

The hardest leg of this swim is always right before the end. Please hang in there. We're approaching the dark trench of this journey. Soon, we'll be headed to meet the sun at the surface again.

Blissfully Blinded

"The enemy will never give up, so you mustn't either."
~A. S. E.

JUST WHEN THINGS were perfect, tragedy hit. The same demon who'd been after me since my youth came back to try and finish me off. I was spending the night at a friend's house when her older brother saw me coming out of the bathroom and asked me to come here. He was friendly and funny, so I thought nothing of it. I should have because he was always putting down the fact that I was dating someone like Liam. He would call him 'nerd boy' and tease me about dating a 'smart guy.'

"What's up?" I asked. "Come sit for a minute. What you still doing up?" he asked. "I had to pee. What are you still doing up?" I asked. "I'm just watchin' tv. I can't sleep for some reason," he said. "Maybe you should drink warm milk," I said. We chuckled. "That's what white folks do, but that junk don't work," he said. "I know, I was just kidding," I said. "What I need is a cup of you," he said.

I frowned with a confused smile on my face and said, "Um, no. I have a boyfriend, remember?" "Smh, man, that ain't even real. That little puppy love y'all got ain't nothin' compared to what I can give you," he said. "I don't... I'm not a slut. And you can call it whatever you want, but I love him," I said, getting up to walk out of the door. "Wait a minute, I'm just playing witchu. Galee! You quick to get serious, ain't cha?" he asked. "I don't play like that. And to be honest, I shouldn't even be in here right now. I'm going back to bed, and I hope you can get some sleep," I said, folding my lips.

As I was leaving, he grabbed my arm and spun me back to him and struggled to walk a squirming me to his bed. "Stop, I'm taken. I told you I don't—" He kissed me, and it was nasty and slimy. "Stop, I'm serious!" I said. "No, you're not. You want this, so I don't know why you even pretending not to," he said. He was large over me, and when I tried to push him out of my way, he laughed. "You so cute, you tryin' to fight me now?" He took my wrists in his hands and laid me on the bed. It was a bit high, so he used himself to scoot me up while climbing up on top of me.

He wouldn't let me talk and kept pushing his tongue in my mouth to keep me quiet. When he did come up for air, he moved one hand to the other to hold both my wrists with one hand and started pulling himself out. "I promise I don't want this! I'm not joking! Stop!" I said. "Shh! You're loud. If my mom or sister hear you, it's over with. You gonna make this bigger than it needs to be," he said.

He was able to push himself inside of me once, and I went crazy! I don't even remember what I did, but whatever it was it had been enough to make him get off of me and throw his hands up. "Whoa, hey, calm down. What's wrong witchu man?" he asked. I ran to the room I was sharing with my friend and called Liam. "Liam...I said no, I swear I said no! Please come get me," I cried. "Renae? Baby what happened?" "He tried to...but I didn't let him," I cried. "Baby, hold on. Who tried to what?" he asked. "Her brother wanted me, but I told him I was with you, and he started saying he didn't care, and it didn't matter and got on top of me and..." "Renae, where's your friend?" he asked. "She's laying right here," I said. "You need to wake her up and tell her," he said. "It's her brother, Liam! She won't believe me!" I cried.

I just started balling and couldn't control myself. My friend woke up from my whimpering. "Porsha? What's wrong, sis? Did Liam do something to you? Sis, did that boy say something to you?" she asked, seeing I was on the phone. I wanted to tell her what had happened with everything inside of me, but I couldn't. My mouth wouldn't say a word. I kept crying with my mouth moving, trying to speak, but all I could do was shake my head.

Just when I was about to try and say something, a figure came to the doorway. "Liam, he's just staring at me," I cried. "Sis, go back to sleep, she's okay. Go back to sleep," her brother said, and she went. She was only half awake, to begin with.

He left the doorway, and I coiled against the wall and asked Liam to stay on the phone with me for the rest of the night, and he did. I couldn't breathe. It hadn't been nearly as bad as what happened with Lamprey, but it was still yet another attack.

Everything came back. I started thinking about how things changed and how everyone turned against me during the first incident. I couldn't go back to that. I couldn't lose my friend and my boyfriend and have everyone hate me again. I had to be smart about this.

I decided the only thing there was to do was to play along. I needed my friend to think everything was a misunderstanding because if she or her family found out what happened, there would be a rising hell to pay, and I would once again be the lying slut claiming to be assaulted. It was bad enough for me when I went through it the first time, I didn't want to go back. And not only that but this time I had a boyfriend. I had a guy who I'd been building a beautiful love with who had pulled me out of the dark headspace Lamprey had left me in. I couldn't let him be ridiculed because of me, either.

When I woke up the next morning, I told my friend that her brother and I tried something, and I freaked out. I told her not to tell her boyfriend or Liam. I told her everything was a misunderstanding and that I was sorry for scaring her the night before. She hugged me and told me it was alright and told me to know that I can talk to her about anything.

When I made it home that morning, my mother, once again...knew. "Porsha, baby, you okay? You look kind of flushed or something," she said. "No, Ma, I'm fine. Just tired," I said. "You and your friend must have stayed up all night, huh?" she asked, smiling. "Yeah, I think I'm gonna go and actually go to sleep now," I said, heading straight to my room.

I called Liam, and he called his friend. We discussed what happened and what, if anything, should be done about it. I hadn't gotten a chance to tell Liam's friend what I had told my friend. She had told her boyfriend despite my instructions and was told the truth about what really happened. She went ballistic! She called me and cursed me out and told me never to come to her house again.

Though I had Liam, all feelings of my freshmen year began to rush back to me like a hurricane of the past. Liam called her and went off. "How could you treat your friend like that? How could you not believe her? Why do you think your brother came and told you to go back to sleep, and why would she be that upset?" he screamed.

I remember getting upset with him for even calling her. I honestly didn't know the right way to handle anything. All I knew was that what was happening was too much for me to deal with. My ex-friend had told girls in the fashion class about what I had said her brother tried to do to me. They teased and pointed at me and talked loud enough for me to hear them, saying things like, "Girl, don't nobody want her ole dusty a*! Why would he need to do that? He could have anybody he wanted to, baby!"

One morning, I told Liam that I wanted to check out. I told him I was ready to die and kept telling him that I wished he was enough to keep me here, but he wasn't. He couldn't understand and was hurt beyond measure. He didn't know how to make things better, and he didn't know what to say to me or what to do.

Eventually, after about a week, things died down, but I was sure not to spend any more nights at my friend's house. We reconciled after a long while, but things were never quite the same between us.

In case you're wondering, I'll go ahead and somewhat soothe you with a spoiler alert from Book #3 of this memoir series. Both Lamprey and my friend's brother reached out to apologize after my rise to fame. Lamprey wrote me a letter via Facebook messenger on my artist page, and my friend passed along the apology from her brother. "My brother told me to tell you that he's sorry for what happened between y'all," she said. "Did he tell you what happened?" I asked. "No, and I didn't ask. I just told him I would tell you. Was it that whole mess from high school that we fell out about," she asked. "Yeah, but we'll let the past be the past. Tell him I forgive him," I said. We've never talked about it again after that.

Things between Liam and I got extremely rocky after that. He kept wanting me to tell him I loved him, and I just couldn't. I couldn't even say to him that we would definitely be together in the future anymore. Overnight, things went from knowing exactly where I was heading to being lost once again.

I hated myself. I couldn't understand how I could find myself in a situation like that twice and not notice the red flags until after it was too late. What had I been thinking? Why was my guard down? Why wasn't I smarter? Why had I tried to hide the truth from my friend by telling her a lie I knew I couldn't keep up with? Everything literally spun out of control, and there was no way for me to stop it.

Liam and I kept trying to be together and kept having faith talks, but the talks went from being hopeful to being dark and ungodly. "Renae, why can't you say it. Why can't you say you're with me because you love me?" he asked. "At the end of the day, God will decide who I'm with. It's not my choice. I have no say in the matter," I said. "That's not true! Why are you saying that? God gives us the choice of free will. You can't tell me just once that you're with me because you're choosing me? I thought you loved me," he said. "It's complicated. Can we just drop the conversation?" I asked.

I want to take this moment to bring awareness to vital signs that may indicate someone's had a traumatic life-changing experience. I found myself deflecting a lot with my boyfriend and trying to sabotage the beautiful love we had. It wasn't that I didn't love him or didn't want him anymore, but I'd slipped back into feeling unworthy. This was the enemy's plan to once again isolate me so that he could have his way with me.

If someone's mood or behavior changes, if they start to be more closed off or even more extraverted and wilder than they were before, it's a good chance they may be dealing with trauma.

Liam and I weren't able to be intimate after that, but we were able to hang on a little while longer. The voices were loud and constantly told me things like '*Liam's only with you because he feels sorry for you*' and '*Liam doesn't want a used up, fat slut like you.*' I was having nightmares regularly and would call Liam after every single one and would have him sleep with me over the phone for the rest of the night.

Caring for me in these times became harsh and taxing for Liam. He no longer had the confidence in our love that he once did. He still treated me kindly, but I didn't receive it well and found myself always trying to pick arguments with him to make us not have to speak to one another.

Being with a guy like Liam after having past wounds ripped open; being reminded of just how used up I actually was, felt similar to how a woman might feel marrying her husband while having him think she was a virgin when she really wasn't. I felt dirty and undeserving, and I felt like our entire relationship was never supposed to happen.

It had to be by chance that Liam and I fell for one another, and had evil not taken its course, the opportunity would have all been worth it.

Color Me Red

"Pain never feels good, even if your body tells you it does. Never forget, the body is an antagonist of the soul."
~A. S. E.

THE ENEMY SEEMED to use everything around me to attack my self-worth once again. My English teacher, Ms. Crawfish, was a sweet lady, but the material was awful. It came time for us to read a book called *Speak*. The name sounded familiar, but I didn't link it to the book my oldest sister showed me on Ayo St.

I thought nothing of it until there was talk about there being a rape scene in the book. I went to Ms. Crawfish and asked her if it was true or not. "Yes, the young lady does go through something," she said. "Um, I can't read this book," I said. "It's required material, La'Porsha. Read the book." "Ms. Crawfish—" "La'Porsha, don't make things difficult. You're gonna be reading worse things than this for college," she said.

Yeah, I canceled college from my mind right then and there. It had never really appealed to me as it was. "Can I talk to you outside?" I asked. She reluctantly agreed. "Ms. Crawfish, I was hurt like this, and I don't wanna read about it," I said. The look on her face seemed flushed. "I'm sorry, La'Porsha. Um, let me see if you can read something else," she said. "Thank you, Ms. Crawfish."

She gave me a book called *The Pearl*, where the baby's head gets blown off at the end. I can see why the Amish stop their education at 8th grade.

Liam and I went on a school field trip to a museum one day with a bunch of classless kids. Liam and I sat near the back of the bus, and right behind us was a bunch of guys gawking at pornographic clips on their phones. They were calling Liam to look back at them, but I looked back first and saw what they were calling him to see. "Don't look. It's something you shouldn't see," I said. "What is it?" he asked. "Does it matter? Don't look," I said.

He ignored them for as long as he could before curiosity got the best of him, and he looked. I was so angry with him that I broke off our relationship. Those guys were disgusting, and as far as I was concerned, Liam was no better than them. The beautiful clean-cut version of himself he'd been showing me was a lie, as far as I was concerned.

When we got back to school, I walked home and wouldn't answer his calls. Eventually, I picked up to warn him to stop calling me. "Renae, let's talk about this, please," he said. "There's nothing to talk about. You're a disgusting pig who made me feel like I wasn't important," I said. "Renae, what was I supposed to do? They wouldn't stop calling my name. I was just trying to get them to stop. I didn't even really see the woman on the screen," he said.

"Wow, so you're an idiot and a liar, huh? How the h* you know it was a woman on the screen and not something else?" I asked. "I didn't get a good look, Renae." "Yeah, just good enough to see that much, huh? Liam, I've been through hell and back and hell and back time and time again, and don't want to be with someone who says he loves and respects me, but would show something different when he gets around a bunch of horny followers. I hope they were worth it!" I said, hanging up the phone.

Liam called right back. "Renae, really? After everything we've been through?" he asked. "That's what the h* I'm asking you! Really? After everything we've been through? You're not as different as you've been making it seem, Liam, and that hurts! This entire relationship I've been hating myself! You understand? I've been trying to change and adjust and open up just to try to be deserving of someone like you because I thought you were too good for me!"

"Renae, I never wanted you to put me on a pedestal," he said. "That's what women do to their kings, Liam! And believe it or not, you put yourself there! How are you gonna spend all this time prying me open and gaining my trust and loving me and respecting me and then pull something like this?" I said. "Renae, so this one mistake wipes out everything else I've done?" he asked. "Oh my gosh! This would have not even been a big deal if it had been a mistake! You deliberately went against what I asked, and you did it in front of the guys who wanted you to disrespect me! You heard them saying that I had you on a leash! You just had to prove 'em wrong, huh? Well, bye dog, 'cause you ain't on a leash no mo'!"

I hung up the phone and wouldn't answer his calls anymore, so he showed up to the house. I started to let him just stand there until the mosquitoes chased him away, but I met him on the deck bench. "Renae, I'm so sorry for disrespecting you. I love you, I do. And you're right, I was an idiot," he said. "Liam, I forgive you, but I don't want this. My heart can't handle being built up by a guy just to be torn down by him. I can't do it," I said. "Renae, I will never make you feel like this again," he said.

After hours of going back and forth, I agreed to continue our relationship, but my heart was closed off and distant. I couldn't find my way back to the happy, joyful me. My mother decided to allow me to decorate my room the way I wanted to and hang pictures all over my wall. I wanted to tac the images up to be artsy, but my dad told me I couldn't.

Liam had been over my house just as he was almost every day. "Ma already said I could put the pictures up like I want to, so that's what I'm gonna do," I barked. "I said you not! I'm the head of this house!" my dad screamed. "Whatever!" I screamed back. My dad grabbed me and choked me against the wall.

Liam heard the commotion from outside, and I saw him through the screen door running towards the house, but my mother raised her hand and stopped him and came running inside. "Duke, move! Why you puttin' your hands on her?" she yelled. "Carolyn, I've had enough of this girl! I can't take it no more! Something gotta change!" he barked.

"Duke, what happened?" she asked. "She runnin' off at the mouth again! I'm sick of her nasty attitude!" he yelled. "If you gonna tell her something, tell her the truth! Don't make it seem like I'm just getting smart with you all out the blue!" I yelled. "See, that's what I'm talking about right there," he said. "Ma, remember how you told me I could tac my pictures on my walls? Well, dad tried to tell me I couldn't and then started screaming about being the man of the house. I can't stand him! He always screws up then comes back like the king of the mountain. This ain't your house, it's our house! And that's my room up there!" I yelled. "This is my house, little girl! And as long as you under my roof—" "I ain't giving no respect unless it's earned! I done told you already," I said.

"Porsha, baby, calm down and go outside with Liam. Poor boy probably having a heart attack. He heard y'all all the way out there! Now, this has got to stop! Duke, it is her room! I did tell her she can do what she wants with her room! You're not even trying to get to know her. You're just throwing your weight around and being a hot head! How do you expect to get anywhere with her like that?" she scorned, looking at my dad. I went outside to meet Liam and told him what happened. "You alright? Are you hurt?" he asked. "No, but if you weren't here, I promise you, it would have been worse. This is what I've been trying to protect you from. My family is not like you think we are. My dad and I have been battling for years," I sobbed.

Liam held me and told me how he wished he could take me away from all of that. "Please don't tell your parents about what happened. I don't want them to stop you from coming over," I said. "I won't talk about it, I promise. Let me tell you something that will make you laugh," he said. "What is it?" I asked. "There was this beautiful, attractive light-skinned girl that I thought was one of the hottest girls in school in the 9th grade." "Um, you sure I wanna hear this story?" I asked. "Yes. Now, listen. She was fine. I walked up to her because my teacher asked me to ask her about singing in the school talent show. She was so icy and blunt that I got nervous. So, I rushed to ask her my question to stop bothering her as soon as possible," he said. "Oh my gosh! No way! That boy was you? You're the one who asked me about the show?" I asked. "Yep. I liked you before talking with you, but even more after," he said. "Oh my gosh, I'm so sorry, Liam! I was...in a bad headspace," I said. "It's fine. I always knew I wanted to know you more after that, and here we are."

Liam became my protector and was always concerned about my well-being from that point on through our relationship. He was always asking questions and making sure I was doing okay at home. I had a faint spell in class one day, and the teachers could barely keep him apart from me. I saw him frantic, but couldn't say anything. He never left my side.

Things died down and almost got back to normal around the time school was ending, though. We spent most of the summer together and even tricked my Granddaddy Joe like Liam was another son of my dad's. Liam and I had a striking resemblance to one another and were often told we could pass for brother and sister.

Liam's parents let him ride to the Delta with my family and visit our extended family. Liam met all my siblings, aunts and uncles, cousins, and my grandparents. We let some of my aunts in the secret plan and went to my grandparents' house. "Well daddy, this another one. This my son," my dad said. "Duke, he shole do look just like you, boy! Well, welcome to the family!" he said.

The house full of people burst into laughter. When we revealed who Liam really was, my granddaddy chuckled and wanted to continue with the theory of him possibly being related to me. On the ride back home, I ended up falling asleep on Liam and slobbered all over his shirt, and he let me. When we pulled into the driveway, Liam woke me up after my family had already gone in the house. "Renae, wake up, baby."

When I raised my head and saw what I'd done, I freaked out. "Why would you let me do that? Oh my gosh, I'm so sorry, Liam," I said. "Renae, I'm gonna be seeing a whole lot worse than this if we're gonna be together, right?" he asked, mimicking what I had told him the first time he came to visit my home. We laughed, he kissed me on my forehead and bid me goodnight.

Liam was gifted a car from his parents, and he asked my parents if it was alright for him to take my sister and me to and from school for the rest of the year. One morning, we were driving to school and I forgot something at home and didn't realize it until we made it down the street. "Hey, could you just back up real quick?" I asked. "Let me turn around," he said. "No, just back up, baby. The house is right there!" I said. "I'm not comfortable with that. Just let me drive, please," he said.

He backed up alright, right into a light pole and dented his car straight down the middle of the bumper. "Crap!" he said. "Should have listened to me," I said. He flashed me a look and pulled into our driveway. I went into the house, laughing, and he got out to examine his first fender bender.

He was very light-hearted about it and nonchalant...or at least, he appeared to be. That mark became somewhat of a thing we could always look at and draw close in laughter.

BLEEDING OUT

"When God isn't the foundation of a family,
parents can hurt children with smiles on their faces.
Never underestimate the detriment of God not being the foundation."
~A. S. E.

WHEN HALF THE summer was over, I made a choice to go to an art school, which was such a regret for so many reasons. The decision was hard because my mother had scared me into thinking that Liam and I would grow apart if we tried to have a long-distance relationship. The school was only a half-hour from home and probably wouldn't have been taxing on Liam and me, but I believed what my mother said and broke things off with Liam. She told me if it was meant to be, and if our love was true, it would survive a little break between us.

It was one of the hardest things I ever did. I mourned Liam, and he mourned me. Before going to the art school, my mother sat me down and had a serious talk with me about open communication. It was the day before my sixteenth birthday. "Porsha, I know things have been rocky around here with you and your dad and everything, but if I let you go to this school, you and I have to have open communication with each other," she said. "I agree. I don't want any secrets between us, either," I said. "Good, now is there anything you've wanted to tell me but haven't that I don't know about?" she asked.

I contemplated whether she already knew something or if she was just trying to open the floor for random conversation. "Um, well, there's one thing I haven't told you about," I said, with tears in my eyes. "What is it, baby?" she asked. "Well, I was...raped," I said. "You were...raped?"

she asked with a frown. "Porsha, are you saying you were...raped?" she asked again. "Yeah." "By who?" she asked. "I can't say," I said. "Oh, you gonna say. What you mean you can't say? When did this happen?" she asked. "Um, a couple years back," I said. "Porsha, if this did happen to you, you're gonna tell us who it was. You don't have a choice. Now spit it out!" she said.

I had already tried putting my past behind me, and Lamprey was long gone. I hadn't really even seen him since around the time of the incident. And I was not about to tell her about the most recent event, not with the anger she was showing. I was not about to tell her who they were so that she could dig all this up and start a war. And what did she mean by *if* this did happen to me? Did she even believe me? *No, she doesn't. She thinks you're disgusting!* So I lied. "I don't know who it was. It happened against the wall at the dance you let us go to in that teen club place," I said. "Against the wall, Porsha?" she asked. "Yeah," I said.

I felt sick for lying to my mother, but I didn't expect her to react the way she did. Then again, I don't think I really thought about her reaction at all. My mother had just finished sitting me down and having a heart-warming moment with me about open communication. I think I just decided to tell her as the start of genuinely open communication with her, but it turned out to be a massive mistake like I'd always thought it would be, especially with my dad in the picture.

My mother sent me to my room and told me to give her a chance to talk with my dad. "Do you have to tell him?" I asked. "He's your dad, yes. And I can't handle news like this on my own," she said.

After about a half-hour, I heard my parents calling for me to come to the den. They were sitting together on the couch and asked me to have a seat on the other couch. "Now tell us what happened," my mother said. My dad already had his nose flared up, so I knew this conversation was going to hell. Not to mention, I couldn't really tell them the full truth without them having an idea of who it was and going after the person, so I had to lie, again.

"It was at the party club Ma let me and Ree go to. I was attacked outside against the wall," I said. My mother's face grew furious! I was shocked and didn't understand her and my dad's reaction. Even if they didn't have the full story, why would they be showing anger towards me? "Porsha, Ima tell you something. I don't know who you think me and ya mama are, but we ain't no fools. And Ima tell you something else, ya lying!" my dad yelled. "I'm not lying! I was raped!" "Shut your mouth, Porsha! Don't you say another word or Ima have you!" my mother yelled.

I couldn't understand or believe what was happening. "Do you even remember what you had on that night?" she asked, referring to going to the teen club. "Um, a blue jean skirt and a blouse, I don't know?" I said, crying. "No, you had on some jeans!" she yelled. "Me and ya mama been married for sixteen years, and the position you describing it happened in ain't even possible!" my dad yelled. "Why are y'all screaming at me like I did something wrong? What is this? Ma, remember when we were watching the documentary of human trafficking, and we got into it? You were saying how you didn't see how women could let something like that happen to them. You said it was too many of them not to escape, and I told you not to judge them. Then you said if you were there, you would have escaped, and I said you can't say what you would've done if you weren't there. When I asked you to turn it off, you said no. I got so angry because I felt like you were judging me by judging them!" I cried. "If this was true, why would you wait so long to tell us?" my dad yelled. "I don't know, I just couldn't get the nerve," I cried. "Two years, Porsha? You must have like it to wait that long," my dad said.

My dad killed my spirit and was no longer a dad to me. But even more than that, he'd taken my mother from me, too. The sight of her sitting in front of him with his arms around her, soothing her like she was the one with the dark secret, was sickening. My mother had never spoken against me the way she did that night. She not only let my dad kill my spirit, but she also helped him do it.

Evil was thick in that den, and they couldn't see me. My parents couldn't see me. Darkness had won. I divorced my parents that night.

I lost all respect for them. My love for them was just about overcome with a deep hatred.

The fight left, and all I could do was scream in internal agony and cry. "Girl! Get out of our face! Go to your room and stay there! And you can forget some sweet sixteen party!" he said. I remained an empty shell in my room that night and wrote desperate cries to God, but I'd been too upset to hear an answer.

I can't really describe the emotions I felt. Rage, bitterness, anger, suicidal, homicidal, and so much more all wrapped in one. I didn't sleep and lay awake until morning. I got up to use the bathroom and when I was walking out, my parents were coming out of their bedroom. "Good morning," my mother said, primping her lip. "Hey," I said, barely audible. "Well, happy birthday," she said. "It's not happy, but thanks," I said. "Well, it not being happy is your own fault," my dad said, bucking his eyes.

"Let's pretend last night never happened," my mom said, patting my dad's chest. "So, what we doing for her birthday?" she asked him. "What you mean? We ain't doing nothin' for it," he said. "It is her *sixteenth* birthday," my mother said, looking at him. "And? Happy birthday," he said, bucking his eyes at me and walking off.

Tears streamed down my face, and I checked out. Liam came over a little later to give me a birthday gift, and I met him on the deck. He saw my face and knew something wasn't right. When I explained to him what happened, he just said, "It's gonna blow over and be alright." He had no encouraging words and showed no anger about what my dad had said to me. It was like he hadn't even heard me. That told me he'd locked me out of his heart and no longer cared about me. I was officially alone.

Hang in there. We've only got a little further to go.

LIFE SUPPORT

"It took my own crucifixions to realize I was more than a conqueror."
~A. S. E.

LIFE AT THE art school couldn't have been a more difficult time for me. When I first arrived, I thought it would be a place where I would meet my new family; my real family. I thought it would be a place where people would understand me, and I would understand them. But even in a school full of young, vibrant artists, I stuck out like a sore thumb.

I was a loner there and didn't really have any real friends. I got along with a group of girls I admired, though. Each of them was exceptionally unique. One was Vietnamese with the sweetest spirit and a country singing voice. Another girl was remarkably athletic and could sing and dance. She reminded me of Sanaa Lathan from Love and Basketball. Another girl was cute as a button and mature. She was quiet and always smiled. And another girl was like an older sister to me. We didn't always see eye to eye, but she was feisty and could act her but off.

Besides all these characters, there was one girl that I really didn't pay much attention to at first. We were sitting in the choir bleachers when the class started a 'clique' discussion. They were trying to pair groups of people together that generally hung out and decide who they thought would remain together after high school.

When it came to me and this other girl, they couldn't find any 'group' we belonged to. I was seated at the very top of the bleachers by myself, and she was sitting at the very top on the opposite side by herself. They laughed at how much alike we were in being to ourselves and placed her and me in a group with each other. "They're both about the same! Put them together!" they laughed.

The girl and I looked at one another and laughed with them. She was my suitemate and was in the adjacent room that shared my bathroom. Her name is Paulette. Yes, that's her real name. After that day, something terrible happened that caused me and Paulette's paths to intertwine in a divine sisterly way. Be patient with me as I bring this full circle. It could take a while.

Our music instructor, we'll call Mr. Starch, had discovered a special 'something' in my voice that he described to be 'rare.' There was a singing competition about to take place that was usually only allowed for seniors, because the singers were extremely skilled and well-seasoned. Mr. Starch, however, felt that my voice was ready to take on senior vocalists all around the nation.

Despite me being a junior, he chose me to join the seniors in competing for the national title. I was honored and lifted. Mr. Starch was a person who always believed that what I had to offer was a pure gift that couldn't really be taught. When I was deciding on whether to go to college and explaining to him that I really couldn't afford to, he was the person that told me, "Kiddo, I'll tell you like this. Your voice does things that I can't teach. It's special, and to be honest, no one can teach you what you already know. Education is great! But if you've got it, you've got it. Period. And you, kiddo, you've got it."

From that moment, I didn't stress about the pressures of my dad wanting me to join the military to pay for college or to even go at all. I focused on what I had, and that was a directly infused gift from my Creator.

When Mr. Starch chose me, the other juniors petitioned him one day when I was absent from class, saying that they felt it was unfair for me to be going to a competition without them being able to at least audition. But Mr. Starch told them he knew what the competition was like and he'd already heard all of our voices. He stood aggressively firm by his decision to send me along with the seniors, while the other juniors stayed behind.

I felt horrible about being in the middle of growing tension and felt terrible for my peers because I understood where they were coming from. But I also trusted and whole-heartedly believed that Mr. Starch knew what he was talking about.

He'd gained my trust through choosing a song for me that I had no doubt in my mind that it was impossible for me to sing. The title was *Your Daddy's Son* from the Broadway show *Ragtime*. I had to mix my falsetto and head voice to reach most of the notes, but somehow someway, God allowed me to make it happen.

I didn't even know what mixing was or head voice or falsetto was until Mr. Starch told me I was using them. I was just singing and getting the sound out any which way it would come. Mr. Starch made me perform my version of Your Daddy's Son for a school showcase, and I caught the attention of the acting teacher who said, "La'Porsha, not only are you an amazing singer, but your connection to this song brought me to tears, and that's very hard to do. If you're ever interested in acting, you let me know." I had brought an acting teacher to tears? Wow!

My dad was supposed to attend and watch me sing, but for some reason, he was running late and missed my performance. When he arrived, everyone raved to him about how I brought the house down.

I just added this to the pocket of moments my dad had missed concerning me, which included, but weren't limited to, not recording my birth but being able to record my sister's and not recording my segment of a gospel singing competition but being able to record every other person who performed.

Back to the senior competition. My grades had been slipping tremendously, and my attitude was the darkest it had been in a while. It started because of a front desk clerk we'll call Ms. Martha. Ms. Martha was loved among all the children and had one of the sweetest spirits you would ever meet. She was known for allowing the children to personally use the front desk phone to call home so that she could keep busy with something else.

She wasn't supposed to allow us to do that and she wasn't allowed to give us the special code we had to dial before making a call, but she did. I had no idea that it was such a big deal. One day, I was in the library upstairs and needed to use the phone. There weren't any staff near the phone, so I thought nothing of it and placed a phone call to my mother from the upstairs library using the code from the downstairs front desk phone.

It must have sent off some sort of signal or something because I got called to the big office and questioned by the principal and assistant principal at that time. "La'Porsha, how did you know the code to make a phone call?" they asked. I didn't think it was as bad as it was, so I told the truth. "Ms. Martha gave me the code to make a call, and I remembered it and used the same code to call from upstairs," I said. "La'Porsha, our administration isn't allowed to do that," they said. "I'm telling the truth, I swear! Ask other kids! She lets many of us make calls sometimes," I said.

"La'Porsha, we've known Ms. Martha for a long time, and she would never do something like that," they insisted. I was appalled and extremely hurt. I didn't want to get Ms. Martha in trouble, but I didn't want them thinking I was a liar either because I wasn't. They called Ms. Martha in the office and questioned her, and she denied everything, knowing that it would cause my record to be permanently tarnished!

I couldn't believe it! My parents came to the school, and I sat in the office with them. "We've spoken to the staff in question, and they deny everything La'Porsha's saying," they said. "You can check the cameras! I promise I'm telling the truth!" I said. "Can you guys check the cameras. I mean, my child is not a liar, and if she's saying you can check the cameras to get the truth, why not take that step?" my mother asked.

I can't remember what bogus excuse they gave or if they lied and said they did, but the whole thing was sick and twisted. They gave me a write-up and put me on probation. When I returned to the dorm building, Ms. Martha was at the desk, crying. "La'Porsha, I am so sorry.

It's ...it was that or I lose my job. Please forgive me," she said. Although her apology didn't really fix anything, a weight was lifted off my shoulders because I now knew why she lied on me, and it was nothing personal. I think my biggest thing was needing to be believed. The situation had brought me back to my parents and how they had treated me after revealing my darkest secret to them.

I withdrew and wouldn't even eat lunch in the cafeteria anymore. I would get my lunch tray and go straight to my room, eat, and watch *Thumbelina*. This was my routine for a few months straight. I escaped into that movie and was able to make it through the second half of the day.

The first half of the day included a geometry class I took at the regular high school in that town. To cope with that, I would plug my ears with my mp3 player. My song list was *You Are Not Alone* by Michael Jackson, *Someone In the Dark* by Michael Jackson, *Living In a World They Didn't Make* by Janet Jackson, and *We Are One* from The Lion King II.

When I would get to class, I would sit there with one ear still plugged up and listen to *They Don't Really Care About Us* by Michael Jackson and *Rhythm Nation* by Janet Jackson. My teacher tried to tell me to cut the music at first, but when we talked outside, he asked, "Why do you listen to music while I'm teaching?" "It helps me concentrate. I hear everything you're saying and understand it better with music. I can also block out the class clowns, and they're ignorant conversations better, too," I explained.

He gave me a puzzled look and then smiled at me. He was an old Caucasian man with a gentle spirit. He said, "I'll tell you what, as long as you can pass my quizzes and tests, I'll let you keep the music, but the moment you fail, the music has to go. Deal?" "Deal!" I said, smiling. Tears began to well up in my eyes. "Hey, what's that? Why are you crying?" he asked. "Nothing. Just been having it kind of rough, and this makes it better," I said.

He gave me a side hug and patted my shoulders. What I told him was only a fraction of the truth. Music had become my life support. It was the only way I was surviving each moment of each day. Even with all the constant infusion of music and Thumbelina, it didn't stop me from angering to the point of chasing a girl literally around the school after she'd pushed my chest and ran off. That incident, unfortunately, made me a bit of a legend there. It also didn't make me numb to cruel things some people said to me.

For instance, there was one guy I admired significantly there. He was unique and extremely talented with art and rap. He and a few others were playing a game about which girls are good for what. He had said the 'Sanaa Lathan' girl was good for wifey and had name another girl good for girlfriend. I have no idea what compelled me to ask him, "What about me?" but it was a question I lamented. "Hm. I say you're good to f*," he said.

The table grew silent and looked with eyebrows raised, feeling embarrassed for me. The other girls let their eyes wander to keep from looking at me. I silently got up and went back to my hole with my music and my movie.

One night, I was sharing something on my computer with my roommate, who I had voted for when she made the top thirteen on American Idol. I looked up to her in many ways. She was an overall friendly and funny person, even though there were some things I didn't understand about her. It took us a minute to see eye to eye because of my weird behavior, but we eventually found common ground and would even have spiritual conversations. She was obsessed with Josh Groban and was the one to introduce me to his incredible gift.

The computer was given to me by my dad. He'd been too cheap to buy me a new one and gave me one he'd used. While I was looking through it with my roommate, a video popped up on the screen. I hurried to try and click out of it, but not before my roomie, and I saw a glimpse of it.

I stared at my screen in disbelief of what I'd seen. The longer I stared at the thumbnail, the more familiar it seemed. I noticed the green couch from our burned down home on Ayo street! When I made that out, I hurried to click exit from the window, but multiple windows of the video had opened on my computer and were simultaneously playing!

I saw the green couch and recognized the woman as my dad's old secretary and saw the teddy bear stand in the hallway that, to this day, my mother refuses to get rid of because she never saw the video, and it's her favorite teddy bear. All this meant the male genitals I was seeing that disgusting woman slobber all over was...my dad!

I threw up and screamed violently and cried. I first called my dad to curse him out like my tongue was built for it, but he didn't answer. So, I called my mother and cursed up a storm in her ear about him. She was appalled and was shocked at my language, but all care left me. When she recognized the height of my rage and the complete absence of my filter, she flew to the school at two in the morning.

When she arrived well after visitation hours, the clerk allowed her to see me, knowing it was an emergency. "How you doing, baby?" she asked. "How the h* you think, Ma?" I answered. "Baby, please, I know it's hard, but can you not curse at me? I'm here for you, baby," she said.

I sat in silence because all my mind conjured up were the harshest, most foul language that ever existed. "Let me show you the video," I said. "Baby, no. Mommy don't wanna see the video. I can imagine what's there, so I don't want to see it. Ya dad and I have been in a rough space and are still trying to get to a good place. This will only hinder progress," she said.

"So, you still want him?" I asked. "Baby, your dad has changed. That video is from when we weren't even together, so how am I gonna hold that against him? I'm sorry you saw what you saw, but we'll get through this, okay?" she said.

I broke down and cried in her arms as she rocked me for about an hour in silent torture. She asked me if I wanted to come home, and I agreed. But I warned her that I didn't want to speak with my dad.

In the beginning, he kept his distance, but when my mother suggested they buy me a brand new computer, he came where I was looking at choices and said, "Hey, can we talk?" "I ain't got nothin' to say to you," I said. "Well, you mind listening?" he asked. "I actually do, but go ahead."

"Baby, I can't tell you how sorry I am for what you saw. That computer was one I barely used, and I thought I cleaned it, but somehow I missed that. I know it was extremely hard to see, but you know ya mama and I are trying to rebuild," he said.

I slowly turned around to meet his eyes with the look of death, but he was so caught up in his selfishness, that he continued despite my silent warning. "Sometimes, it's best to keep things to yourself if it's not going to help the here and now. This is just another hurdle me and ya mama now have to try and get over," he said.

He said it! He actually said what I thought he was about to say! I was blown away. "Are you telling me I should have just dealt with it on my own?" I asked. "No, baby, I'm just...never mind," he said, slowly walking back over to join my mother.

Fresh tears fell on my cheeks, but before they hit, I *knocked* them away. *Don't you dare waste any more tears on this non-family you don't have*, I told myself.

I had tried to reconnect with Liam. I was so lonely, and I missed him. It had been a grave mistake to ever let him go. We stayed together for about three weeks before he decided that his heart was no longer with me, and he couldn't do *us* anymore. I mourned him by watching a scene from *New Moon* when Jacob leaves Bella crying the rain and breaks up with her. I didn't watch the movie, just that one clip redundantly in the shared area at the end of my hall. I looked like a zombie by the eyes, so much so that an administrator walked me to my room and tucked me into bed like a baby. I was highly suicidal, and she knew it.

My faint spells picked up drastically while attending the school as well due to stress. So with all this taking place, when Mr. Starch chose me to represent our school with the other seniors, the assistant principal later told me that I couldn't go because of my poor grades. I hadn't really been focusing, I'd just been trying to get by and get back to my hole with my music and my movie as quickly as I could and interact with the students and staff there as least as possible.

My faint spells caused me to have to call home a lot. My dad and mother decided to accuse me of faking in the most childish way possible. One day, they had picked me up and started talking to each other like I wasn't there. "You know what I would do when I was in school and would get in trouble or just didn't want to be there?" my dad asked my mother. "What?" my mother asked, already knowing what he was going to say. "I would pretend to faint," he said. "What? Naw..." my mother said, sarcastically.

When we got home, they told me that if my behavior continued, they were going to take me out of the art school and send me to boot camp. "Porsha, what do you need? Tell us what you need? Counseling?" my mother asked. "What are you talking about, my faint spells? I don't know! If the doctors can't tell you how can I? But just because they can't diagnose me doesn't mean I'm faking! That's ignorant to even think!" I yelled.

"It's this! It's this, Porsha! Your attitude and the way you always talking to us! You don't even treat us like we're your parents!" my mother cried. "You really wanna go there? Y'all don't act like it! You cry 'respect, respect, respect'! Where's mine?" I asked. "You have to give it to receive it," my dad said. "I'm glad you know it!" I said.

All these types of arguments had been going on and contributing to my misbehavior. So although Mr. Starch believed in my talent enough to go compete, Ms. Toad, being the snake I felt she was, told me I wouldn't be able to go. "Your grades are horrible, and you would be gone and miss too much work," she said, with my parents in the office. "What can I do? Please! Mr. Starch believes in me so much and has even had to defend his decision against my peers. I can't let him down!" I said.

Ms. Toad looked at me with a smirk and said, "I'll tell you what. If you raise your grades in the next two weeks from where they are now, then you'll be off academic probation and will be able to go. But honestly, I don't see it happening," she said.

"You've got a deal! I'm going to work harder than you ever thought I could," I said, smiling. I did just that. I was headstrong in my books, and my grades shot up! Part of me felt like she made the deal because she didn't think I could do it. That drove me to work overtime at proving her wrong.

After two weeks of slaving to pull my grades up, I met the requirements with flying colors! My parents met back up with me, and we sat in Ms. Toad's office once more. "Well, you surprised me," she said smirking. "But if I'm being honest, I still don't think you should go. You're going to miss a lot of work and have to play this catch-up game all over again when you get back," she said.

What was I hearing? "No, please I can do it! What about our deal?" I asked. "A deal is a deal, but the last say is up to your parents. If they say you can go, then alright," she said. My parents looked at me, contemplating and smirking and sent me out of the office to speak more with Ms. Toad.

They called me back in, and I thought they were about to give me the best news of my life, but instead, my parents looked me in the face and said, "Porsha, we've talked it over, and as hard as it is to say this, we can't let you go." I stood there in silent shock with tears on my face. "What?" I got weak and took a seat in a chair. "What are you saying? How are you taking her opinion over what I've just done? Are you telling me I worked my butt off for two weeks straight for nothing?" I screamed. "You did what you were supposed to been doing, Porsha!" my mother said.

I stormed out of the office down the concrete pathway to the dorm building. "La'Porsha! La'Porsha!" my mother called. Eventually, I stopped and swung around. "See how you actin'?" my mother asked. "Shut up! Shut up, Ma! Shut up and leave! Get out of my face! Go!" I screamed in agony. My parents put up their hands and walked away, leaving me there in my own torture.

The girl I mentioned earlier about being a great actress saw me falling to the ground and crying. "Baby, get up! Come on, get up! You stronger than this, baby. Come on, you a fighter, Porsha, get up," she said. I don't know how much of everything she'd seen, but she came in like a boxing coach and helped walk me to the room she shared with Paulette.

Paulette sat on her bed like a wise mother and consoled me. The other girl's name was Courtney. "Porsha, look at me. Baby, look at me! You are a fighter, Porsha! You are a warrior! I don't have to know what's going on, but I know you're under attack! Don't let them see you down like this! Porsha, I swear you have so much power in your voice, they can't stop you no matter what! Not if you don't let them," she said.

I tried to raise my eyes to hers, but I couldn't. Courtney went to get a tissue and wiped the snot from my nose and the tears from my eyes and held my face on her fingertips. "Stop it! Pick your head up! Don't hang it down low. They ain't worth it, baby! The best revenge is success! It's hard now, and sometimes you can't see the light with your eyes, but it doesn't mean it's not there. Go deeper and further and don't quit!" she said.

When I tell you her pep talk to me was everything! She and I hadn't always seen eye-to-eye up to this point, but the fact that she put our differences aside and spoke life into a soul she saw dying at that moment, was everything to me!

Paulette allowed Courtney to finish and said, "Sis, I don't know what's going on, but I know the enemy wants you, honey. I be seeing you around here and I don't know everything, but I've heard some thangs about you. From what I gather, almost every person at this school want what you got, and that's why they hate you. That's why they talk about you. That's why they turn against you. They're afraid of you and intimidated by your gift. Honey, you don't dim your light for them, you pass them some d* shades and shine, baby!" she said.

I've lost touch with Courtney due to our busy lives as she's very successful herself, these days, but Paulette and I have remained friends for over ten years now. She is my very best friend, and no one could ever take her place. These two girls saved my life that day because I was crucified...again. They revived me with their love.

I eventually gained the physical strength to walk back over to my side of the suite and plugged up my music, then watched my movie. Let's take a listen to *Nearer, My God, To Thee* by BYU Vocal Point & BYU Men's Chorus.

Critical Condition

"When spiritual wounds are made, the only blood donor that matches what you need is Christ, the Son of I Am."
~A. S. E.

THEN, I DID something I hadn't done since the incident with Lamprey. I prayed, cried, and worshiped God. With every note, I journeyed a little closer to the light. I could feel my spirit growing warm, and the taxing darkness fading away.

My faith in God hadn't really been shaken to the point of not believing in Him or wanting to please Him, but my identity and self-worth had been entirely dark washed. I no longer knew my purpose or value to God, and because of that, I felt He didn't care what I did or with whom I did it. In my mind, God had allowed me to slip through the cracks. He'd placed me not only in a dysfunctional world but in a dysfunctional home.

In the middle of my praise, I started wondering why I didn't hear His voice when I'd invited Lamprey over or when I'd kept going with Carmen or when I'd got in the car with the couple or when my friend's brother called me to his room, why hadn't I used the wisdom God gave me to refuse. Just as I thought it, He answered me with a voice sweetly brushing against my ear that I hadn't been in a place to hear in a very long time. "*I am not him. I am not Lamprey or any of the others that have hurt you. I would never force Myself upon you. I've mourned your love just as you have Liam's and your parents'. I've wanted to intervene, but to do that, you would have had to choose Me. I sent warnings and messages by way of people and the dreams I gifted you, but they went ignored. I know you're broken and tired.*

If you will Me to come to you and be with you and surrender your heart and your mind and your body and the very depths of your soul to Me, I will come and rest upon you with a sacred love unmatched to any other impersonation of love you've ever come to face. If you give Me all of your being, I will give nothing short of My deepest love, My endless mercy, My abundant grace, and My overwhelming favor to you and to anything that is of you."

The words caused my spirit to sink into deep worship and praise for My God, who'd just finished declaring that He not only still *loved* me, but He still *wanted* me. The Almighty holy, sovereign, righteous, just, and everlasting Creator thought me important enough to fervently pursue my heart while still allowing me the gift He'd never take away from me; free will. And even if I willed sin to be my master, He, the Most High, called on my hand in marriage. He, the Almighty, appealed to me by comparing Himself to my transgressors, who weren't even worth being uttered from His holy lips.

He gifted me peace and settled my internal storm. He soothed the aches of my gut and began mending all pieces of my heart. He began healing the heart broken by so many vessels of the enemy. Then I heard my name over the intercom being called. The clerk pointed me outside where my mother's car was parked. They had wrapped my favorite sub sandwich, Philly cheesesteak, with a card and a letter saying how much they loved me and to try to keep my head up.

Before now, I would have thrown it back at them, but God had minutes ago given me a peace that passed all understanding, even my own. I accepted the gift with as best of a smile as I could make on my emotionally drained face and receded back to my room with my music, my movie, and now, my God.

While the seniors were away, the dance teacher trusted me to be her assistant in putting together her dance recital. My dad showed up to support the junior showcase I was a part of as well as the recital. I think this was a day all departments showed their stuff to visitors or something like that.

My dad told me how awesome I was and how much he enjoyed the show. He much later revealed to me that he went home that night and cried to my mother, "My baby didn't belong there. She stood out so obviously. She should have been on that trip," he said. "I let you make the decision as the head of the house," my mother said. "I know, and I take full responsibility. But this is one time I wish you would have gone against me and sent her on the trip. I could see her trying to be her best and cover up the pain of her being left behind, and it cut me deep," he said, with tears flowing from his eyes.

When it came time for the junior competition, my dad decided to join me to try and show his support and make up for the first missed trip. It wasn't the same, but it was nice to get along with him without arguing even once. He was supportive and rooting for me as my mother would have been. He kept calling her and bragging and keeping tabs on everything.

Then my voice completely disappeared. He was distraught and didn't want me to mess up. I told him that my Father was with me, and would make everything alright. As soon as I took the stage to sing *One Night Only* from Dreamgirls, my voice returned for that moment only, I received a standing ovation, won second place overall, and then my voice left again.

My dad and I laughed about it, acknowledging how much I wasn't in control of anything and how God allowed my voice to return momentarily to accomplish all that I had. Things seemed a little lighter for a while.

My class took a trip to New York to sing Rene Clauson's *Memorial* at Carnegie Hall with a college chorus and full orchestra. It was an experience that was topped only by me witnessing Lion King live on Broadway for the first time. That experience changed my life! That was the moment I became my version of Simba and decided that I would always 'remember' who I was.

That's not to say I didn't face struggles and more rejections, but they never quite broke me down the same way they had been able to.

My high school sweetheart, Liam, had agreed to still take me to prom before breaking things off with me. Since the special night was approaching, he called me asking if I still wanted to go, and I said yes. The night was magical. His parents had rented a black SUV that resembled the one-off of the Twilight movie, and he rode me down the long pathway in Percy Quinn Park, listing to *Float On* and other oldies.

I couldn't even bring myself to look at him, he was so beautiful. I stared out the window, and he noticed my nervousness and grabbed my left hand and kissed it. "Let's just focus on tonight," he said. I smiled.

We sat down for a while, watching people dance the night away until a slow jam played. He stood up and asked, "May I have this dance," with the sexiest smirk I'd ever seen him make. I place my hand in his and let him guide me to the dance floor. "I'll do my best if you do yours," he said, smiling. "I can't dance either, so let's wing it," I said, mentally referencing Thumbelina.

He was so smooth, I was shocked and couldn't stop blushing and making nervous giggles. He'd made my dreams come true. He had been my Prince Cornelius and had allowed himself to 'be my wings' for that special night.

Then, he lowered his hand on my back and drew me nearer and whispered in my ear, "Let's get back together." "What? Are you playing or serious," I asked, smiling and hopeful. "Maybe this is just what I needed... this right here, to remind me of our connection," he said. "Yes! Nothing would mean more to me," I said. "We'll take it slow, but a chance can't hurt, right?" he asked. "Right," I said through my smile.

We eventually went back to his place, and he invited me to spend time with him in the living room. "Hey, are you serious about us trying again?" I asked. "You don't believe me?" he asked. "I want to, I'm just scared. What if what you feel isn't real?" I asked. He stepped up to me and kissed me long and passionate and gentle. "Does that feel real?" he asked. "Yes," I smiled.

That's what you think. Just wait. [voices] I ignored the voices. The rest of the night was a dream, and unfortunately, the next day, I was startled right out of that dream. Liam called me. "Hello?" I answered. "Hey, you busy?" he asked. "No, what's up?" I asked. "I feel bad for saying this, but

I'm rethinking things, and maybe you were right. Maybe I got caught up in the moment," he said. "Liam, please. No, don't do this. Last night was real! I felt it! What happened between then and now?" I asked.

"Well, I asked my mother about us getting back together, and she didn't think it was a good idea," he said. "What? Why? Is it because of my past or my family?" I asked. "No, she just saw how hard I took it when you broke things off the first time and how bad of a place it left me in," he said. "I mean, I understand, Liam, but I was in a bad place too! Things are different now. They're better," I said. "I'm sorry, I just don't know," he said. "Is it because of the last [assault] incident?" I asked. "I mean, it's everything. I don't even know what to believe with that or anything else... I just, I don't know, Porsha. I mean, even you said it. How can you find yourself in that situation more than once? And I believed you when you said you loved me and look how that turned out," he said.

My heart was sucker-punched. He didn't believe me anymore? How could I give him an answer to the question I couldn't even answer myself. I had no idea how I ended up in such similar situations more than once. I felt he was right. I should have been smarter and thought quicker. But I couldn't change any of that now, or could I? "Okay, if it makes you feel better, I wasn't raped. Okay? I wasn't raped! I'm not damaged goods. I was just troubled. Does that help?" I asked. "Porsha, is that true?" he asked. "Would it make a difference?" I asked. "Well, it might I don't know, just tell me."

He seemed to be reconsidering being with me if it was the truth, so out of a failed desperate attempt to keep him in my life and not lose him again, I said, "Yes. None of that stuff is who I am. I'm just a regular girl who was depressed for a while. See? Everything that happened in our relationship is normal stuff that relationships go through. It's nothing we can't get past together. Now, can we put the past behind us and build us back up again?" I asked.

He was quiet for a moment and said, "Yeah, I guess." "Come to the movies with me today? My mom is taking us to Brookhaven with my older sister visiting. Please come?" I asked. "Uh, I don't think I feel up to it," he said. "Please," I begged. After a long silence, he agreed.

When the movie was over, we started talking about the conversation we'd had earlier that morning. Liam revealed that he still wanted to back out, so I turned to my mother for help. "Ma, can you please talk to him. I don't want to lose him, and I think he's scared to give us another chance," I said. "Porsha I can't make someone like you. That's his decision," she said. "This all started because you told me to break up with him!" I said. "I'll talk with him," she said.

They talked for a while, and then he walked back towards me. "Well, what did she say? Did she tell you how much I loved you?" I asked. "I'm sorry, Porsha," he said. I raced to my mother. "What did you say to him?" I asked. "I didn't say anything but what I felt! I told him that I felt y'all should be friends, and—" I stormed away from her before letting her finish and got into the car. "Porsha, I'll never stop caring about you," he said. "I'm just no longer good enough to be with?" I asked. "I'm sorry. Maybe if you had asked me six months ago when my heart was still hanging on, I would've said something different, but I just can't now. Just please promise me you won't give up on yourself," he said.

I looked out of the window and cried all the way back home. How could I have gained the love of my life back and lost him in the same twenty-four hours? I tried to turn my focus back to God and keep pressing forward. But my flesh boiled with sorrow and anger at how unfair I thought my life was to this point.

As I'm writing this, I'm realizing exactly what happened here. I'd just reconnected to my Creator and re-centered myself in Him. The very first time Liam entered my life, I believe God was using him to pull me out of the dark. But this time, the enemy used him to place me back there. It's amazing how we never stop to think that we're all vessels and we're always being used by one master or another. Just because someone served one purpose at a particular time in your life doesn't mean they'll always serve that same purpose every time you run into them again. People[puppets] don't really change, they simply switch between two [puppet]masters.

I decided to try out for American Idol before my senior year and was given an ultimatum by the same crooked administrators at the arts school. My parents and I were told I had to choose between attending the school or trying out for the singing competition because they had already had a student go through Idol and didn't want to support another student going through that. By this time, my parents had come to realize how they'd been deceived and convinced by Ms. Toad in not allowing me to compete, and they deeply regretted it. They stood their ground with a fierce vengeance. "We fully support her decision to follow her dreams and try out for Idol," my dad said, firmly. "She'll be okay, even if she doesn't make it. But we're not about to pass on this opportunity for her based off of what might or might not happen," my mother chimed in.

[Sneak peek from Book #3 of this memoir series.] The same administrators that had allowed a staff's word to ride over mine at the school ended up reaching out to me with a proposal. While on American Idol, they offered to 'promote' me if I let people know I attended their school. I respectfully wrote her back saying, "I appreciate your kind offer, but I respectfully decline." What I really wanted to write was, "Really, you'll promote me? Oh, how kind of you, but no thanks. I think my God's got that part covered. No need for snakes in my grass," but I said nothing of the sort. [I'm crying laughing aloud!]

I chose to try out for Idol with my sister. I went to New Orleans and sang *Have You Ever Been In Love* by Celine Dion. I received a standing ovation from all who heard me in the echoing arena, but was told I should come back next year because I was young and wasn't what they were looking for. I was pulled to the side by a producer saying that my voice wasn't understood because it was too big, and they were looking for something more sweet and subtle. This broke my spirit, and reinforced my dad's notion that I was chasing a pipe dream. He became adamant about me seriously considering the military or college.

I held to my guns against my dad and my 2nd JROTC instructor about me being on American Idol. We were even given a class assignment that made us have to choose jobs and budget a household. I chose being a 'contestant on American Idol'. "Mays, you need a plan B. That's not a real job," my instructor laughed. My classmates laughed at my crazy faith, but they believed me because of how much I believed in myself.

I decided not to return to the art school for my senior year and to return to McComb High. With me moving back in the house and being home full time again, things between my dad and I heated up once more. The fights were physical and often drew blood from my lips or left huge lumps on my forehead. I even pulled a knife on him once, and had it not been for my mother standing between us, I would have taken his life.

I skipped most of my senior year, but when I did attend school, my days were nothing short of eventful. I was full-on back to rebelling against God and re-entered a 'companionship' with a much older woman in her thirties in Amite, LA. I had met her through a 'friend finding' website while I was at the art school. Over the period of my junior year, we grew close, but I'd ended things after hearing God profess His love for me.

At the same time, I had signed up to be in every single class Liam was in with hopes of his heart letting me in one final time to prove myself worthy of him. But he had moved on with a girl we'll call Joy. Joy had a limp to her walk due to being crippled. He and Joy had known each other since elementary. It hurt because I'd become good acquaintances with Joy, but I wished them both the best.

I begged Liam one night to attend a football game with me. It was something he'd told me he had never done before, so I wanted to share that experience with him and make another memory to hold to. He lied and said he had tons of homework and didn't feel like going. So, I figured I'd start on my calculus homework. I hit a problem I couldn't solve and texted him for help. When he didn't respond, I called and heard the football game in the background. "I thought you said you had homework and didn't want to go," I said. "I did, but Pilch—" "Pilch? I asked you to go to the game and you adamantly refused so you could with Pilch? Liam, if you didn't want to go with me, you should have just said so," I said. "I didn't want to hurt your feelings," he said. *Oh, hush.*

He's trying to get you out of his life! You're yesterday's trash! [voices] "I'm not glass, I won't break. Have fun. Bye," I said.

He had started making it extremely clear to me that he no longer cared about me. One day, I had another weak spell, and he stepped over me and walked out of the classroom. When the teachers were able to bring me to, I caught him enjoying his lunch with his friends and with Joy. I knew then, not only had I lost the love of my life forever, but I lost my soul mate.

One day Joy just up and randomly told me he was talking to her about how hard it was being in a relationship with me. She was telling me personal things he was saying to her about me and about some of the darkest moments of my life that were private, and it sounded like he was trying to use the relationship we had like some kind of sob story to gain brownie points with Joy.

I slowly turned to her and asked, "Okay, and what did *you* say while he's telling all my business?" I asked. "I was just listening to—" "Why the h* you telling me all this anyway?" I asked. "I...I don't—" "You know what, you come in my face again with some bull like this, Ima smack you! Move!" I said, nudging her out the way, storming down the hall.

I stormed in our Physics class we took together and caught him in his desk and slapped him. "Let me tell you something, b*, if you wanna screw some lil' limpin' hoe that's fine by me, but don't you dare...say... my...name. Don't act like y'all don't have enough to talk about already. You wanna be a doctor, and she is what she is ...that's plenty of conversation!" I scolded.

The whole class laughed at Liam, asking him what happened. "I don't even know what you're talkin' about," he said. "Really, punk? You're gonna lie? Hmm, now I see the real reason you didn't want me back. It bothers you that your balls are smaller than mine," I said, tilting his forehead back with my fingers. "I've warned you, Liam. And if you think I'm lying or bluffing about *this*, try me," I said in my lowest voice register.

Just then, the Physics teacher walked in and said, "Hey what's—" "I'm going home...today ain't the day," I said, walking out. I waltzed straight to the outdoor section that was in front of the school, sat on the bench and used my cell phone to call my mother. When she arrived, I cried my eyes out to her, saying how betrayed I felt by Liam. "Baby, there are other guys," she said. "Ma, no! I've given so much to Liam. You don't even understand," I cried.

I was referring to the fact that just as Liam began talking to Joy, he'd come to my house to tutor me. I was relentless in trying to convince Liam to get back together with me all senior year. This particular day, I reminded him that I was his first. "Well, my brother says technically, you weren't my first." "Liam, what does that even mean? We had sex," I argued. "Yeah, but I didn't c*, and my brother says since I didn't do that, it doesn't count as 'me losing my virginity.'" "So are you ashamed of what we did?" I asked. "I'm sorry, but no. I don't see you as my first. I mean, why would I want to? We didn't last. I'm sorry if that hurts, but it's the truth," he said.

Tears began flowing down my face. "See? I'm leaving. I wasn't trying to make you feel bad," he said. "Liam, no! Wait...please. I...You're right. I'm sorry for expecting you to cherish our first time the way I do. But, regardless of if you love me or not, I still love you. I want to be your first," I said. "Renae—" "I'm not talking about sex. Let me be the first to make you.." I said.

Liam thought for a moment. I grew sick, but hid it well. I couldn't shake the porn images out of my head, but for Liam, I was willing to do anything. I kneeled before him sitting on my bed in my attic room, and served him. When he released, my throat burned, and I ran downstairs to the bathroom. I spit and rinsed my mouth, then went to the washroom to recollect myself. Liam found me there. "Are you okay?" he asked. "Yeah, I'm good. I promise," I said. "You're lying. See, this is why I didn't want to—" "Liam, I'm fine. I didn't have a flashback or anything. I'm just not...used to that. Did you enjoy it?" I asked. "What do you think?" he asked. I laughed while beginning to cry and he hugged me. "We'll figure things out, I promise. I still love you, I'm just not in love," he said.

I didn't tell my mother any of this in depth, but I hinted that Liam and I had done intimate things together.

My teacher didn't even report me. He told me later that he figured I needed that time alone for how upset I was.

That wasn't the only time I had gone off in class. With my dumb, love-struck behind signing up for every class Liam was in, which were many college AP courses, I was struggling... big time. It was hard for me to keep up with the material, but Liam had been helping me almost every day after school, which had always been my plan.

Unfortunately, his help didn't really matter when it came to physics. That was one subject I just couldn't get a handle on. I was asking a question to the teacher one day, and smart-mouthed snobby 'mean girl', Amy, decides she wants to vent her frustration out to me. She was the same one from Mr. Crab's Class. "Oh my gosh! Really? It's simple, and if you're not getting it, then tutor after school or something! Maybe if you actually did your homework, you would understand this!" she vented.

I looked at the teacher, waiting for him to say something, but he... said...nothing. I got out of my seat and said, "Hoe, say it to my face! Shut yo privileged a* up! You don't know anything about me to be talkin' to me like that. I'm sorry if all students can't get it as quick as you, but while I'm learning and asking whatever question I'm asking to the teacher, you shut your mouth," I told her.

She went silent and rolled her eyes. "And when they get stuck, I'll come and pop 'em back into place for you, m'kay?" I said. "You know what? I'm writing you a referral," the teacher said. "Oh really?" I asked, smiling. "You don't get to take over my class and get away with it," he said. "If *you* had taken over your class and addressed that nasty attitude sittin' over there, I wouldn't have had to. So go on and write ya referral, but it'll be your last time makin' a bad judgment call like this," I warned.

I gathered my books and walked out. I hung out in the outside eating area until it was time for lunch. When the bell rang, I went into the cafeteria and found a table. When the teacher saw me eating alone, he came and sat at my table. "Hey, I thought about what you said, and you were right. I should've said something," he said. "And why didn't you?" I asked. "I don't know, but I'm not writing you up. And if you need tutoring, let me know," he said. "Thanks," I said with a straight face. "Sorry for cursing in your class," I added. "I didn't even know you used language like that," he said. "I usually don't, but haven't really been myself in a while," I said. "Well, you'll figure it out, and I tell you what. If you can commit to letting me tutor you, I'll count our sessions towards your passing grade. Deal?" he said. "Yeah, "I said. He got up and left.

All AP classes weren't bad. There was my psychology class that I always fell asleep in because I didn't feel like hearing about crazy people having sex with dead people. And then there was my English class that was interesting and hype because of the quirky teacher we had who would always get overjoyed when students brought her Mountain Dews.

One day, in psychology, while I was sleeping, the teacher thought she'd show the class something kind of neat and used me as an example. She would always have soft, soothing music playing and the class would be talking so the chorus of voices would put me to sleep. She had been calling my name to wake up for a very long time, but I hadn't responded. Then, she had the class to get extremely quiet, and she turned off the music. As soon as she stopped the music and there was utter silence, I popped up like someone had screamed in my ear.

The class laughed, and so did I when she explained what had just happened.

I was known for skipping anytime we had a test or essay due in English. "Where's La'Porsha?" she would ask. The class would laugh and say, "She's absent," knowing why I wasn't there. I only skipped because when it came to 'reading comprehension,' I would always see something or hear something different than much of the class.

The teacher would ask questions like, "What was the author trying to say?" I felt the answers should have been able to be fluid. If people misunderstand one another when speaking directly to one another, how much more do we misunderstand metaphoric fiction novels and poetry?

My answers were always 'not what the author meant,' so I gave up on trying to figure out somebody I couldn't even converse with.

There were also the hard days of English when we'd have to watch things like the gory, spooky Macbeth, and the rape story of The Canterbury Tales. Then, we had to read all sorts of vulgar material and be tested on them. I skid my way through class with spark notes and other devices.

There was a girl in our English class, we'll call Mary, that all the guys liked because she wasn't into boys and she was headstrong in her books and athletics. I secretly envied her because she was the kind of girl I always wished to be. I had a deep admiration for her conservative way, but one day, while Liam and I were still on good terms and studying together, he told me that if he ever had a daughter, he would want her to be like the girl from our English class. He had also stated how she would be the kind of woman he would want to marry. "Not like me?" I asked. He stayed silent, knowing his statement had caused pain.

If I could undo every defiling thing that's been done to me and that I've participated in, I would, if it meant a chance to be your Mary. Those were my thoughts, but all that came from me were tears and a tortured frown aimed at Liam. "I'm...I'm sorry. I didn't think me saying that would affect you that way," he said. "So how did you think that statement would affect me, or did you even care?" I shouted. "Porsha—" "Really? Since when do you call me that?" I asked. "What was so bad about my statement? It's the truth! I mean, be honest! If you had a daughter, would you want her to be like you or like Mary?" I stood in agonizing shock because he was right. "Exactly. Look, I'm confused. You say we can be friends, but when I try and talk to you like a friend, you flip out. Maybe a friendship with us is just not gonna work," he said. "You're right," I cried. That was the last day he 'tutored' me in Calculus.

One funny day after that, our English teacher decided to ask us about what kind of utopia we would build for ourselves. When it was my turn, I said, "I would be the queen of a kingdom where women are catered to, protected, respected, adored, loved..." "Ooooo, I'm liking this, go on," the teacher urged. "Wait for it, there's a catch knowing Porsha," my friend D. C. said. "...and all men who wanted to enter had to come before me to be personally castrated before becoming a part of the kingdom," I finished.

Every guy in the class held their privates and bent over and looked straight to Liam. "Man, what you do to her?" they asked, laughing. "She was like that when I met her," he said, shooting me a look. We smiled and laughed.

I'd also had a few respectfully objective words for my English teacher when Liam started bragging on the fact that he purposely wrote his essays to be unreadable so that he could get passing grades. He said that since he had a reputation for making good grades, the teacher would often just give him with an A or B, depending on the day and would say, "I can't read this, but I know it's good."

I called them out on it and ruined that lil' essay love affair. "If you can't read it, he needs to type or do it over...or you can just start giving me an A or B, your choice," I said, smiling. Liam stared at me with his mouth open in disbelief that I had ruined his easy essay grades.

I sucked at writing essays, but there was this one time I actually tried my best and got a 70 for it. When I questioned the teacher about it, she said my grade was so low because the essay didn't sound like me. "I would hope I write differently than how I talk," I said, raising an eyebrow and frowning the other. "Shoo, Shoo, that's the grade," she said. That was the first and last time I tried in her class.

There did happen to be one major outlet for me during this horrid time. I agreed to play Evilene in The Wiz play that was put on by a man we'll call Mr. Z. I wanted to play the part of Dorothy so that I would sing her songs, but he said the 'anger came natural' for me. Go figure. Mr. Z remains to be one of my closest, dearest, and most trusted mentors.

When he and I first met, I was about as rough as they came. But he cultivated me and encouraged me to channel my wisdom and emotions. The only disagreement we ever had was when he first called me a

Prophetess. In my mind, that meant witch or psychic, so I rebuked that statement with a whole lot of attitude.

As time went on, he gently nudged me to walk in my purpose. In many ways, he tamed me and brought me back to at least a neutral state in God, which was still very horrible, but it was better than the darkness I was in.

I was the best Evilene they'd ever seen. I would make my entrance from the back of the auditorium and scare audience members before taking my seat on stage in a chair that was so big, my legs naturally stretched straight out in front of me.

Since I was a senior, my sister, who was then a freshman, cooked up a little senior prank on me. During my last scene, when the bucket of water melts the witch, they usually used confetti. But on the very last night, they used real cold water, and I forgot my lines and was rolled off stage, literally frozen in my chair.

The play had amazing actors and even more fantastic music. It was a masterpiece. I had also become the top girls singles tennis player at the school. Tennis was a huge outlet for me. The coach tried to put me on doubles, but it never worked because I hogged the court. I still enjoyed playing with my sister, Ree, in doubles sometimes.

The coach would call us Venus and Serena. I was Serena, for many reasons. I played hard and fair, and whenever I felt misjudged or cheated by the other team, I made them pay for it. I think I got voted most talented in the yearbook by my peers, which was sweet.

I finished the year out with a bang...that no one expected. Pilch would always call me perpetrator any time he passed me in the hall. He said this because I skipped over half of the year. It didn't go on my record, because I was smart with it. I won't mention how I skipped because I want all you kids to be better than I was and actually stay in class.

It was decided that I would sing the class song for class night. It was the program where all awards and scholarships were named. I sang *Because You Love Me* by Celine Dion. I remember seeing Liam seated right on the front row from the stage, and I broke down and cried. The seniors thought I cried because it was our night, but I lamented the love I felt I lost and would never see again after graduation. He had been the only guy to truly try and love past my demons.

At graduation, my name got called to stand and be applauded with all students who had a 3.0 GPA to 3.5 GPA. My peers looked at me in disbelief and laughed and shook their heads. "Ooooo, ain't no way! How in the world, La'Porsha?!" they shouted. "Fava!" I shouted, doing my happy dance. My own family sat there, perplexed at how it had been possible for me to come out shining like that. I looked at them, shrugged my shoulders, and laughed.

That night should have been the happiest night of my life, but it was the night I'd grown the most scared. What would I do, now? Where would I go? I was done with school, period. I became anxious about the future and couldn't turn my thoughts off.

Somehow, I rested for the night and woke up the next day feeling like I'd awakened in the middle of an ocean. I was overwhelmed, so I ate leftovers from my graduation meal and watched movies until I felt comforted. What was next for me? I had auditioned for an arts college in Los Angeles and received the full scholarship in the amount of $15,000, but it wasn't nearly enough to pay my way. No matter how things seemed, I wasn't going to the military.

I was very nervous about being at home all day with my family since we were always getting into it, so I made myself scarce.

I started spending most of my time hanging with Mr. Z. I worked on art and music from morning to late evening. My family barely saw me, and it was better that way.

Alright! Head on up to the surface. You did amazing! I'm so proud of how you were able to navigate these treacherous waters. Feel that warm sand oozing between your toes? Rest here, take it all in, and prepare yourself for the next terrain. Maybe take some time and reflect. Take a listen to *God Only Knows* by For King & Country. Let's meet up a little later! Until then, take care!

BATTLE MEMOIR SERIES: BOOK №2

Trained On the Battlefield

Sneak Preview...next page

Bye-bye, Baby

"Why would you let me fall asleep?!', he exclaimed with a dark hunger for my suffering in his voice. His eyes grew dark, and I recognized his present spirit. He'd come back to finally finish me off. "What do you mean? You were tired, and fell asleep," I answered, trying to acquire some brave, nonchalant tone in my voice, despite the rapidly growing dread in my gut. "No, you let me fall asleep on purpose," he insisted with a sinister smile. He slowly nodded his head to reaffirmed the accusation he stated, and his body began to shiver.

I was all too familiar with the 'evil shakes,' so I slowly slid off the left side of our shared mattress, bent over to swiftly pick my sleeping daughter up out of her baby sleeper, and stood erect, staring at my husband as he sat still as a statue with his right shoulder limp, and his hands and feet crossed. "I don't know what you're feeling or why you're upset with me, but I'm going to let you figure it out," I said, trying to sound stern.

Just as I started toward the bedroom door with my daughter in my arms, he abruptly slid off the right side of the bed right into the pathway of the door. "Where are you going?" he asked, his voice low and hauntingly groggy. "I'm going to the restroom," I answered. "Why?" he asked. "Why does anyone go to the restroom? I need to pee," I said. "Okay, you can go, but put Nay down. She's sleeping," he said. "Ha...nice try. She's coming with me. Since when do I leave my daughter alone with you?" I aggressed. "Hm. Your daughter?" he asked rhetorically. "H* yeah, my daughter," I replied with a lash of anger. "Well then, pee on yourself. You're not leaving this room," he said with snarky confidence.

For the next few moments, we intensely starred at one another. I knew his eyes well enough to make out his thoughts loud and clear. I suspected he was mentally gearing up to attack me, so I, in turn, mentally geared up to defend myself and my daughter. Almost simultaneously, he swiftly lunged towards us, and I just as swiftly whirled my daughter around to not be positioned in between him and myself. He grabbed my hair, yanked my head back enough to cause a sharp pain in my neck, and whispered in my ear, "Put her down, Renae."

I winced at the pain of his pull and reluctantly obeyed. I gently placed my daughter back down in her sleeper, and as soon as he noticed my hands were no longer in contact with her, he yanked me even harder than before and threw me onto the mattress. Before I'd been able to flip my body over, he'd climbed on top of my back, pinning me down with his weight. He mashed my head into the covers for what seemed to be forever, and just as I was losing strength, I felt all his weight lift off my back.

In reaction to barely being able to breathe, I rolled on my back, thinking that I'd be able to catch my breath. I was wrong. I lay there just enough time to semi-focus in on his smiling face looking down at me, enjoying the sight of me struggling. He got on top of me again and put his hands around my throat. He began squeezing the life from my body, his eyes iced with a sinister expression of the non-remorseful desire to vigorously accomplish my demise.

I tried to act as I usually would and show my unwavering determination not to allow him to win. I managed to squeeze out a couple words that sent him over the top. "I..iss...th..tha...t...all, ccc...cco..cow..ard?" I struggled. "Renae, you're about to die by the hands of your lover," he melodically boasted.

I'd grown accustomed to his empty threats on my life, but I couldn't shake the eerie sense that this wasn't a drill. Tonight would be the night I die. As he began jolting his hands to reaffirm his tight grip around my neck, I forced my eyes to roll to the left of me and saw my daughter still soundly asleep. My mind betrayed me, and I must have allowed my expression to reflect my secret thoughts at that moment. All I could think of was that I was...leaving. I was really leaving my baby, my borrowed angel, in the hands of this monster; the same monster who'd tortured me for laughs, the same monster who'd bragged about molesting a 3-year-old toddler, the same monster who preyed on misfits and vulnerable women.

I'd become angered with myself at the thought that I could be so weak to allow something like this to happen. Why hadn't I left sooner, or fought harder, or been smarter? In a matter of seconds, all my choices mercilessly haunted me as I felt myself leaving my daughter behind. *"No! This can't happen! It can't end this way!"* I thought. At that very instance, my daughter had saved my life. My husband saw the desperate cry for help in my face, and it'd made him feel as if he'd won this sick battle of power. So, he released his grip on my neck just as I'd almost completely faded out.

My vision was blurred, but I noticed a bright light appear, and then darkness. It was the light from the stairwell. He'd left the room to go downstairs. I'd been too weak to try and escape with my daughter, so I mustered up the strength to lift her into my arms once again and cuddle her tightly. It was very apparent that my plan to escape would have to be expedited. I'd have to make my move the next day. It was now or never. Of the three years we'd been married, I'd never been that close to leaving the earth by his hands. A counselor had once told me that if he'd threatened to take my life before, he'd eventually get to the point of doing it. With the way the night had gone, I was sure that his next attempt would be a success, and I'd be no more.

As I listened for his footsteps back up the stairwell a moment longer, I'd heard a car crank and pull out of the driveway. I expected his return, but to my relief, he'd disappeared for the remainder of the night.

When I'd mentally decided to go through with evicting him from my and my daughter's life the next day, I felt a heavy presence blanket my sleeping baby girl and me. *"Daughter, I am with you."* "BH? Father, is that you?" I asked aloud. *"I will never leave you nor forsake you. Trust in me with all your heart. For, if I stand with you, who can come against you?* "Father, please, forgive me for what I've done. Forgive me for what I must do. BH, I never meant to forsake you. And I never meant to bring a child amid these circumstances. Now, she has to grow up without a father; I have made her another statistic. I've made her the product of a broken home. Lord God, please, Father, forgive me!" I sobbed with a tear broken voice that I'd managed to sound just above a whisper. *"My grace for you is sufficient, and my mercy over your life is everlasting, so long as you trust me with everything that you are. I love you. I've given you hope in blessing you with a child, that you may be reminded of who and whose you are. You are Kokumo, the woman that shall never spiritually die again. You are ASE, the woman full of life. You are the daughter of The Most High, child of the Alpha and Omega. You are La'Porsha Renae."*

I'd fallen peacefully asleep to the sound of God's whispers of affirmation about my value and identity. To my surprise, my daughter and I had experienced the most profound, most peaceful slumber we'd had in a long time. I'd like to believe BH had sent His angelic warriors to encamp around us that night so that I'd be well-rested for what was to come the next morning.

CPSIA information can be obtained
at www.ICGtesting.com
Printed in the USA
LVHW050156150720
660704LV00002B/25

9 781631 29603